The House and Senate in the 1790s

Perspectives on the History of Congress, 1789–1801

Kenneth R. Bowling and Donald R. Kennon, Series Editors

Inventing Congress: Origins and Establishment of the First Federal Congress

Neither Separate nor Equal: Congress in the 1790s

The House and Senate in the 1790s: Petitioning, Lobbying, and Institutional Development

The House and Senate in the 1790s

Petitioning, Lobbying, and Institutional Development

Edited by Kenneth R. Bowling and Donald R. Kennon

PUBLISHED FOR THE
UNITED STATES CAPITOL HISTORICAL SOCIETY
BY OHIO UNIVERSITY PRESS • ATHENS

Ohio University Press, Athens, Ohio 45701

Ohio University Press books are printed on acid-free paper ∞™

10 09 08 07 06 05 04 03 02 5 4 3 2 1

Library of Congress Cataloging-in-Publication Data

The House and Senate in the 1790s: petitioning, lobbying, and institutional development / edited by Kenneth R. Bowling and Donald R. Kennon.
p. cm. — (Perspectives on the history of Congress, 1789–1801)
Includes bibliographical references and index.
ISBN 0-8214-1419-4 (alk. paper)
1. United States. Congress — History. 2. Petition, Right of — United States — History. 3. Lobbying — United States — History. 4. United States — Politics and government — 1789–1815. I. Bowling, Kenneth R. II. Kennon, Donald R., 1948– III. United States Capitol Historical Society. IV. Series.
JK1041 .H68 2002
328.73′09′033 — dc21 2001054591

Contents

Preface

The 1998 and 1999 United States Capitol Historical Society conferences on Congress in the 1790s looked at petitioning, lobbying, and the institutional development of the House and the Senate.

The first paper in this volume was delivered at the 1994 conference entitled "Inventing Congress." In it, John P. Kaminski, coeditor of *The Documentary History of the Ratification of the Constitution,* analyzes the issue of Congress, its structure and powers, during the writing and ratification of the Constitution in 1787 and 1788. Significantly, he points out that both Federalists and Antifederalists recognized the various structural components—bicameralism, term of office, and source of salary, for examples—as important checks on the vastly expanded powers of the proposed Congress.

The fifth annual conference in 1998, "Seeking Justice and Influencing Congress: Petitioning and Lobbying, 1789–1801," sought to call to the attention of scholars the wealth of congressional history that has long laid buried, particularly in House and Senate records at the National Archives.

"Petitioners and Their Grievances: A View from the First Federal Congress" was delivered by William C. diGiacomantonio, associate editor of the *Documentary History of the First Federal Congress.* Intending his remarks as a kind of popular history of the First Federal Congress, he argues that the number and variety of the petitions submitted attest to the expectations that Americans had of their new government and provide insight into their concepts of civil rights, citizenship, and entitlement. His overview divides the petitions into classes: commercial (trade policy and revenue collection), public credit (policy and terms), general welfare (morality, civil rights, and the protection of citizens), arts and sciences (copyright, patent, and subsidy), public lands (titles and sales), government organization (elections, compensation, and unfinished business of the Confederation Congress), and, the largest group, Revolutionary War claims (pay, pensions, and compensation for property).

Jeffrey L. Pasley, professor of history at the University of Missouri-Columbia, entitled his paper "Private Access and Public Power: Gentility and Lobbying in the Early Congress." Defining the process of lobbying as an attempt by an individual or a group to personally make their case to Congress or individual congressmen, Pasley distinguishes the process from that of petitioning while recognizing the efforts of several petitioners who also engaged in the process, most notably the Quakers and antislavery societies. He looks in depth at the case of Ohio Company lobbyist Manasseh Cutler and the role of Jonathan Dayton while a member of Congress from New Jersey. In both, he stresses the role and importance of gentility as an avenue of access.

In "Rites of Passage: Postal Petitioning as a Tool of Governance in the Age of Federalism," Professor Richard R. John of the University of Illinois at Chicago and his graduate student Christopher J. Young argue against the dismissive view of the Federalist legacy. They detail the impact of petitioning on the institutional development of the United States Post Office, particularly its extension westward, and conclude in part that, despite toying with the abolition of the federal postal service, the Jeffersonians continued the expansion of the system nourished by the Federalists and responded positively to the logical next step, petitions calling for federal support to build the roads on which the mails were conveyed.

Marion Nelson Winship, who is completing a doctoral dissertation at the University of Pennsylvania, focuses on western rhetoric and on the most prominent of Kentucky Republicans, John Breckinridge, in her "The 'Practicable Sphere' of a Republic: Western Ways of Connecting to Congress." She argues that it is a mistake to view the democratic societies as vehicles for popular expression of local issues as if there were no communication among them and that bringing down the Federalists, not the expression of western needs, was the overarching purpose of their often sarcastic, polemical demands of Congress.

In the final paper of the day, "Contesting the Character of the Political Economy in the Early Republic: Rights and Remedies in *Chisholm* v. *Georgia*," Professor Christine A. Desan of Harvard Law School argues that the famous and often studied case should be considered in the context of the political economy that followed in the wake of the ratification of the Constitution. In particular, she contrasts the then prevailing legislative venue with the emerging judicial venue as remedies for the assertion of property rights.

The sixth annual conference in 1999 was entitled "The Institutional Development of Congress in the 1790s." Its purpose was to look at Congress from the end, rather than the beginning, of the decade.

Political scientist David J. Siemers of the University of Wisconsin-Oshkosh spoke on "Electoral Dynamics of Ratification: Federalist and Antifederalist Strength and Cohesion, 1787–1803." In a statistically based argument, he traces the cohesion of Antifederalists during the first four congresses and their resurgence in the Fifth Congress, by which time they had formed a stable alliance with disgruntled Federalists who followed the leadership of James Madison.

Terri D. Halperin, visiting assistant professor of history at the University of Richmond, spoke on "The Special Relationship: The Senate and the States, 1789–1801." Beginning with a discussion of the important provisions in the Constitution that acted to weaken the relationship between the Senate and the states and the amendments proposed to rectify that situation, she details a decade of Senate history that witnessed a negotiation of the relationship between the federal government, the senators, and the state legislators. In doing so, she brings forward the little known, but institutionally important, exchanges between North Carolina and its senators.

Senate historian Richard A. Baker entitled his paper "The United States Senate in Philadelphia: An Institutional History of the 1790s." In it he discusses the physical setting of the Senate, its officers, leadership (including Vice Presidents John Adams and Thomas Jefferson), administration, and rules. Baker concludes with an exploration of four controversies that brought public scrutiny on the Senate and caused senators to set precedent and consider the way it conducted business: the question of whether to seat Albert Gallatin of Pennsylvania in 1794, the ratification of the Jay Treaty in 1795, the rejection of John Rutledge's nomination as chief justice that same year, and, at the end of the decade, the impeachment trial of William Blount.

Raymond W. Smock, former historian of the House of Representatives, emphasizes the role of democracy in "The Institutional

Development of the House of Representatives, 1791–1801." After stressing the foundation laid by the First Federal Congress, he discusses the establishment of standing committees and the role of the leadership, calling in particular for additional study of the early Speakers of the House.

The House and Senate in the 1790s

John P. Kaminski

From Impotence to Omnipotence

The Debate over Structuring Congress under the New Federal Constitution of 1787

FROM MAY TO SEPTEMBER 1787 a convention of delegates from twelve of the thirteen states sat in Philadelphia to propose alterations in the Articles of Confederation that would preserve the Union, strengthen the Confederation Congress, and fulfill the promise of the Revolution. Dr. Benjamin Rush of Philadelphia, writing in the nationally circulated *American Museum,* asserted that though the War for Independence was long over, the American Revolution continued: "It remains yet to establish and perfect our new forms of government; and to prepare the principles, morals, and manners of our citizens, for these forms of government, after they are established and brought to perfection."[1] A correspondent in the *New Haven Gazette,* using the pseudonym "The People," believed "our Revolution is yet but half completed; we have escaped the evils which threatened us from a foreign quarter, but we have not attained the positive blessings which we promised ourselves from the establishment of a free and independent empire. The truth is, such an empire is not yet established. In vain have we, for four years, pursued a phantom, a shadow without substance, an effect

[1]Rush's essay is printed in John P. Kaminski and Gaspare J. Saladino, eds., *The Documentary History of the Ratification of the Constitution,* 16 vols. to date (Madison, Wis., 1976–), 13:45–49. Hereafter cited as *DHRC.*

without a cause."[2] Dr. David Ramsay of South Carolina, Benjamin Rush's former student, agreed that "the revolution cannot be said to be completed till an efficient form of government is established."[3] Such a task was daunting. John Adams knew that "it is much easier to pull down a Government . . . than to build [one] up."[4]

Virtually all Americans were dissatisfied with the Articles of Confederation. Nearly everyone wanted and expected the Philadelphia Convention to give Congress additional powers, particularly to levy a tariff and regulate commerce. Some people, such as Confederation Secretary at War Henry Knox, wanted greater change. He argued that "a patch work to the present defective confederation" would merely delay the crisis. He urged the complete replacement of the Articles with "an energetic and judicious system."[5] George Washington agreed that the convention should "adopt no temporising expedient, but probe the defects of the Confederation to the bottom, and provide radical cures."[6] In any event, Congress — the only branch of the government under the Articles of Confederation — was sure to be changed by the Constitutional Convention.

All of the delegates who met in Philadelphia wanted to preserve the Union by strengthening the powers of the general government either by amending the Articles of Confederation or by creating an entirely new government armed with coercive power over the states and individuals. Equally important, many Americans wanted to limit the powers of the state governments, which were dominated by popularly elected assemblies that all too often enacted legislation that violated the rights of minorities. By strengthening the powers of Congress, restraining the state assemblies, and controlling the licentiousness of the people, the nation would preserve the principles of the Revolution. A widely reprinted article in the *Pennsylvania Gazette* of September 5, 1787, declared that 1776 would be remembered "for a

---

[2]"The People," *New Haven Gazette,* Oct. 11, 1787.

[3]David Ramsay to Benjamin Lincoln, June 20, 1788, Lincoln Papers, Massachusetts Historical Society (MHi).

[4]John Adams to James Warren, Jan. 9, 1787, Adams Letterbook, MHi.

[5]Henry Knox to George Washington, Mar. 19, 1787, W. W. Abbot and Dorothy Twohig, eds., *The Papers of George Washington,* Confederation Series, 6 vols. (Charlottesville, 1992–97), 5:96.

[6]George Washington to James Madison, Mar. 31, 1787, ibid., 5:116.

revolution in favor of *Liberty*" against an arbitrary, tyrannical imperial government; and 1787 would be remembered "for a revolution in favor of *Government.*"[7]

The structure and power of the new Congress took center stage in both the Constitutional Convention and the debate over the ratification of the Constitution. Despite the problems associated with the state legislatures and with the Confederation Congress, most Americans still believed that legislatures should be the supreme branch of government and that within any legislative body the majority ought to prevail. No matter what structural changes might occur in the Articles of Confederation, America's new government surely would remain centered in and dominated by a representative legislature. Consequently, it is not surprising that the first and longest article of the new Constitution provided for Congress.

Throughout the country (before, during, and after the sitting of the Constitutional Convention) individuals pointed to the danger of granting additional powers to the unicameral Confederation Congress. Although Americans universally gave lip service to Montesquieu's maxim in favor of the separation of powers, the authors of the state constitutions had in practice made the lower houses of the state legislatures supreme, while at the federal level the Articles of Confederation created a government with *only* a legislative branch. Legislative assemblies exercised overwhelming power within their states, and they often abused that power. The Confederation Congress had supreme authority within its sphere, but it had no power or means to enforce its will. Most delegates to the Philadelphia Convention wanted to strengthen Congress and rein in the states. To a great extent, the problem faced by the delegates was a legislative dilemma—how to restrain the state legislatures and empower Congress while protecting the people from legislative abuse. Especially troubling was how to grant additional power to the unicameral Confederation Congress. These legislative dilemmas were attended to by James Madison in *Federalist* No. 51. "In framing a government which is to be administered by men over men, the great difficulty lies in this: You must first enable the government to control the governed; and in the next place, oblige it to

---

[7]*DHRC,* 13:192.

control itself." The electoral process had long provided the people with the most important method of control over their legislatures. However, according to Madison, "experience has taught mankind the necessity of auxiliary precautions." The delegates to the Constitutional Convention provided Congress with many new powers but also created several significant auxiliary precautions to restrict the abuse of these new powers. These auxiliary precautions included certain structural components that established a formidable system of checks and balances.

Antifederalists argued that the Constitution gave Congress too many powers. Some were unobjectionable, including the powers to borrow money; regulate foreign and domestic commerce and trade with Indians; establish rules for naturalization and bankruptcies; coin money and regulate its value; fix the standard of weights and measures; provide punishment for counterfeiting, piracy, and crimes on the high seas; establish post offices and post roads; grant patents and copyrights; and even declare war. But other powers were too broad or were not properly restricted. These included the powers to levy and collect taxes of all kinds to pay the country's debt and to provide for the common defense and general welfare; create inferior courts; raise and support armies and a navy; provide for organizing, arming, and disciplining the state militia; provide for calling up the militia into federal service; and exercise exclusive jurisdiction over an immense federal seat of government. And Antifederalists believed any other powers needed could be justified by the "sweeping clause" that authorized Congress "to make all laws which shall be necessary and proper for carrying into execution the foregoing powers, and all other powers vested by this Constitution in the government of the United States, or in any department or officer thereof."

Antifederalists also suspected the effectiveness of the limitations placed on Congress in Article I, section 9, of the Constitution. The prohibition of Congress stopping the African slave trade before 1808 was declared inhumane and impolitic. The indefinite time frame in which the writ of habeas corpus could be suspended alarmed Antifederalists. Some Antifederalists like George Mason did not want a complete prohibition of ex post facto laws, preferring to keep that option open for Congress in noncriminal matters. The requirement for "a proper appropriation and accounting" of all moneys spent was too diffusive; Antifederalists wanted a set scheduled publication of its financial affairs. The prohibitions on passing bills of attainder and issuing titles of nobility merely proved to Antifederalists that this was not a government of strictly delegated powers.

With this vast array of powers, Antifederalists asserted that Congress's authority would "extend to every case that is of the least importance—there is nothing valuable to human nature, nothing dear to freemen, but what is within its power."[8] Referring to the general welfare clause, the necessary and proper clause, and the supremacy clause in Article VI of the Constitution, Antifederalists charged that the new Constitution would establish the dominance of Congress over the states and the people despite the protections in state constitutions and bills of rights. George Mason pointed out that when the people of Virginia formed their state constitution, they also adopted a Declaration of Rights. Whereas Virginians "would not trust their own citizens, who had a familiarity of interest with themselves," with the new Federal Constitution, they would give up a great part of their rights to a far-off government controlled in Congress by a northern majority totally unsympathetic to the South.[9] Mason wanted a clause in the Constitution reserving to the states all powers not delegated to the federal government. Such a clause, he noted, existed in the Articles of Confederation, even though the Articles provided for a far weaker general government. "Why not then have a similar clause in this Constitution?" "Unless this was done, many valuable and important rights would be concluded to be given up by implication," said Mason, adding that he saw no "distinction between rights relinquished by a positive grant, and [those] lost by implication. Unless there were a Bill of Rights, implication might swallow up all our rights."[10] All of the seven state ratifying conventions that proposed amendments to be taken up by the First Federal Congress recommended that the new Congress have only *expressly* delegated powers. All other powers were to remain with the people or their respective state governments. Fearing

[8] "Brutus" I, *New York Journal,* Oct. 18, 1787, ibid., 13:414.

[9] George Mason speech in the Virginia Convention, June 11, 1788, ibid., 9:1157.

[10] George Mason speeches in the Virginia Convention, June 16, 1788, ibid., 10:1326, 1328.

that those clauses in the Constitution that specifically prohibited Congress from certain actions—granting titles of nobility for example—might be interpreted to mean that Congress had all other powers, the Virginia and North Carolina conventions asserted that these particular limitations on Congress were to be considered as being "inserted merely for greater caution."[11]

The purpose of the debate over the structure of Congress was to determine whether the federal legislature was organized properly to exercise the powers assigned it by the Constitution. Federalists argued that for too long Americans were "so fearful of giving their rulers powers to do hurt, that they never have given them power to do good."[12] The Constitution was to give Congress limited delegated powers that would be implemented safely, efficiently, and effectively by a Congress that was powerful but restrained by an elaborate system of checks and balances. Antifederalists disagreed. The American Revolution, they said, that separated the colonies from Great Britain "was not more important to the liberties of America than that [revolution] which will result from the adoption of the new system. The *former* freed us from a *foreign subjugation,* and there is too much reason to apprehend that the *latter* will reduce us to a *federal domination.*"[13] Antifederalists contended that the Constitution gave Congress vast powers both explicit and implied; and that the structure of Congress, without a bill of rights limiting it, would allow the abuse of these powers. Both sides agreed that at the time of the Revolution, when the Articles of Confederation were drafted, "the publick rage was on the side of liberty. The reigning disposition then was to secure the highest degrees of liberty to the people, and to guard against every possible instance of oppression in their rulers. The consequence is want of sufficient energy in government. We have had a surfeit of liberty; and, to many, the very name has now become nauseous."[14]

The Constitutional Convention agreed to alter the structure of Congress, increase its powers, and limit the powers of the states. Delegates

---

[11]Ibid., 18:205, 319.

[12]"Atticus" III, *Independent Chronicle* (Boston), Nov. 22, 1787, ibid., 4:299.

[13]"The Republican Federalist" III, *Massachusetts Gazette,* Jan. 9, 1788, ibid., 5:661.

[14]"Cornelius," *Hampshire Chronicle* (Springfield, Mass.), Dec. 18, 1787, ibid., 4:415–16.

to the convention divided over the structure of Congress depending on whether they represented a large state, a small state, a southern slave state, or a northern state. (With the exception of Massachusetts, all of the northern states still had slaves, although slavery was far less important to their economies. Most northern states had passed gradual emancipation acts, while in all of them there was significant abolitionist sentiment.)

When the future powers of Congress and the restrictions on the states were discussed in the convention, delegates usually divided along ideological lines—nationalists versus state-oriented delegates. New York's three delegates split—Alexander Hamilton was a committed nationalist; Robert Yates and John Lansing, Jr., were recognized as "antifederal" men. Some confirmed opponents of a strong central government, such as Elbridge Gerry of Massachusetts, came to Philadelphia so frightened by the "excesses of democracy" that they initially supported significant increases in congressional power. Gerry's long-standing commitment to the republican ideals of limited government eventually crept back as fears of Shays's Rebellion faded and as the convention increased the powers of Congress. Some large-state delegates (such as Virginians Edmund Randolph and George Mason), who had come to Philadelphia seeking significant increases in congressional power, lost their enthusiasm for a strong Congress when it was decided that the Senate should be apportioned equally among the states, thus lessening the control of Congress by the large states. Some small-state delegates (such as William Paterson of New Jersey and Oliver Ellsworth of Connecticut), who had come to Philadelphia seeking to protect the interests of the small states, agreed to enlarge Congress's powers once state equality was guaranteed in the Senate. Similar alignments existed during the public debate over the ratification of the new Constitution.

A small group of nationalists led by James Madison felt that the only way effectively to limit the states' ability to violate the rights of minorities (creditors, former Loyalists, Quakers, etc.) was to give Congress the extreme power to veto any state legislation. Probably because such a provision might doom the Constitution, the convention rejected Madison's congressional veto power in favor of a supremacy clause with the implied power of the federal judiciary to strike down state laws that contravened the Constitution, federal laws, or treaties. Madison left Philadelphia believing that this substitution would be inadequate to control the states, allowing their legislatures to continue unsound policies and discriminatory practices.

During the ratification debate, Americans became Federalists or Antifederalists for various reasons. Federalists from large and small states, from the North as well as the South, although admitting that the Constitution had flaws, publicly supported virtually all of the provisions concerning the Constitution. James Madison suggested that the new Constitution need not be perfect—only that it be less imperfect than the Articles of Confederation. Even if their home state would suffer from a particular constitutional provision, Federalists put the best light on that provision. Sometimes this support took the form of taking the high ground of sacrificing the interests of one's home state for the general welfare of the country or as a concession exchanged for other advantages. Supporters of the Constitution did not want to raise doubts about any constitutional provisions. Antifederalists, however, publicly opposed many of the constitutional provisions concerning the new Congress, depending on what might best appeal to their constituents. Sometimes this meant that Antifederalists in different sections of the country took diametrically opposing stances. For instance, large-state Antifederalists opposed the equal representation of the states in the Senate and the underrepresentation of their state in the House of Representatives; small-state Antifederalists favored equal representation in the Senate and were not at all concerned that their states were overrepresented in the First Congress. Southern Antifederalists argued that the Constitution gave Congress the power to abolish slavery (and Virginia Antifederalists criticized the protection of the slave trade until 1808), while northern Antifederalists were highly critical of the fugitive slave clause of the Constitution, the protection of the slave trade, and the extra representatives and presidential electors given to the southern states by the three-fifths clause. Northern Federalists argued that the Constitution would eventually lead to the end of slavery; southern Federalists assured their constituents that the Constitution gave Congress no power that would endanger slavery.

The basic principles of federalism and separation of powers were the most fundamental safeguards restricting Congress's power. The former allocated power between the new federal government and the component states, while the latter created an interior tension between the branches of the federal government.

The controversy over federalism underlay all other issues in the debate over the ratification of the Constitution. Antifederalists argued that Congress's vastly increased powers—especially because they anticipated a broad interpretation of the general welfare and necessary and proper clauses—signaled the annihilation of the state governments as anything but administrative districts, occupying the same status as the counties within states. Federalists vehemently denied this charge and asserted that the Constitution created a federal republic in which the federal government had only delegated powers. Powers not delegated to the federal government were reserved to the states.[15] States surely would be vigilant against any usurpation of power by Congress. In addition, Federalists used the doctrine of delegated powers to justify the omission of a bill of rights in the Constitution. Because Congress would have only delegated powers, it had no power to infringe religious liberty or the freedom of the press. Furthermore, any list of rights would imply that those rights not listed were unprotected from the actions of Congress, or imply that power existed to legislate on rights or on anything in general unless prohibited.

In addition to federalism, the concept of separation of powers was used to limit the new Congress under the Constitution. In the Constitutional Convention both the Virginia and the New Jersey plans called for a separate executive and judiciary in addition to Congress. In fact, the only argument concerning the separation of powers during the

---

[15]James Wilson first enunciated this interpretation—in its most extreme form—in a speech at the statehouse in Philadelphia on October 6, 1787. "When the people established the powers of legislation under their separate governments, they invested their representatives with every right and authority which they did not in explicit terms reserve; and therefore upon every question, respecting the jurisdiction of the house of assembly, if the frame of government is silent, the jurisdiction is efficient and complete. But in delegating federal power, another criterion was necessarily introduced, and the congressional authority is to be collected, not from tacit implication, but from the positive grant expressed in the instrument of union. Hence it is evident, that in the former case every thing which is not reserved is given, but in the latter the reverse of the proposition prevails, and every thing which is not given, is reserved" to the people or the states (ibid., 13:339).

ratification debate came from Antifederalists who took exception to the distribution of particular powers to the branches, or who maintained that the new Constitution did not sufficiently separate the branches; in particular, they focused on the executive and judicial powers of the Senate and its intimate connection with the president. A privy council, Antifederalists argued, should be created to assume the executive duties of confirmation of appointments and advice and consent to treaties. The judicial responsibility of trying impeachments should lie elsewhere—the federal or state judiciary—especially if the Senate was to participate in the appointment process. Furthermore, the office of the vice president should be eliminated, and the Senate should elect one of its own members to preside. Federalists argued, however, that a complete separation of powers among legislative, executive, and judicial branches was unnecessary, if not impossible, and would create continual governmental gridlock. The branches had to be sufficiently independent of each other to create checks and balances that would protect against the abuse of power, but they had to work together so that government could function.

The most fundamental structural component of Congress—bicameralism—was closely linked to both separation of powers and federalism. Bicameralism received broad, but not universal, support. In the Constitutional Convention, delegates from small states, fearing domination by large states, advocated the retention of the unicameral Confederation Congress with equal state representation. But most of the delegates to the convention came from states with bicameral legislatures. (Only Pennsylvania, Georgia, and the independent republic of Vermont had unicameral legislatures.) William Paterson of New Jersey argued that bicameralism was beneficial in state legislatures that were all powerful; but in Congress, whose "objects are few and simple," it would be an unnecessary expense. People, Paterson suggested, complained that Congress was too weak and could not act—not that Congress needed two houses to check each other; representatives from the different states would serve as sufficient checks upon each other. Gov. Edmund Randolph of Virginia responded that the only reason why the unicameral Confederation Congress had been safe so far was because of "the general impotency of that body"—it had no power to act on private individuals and it had no means to enforce its will on the sovereign and independent states. James Wilson of Pennsylvania warned his fellow delegates about the dangers of legislative despotism. Without restraints on the legislature, "there can be neither liberty nor stability." In a single house, the only check came from "the virtue & good sense of those who compose it." This was inadequate. The convention, by a vote of seven states to three, with one divided, voted in favor of bicameralism.[16]

There also was little controversy about bicameralism in the debate over ratifying the Constitution. Baptist minister Joseph Spencer of Orange County, Virginia, was one of only a few Americans who spoke out against a two-house Congress. Writing to his neighbor, Spencer told James Madison that he "utterly oppose[d] any Division in [the] Legislative Body. The more Houses, the more parties, the more they are Divided; the more the Wisdom is Scattered. Sometimes one house may prevent the Error of another & the same stands true of twenty Houses. But the Question is, whether they do more good than harm. The Business is certainly thereby retarded & the Expence inhanced."[17] But Edmund Pendleton of Virginia saw the "wisdom of 2 branches in the Legislature." It was "proven from reason & Sanctified by our own State System."[18] James Wilson, hating his own state's unicameral assembly, embraced federal bicameralism. The two houses of Congress would "act with more caution, and perhaps more integrity, if their proceedings are to be under the inspection and control of another, than when they are not. From this principle, the proceedings of Congress will be conducted with a degree of circumspection not common in single bodies, where nothing more is necessary to be done, than to carry the business through amongst themselves, whether it be right or wrong." Wilson explained that "in compound legislatures, every object must be submitted to a distinct body, not influenced by the arguments or warped by the prejudices of the other." Wilson predicted that because "there will be more circumspection in forming the laws, so there will be more stability in the laws when made. Indeed one is the

[16]The quoted speeches came from the debates on June 15 and 16. See Max Farrand, *The Records of the Federal Convention of 1787*, 3d ed., 3 vols. (New Haven, 1937), 1:254, 256, 260.

[17]Joseph Spencer to James Madison, Feb. 28, 1788, *DHRC*, 8:425.

[18]Edmund Pendleton to Richard Henry Lee, June 14, 1788, ibid., 10:1626–27.

consequence of the other; for what has been well considered, and founded in good sense, will, in practice, be useful and salutary, and of consequence will not be liable to be soon repealed. Though two bodies may not possess more wisdom or patriotism than what may be found in a single body, yet they will necessarily introduce a greater degree of precision" that would be reflected in the laws. Wilson warned that "an indigested and inaccurate code of laws is one of the most dangerous things that can be introduced into any government."[19]

Bicameralism at the federal level would check a greatly strengthened Congress. Two houses, elected for different terms by different constituents, would serve as an internal check on one of the three separated branches—thus a check on a check. The convention then agreed that one house of Congress should be weighted toward the large states with proportional representation in the House of Representatives, while the Senate with its equal state representation would give small states the advantage. Bicameralism also served another function. The House of Representatives would be elected directly by the people every two years; the Senate would be elected by the state legislatures, one-third every two years. The former provided a national forum for the people; the latter represented the interests of the states, preserving a federal component in the new Constitution: therefore, as "a child may have a resemblance of both its parents," so the new Constitution would have attributes of both a national and a federal government.[20] During the ratification debate, Antifederalists denied that the new government could have these dual attributes. With the exception of their denunciation of the lack of a bill of rights, Antifederalists' primary argument against the Constitution was that it created a consolidated—a national—government that would annihilate the states as sovereign entities. Patrick Henry stumbled on the first three words of the preamble: "We the People." Federal governments did not know people—they were unions of states. States, he said, "are the characteristics, and the soul of a confederation. If the States be not the agents of this compact, it must be one great consolidated National Government."[21]

---

[19]James Wilson speech in the Pennsylvania Convention, Dec. 1, 1787, ibid., 2:452.

[20]"Atticus," *Independent Chronicle,* Nov. 22, 1787, ibid., 4:298.

[21]Patrick Henry speech in the Virginia ratifying convention, June 4, 1788, ibid., 9:930.

Other structural elements of Congress generated greater debate. Antifederalists charged that both the House of Representatives and the Senate were far too small. The Constitution specified that the first House of Representatives would, if all thirteen states ratified the Constitution, consist of sixty-five members. Compared with tiny Rhode Island's assembly of 70, the 160 members of the Virginia House of Delegates, and the 400-member Massachusetts House of Representatives, the U.S. House of Representatives woefully underrepresented America. George Mason objected that "there is not the Substance, but the Shadow only of representation; which can never produce proper Information in the Legislature, or inspire Confidence in the People: the Laws will therefore be generally made by Men little concern'd in, and unacquainted with their Effects & Consequences."[22] Mason's fellow Virginian Richard Henry Lee saw but "a mere shred or rag of representation" in the House of Representatives.[23] An anonymous newspaper writer predicted that despite the popular election of representatives, "their dignity, being necessarily great in proportion as their number is small, fair and unbiassed elections are scarcely probable, if not impracticable."[24]

Federalists defended the size of the House of Representatives. Because Congress would only legislate in general matters, which concerned the interests of the country as a whole, it was unnecessary for representatives to have minute knowledge of local affairs. A larger representation would be too expensive. (Antifederalists regularly charged that the new government would be excessively expensive.) If all thirteen states had sent their full allotment of delegates (seven) to the Confederation Congress, it would exactly equal the number of representatives and senators allocated for the First Congress.[25] Federalists also alluded to the extremely high growth rate of the American

---

[22]George Mason's objections enclosed in his letter to George Washington, Oct. 7, 1787, ibid., 13:348.

[23]Richard Henry Lee to Gov. Edmund Randolph, Oct. 16, 1787, ibid., 14:368.

[24]"The Impartial Examiner" III, *Virginia Independent Chronicle,* June 4, 1788, ibid., 10:1578.

[25]Each state could send between two and seven delegates to the Confederation Congress. Thus a full representation of ninety-one delegates would equal the sum of sixty-five representatives and twenty-six senators in the First Federal Congress. Most states, however, usually elected no more than five delegates, of which only two or three served at any one time.

population, which doubled every twenty-five years. Within three years of the adoption of the Constitution, a census was to be taken and it was anticipated that at the ratio of 1:30,000 there would be 100 representatives in the House. Twenty-five years later that number would grow to 200. In fifty years it would swell to 400 representatives; 800 in seventy-five years. There was no need to worry about the adequacy of the representation under the new Constitution.[26]

Antifederalists persisted. Citing Article I, section 2, of the Constitution—"The number of Representatives shall not exceed one for every thirty Thousand, but each State shall have at Least one representative"—Antifederalists argued that one representative per state would meet this minimum constitutional requirement. Furthermore, the small number of representatives meant that they would be elected either in extremely large election districts or maybe even in statewide elections. In either case only demagogues or the wealthiest, most prominent individuals would be elected, converting what was supposed to be the most democratic element of the new government into an assembly of aristocrats. Federalists quietly agreed with this assessment. They wanted large election districts to assure the election of the "natural aristocracy"—the most meritorious and virtuous who would properly represent their districts. These well-qualified representatives would attend Congress, listen to the debates, and make the best judgment from the available information.

Antifederalists argued that the representatives ought to mirror the people they represented. "O," in the Boston *American Herald,* maintained that "in order for one man properly to represent another, he must feel like him, which he cannot do if he is not situated like him."[27] Another writer asked "where is the people in this House of Representatives? Where is the boasted popular part of this much admired System? Are they not couzin germans in every sense to the Senate? May they not with propriety be termed an Assistant Aristocratical Branch, who will be infinitely more inclined to co-operate and compromise with each other, than to be the careful guardians of the rights of their constituents."[28]

---

[26]See Rufus King and Nathanial Gorham's response to Elbridge Gerry's objections, post-October 31, 1787, *DHRC,* 4:186.

[27]"O," *American Herald* (Boston), Feb. 4, 1788, ibid., 5:855.

[28]"John De Witt," *American Herald,* Nov. 5, 1787, ibid., 4:198.

Antifederalists were appalled at the small size of the Senate. If all of the states ratified the Constitution, there would be but twenty-six senators. With a quorum of fourteen, eight senators could agree to or defeat a bill or an appointment, while ten might ratify treaties that would become the supreme law of the land. Far too much power would be concentrated in the hands of too few. Because of its small size, the Senate could easily be corrupted by bribes from European countries interested in the passage or rejection of treaties or from private individuals seeking an appointment. Following the tradition of British monarchs, the new executive branch could influence a few senators and easily alter the outcome of any issue. Federalists pointed out, however, that the Senate would grow as new states joined the Union. Kentucky and Vermont would soon be admitted as full-fledged states, and Maine, Tennessee, and five new states carved from the Northwest Territory would not be far behind.

Considerable debate occurred over the terms of both representatives and senators. Looking back to England, Americans were well aware of the ongoing struggle over the tenure of the House of Commons. The Triennial Act (1641) was hailed as a bulwark against the arbitrary authority of the Stuart kings to rule without Parliament. Robert Whitehill of Pennsylvania drew on this history:

> It is strange to mark . . . what a sudden and striking revolution has taken place in the political sentiments of America, for in the opening of our struggle with Great Britain, it was often insisted that annual parliaments were necessary to secure the liberties of the people, and yet it is here proposed to establish a House of Representatives which shall continue for two, a Senate for six, and a President for four years! What is there in this plan indeed, which can even assure us that the several departments shall continue no longer in office? Do we not know that an English Parliament elected for three years, by a vote of their own body, extended their existence to seven, and with this example, Congress possessing a competent share of power may easily be tempted to exercise it. The advantages of annual elections are not at this day to be taught, and when every other security was withheld, I should still have thought there was some safety in the government had this been left.[29]

[29]Robert Whitehill speech in the Pennsylvania Convention, Nov. 28, 1787, ibid., 2:395–96.

Since the beginning of the Revolution, most of the American states elected their assemblies annually. John Adams had recommended annual elections for most state offices in his 1776 pamphlet *Thoughts on Government.* Quoting Alexander Pope, Adams wrote:

> Like bubbles on the sea of matter borne,
> They rise, they break, and to that sea return.[30]

Connecticut and Rhode Island elected their assemblymen every six months. The Articles of Confederation provided for the annual election of delegates to Congress. Dr. John Taylor told his fellow Massachusetts Ratification Convention delegates in 1788 that annual elections have "been considered as the safeguard of the liberties of the people . . . and the further we deviate therefrom, the greater is the evil."[31] Annual elections were said to be sanctioned by God as they coincided with the annual renewal in nature and the revolution of heavenly bodies.[32] Annual elections were an annual recognition of the sovereignty of the people.[33] Federalist Thomas Dawes of Boston thought that Antifederalists' concern about the length of the term missed the point. He praised the provision that allowed the people to vote directly for their representatives in Congress. Under the Articles of Confederation, delegates to Congress were elected in any manner decided by the state legislatures. In fact, most legislatures directly elected their state's delegates to Congress. The election provided by the new Constitution was an "acquisition of a new privilege . . . in favour of the people, if they are even chosen for forty years instead of two years."[34]

Federalists readily defended the two-year term of representatives. A Virginia pamphleteer gave numerous reasons for biennial elections: the long distances to travel, the need to become acquainted with federal measures, and the difficulty of getting men of ability to run for

---

[30]Robert J. Taylor, ed., *Papers of John Adams* (Cambridge, Mass., 1979), 4:90.

[31]John Taylor speech in the Massachusetts Convention, Jan. 14, 1788, *DHRC,* 6:1185–86.

[32]Charles Turner speech in the Massachusetts Convention, Jan. 14, 1788, ibid., 6:1187n.

[33]William Findley speech in the Pennsylvania Convention, Dec. 5, 1787, ibid., 2:506.

[34]Thomas Dawes speech in the Massachusetts Convention, Jan. 14, 1788, ibid., 6:1186.

short terms all justified the biennial election.[35] "Plain Truth" in Pennsylvania contended that "Annual elections in a federal government would beget confusion; it requires years to learn a trade, and men in this age are not legislators by inspiration." They must have time on the job to learn their profession.[36]

Fisher Ames of Massachusetts acknowledged that frequent elections had "been sanctified by antiquity, and . . . more endeared to us by our recent experience, and uniform habits of thinking." But Ames suggested that "a right principle, carried to an extreme, becomes useless." Obviously election for a day or for a lifetime would be unacceptable. The truth must lie as usual somewhere between the extremes. He believed that "the terms of election must be so long, that the representative may understand the interests of the people, and yet so limited, that his fidelity may be secured by a dependence upon their approbation." Ames wanted the advocates of annual elections to consider whether biennial elections would be harmful. "For it does not follow, because annual elections are safe, that biennial are dangerous. For both may be good." Adopting two-year terms did not put America on a path to lengthier terms of office. In England, Parliament could change the length of the Commons' term by a simple law; in America the term was set by the Constitution and would be difficult to change. He endorsed biennial elections because of the extent of the country, because of the kinds of legislation to be considered, and because they would perfect the "security of our liberty." Ames appreciated the protection biennial elections gave representatives from the volatile swings in popular opinion.

> A democracy is a volcano, which conceals the fiery materials of its own destruction. These will produce an eruption, and carry desolation in their way. The people always mean right, and if time is allowed for reflection and information, they will do right. I would not have the first wish, the momentary impulse of the publick mind, become law. For it is not always the sense of the people, with whom, I admit, that all power resides. On great questions, we first hear the loud clamours of passion,

[35]"A Native of Virginia," *Observations upon the Proposed Plan of Federal Government* (Petersburg, Va., Apr. 2, 1788), in ibid., 9:661–62. See also George Nicholas speech in the Virginia Convention, June 4, 1788, ibid., 9:923–24.

[36]"Plain Truth," *Independent Gazetteer* (Philadelphia), Nov. 10, 1787, ibid., 2:222.

artifice and faction. I consider biennial elections as a security that the sober, second thought of the people shall be law. There is a calm review of publick transactions, which is made by the citizens who have families and children, the pledges of their fidelity. To provide for popular liberty, we must take care that measures shall not be adopted without due deliberation. The member chosen for two years will feel some independence in his seat. The factions of the day will expire before the end of his term.[37]

The Senate, according to James Madison, was to be "the great anchor of the Government." The Constitutional Convention struggled over the method of its appointment and term of office. Election of senators by the House of Representatives, by the president, by electors chosen by the people, and by the state legislatures were all considered before the latter was finally selected. Suggested terms of office ran from good behavior to nine, seven, six, five, and four years. When the term of office for the House of Representatives was set at two years, the convention agreed on six years for the Senate. The sting of this lengthy term was softened by staggering the election of one-third of the senators every two years.[38] The staggered election convinced many that senators would keep "in mind that they are one day to return to the body of the people, and they ought not to be too much under the impulse of popular prejudices for it is sometimes necessary to save the people from themselves."[39]

Relatively little controversy occurred during the ratification debate over the method of electing the Senate. Federalists praised the election of senators by state legislatures as a vast improvement over the appointment of hereditary members of the House of Lords by the British monarch. Senators would "have *no similitude to nobles.*"[40] Edmund Pendleton thought the indirect election of senators seemed "admirably contrived to prevent Popular Tumults, as well as to preserve that Equilibrium to be expected from the Ballancing Power of

---

[37]Fisher Ames speech in the Massachusetts Convention, Jan. 15, 1788, ibid., 6:1189–93.

[38]James Madison to Thomas Jefferson, Oct. 24, 1787, ibid., 8:99.

[39]Alexander White to the Citizens of Virginia, *Virginia Gazette* (Winchester), Feb. 29, 1788, ibid., 8:440.

[40]"An American Citizen" (Tench Coxe) I and II, *Independent Gazetteer,* Sept. 26 and 28, 1787, ibid., 13:250, 264.

the three branches."[41] Federalists also used the election of the Senate by state legislatures as proof that the states would not be annihilated by the new Constitution, because without the state legislature, "there can be no senate."[42] Antifederalists belittled this proof. "Who is so dull as not to comprehend that the *semblance* and *forms* of an ancient establishment may remain after the *reality* is gone."[43] Other Antifederalists complained that rendering senators "more independent of the people" precluded the people "from having any decisive influence on their conduct."[44]

Antifederalists condemned the six-year term. Philadelphian Samuel Bryan writing as "Centinel," America's most vociferous Antifederalist essayist, predicted that "the term and mode of its appointment will lead to permanency."[45] John Taylor of Massachusetts agreed. "To be chosen for six years, but a shadow of rotation provided for, and no power to recall" meant that if men "are once chosen, they are chosen forever."[46] Political societies in Danville, Kentucky, and in western Virginia debated the Constitution and each suggested three-year terms for senators with staggered election of one-third of the Senate annually.[47] George Mason in the Virginia Convention predicted that, with six-year terms, no recall, and no mandatory rotation, senators "will fix themselves in the federal town, and become citizens of that town more than of our State. They will purchase a good seat in or near the town and become inhabitants of that place."[48]

Federalists felt that the responsibility vested in the Senate justified the longer term of office. "A Freeholder" in Virginia suggested that senators "might be too dependent on the will and fluctuating opinions of annual Assemblies, if they were not elected for a time which would

---

[41]Edmund Pendleton to James Madison, Oct. 8, 1787, ibid., 13:355.

[42]James Wilson's speech in the Pennsylvania Statehouse Yard, Oct. 6, 1787, ibid., 13:342.

[43]"Centinel" (Samuel Bryan) II, *Freeman's Journal* (Philadelphia), Oct. 24, 1787, ibid., 13:459.

[44]"The Impartial Examiner" II, *Virginia Independent Chronicle*, June 4, 1788, ibid., 10:1578. See also George Mason's "Objections to the Constitution," ibid., 13:349.

[45]"Centinel" I, *Independent Gazetteer*, Oct. 5, 1787, ibid., 2:165.

[46]John Taylor speech in the Massachusetts Convention, Jan. 19, 1788, ibid., 6:1257–58.

[47]Ibid., 8:411–12; 9:770, 774.

[48]George Mason speech in the Virginia Convention, June 14, 1788, ibid., 10:1292.

not only give them experience, but confidence to exercise their own judgments, when evidently in the right, without fear of being recalled by their constituents." Furthermore, their tenure, along with the president's, would "be essential to give stability to government, and uniformity to the execution of the laws; as well as to give foreign ministers the necessary confidence in government, when they negotiate treaties, on which the welfare, very possibly the existence of the states may depend."[49] James Madison felt the terms were "moderate," while Pendleton favorably compared the ratio between the federal House of Representatives and Senate (2 to 6) with the Virginia assembly and senate (1 to 4).[50] Zachariah Johnston, an influential farmer from western Virginia, succinctly stated the Federalist position in the Virginia ratifying convention: "The terms of elections are short, and proportionate to the difficulty and magnitude of the objects which they are to act upon."[51]

Closely coupled with the issue of the length of congressional terms was the question of whether mandatory rotation in office would have been beneficial. The Articles of Confederation provided that delegates to Congress could serve only three years within any six-year period; while the Pennsylvania, Delaware, and Virginia constitutions all had provisions for mandatory rotation in office for legislators. The new Constitution eliminated all mandatory rotations in office. Antifederalists saw rotation as one of the "grand bulwarks of freedom."[52] It was "a security which the people owe to themselves, for the fidelity of their servants; and perhaps the only good security they can have." It was the only way to require public officials "in a private capacity [to] feel all the good and evil effects resulting from their administration."[53] George Lee Turberville, a Virginia planter, objected to the loss of

---

[49]"A Freeholder," *Virginia Independent Chronicle*, Apr. 9, 1788 (extraordinary), ibid., 9:722.

[50]James Madison to Thomas Jefferson, Oct. 24, 1787, and Edmund Pendleton to Richard Henry Lee, June 14, 1788, ibid., 8:101; 10:1627.

[51]Zachariah Johnston speech in the Virginia Convention, June 25, 1788, ibid., 10:1531.

[52]"A Real State of the Proposed Constitution in the United States," *Independent Gazetteer*, Mar. 7, 1788; "An Officer of the Late Continental Army," *Independent Gazetteer*, Nov. 6, 1787, ibid., 2:212; Pennsylvania Petition against the Confirmation of the Ratification of the Constitution, January 1788, ibid., 2:771.

[53]"Republicus," *Kentucky Gazette*, Feb. 16, 1788, ibid., 8:378.

"That truly republican method of forcing the rulers into the character of Citizens again by incapacitating them for service for a given number of years after having been as many in Office." Such "a Barrier against oppression" could only be opposed by ambitious men seeking high offices.[54]

Massachusetts Chief Justice William Cushing, a Federalist, thought otherwise. A mandatory rotation in office "would be an open down-right abridgment of the people's liberties & right of Election—& a bold stroke for any Constitution makers to attempt; besides that it might prove dangerous to the *Commonwealth* in being obliged to bring in, new and unexperienced men, perhaps in an all hazardous moment, a time of war, instead of their tried & faithful Servants, whom they would wish to choose."[55] Judge Caleb Wallace of Kentucky agreed. It seemed illogical that "a man should be excluded from office as soon as by experience he is qualified to fill it."[56]

Debate also occurred over Congress's power to set their own salaries and to have their salaries paid from federal funds instead of by the states. Antifederalists charged that members of Congress would create "lucrative establishments" by "paying themselves at pleasure" independent of any control by the states.[57] John Taylor reminded the Massachusetts Convention that delegates to the Confederation Congress had always been paid by their home states. Since no state ever failed to pay its delegates, Taylor could see no reason why we should "leave the good old path." In fact, before the Revolution it was thought to be a grievance when the crown tried to pay the salaries of governors and judges, thus decreasing "their dependence on the people."[58] Gen. Elisha Porter responded that some states had failed to send delegates

---

[54]George Lee Turberville to James Madison, Oct. 28, 1787, ibid., 8:127. See also Samuel Nasson speech in the Massachusetts Convention, Feb. 1, 1788, ibid., 6:1398.

[55]William Cushing's prepared speech for the Massachusetts Convention, c. Feb. 4, 1788, ibid., 6:1433–34. See also Theophilus Parsons speech in the Massachusetts Convention, Jan. 23, 1788, ibid., 6:1326.

[56]Caleb Wallace to William Fleming, May 3, 1788, ibid., 9:782.

[57]"Philanthropos," *Virginia Journal,* Dec. 6, 1787; Joseph Spencer to James Madison, Feb. 28, 1788; Patrick Henry speech in the Virginia Convention, June 5, 1788; and "The Republican Federalist" VII, *Massachusetts Centinel,* Feb. 6, 1788, ibid., 8:210, 425, 9:961.

[58]John Taylor speech in the Massachusetts Convention, Jan. 21, 1788, ibid., 6:1283–84.

to the Confederation Congress because they had no money. Such also was true of some Massachusetts towns that were financially unable to send delegates to the state legislature. He appreciated the legislature's willingness to pay convention delegates out of state funds because they were assembled "for the general good." Such would be the case for members of Congress.[59] A Virginia newspaper writer saw "not the least ground for apprehension or fear." The president would veto any exorbitant increase Congress would propose for itself. Furthermore, by the time members of Congress would reach the age to satisfy the qualifications for office, "their integrity will be tried, and their abilities known and approved: most of them probably will be past, 'the hey-day in the blood,' weaned from the intoxicating dissipation of youth, and the hot allurements of pleasure."[60] A Virginia pamphleteer argued that the "many men of talents and virtue, from amongst whom the Congress will doubtless be chosen," would never "pass a law to give themselves immoderate salaries." But even if they did, "what would be the mighty evil to this extensive continent, from eighty or ninety persons having salaries larger than perhaps their services might merit?"[61] He also suggested that Congress needed to adjust its salaries to the ravages of inflation that would inevitably occur.

In addressing the Virginia Convention, James Madison hoped to explain, "to the satisfaction of every one," why the Constitutional Convention gave Congress the power to adjust its own salaries and to pay them from federal funds. If practicable, he said, Congress's salaries should have been specified in the Constitution "so as not to be dependent on Congress itself, or on the State Legislatures." Unfortunately, inflation made it impossible to set salaries permanently "as what may be now an adequate compensation might, by the progressive reduction of the value of our circulating medium, be extremely inadequate at a period not far distant." Furthermore, it would be inappropriate to allow the state legislatures to pay the salaries of members of Congress

---

59Elisha Porter speech in the Massachusetts Convention, Jan. 21, 1788, ibid., 6:1284.

60"Civis Rusticus," *Virginia Independent Chronicle,* Jan. 30, 1788, ibid., 8:335–36. The quote, "the hey-day in the blood," is taken from *Hamlet,* act 3, scene 4.

61"A Native of Virginia," *Observations upon the Proposed Plan of Federal Government* (Petersburg, Va., Apr. 2, 1788), *DHRC,* 9:667.

"because it is improper that one Government should be dependent on another." Under the Confederation, states paid the salaries of their members of Congress, "which enabled the States to destroy the General Government." Furthermore, Madison argued that no state legislature had abused its power to set its own salary because the people would indignantly reverse such an act. Such would be the case in Congress if they increased their salaries inappropriately. "The certainty of incurring the general detestation of the people will prevent abuse."[62]

Finding Madison's reasoning unconvincing, John Tyler responded by taking a completely different tack. By not having permanently fixed salaries in the Constitution, Congress might set them so low "that none but rich men could" afford to serve, thus creating a de facto aristocracy. To compare the congressional situation with past history in the Virginia legislature was inappropriate. Virginia legislators were immediately responsible to their constituents; Congress would not be.[63] Madison disagreed. Any change in the Constitution would be "equally or more liable to objections." Inflation and state dominance over Congress were legitimate concerns. Madison saw little to fear from Tyler's arguments. The people would never elect representatives who would arbitrarily reduce salaries to form an aristocracy. If, however, Congress did lower salaries, making it impossible for meritorious men to serve, states could supplement their salaries. Nonadjustable salaries decimated by inflation were far more likely to keep meritorious men from serving.[64]

Antifederalists, along with numerous Federalists, decried the fourth section of Article I, which gave Congress the power to regulate federal elections. Using this authority, members of Congress could perpetuate their own reelection and become "omnipotent." Young John Quincy Adams saw this power as "insidious, because it appears trivial, and yet will admit of such construction, as will render it a very dangerous

[62]James Madison speech in the Virginia Convention, June 14, 1788, ibid., 10:1262.

[63]John Tyler speech in the Virginia Convention, June 14, 1788, ibid., 10:1263. William Grayson shared Tyler's fears and used the British House of Commons to show how salaries could be eliminated to stifle competition and eventually obtain lucrative positions.

[64]James Madison speech in the Virginia Convention, June 14, 1788, ibid., 10:264, 266.

instrument in the hands of such a powerful body of men."[65] Federalists denied any sinister intent. This provision merely gave Congress the means of self-preservation by allowing it to call an election if a state was militarily occupied or if a recalcitrant state legislature refused to call an election. Congress could also correct serious malapportionments in congressional districts.[66]

Once elected, members of Congress were immune from some important restrictions provided in the Articles of Confederation. Delegates to the Confederation Congress faced annual elections, served no more than three years within any six-year period, and the states retained the power to recall any or all of their delegates. These restrictions made members of Congress "the servants of the people." Under the Constitution "our federal rulers will be masters and not servants."[67]

"Brutus" thought it only proper that the state legislatures retain the power to recall their representatives. "It seems an evident dictate of reason that when a person authorises another to do a piece of business for him, he should retain the power to displace him, when he does not conduct according to his pleasure." Recall had not been abused under the Confederation and "Brutus" saw no ill effects likely under the new Constitution. "It may," he said, "operate much to the public benefit."[68] "Federal Farmer," the most celebrated Antifederalist essayist, wrote the most compelling argument in favor of recall. The drafters of the Articles of Confederation thought it essential that members of Congress could be recalled by their states. This principle should also apply under the new Constitution. "We must," he argued,

> trust a vast deal to a few men, who, far removed from their constituents, will administer the federal government; there is but little danger these men will feel too great a degree of dependance: the necessary and important object to be attended to, is to make them feel dependant enough. Men elected for several years, several hundred miles distant from their states, possessed of very extensive powers, and the means of

---

[65]Adams to William Cranch, Oct. 14, 1787, ibid., 4:73.

[66]"Landholder" IV (Oliver Ellsworth), *Connecticut Courant,* Nov. 26, 1787, ibid., 14:233–34.

[67]Martin Kingsley speech in the Massachusetts Convention, Jan. 21, 1788, ibid., 6:1291.

[68]"Brutus" XVI, *New York Journal,* Apr. 10, 1788, ibid., 17:68.

> paying themselves, will not, probably, be oppressed with a sense of dependance and responsibility . . . . the principle of responsibility is strongly felt in men who are liable to be recalled and censured for their misconduct.

Recall had not been abused by the states under the Articles, and probably would not under the new Constitution. It would "be a valuable check." Senators particularly should be subject to recall because representatives would be elected more frequently, and, being chosen by the people, it would be more difficult for them to recall their representative than for the state legislatures to recall senators. "Federal Farmer" worried most about "interested combinations and factions . . . in the federal government . . . all the rational means that can be put into the hands of the people to prevent them, ought to be provided and furnished for them. . . . The circumstance of such a power being lodged in the constituents, will tend continually to keep up their watchfulness, as well as the attention and dependance of the federal senators and representatives."[69]

Coupled with the loss of the power to recall, Antifederalists decried the loss of the power to instruct members of Congress. Under the Articles of Confederation, delegates to Congress could be instructed by their state legislatures and be recalled if they failed to follow their instructions. According to "A Farmer" in Pennsylvania, although some complaints had surfaced about the mandatory rotation requirement of Congress, "the power of instructing or superceding of delegates to Congress under the existing confederation, hath never been complained of."[70] Some state constitutions specifically provided for the people's right to "assemble to consult upon the common good; give instructions to their representatives"; and petition for redress of grievances.[71] But once elected, federal senators and representatives would be "under no constitutional check or controul from their constituents, either by instructions, being liable to be recalled, or otherwise." No "citizen or the legislature of any particular State, nor of all the citizens and legislatures of all the States" had any power "either to give any

[69] *An Additional Number of Letters from the Federal Farmer to the Republican* . . . (New York, May 2, 1788), in ibid., 17:304–5.

[70] "A Farmer," *Freeman's Journal*, Apr. 23, 1788.

[71] See Article XIX of the Massachusetts Declaration of Rights, *DHRC*, 4:444.

legal instructions to a single member of Congress, or to call him to account for any part of his conduct relative to the trust reposed in him."[72] The Virginia, New York, and North Carolina ratifying conventions each proposed amendments to the Constitution guaranteeing the right to instruct their representatives and senators.[73]

Federalists responded by sometimes asserting that state legislatures did possess the power to instruct their representatives in both houses of Congress. Rufus King in the Massachusetts Convention suggested that "from time to time," "the state legislature, if they find their delegates erring, can and will instruct them. Will not this be a check? When they hear the voice of the people solemnly dictating to them their duty, they will be bold men indeed to act contrary to it. These will not be instructions sent them in a private letter, which can be put in their pockets—they will be publick instructions, which all the country will see, and they will be hardy men indeed to violate them."[74] Other Federalists agreed that the representatives of a free people, always desirous of being reelected, would not "dare to act contrary to the instructions of their constituents." To believe otherwise would call into question all safeguards in government, even the Antifederalists' boasted bill of rights.[75] Theophilus Parsons justified the omission of the powers to instruct and recall. With the sword of Damocles hanging over their heads, representatives would "lose all ideas of the general good, and will dwindle to a servile agent, attempting to serve local and partial benefits by cabal and intrigue."[76]

A key feature of the Constitution provides for amendments. Congress could propose amendments with a two-thirds vote by both houses. Ratification of amendments would be achieved by approval of three-fourths of the states. James Madison sought to implement this provision by proposing a bill of rights and four structural amendments to the

---

[72]"Cornelius," *Hampshire Chronicle,* Dec. 11, 1787, ibid., 4:411.

[73]The wording in these recommendatory amendments is virtually identical to that in the Massachusetts Declaration of Rights of 1780. See ibid., 18:202, 299, 316.

[74]Rufus King speech in the Massachusetts Convention, Jan. 19, 1788, ibid., 6:1257, 1260–61, 1263. See also speeches by Francis Dana and Charles Jarvis in the Massachusetts Convention, Jan. 18 and Feb. 4, 1788, ibid., 6:1242, 1426.

[75]"Cassius" VI, *Massachusetts Gazette,* Dec. 14, 1787, ibid., 4:424.

[76]Theophilus Parsons speech in the Massachusetts Convention, Jan. 23, 1788, ibid., 6:1326.

William C. diGiacomantonio

Petitioners and Their Grievances

A View from the First Federal Congress

THE NUMBER AND VARIETY of petitions to the First Congress attest to the people's expectations of their new federal government and the Constitution; their concepts of civil rights, citizenship, and entitlement; their ideas for economic growth and westward expansion; their material aspirations; and their understanding of the Revolutionary War, their role in it, and their obligations to those who suffered to secure independence. More than any other type of document, these petitions reveal the minds, sentiments, and conditions of men and women from 1789 to 1791. This survey of who petitioned—and what they petitioned for—is intended as a kind of popular history of the First Federal Congress. By recovering stories from the documentary record, we can hear again what the First Congress meant to the people it represented.

By early March 1790 the House of Representatives of the First Federal Congress had been debating Alexander Hamilton's Report on Public Credit almost daily for a month. Members appeared tired and bewildered to Pennsylvania Sen. William Maclay—and they were not the only ones.[1] Congress's increasingly crammed agenda became the

[1]Kenneth R. Bowling and Helen E. Veit, eds., *The Diary of William Maclay and Other Notes on Senate Debates*, vol. 9 of *The Documentary History of the First Federal Congress, 1789–1791*, 14 vols. to date (Baltimore, 1972–), pp. 202, 203, hereafter cited as *DHFFC*.

subject of critical commentary in the press. One wag, signing himself "Mathematicus," offered a reward to "men of genius" for calculating how long it would take Congress to complete all its business if it had taken four weeks to debate the first four resolutions on Hamilton's report.[2] Adding to the backlog was a flood of petitions that, just one week after Mathematicus wrote, Rep. Theodorick Bland of Virginia proposed to stem by moving to automatically submit all that related to monetary claims to the relevant executive department head. The next day alone, the House received five petitions for Revolutionary War claims, lending urgency both to Bland's motion and another by Elias Boudinot of New Jersey for the creation of a standing committee on claims. Yet the House consistently declined to take such streamlining measures.[3]

"Why is so much attention paid to trifling memorials?" asked the editorial writer "Candidus" midway through the session. "And why should we support men at Congress to trifle away their time upon them? The answer to questions of this kind is obvious," he insisted.

> Justice is uniform. It is the same when administered to an individual, a state, or a nation. . . . There is a mutual dependence between the supreme power and the people. And since the whole government is composed of individuals, does it appear inconsistent that individuals should be heard in the public councils? Much depends on public opinion in matters relating to government. Some deference therefore should be paid to it. In order to gain the confidence of the people they must be fully convinced that their memorials and petitions will be duly attended to when they are not directly repugnant to the interest and welfare of the community.[4]

Whether one was a senator or an orphaned child of a Continental soldier, all citizens claimed an equal right to justice by their right to petition. The preamble to the Constitution had proclaimed the establishment of justice as one of the purposes of government. Petitions are instructive for revealing how citizens thought Congress ought to dispense justice.

---

[2]*Daily Advertiser* (New York), Mar. 4, 1790.

[3]*DHFFC,* vol. 12 (Helen E. Veit, Charlene Bangs Bickford, Kenneth R. Bowling, and William C. diGiacomantonio, eds.), pp. 692, 698, 716–17, 724.

[4]Extract from a "Speculation" printed in the *Farmer's Journal* (Danbury, Conn.), May 27, 1790.

Unlike their counterparts in England's House of Commons (where petitions against new taxes, for example, were routinely banned),[5] members of the First Congress were unencumbered by weighty traditions qualifying the people's right to petition. Consequently, the more than six hundred petitions presented to the First Congress broached almost every subject that could come under the scrutiny of a deliberative body in the last decade of the eighteenth century. The belief, inherited from the practice of the colonial assemblies, that petitions should derive from personal, not broad, ideological grievances was put aside as congressmen dutifully presented their constituents' petitions on such matters of communal welfare as the institution of slavery, the prohibition of rum, and the standardization of printings of the Holy Bible.[6]

Commercial Petitions

Regulating interstate and foreign commerce was one of the most eagerly anticipated functions of the new government. Unlike the Articles of Confederation, the Constitution enabled Congress to respond in a comprehensive way to foreign trade restrictions by imposing retaliatory measures; to encourage the promotion of domestic manufactures by taxing the importation of the same goods manufactured abroad; and to promote American shipbuilding and a merchant marine by discriminating against goods imported in foreign bottoms. But all this had to be balanced with jealously guarded sectional interests and the overarching need to maintain a high level of imports because the collection of tariff duties was the only politically viable means of raising revenue.

Greeting that "happy Period" when "one uniform efficient Government should pervade this wide-extending Country," citizens began to petition about general trade policy within days after Congress took up the subject. Indeed, one of these petitions—from the tradesmen, manufacturers, and others of Baltimore—was the first petition to be

---

[5] P. D. G. Thomas, *The House of Commons in the Eighteenth Century* (Oxford, 1971), pp. 17, 69.

[6] Raymond C. Bailey, *Popular Influence upon Public Opinion: Petitioning in Eighteenth Century Virginia* (Westport, Conn., 1979), p. 39.

presented to Congress, ten days after the House convened. These petitions have several distinguishing and significant characteristics in common. In terms of wording, their impact relies on a handful of key repetitive phrases: the present "melancholy State" of the country; becoming "independent in Fact as well as in Name"; the government as the "Supreme energetic System" laying its "protecting hand" over "the whole Empire."[7]

In terms of these petitions' origins, commerce's appeal to class interests naturally incited class action. Tradesmen, mechanics, manufacturers, and shipwrights from Boston, New York, Philadelphia, Baltimore, and Charleston petitioned as groups, or smaller groups petitioned claiming to speak for larger groups. Thomas B. Wait informed Rep. George Thatcher of a meeting of no more than twenty merchants and a few of his other constituents of Portland, Maine, who immodestly claimed to speak for the entire town by beginning their petition "*Portland* district of Main, humbly shews." Wait went on to mock the inference that "the application, therefore, is made, not only by the Inhabitants who are voters, but by those also who are not—by the women, children, infants, & embryos—by the soil, the . . . sticks and the stones."[8]

Trade-related petitions were often the results of relatively sophisticated campaigns. Several trades meeting within the same seaport coordinated their appeals for protection and established committees of correspondence to consult with similar interest groups in other cities.

After specific rates had been set under the first impost, tonnage, and coasting acts, petitions continued to pour into Congress seeking modifications of duties and bounties on such goods as molasses, hemp, cotton, mustard, paints, hides, and tea. Two petitions kept general trade policy on the agenda. One was signed by forty-one ship captains virtually stranded in Charleston, South Carolina, harbor because of the "usual partiality" for foreign carriers, according to "some circum-

---

[7]*DHFFC,* vol. 8 (Bowling, diGiacomantonio, and Veit, eds.), pp. 343–46 passim. This volume and its companion, vol. 7 of the series, are the source for all the petition histories discussed in this paper; readers are referred to their indices. Bibliographic citations therefore are routinely omitted, except when the reference is to a direct quotation or to new information not contained in vols. 7 or 8.

[8]Ibid., 8:415 and note.

stances that are incomprehensible to your petitioners but which they trust the wisdom of Congress will ascertain."[9] The petition was referred to a committee that was eventually discharged without reporting. The other petition, from merchants and traders of Portsmouth, New Hampshire, received much more attention both in the House and in the press. It urged retaliation for foreign nations' discriminatory trade policies. Such measures were incorporated into a Madison-sponsored Trade and Navigation Bill that made Anglophiles cringe and that never passed into law.

It was this petition that prompted Rep. James Jackson of Georgia to complain about New England's protectionist begging, which he contrasted with the South's own patient suffering for the general economic welfare. Was his state "to be saddled the more," he asked, just because it was not "clamorous"?[10] It is true that, geographically, the overwhelming majority of petitions to the First Congress—about 85 percent—did in fact come from the northern states; Pennsylvanians alone submitted as many petitions as did Americans residing south of the Mason-Dixon line. But one Boston correspondent inverted Jackson's logic by suggesting that the imbalance only went to prove that northerners "are in a suffering condition, and it is thus that their sufferings are declared. What are we to infer from the silence of the citizens to the southward? That their comparative situation is better, and they therefore are contented."[11]

Supporters of tonnage discrimination against foreign nations nonaligned by commercial treaties with the United States cited the steep decline of New England whale and codfish industries as evidence of the need for retaliatory measures. Along with its own petition for the encouragement of fisheries, the Massachusetts legislature forwarded petitions it had received from the towns of Nantucket, Gloucester, and Marblehead. The last contained a chart listing in pathetic detail the poverty of each of the town's wards according to its number of widows, orphans, and the quantity of fuel it had left to carry them through the winter.

---

[9]Ibid., 8:355

[10]Ibid., vol. 6 (Bickford and Veit, eds.), pp. 1968–73.

[11]*Gazette of the United States* (New York), June 9, 1790.

When Congress first sought to supplement the revenue from tariffs by considering the more odious option of excise taxes on domestic products, it prompted petitions from snuff and tobacco manufacturers and coachmakers in New York, Philadelphia, and Baltimore. The Duties on Distilled Spirits Act (HR-110) ignited more widespread opposition than any other legislation, but only two petitions against it arrived before the First Congress adjourned. The petitioners were tradesmen and farmers of Philadelphia and Lancaster Counties, Pennsylvania, who attacked the odious history of the tax. Their western neighbors finally rose in revolt against this legislation in the short-lived Whiskey Rebellion three years later.

Petitions from the inhabitants of Rhode Island's seaports, and on behalf of the merchants of North Carolina, highlighted the interesting constitutional dilemma posed by those two states' foreign status pending their ratification of the Constitution. An amendatory Collection Act (HR-23) passed in the last days of the first session temporarily exempted the two states from the commercial burdens placed on foreign countries. North Carolina ratified before the expiration of the four-month deadline, but Rhode Island Antifederalists were unswayed. The punitive measures threatened by the Rhode Island Trade Bill (S-11) were only barely averted by that state's reluctant ratification in May 1790. Other petitions relating to the enforcement of Congress's various trade and revenue acts included appeals for designating additional ports of entry, mitigating fines and penalties, and increasing the compensation of revenue officers.

Besides seeking to handicap foreign imports by means of protective tariffs, at least some industrial pioneers thought the encouragement of manufactures ought to extend to the more modern sounding alternative of direct government subsidies. Cotton manufacturers in Philadelphia and Beverly, Massachusetts, sought just this in the context of larger aid packages that also included tariff protection. A third petition sought a loan or bounty for a malt liquor distillery in Haverhill, Massachusetts. The most controversial petition of this type came from the German-born John Frederick Amelung, whose glass factory in Frederick County, Maryland, had suffered a devastating fire in early May 1790. His petition, presented to the House three weeks later, led to a committee's favorable recommendation of a loan. But the proposal was eventually defeated after a lengthy floor debate that questioned the constitutionality of such a subsidy, the state of the treasury, and the fairness of loaning money to "foreigners."[12]

Public Credit Petitions

The availability of a reliable federal revenue through enforceable imposts and excises allowed the First Congress, during its second session, to address the most difficult and complex issue before it: the support of public credit. When the session convened in January 1790, the federal debt—including principal and interest—stood at $54 million; one-fifth owed to foreign creditors in Holland, France, and Spain. After some of the most lengthy and contentious debates on the floor of the House, and several months of seesawing votes on the subject, the House agreed to an assumption of the states' individual war debts that added another $25 million to the total debt finally provided for under the Funding Act (HR-63) of August 1790.

Before the act was passed, Congress received two petitions requesting that Congress meet the government's fiscal obligations; after the act was passed, it received ten more petitions disputing the way Congress did it, mostly protesting the reduction of the interest on the national debt from 6 percent to approximately 4 percent while leaving the original rates on the foreign debt intact. Prominent public figures and Continental army officers lent their names and influence to these appeals; Pennsylvania Supreme Court Justice Thomas McKean signed two of them and delivered one of them personally. Despite efforts to rally a continent-wide petition campaign, all but one of the petitions came from individuals or groups of public creditors in Philadelphia, New Jersey, and Boston. The remaining petition came from neither an individual nor a special interest group, but the General Assembly of the Commonwealth of Virginia. It was presented, appropriately, to the Senate—the body that represented the states in Congress. Although it was tabled without any known debate, Virginia's petition remains significant for two reasons: it was one of only two petitions the First

---

[12] *DHFFC,* vol. 13 (Veit, Bickford, Bowling, and diGiacomantonio, eds.), p. 1549.

Congress received from a state legislature, and it declared the unconstitutionality of an act of Congress fully eight years before the Virginia and Kentucky Resolutions against the Alien and Sedition Acts.

Several of the petitions relating to public credit share the distinction of being the longest petitions submitted to the First Congress. Though singular in that regard, they share several significant rhetorical elements with the petitions relating to trade policy. They provide a "melancholly Retrospect" of an earlier period "when complicated Want enfeebled, and impending Ruin agitated, their Country." Contrasting the promise of an "efficient government" with "the imbecility of the former Union," they hint at a stalled Revolution in which "the Triumphs of Independence" were incomplete while fettered by indebtedness.[13]

General Welfare Petitions

In steering their focus away from narrow self-interest by repeated references to plighted faith and national honor, many of the public credit petitions invoke the larger theme of national character and the legislature's impact on it. But another group of petitions were based more explicitly on Congress's perceived obligation to improve national character by legislation. Only one of these petitions made explicit reference to the Constitution's preamble. Yet they all directly and dramatically raised the issue of Congress's "implied powers" to provide for the general welfare.

The most famous of these petitions were the three submitted in February 1790 by Quaker or Quaker-sponsored antislavery groups in Philadelphia and New York. They sought better conditions for Africans during the infamous "Middle Passage" and even alluded to the eventual abolition of slavery. No other petitions to the First Congress unleashed the passionate rhetoric that these three did; none took up as much of Congress's time; and none produced a more thorough documentary record of the sophisticated lobbying campaign that accompanied it. This campaign included, in some form, all the activities

---

[13]Ibid., 8:260, 261, 275.

that political pressure groups engage in today: the Quaker petitioners gathered supporting evidence, attempted to educate legislators and the public through the media, recruited influential allies, orchestrated more broad-based and geographically diverse petition campaigns, testified before a congressional committee, and approached individual members at dinners, in their homes, on the streets, and even in their seats on the floor via letters delivered by the House doorkeeper.[14]

Neither congressmen nor their constituents would soon forget how "the dignity and honor of the House were greatly lessened by the torrent of Abuse" that southern members directed against the Quaker petitioners who looked down upon them from the gallery above.[15] Besides prompting serious questions about the Quakers' right to petition based on their neutrality during the Revolutionary War, the antislavery petitions led congressmen to consider the role of religious sentiment in framing public policy. The constitutional limitations, on the other hand, were clear. After a total of nine days' debate, which included the first documented filibuster in congressional history,[16] the House simply tabled an amended committee report that restated Congress's power to regulate commerce at the same time it acknowledged its powerlessness to halt the slave trade before 1808, emancipate slaves already imported, or interfere in their treatment within state boundaries.

Pennsylvania Rep. George Clymer had lumped the abolition of slavery together with the prohibition of rum as the two greatest glories to be expected of the new Constitution.[17] Spearheaded by Clymer's friend Dr. Benjamin Rush, Philadelphia's College of Physicians petitioned Congress to discourage the use of distilled spirits that "tend

---

[14]For a full account of the lobbying effort, see William C. diGiacomantonio, "'For the Gratification of a Volunteering Society': Antislavery and Pressure Group Politics in the First Federal Congress," *Journal of the Early Republic* 15 (1995):169–97.

[15]Elias Boudinot to William Bradford, Jr., Mar. 25, 1790, Wallace Papers, Historical Society of Pennsylvania, Philadelphia.

[16]William Smith to Edward Rutledge, Feb. 28, 1790, in George C. Rogers, Jr., ed., "Letters of William Loughton Smith to Edward Rutledge," *South Carolina Historical Magazine* 69 (1968):108.

[17]George Clymer to Dr. Benjamin Rush, [June 18], 1789, Gilder Lehrman Collection, Pierpont Morgan Library, New York.

equally to dishonor our Character as a Nation, and to degrade our Species as intelligent Beings." They professed the belief that the "Wisdom and Power" of the legislature could abolish behavior that "Reason and Religion" had failed to restrain.[18]

Petitions that Congress take measures "to prevent the publication of any inaccurate editions of the holy bible" linked public policy and moral sentiment even more directly. In May 1790 the Congregational clergy of Massachusetts addressed a circular letter appealing to all other Christian denominations to "confer & unite with us in one Petition, & thus to concentre the whole Christian interest in America."[19] Only the Baptist Associations of New England joined them. Sadly for students of the First Amendment, both petitions were tabled without debate.

The question of whether persons who conscientiously objected to bearing arms deserved a "peculiar indulgence" for their religious scruples was a subject brought before the First Congress by four petitions from Quaker Meetings in Philadelphia, New York, New England, and Baltimore. Many congressmen supported the petitioners' argument that the free exercise of religion was one of the "Blessings of Liberty" that the Constitution had been expressly formed to secure.[20] None are known to have publicly endorsed the petitioners' expressed tenets against making war.

The impact on an apprentice's productivity more than the salvation of his soul seems to have been the motivating factor behind a petition of the Manufacturers, Mechanics, and Inhabitants of Philadelphia as well as an earlier petition by John Amelung seeking militia duty exemption for employees of his glass factory. In addition to lost man-hours and the expense of equipping an apprentice, the Philadelphia petition claimed that masters risked weakening their authority and exposing "the flexible and ductile minds of young people" to "scenes and situations, from which morality seldom returns without a taint."[21] The petition, circulated in newspapers between New York and Baltimore, reportedly garnered 1,729 signatures. Although it was never submitted

[18] *DHFFC*, 8:313, 314.
[19] Ibid., 8:307–8.
[20] Ibid., 8:225.
[21] Ibid., 8:227.

to Congress, it represents an eloquent expression of America's unique melding of economic shrewdness with religious moralizing.

The Philadelphia petition cited the danger to the health of an apprentice while engaged in militia training. The First Congress received three petitions relating more directly to public health. The petition of the Boston Marine Society for the establishment of hospitals for "aged and disabled seamen"[22] was referred to Hamilton, whose favorable report met with qualified approval but no legislation by the Second Congress. The petition of the Merchants and Inhabitants of Baltimore was more ambitious in asking for the establishment of a "health-office . . . for protecting them from the infectious and epidemical diseases, brought by passengers and others arriving from foreign countries."[23] As with the Boston petition, a committee recognized the merits of such a measure but postponed further action until a general plan benefiting all major American seaports could be adopted.

Arts and Sciences Petitions

Because petitions reveal citizens' assumptions about the government's role in their lives, and what grievances they thought it capable of relieving, petitions that were envisioned but never presented are as instructive as those that actually made it to the floor of Congress. An example is Rev. Jedidiah Morse's petition requesting free postal delivery of information he was soliciting for the revised version of his soon-to-be famous primer, *The American Geography.* Fortunately, other means of encouragement were available to Morse. On May 12, 1789, he petitioned the House for copyright protection for his book by either a general bill or a private act that would also secure it against "mutilations, alterations, and abridgments."[24] Originally copyright protection was combined with patent protection as the goal of a single Copyright and Patent Bill (HR-10). A total of twenty-three patent petitions and six petitions seeking copyrights for books and maps were received by the First Congress before it passed separate patent and copyright acts in the second

[22]Ibid., 8:309.
[23]Ibid., 8:308.
[24]Ibid., 8:36.

session. One of the copyright petitioners petitioned again in the third session for an increase in the penalties for breach of copyright.

The most strenuous, perhaps meddlesome, and certainly most publicized of these petition attempts relating to the encouragement of the arts and sciences was that of the inventor John Fitch. In competition with fellow petitioner James Rumsey, Fitch laid claim to unlocking the economic potential of America's vast interior by various improvements to steam-powered navigation. The first of his four petitions to the First Congress sought a patent; the other three challenged various provisions of patent legislation. Fitch preceded his last petition attempt by canvassing individual members of both houses for their expected levels of support. Of those he approached, only James Jackson of Georgia "refused an audience," noted Fitch. "I suppose because he thought me to be a quaker."[25] Fitch's written tally is a rare and fascinating record of early congressional lobbying.

In addition to seeking copyrights and patents, at least five men thought the First Congress should provide encouragement for the arts and sciences in more direct ways. Three sought cash rewards for various accomplishments: a cure for hydrophobia, the publication of a road atlas, and the "discovery" of a new method for the desalinization of seawater. The noted cartographer John Churchman sought direct government subsidies for an expedition to the Arctic and other scientific experiments aimed at solving the puzzle of how to determine latitude at sea by magnetic variations. A fifth petitioner, John MacPherson, accused Churchman of plagiarizing his own lengthy and obtuse public lectures on the subject. In a later petition to the Second Congress, MacPherson added the charge of fraud, reassuring the Senate that, unlike Churchman, "I do not wish to obtain Sea Otters and Seal Skins by deceiving my Country."[26] MacPherson's First Congress petition requested money to go to France to vindicate his theories before a more enlightened scientific community.

In May 1790 the House received a petition from more than a dozen merchant mariners being held for ransom by Barbary pirates in the Mediterranean. Although they were entering upon their fifth year of

---

[25]Ibid., 8:73.
[26]Ibid., 8:11.

"slavery," as they called it, their requests for Congress's intervention sound remarkably patient. They were "sensible of the Multiplicity of Business" facing Congress, and realized that "untill such time as affairs so important was adjusted at home nothing Could be done abroad." Few Americans had as much to hope for from the emergence of a strong government that would enable their country to take its place among the political and military powers of the world. Consequently, their petition, even more than those on commerce and public credit, was laden with allusions to "the Rising Empire." "I experienced American Independence," Richard O'Bryen, the captives' spokesman, reminded Congress. "Let them consider the Basis on which the[y] at first formed thire Empire."[27] The Senate authorized the president to redeem the captives when the money became available, but later rescinded the order until the state of the treasury improved. The captives, who by 1796 numbered 119, were all ransomed according to a treaty ratified that year, and Richard O'Bryen went on to become America's consul to his former captors.

Disposition of Public Lands

Few issues test a government's claim to sovereignty as manifestly as the power to dispose of public lands as it sees fit. Most of the ten petitions the First Congress received on the subject of public lands dealt with the consequences of the Revolution's drastic impact on patterns of settlement. Some of the petitions sought to facilitate the purchase of new titles to unappropriated lands. Surprisingly, more sought to reverse or slow the effects of the land-hungry Revolution by securing old titles.

The related petitions of Andrew Ellicott and Nathaniel Gorham represent these two trends. Ellicott, deputy surveyor in the office of geographer of the United States, petitioned for funds to complete the survey of New York's western boundary. The Confederation Congress had already agreed to sell to Pennsylvania what lay beyond: the so-called Erie Triangle. Nathaniel Gorham and his business partner, Oliver Phelps, thought they had already bought the land from

---

[27]Ibid., 8:3–4.

Massachusetts before that state ceded it to the Confederation. Publicly, Gorham's petition sought to give him a voice in the determination of the boundary line; privately he may have sought to delay the business until the Erie Triangle was settled with enough New Englanders to create a fait accompli. The petition attempt failed, and Ellicot's boundary line subtracted 200,000 acres from his tract, speeding Gorham's eventual forfeiture of two-thirds of his six-million-acre tract.

Because the Federal Congress did not pass a uniform system for disposing of public lands until 1796, speculators such as Hannibal Dobbyn and George Scriba petitioned the First Congress directly for land purchases of as much as four million acres for as little as twenty cents an acre. Most congressmen were unaware that Scriba's venture was a front for the noted New York land speculator William Constable. Constable believed that Hamilton failed to report a land sales system to the First Congress because the success of Constable's sales agent in Europe had convinced the secretary of the treasury of the feasibility and greater profitability of selling smaller tracts directly to immigrants. Members of the First Congress also saw advantages to selling smaller tracts in a more orderly way, but not necessarily with an eye toward the economic bottom line. Hannibal Dobbyn's intention to bring over masses of fellow Irishmen alerted Connecticut's Rep. Roger Sherman to the dangers of an influx of persons unused to republican government, who "might tend to disturb the harmony and tranquillity, and embarrass the operations of the government."[28]

Four petitions sought to settle disputed land titles either caused or prolonged by the Revolution. Congress rejected the French Canadian Marquis de Chartier de Lotbiniere's petition for title to his ancestral manors along New York's Lake George and Lake Champlain, which had been in litigation since the Seven Years' War. Similarly, it made no reply to the petition from a group of German Pietists who lost their lands in North Carolina for refusing to swear an oath of allegiance to the Revolution out of religious conviction. Congress did endorse Alexander Fowler's pre-Revolutionary claims to a land bounty as a former British officer, but it refused to intercede when the United Land Companies appealed Virginia's nullification of their titles purchased di-

[28]Ibid., 12:51.

rectly from Native Americans prior to the Revolution. Associate Justice of the Supreme Court James Wilson petitioned on behalf of the company, which numbered Senators Robert Morris and Charles Carroll among its investors.

Government Organization

A large number of petitions submitted to the First Federal Congress dealt not with large questions of state policy or general welfare, but administration. Congress received a predictable number of petitions from office seekers for congressional staff positions. The qualifications most frequently cited were past attachment to the revolutionary cause and present economic distress, no doubt contributing to the impression that the inferior offices were mere sinecures.

Putting its own house in order meant, among other things, resolving disputed elections of its members and addressing unresolved grievances the First Congress had inherited from its predecessor, the Confederation Congress. The House received a petition from physician and historian David Ramsay seeking to unseat William Smith, his successful opponent in the first federal election for Charleston, South Carolina's, representative. It received several petitions to invalidate the election of the New Jersey delegation because of voting irregularities. All of these petitions helped establish important precedents relating to rules and procedures, such as the investigative role of committees, the status of seated members pending a ruling, and the relevance of state laws in congressional rulings on election qualifications. The debate over the New Jersey election, which was closely followed in the press, borrowed some of its intensity from the upcoming debate over moving the seat of government to Philadelphia, a measure that New Jersey's seated members were expected to support. Ramsay's petition also became an important forum for discussing the tangential themes of citizenship and the fear of residual loyalism.

All but a few of the petitions traced to the Confederation Congress's unfinished business related to claims for extraordinary expenses or additional compensation for employees of the Confederation: commissioners for liquidating the accounts between the United States and various states, agents for settling the accounts of the army's last remaining garrisons at Pittsburgh and West Point, commissioners for negotiating treaties with the Indians and Moroccans, and even the household steward of the presidents of Congress.

Most of the petitions were referred to the secretary of the treasury. Hamilton either never reported on or dismissed the majority of them on grounds that it would admit a "mischievous" precedent "which would be likely to lead to numerous applications and much embarrassment." He would allow a claim, he declared, only when it would not "form an inconvenient precedent, or contravene any rule, the maintenance of which is necessary to the preservation of order."[29] The influence of powerful friends and family could not sway the final issue. Thus Hamilton took no action on the petition of Representative Sherman's son, Isaac, who sought a higher salary as a government surveyor than that earned by surveyors who, because of the threat from Indians, never carried out their tasks.

Imputations arising from a congressional inquiry into his public accounts in 1785 had induced Sen. Robert Morris, former superintendent of finance, to appeal to the Confederation Congress for a final investigation and exoneration of his activities. Unfortunately, Congress was never able to collect a quorum to meet with Morris before the First Congress came into being. Understandably, both the House and Senate felt called upon to respond with some delicacy when he petitioned both bodies in February 1790. Morris's was the only petition to the First Congress submitted by one of its sitting members. His colleagues in the Senate agreed to the request for a new examination into his accounts, but their resolution was tabled in the House, where two separate committees each concluded that a detailed reexamination was both impossible and superfluous. Both houses did indulge one of Morris's requests, and took the rare step of inserting his petition in their respective journals.

When the Federal Congress convened in 1789, and for many years thereafter, the post office constituted the largest and most visible federal presence in the Republic. Of all government operations, it touched the most number of citizens in the most direct way. Under

---

[29]Ibid., 8:114, 93, 117.

the Confederation, this operation was run under a special ordinance with minimal congressional oversight. The First Congress failed repeatedly to improve upon the Confederation establishment, although it did receive seven petitions regarding modifications of existing contracts or settlement of past accounts with independent carriers. Surprisingly, given the lengthy debate sparked on the floor of the House by the subject, only one petition related to the establishment of new post roads.

A petition, from Mary Katherine Goddard, challenged her recent dismissal as postmistress of Baltimore and was accompanied by some of the most extensive documentation generated by any petition attempt in the First Congress. Her petition correctly cited the Washington administration's policy "that no Person should be removed from Office under the present Government, unless manifest misconduct appeared." In Goddard's case, the "misconduct" in question may have been her close association with the recently removed postmaster general, Ebenezer Hazard, whose own last days in office were clouded by charges that he had obstructed the circulation of Antifederalist newspapers during the debate over the Constitution. Ironically, Goddard's cause may have also been damaged by her brother's own well-known Antifederalism. The only explanation given that she herself considered "worthy of either notice or belief" was that a man's physical abilities were better suited to the task at hand.[30] Samuel Osgood, Hazard's successor as postmaster general, sidestepped the written protest lodged in support of Goddard by more than two hundred of Baltimore's most prominent residents, including the governor and the French consul. Their letter, Osgood's noncommittal reply, a schedule of the Baltimore post office's lucrative receipts, and another document labeled "Observations" accompanied Goddard's petition to the Senate.

Like a stretch of post road, the location of the federal capital was viewed as a catalyst for economic development. No fewer than twenty-six sites vied for this unprecedented infusion of government spending while the subject was under consideration in the First Congress. Nine sites brought their appeals by petition: a district in New Jersey and

---

[30]Ibid., 8:234.

Pennsylvania surrounding the Falls of the Delaware River; Lancaster, York, Reading, Carlisle, Germantown, and the counties around Philadelphia, Pennsylvania; and Baltimore and Georgetown, Maryland. Only the first two of these petitions are extant. But secondary reports such as newspaper summaries indicate that all of them composed a similar genre. Like chamber of commerce advertisements, they included maps and charts painstakingly detailing the number of masons, bakers, and clock and watchmakers that each locality boasted. References to navigation, commerce (real and potential), military defensibility, the quantity and types of fish, lumber, stone, artisans and manufacturers, the salubrity of the air, the fertility of the soil, and the centrality and accessibility to points north, south, and especially west, are all literary elements in these sometimes amusing displays of boosterism.

Petitions to alter or influence the location of federal courts probably shared in part this fever for municipal self-promotion. At least nine localities petitioned the First Congress on the subject. And although only one of their petitions remains extant, it is clear from it and from descriptions in the House Journal that the petitioners also argued their cases on grounds of convenience and access of the greatest number of people to the legal transactions necessitated by the federal government's expanding civil, admiralty, and revenue jurisdiction.

Only two petitions, from the same petitioner, prayed Congress for compensation and expenses incurred by a federal court clerk. Seven petitions were submitted by clerks and higher-ranking officials employed in the executive branch. All were successful, including one that prayed for compensation for expenses incurred by clerks in following Congress from New York to Philadelphia in late 1790.

There remains one other executive branch petition that perhaps merits special notice. Its roots are buried in the darker consequences of the Revolutionary War, but it is not merely a claim for the settlement of a government contract. It falls through the cracks, where any attempt to focus light only casts the subject deeper into shadow.

On August 11, 1789, Atcheson Thompson petitioned "that he may receive payment for sundry articles of clothing and other supplies furnished to George M[organ]. White Eyes, an Indian youth of the

Delaware tribe, by order of the President of the United States."[31] The petitioner was presumably a New York City merchant or tailor. The individual named in the petition was the son of a prominent Delaware Indian chief murdered by his American allies in 1778. In recognition of his father's services, George Morgan White Eyes was sent to Princeton in 1779 to be educated at Congress's expense. In 1788, the approximately sixteen-year-old boy was withdrawn from his last year at the college and sent to New York City by his congressionally appointed guardian to await further instructions. There followed a year of silence and neglect from the board of Treasury. Now totally destitute, and eager either for a government job or the money to return to a home he had never seen, the son of a former chief appealed directly to his "Brother" chief, George Washington. The president subsequently authorized Thompson's expenses, but the question of who was to pay the bills lingered. A month after Thompson petitioned, Washington paid the bill; he was probably reimbursed by Secretary of War Henry Knox from money Congress appropriated the next year for "Cloathing[,] a Horse and Money . . . to carry [White Eyes] back to his own Country."[32] The young man—probably not imbued with respect for American ways, as Congress originally intended—settled in a Delaware Indian community in the Northwest Territory, where he was killed in a drunken brawl eight years later.

Revolutionary War-Related Claims

The overwhelming majority of the petitions submitted to the First Congress were direct by-products of the War for Independence—from veterans, their dependent survivors, or civilians with war-related claims.

Former officers in the Continental army petitioned about the lifetime half-pay service pension they had been promised during the darkest days of the war, which was later exchanged, or commuted, for the equivalent of full pay for five years. These commutation petitions sought changes in their entitlement based on disputes about the rank

[31] Ibid., 8:137.
[32] Ibid., 6:1917.

they held at the end of the war. Other officers and soldiers claimed allowances for the depreciation of the paper money payments they had received during the war, and for miscellaneous extraordinary expenses. Among the latter were three former officers seeking indemnities for the British army pensions they had forfeited by joining the Continental army.

Revolutionary War officers formed a special interest group uniquely poised to influence legislation. One of the achievements of the Continental army was the creation of a continent-wide confraternity known as the Society of the Cincinnati. Its members—like the original Cincinnatus of ancient Rome—were willing to surrender the sword for the plow. But they were not willing to surrender the camaraderie or ties of mutual support that saw them through the war, linking Virginian with Pennsylvanian and Marylander to Rhode Islander in a way few other institutions could. Opponents feared the emergence of an antidemocratic "fifth column" aping European aristocratic orders.

There is no overt proof that members formed a united front on broad questions affecting veterans' benefits as early as the First Congress. The extent to which membership in the society may have helped individual petitioners remains equally difficult to determine. But it is likely that, in pressing their individual and joint claims, some petitioners who were also members of the society relied on that special bond with each other and with the twenty-five senators and representatives in the First Congress who were either charter or honorary members of the society. It certainly may have played a role in the decision of the officers of the army's Massachusetts Line to have the group's chairman, Benjamin Lincoln, submit a draft of their petition to secretary of war and fellow member Henry Knox. Or it may have played a role in member Alexander Hamilton's actual drafting of a petition for the New York chapter's president, Baron von Steuben, or in William Jackson's request that Otho Holland Williams write to Sen. William Grayson on his behalf for the post of secretary of the Senate. Williams's intervention was helpful, Jackson thought, because, "as a Soldier, your interest will have double weight in that question."[33]

---

[33]William Jackson to Otho Holland Williams, Jan. 30, 1789, Otho Holland Williams Papers, Maryland Historical Society, Baltimore.

One class of petitioners whom the war forced into a type of nationality limbo were Canadians—French and Anglo alike—who, like Prudent La Jeunesse, sought relief "in consideration of having espoused the cause of the United States, early in the late war, [and] of having abandoned his residence in Canada, to follow its fortunes." Refugee of the unpredictable fate that kept Canada from becoming the "Fourteenth Colony," La Jeunesse found himself "distitute of Freinds and Aquaintances in this to him a strange Country."[34] He reminded Congress how he had raised and led Canadian volunteers to participate in the victories at St. Johns, Chambly, and Montreal, only to end the war as chief baker at West Point. Congress denied his appeal for charity and La Jeunesse spent his later years in the poorhouse at Plattsburg, New York.

Congress's severe austerity consistently foiled petitioners' confidence that "every member of your Honorable Body, who lived in those times, which tried men's souls, will take a lively interest in contributing, liberally, to the necessities of those veteran Officers and soldiers, who may be wasting their last days, under the hard hand of poverty."[35] Congress was prepared to practice noblesse oblige only when it felt contractually bound to do so, or to reward particularly meritorious service. Each of these criteria is illustrated by the petitions of two soldiers whom the war brought from Germany to America by very different routes.

The first was Nicholas Ferdinand Westfall. A sergeant major in the Hessian forces, he fell under the spell of propagandistic handbills advertising Congress's offer of free land for Hessian noncommissioned officers who deserted, with bounties for every additional man they induced to desert with them. Westfall escaped from Gen. John Burgoyne's doomed army with twelve cohorts on August 8, 1777. Nine days later six of them showed up in the American camp at Saratoga. Westfall later settled on a farm and married—presumably a German woman, because she later went with their children to Germany to try to recover his estate there. They failed, leaving Westfall "in a very indigent and helpless condition," from which he petitioned Congress for

---

[34]*DHFFC,* vol. 7 (Bowling, diGiacomantonio, and Bickford, eds.), p. 167.
[35]Ibid., 7:181.

relief.[36] The petition was referred to Secretary of State Thomas Jefferson, who, with characteristic thoroughness, computed down to the dollar and cents what expense Westfall's deserters had saved the United States by not having to field an equivalent number of Continental soldiers. This amount ($336), along with 100 acres of land in the Western Territory, were granted to Westfall under the Widows, Orphans, and Invalids Act of March 1792.

The second petition came from Baron Frederick Wilhelm von Steuben. He is usually represented as a down-and-out mercenary soldier with a padded résumé. But the story that emerges from the ample documentation accompanying his First Congress petition is that of a gentleman of leisure, who only reluctantly responded to the constant entreaties to aid the cause of American independence from his high friends at the court of Versailles. Although constrained, for political reasons, to offer himself as a volunteer without pay, Steuben later remembered telling a congressional committee shortly after his arrival in the United States in 1777 that he expected his expenses to be defrayed, "as was customary," he told them, "with Officers of distinction in Europe."[37] Other emoluments—compensation for the loss of various service pensions from European princes—were alluded to. These vague agreements in place, Congress sped the Baron on his way to become the famous disciplinarian who reorganized the Continental army after the demoralizing winter at Valley Forge. Promoted to inspector general with the rank and pay of major general, Steuben soon absorbed the office and functions of adjutant general as well, thereby becoming Washington's de facto chief of staff.

The Confederation Congress granted Steuben honorific tokens and arrearages of pay. But his First Congress petition related to his larger claim to expenses and indemnities. Secretary of the Treasury Hamilton's report on the petition concluded that whether Steuben's verbal agreement with Congress in 1777 constituted a contract or not, it was "most consistent with the dignity and equity of the United States, to admit it as the basis of a final adjustment of his claims."[38] The Steuben Act

---

[36]Ibid., 7:293.
[37]Ibid., 7:212.
[38]Ibid., 7:242.

of June 1790 awarded a $2,500 annuity, which a disappointed Steuben threatened but failed to appeal before his death four years later.

Approximately one-third of all the Revolutionary War–related petitions to the First Congress concerned invalid pensions—requests for new ones, or arrearages on old ones. Disabled officers were entitled to half pay for life (upon return of their commutation). Noncommissioned officers and soldiers were entitled to no more than five dollars per month, with proportional allowances for partial disabilities. Providing the same disability benefits to seamen established a rare parity between them and their fellow fighters on land. Like the army's hospital department, the Continental navy was plagued by poor administration, haphazard oversight, and frequent congressional reorganizations that resulted in several contested claims to compensation. One of these, from five navy and two marine captains seeking the same half-pay benefits as army officers, was not aided by the fact that the group's principal spokesman, "Commodore" James Nicholson, was father-in-law to two members of the First Congress, Sen. William Few and Rep. Joshua Seney.

Among the invalid petitions to the First Congress was one submitted on behalf of five Oneida and Tuscarora Indians, and the widows of two others, by their perhaps aptly named attorney, Cornelius Van Slyck. The petitioners are not otherwise identified in the House Journal, and in fact one was neither an Oneida nor a Tuscarora, but a member of the Caughnowagas, Catholic Mohawks based near Montreal. At least two of them had commanded large groups of Indian scouts who helped defeat Burgoyne at Saratoga in 1777. Another joined in Gen. John Sullivan's devastating raid against the Iroquois in 1779. All seven petitioners based their claims on army commissions they had been granted by the Continental Congress in 1779 in gratitude for not joining their former allies among the Six Nations. Knox's report on their claim does not address directly the status of these once useful allies, but we can infer the neglect they were subject to. Two years after the war, Congress felt the need to pass a resolution specifically recommending that the Indian officers' accounts be settled like any other officer's. New York State made good only their depreciation in pay. By the time they appealed to the First Congress, their claims to half pay or invalid pensions were precluded by the various acts of limitation.

Combatants were not the only ones to submit war-related petitions. Eight civilians requested the same compensation for depreciated money payments as the Continental Congress had guaranteed army personnel. Many more civilians sought compensation for services they had provided as commissaries, staff clerks, blacksmiths, even a special emissary to the French court. Two petitioners—one a French Canadian and the other a Dutchman—sought compensation as propaganda writers and liaisons to their native countrymen.

One of the rewards of researching petitions to the First Congress is the appreciation it reawakens for the fact that the war for American independence was not entirely won by Anglo-Americans. To the list of German mercenaries, French Canadian volunteers, Dutch propagandists, and Oneida chiefs should be added the name of Jehoiakim McToksin—a member of the Stockbridge, or Moheconnuck, Nation, and the only other Native American known to have petitioned the First Congress. McToksin sought and received compensation for his services as an interpreter and guide during Sullivan's expedition against the Iroquois. Massachusetts Rep. Theodore Sedgwick seems to have ably managed the business; he presented the petition, submitted the favorable committee report on it, and even collected affidavits written on McToksin's behalf. Sedgwick resided at Stockbridge and no doubt felt at ease in matters relating to the Stockbridge Indians. But we are left to wonder about his fellow members' feelings when we read a newspaper account that "the singularity of this petition was the subject of much pleasantry"—some of it, almost certainly, at McToksin's expense.[39]

By far the greatest number of Revolutionary War–related petitions submitted by civilians sought compensation for money and supplies advanced and property damaged or destroyed. The best-known properties treated in this way were William Dewees's estate outside Philadelphia, which the British army raided and the Continental army later made famous as their winter encampment at Valley Forge, and Stephen Moore's 1,617 acre tract along the Hudson River, which the army had occupied continuously since 1778 and which the First Congress finally purchased outright under the West Point Act (HR-76) of July 1790.

---

[39]Ibid., 7:7.

Widows and orphans of Continental army officers killed while in service constituted another large group of civilian petitioners. A congressional resolution of 1780 recommended that the states extend to dependent survivors their husbands' and fathers' service pensions. Most of these petitions met a predictable fate: in cases where the benefit was due, it had already been paid; where it was not due, or an augmentation or interest on a late payment was sought, the claim was rejected because it "would involve the inconvenient precedent of unsettling an established rule."[40] Two interesting questions were raised by these petitions. The first was whether army officers fatally wounded at the Battle of Bunker Hill on June 17, 1775, were to be considered officers of the Continental army, since—as Hamilton pointed out—the Continental army might not be said to have come into existence until Washington arrived to take command ten days later. The second was whether the destitute mother of a son killed in action had some claim to an allowance. The answer to each was negative.

Petitions relating to the settlement of wartime accounts came from both soldiers and civilians. These included claims for miscellaneous expenses, such as Lewis Costigin's room, board, and bribery expenses while spying in British-occupied New York City; and two army volunteers' claims for money to return to their native Germany and France. Also, in this category are petitions seeking compensation for private money or credit expended by military officers in a public capacity. Debtor's prison literally awaited Timothy Pickering before a Special Appropriation Act (HR-100) acceded to his petition by granting him $40,000 to discharge private debts he had contracted on behalf of the public as quartermaster general during the last years of the war.

Pickering was not the most famous Revolutionary War figure rescued from private ruin by a petition to settle his past accounts. Maj. Gen. Nathanael Greene had earned widespread admiration as Pickering's predecessor and later as the victor in the brilliant war of attrition against Lord Cornwallis's army in the Carolinas. Grateful southerners lavished the Rhode Island Quaker with gifts of plantations and slaves. But his early death in 1786 bequeathed a precarious estate to his widow. In March 1790 Catherine Littlefield Greene resubmitted

[40]Ibid., 7:259.

her husband's Confederation Congress petition seeking relief from demands against his estate brought on by the bankruptcy of John Banks and Company, a military supplier whose debts Greene had been forced to stand as surety in exchange for a guarantee to provision his troops in the last year of the war. "Kitty" Greene's case attracted the support of many influential figures at the seat of government, because of her own personal charisma and her husband's military reputation. Henry Knox and Alexander Hamilton helped to draft her petition. Others joined them in collecting reams of evidence, the primary aim of which was to prove that the private credit Greene extended on behalf of his troops was not really part of a secret partnership agreement with the soon-to-be bankrupt supplier. The other underlying obstacle, Greene recognized, was that Congress, "to save themselves from paying the tax of a Shilling, would Sacrifice the Widow and Orphans of a General Who, alas can no longer Serve them."[41] Hamilton refrained from submitting his favorable report on Greene's petition for almost a year and a half; internal evidence indicates that he was receiving corroborative evidence right up until the last day. There are twenty-six attachments in all: affidavits, certificates, and copies of letters and contracts. After extensive debate, the Second Congress finally granted Greene's estate an indemnity of £8,688.

Catherine Greene's petition, like Steuben's, was rare for the support it enjoyed among so many highly placed public figures intent on securing a favorable outcome. In Steuben's case, lamented Senator Maclay, "invention has been tortured to put Money into his hands."[42] Among the rest, those that escaped being tabled immediately were generally dismissed by Knox or Hamilton because of a strict adherence to various statutes that cut off the eligibility of certain types of claims after a given date. Any relaxation of these so-called acts of limitation, they frequently reminded Congress, would cause "such an inundation . . . [as] would probably occasion disgust."[43] Secretary of the Treasury Hamilton advised Congress that "the impossibility, from the extraordinary circumstances of the times . . . to do justice, the inextricable

---

[41]Ibid., 7:495–96.
[42]Bowling and Veit, *Maclay's Diary*, p. 270.
[43]*DHFFC*, 7:376.

confusion, and incalculable expense" of offering civilians depreciation allowances, for example, militated powerfully in favor of leaving the matter "where the rules and principles of settlement at the Treasury have left it."[44]

Nowhere was this policy more rigidly applied than with the approximately 150 invalid petitions submitted to the First Congress. Cases like Henry Carman's seem to bear out Knox's assumption that an appeal to Congress was probably not well founded to begin with if it had failed to persuade the local authorities responsible for maintaining the pension rolls, whose information was deemed more reliable. Carman petitioned the House because of a disability he claimed was caused by a bullet to his shoulder that "caused his left arm to perish." In his report, Knox verified that Carman had served in the New York militia, but he was not convinced the wound dated from Carman's time of service. An affidavit by five of Carman's neighbors, later submitted to the War Department by the local examining board, testified that he had "received his wound in his own house, by the accidental discharge of a pistol which was laid on a shelf by one of the party with whom the said Carman had been in pursuit of a cat."[45]

With other invalid petitioners, it is harder to look the other way. Thomas Simpson began his military career at the age of twenty in New Hampshire's "Corps of Rangers." Between 1775 and 1779 he rose from private to captain lieutenant and saw action at Quebec, Saratoga, and Monmouth. In that time he lost his left eye to smallpox, had an inextractable musketball lodge near one of his kidneys, and had his right leg crushed by the fall of a horse. Knox denied his request for an increase from a quarter pension to a half pension, on the familiar grounds that "it would operate perniciously for the United States to encrease or modify the pensions which have been assigned to the Invalids by the respective States."[46]

Thomas McKinstry left his native Columbia County, New York, to join a Massachusetts regiment outside Boston just weeks after Lexington and Concord. During the Continental army's retreat from Canada

---

[44]Ibid., 7:5.
[45]Ibid., 7:345.
[46]Ibid., 7:343.

in early 1776, he was stricken with smallpox and in that state was forced to "cross and recross the lake [Champlain] several times in an open boat exposed to the weather." A want of medicine and fresh provisions combined with the effect of some other undisclosed disease contracted in his eyes left McKinstry on the verge of total blindness, applying as a pauper for public relief. Yet the New York examiners ruled that these circumstances "were not of such a decisive nature as to entitle him to a pension."[47] And again Knox stood by the state's ruling, citing additionally the acts of limitation. Truly, the letter killeth.

Not until March 1792 did Congress enact legislation altering the manner of establishing or changing a claim. In the absence of such new legislation, petitioners could only claim a change in their pension status if they were mentioned by name in one of the two private acts: the Disabled Soldiers and Seamen Act (HR-88), and the Widows, Orphans, and Invalids Act passed by the Second Congress.

In other areas, however, the common people's impact on the legislation of the First Congress was significant. By extending their influence beyond the act of electing their congressmen, the people's petitions voiced interests and concerns that in some cases translated directly into legislation. In this category were petitions relating to copyrights and patents, federal revenues and their collection, the federal debt, the location of the capital, and the land office. In other cases petitions prompted some debate and appropriate legislation was considered; among these were the Quaker antislavery and militia exemption petitions and the petitions relating to public hospitals.

---

[47]Ibid., 7:350.

Jeffrey L. Pasley

Private Access and Public Power

Gentility and Lobbying in the Early Congress

LOOKING BACK FROM the late twentieth century, an era of aggressive, unapologetic interest-group politics in which tens of thousands of people make their livelihood as lobbyists in the national and state capitals, it is commonly assumed (and asserted in journalistic and social scientific accounts) that lobbying is a natural outgrowth of representative government, that the one must have existed as long as the other. How could any legislative body exist without generating a group of people committed to influencing it?[1]

However, any effort to document this assumption by surveying the historical literature on lobbying in the early United States runs into unexpected roadblocks. There are only a handful of scholarly books on the history of lobbying in America, and none of them deal with Congress before the Civil War. Several works deal with the American colonies' lobbying of the British government, while two others analyze

[1]A typical statement comes from the political scientist Lester W. Milbrath: "Lobbying is probably as old as government," he writes, then briskly carries his historical narrative from the dawn of government to 1946 in two paragraphs (Milbrath, *The Washington Lobbyists* [1963; reprint ed., Westport, Conn., 1976], pp. 12–13). For other examples, all using some variation of the "old as government" line, see James Deakin, *The Lobbyists* (Washington, D.C., 1966), pp. 52–77, esp. p. 53; Karl Schriftgiesser, *The Lobbyists: The Art and Business of Influencing Lawmakers* (Boston, 1951), pp. 3–21, esp. p. 3; Colleen McGuiness, ed., *The Washington Lobby*, 5th ed. (Washington, D.C., 1987), pp. 1–3.

the rise of reformist pressure groups during the Progressive Era. Apparently, only one book in the whole historiography of American politics takes the history of congressional lobbying as its primary subject, and it focuses exclusively on the period when Ulysses S. Grant was president. A few other works cover individual figures who lobbied or individual incidents where lobbying occurred, but mostly long after the 1790s.[2] Some sense of the scale of this problem can be seen in Joel H. Silbey's twenty-three-volume compendium of articles on the history of Congress. This extensively indexed series features exactly *two* references to lobbying, and one of these was an article version of the book on lobbying in the age of Grant. To say the least, historians of Congress have not been too interested in lobbying. In going through the literature, one detects a strong preference for great floor debates and high-profile decisions, the kind recorded in roll call votes on big issues such as slavery and war, rather than the more prosaic, technical, and financial matters on which lobbyists, like Congress itself, tend to spend most of their time.[3]

It is important to be clear about what is meant here by *lobbying*. The word should not be used to denote simply *any* effort to influence Congress. Petitions, letters, newspaper articles, and such are all ways in which Congress can be pressured, and they are certainly tools that

[2]A survey of library catalogs and electronic databases turned up the following works: Alison Gilbert Olson, *Anglo-American Politics, 1660–1775: The Relationship between Parties in England and Colonial America* (London, 1973); idem, *Making the Empire Work: London and American Interest Groups, 1690–1790* (Cambridge, Mass., 1992); Michael G. Kammen, *A Rope of Sand: The Colonial Agents, British Politics, and the American Revolution* (New York, 1974); Rebecca Starr, *A School for Politics: Commercial Lobbying and Political Culture in Early South Carolina* (Baltimore, 1998); Margaret Susan Thompson, *The "Spider Web": Congress and Lobbying in the Age of Grant* (Ithaca, 1985); Elizabeth Sanders, *Roots of Reform: Farmers, Workers, and the American State, 1877–1917* (Chicago, 1999); and Elisabeth S. Clemens, *The People's Lobby: Organizational Innovation and the Rise of Interest Group Politics in the United States, 1890–1925* (Chicago, 1997). There are also two biographies of prominent nineteenth-century lobbyists: Lately Thomas, *Sam Ward: "King of the Lobby"* (Boston, 1965); and Glyndon G. Van Deusen, *Thurlow Weed: Wizard of the Lobby* (Boston, 1947). Only a few these works take lobbying as their primary subject, and only one (Thompson) can really be considered a history of lobbying Congress. The historical literature on lobbying in the 1790s is limited to studies of particular incidents and individuals. These will be cited below. The works listed in note 1 all contain breezy, journalistic capsule histories of lobbying. For the early period, they typically content themselves with mentioning the constitutional guarantee of the right to petition.

[3]The compendium mentioned is Joel H. Silbey, ed., *The Congress of the United States, 1789–1989,* 23 vols. (Brooklyn, N.Y., 1991).

lobbyists may use. However, they are not the kinds of influence on Congress that the political term *lobbying* was invented to describe. The term was inspired by the image of people loitering in the anterooms and hallways of government buildings, especially legislative chambers, hoping to guide government policy.[4] Hence my definition: lobbying occurs when some group or individual, typically a private economic interest seeking benefits or protection, makes its case *personally* to government decision makers, often but not necessarily through some sort of specially deputed emissary. This is certainly the kind of lobbying regarded as typical in our time, when virtually all significant economic interest groups, be it industries, professions, occupations, or individual corporations, maintain Washington offices or retain lawyers and consultants to help ensure favorable treatment from the national government. Typical subjects for modern lobbying would be preserving a industry's tax break or heading off a costly regulation.[5]

It is this type of lobbying—the personal buttonholing of lawmakers by paid agents of special interests—that professional historians have particularly neglected in their studies of early congressional history. One of their reasons has been a conviction (differing sharply from the less well-informed assertions of journalists and political scientists focused on twentieth-century lobbying) that there was not much of it happening in the early period. Former House historian Raymond Smock has written that in the First Federal Congress "there were no lobbyists, at least as we describe them today." The only thing close to lobbying that Smock could detect were the activities of various land companies and the furious politicking of the competitors for the site of the permanent capital, a process that has been described very fully by Kenneth Bowling. Even Bowling found relatively little personal lobbying over the seat of government issue. Most of the site promoters

---

[4]H. L. Mencken, *The American Language: An Inquiry into the Development of English in the United States,* 4th ed. (New York, 1965), p. 148; William A. Craigie and James R. Hulbert, eds., *A Dictionary of American English on Historical Principles* (Chicago, 1942), 3:1436–37; Mitford Matthews, ed., *A Dictionary of Americanisms on Historical Principles* (Chicago, 1951), 2:1951; J. A. Simpson and E. S. C. Weiner, *The Oxford English Dictionary,* 2d ed. (Oxford, 1989), 8:1074.

[5]Jeffrey H. Birnbaum and Alan S. Murray, *Showdown at Gucci Gulch: Lawmakers, Lobbyists, and the Unlikely Triumph of Tax Reform* (New York, 1987); Jeffrey H. Birnbaum, *The Lobbyists: How Influence Peddlers Get Their Way in Washington* (New York, 1992).

worked through petitions, private letters, and the press, and a few were themselves members of Congress. The only site that had a lobbyist in the sense used here was Lancaster, Pennsylvania, whose chief landowner, William Hamilton, reluctantly traveled to New York in a futile campaign to entice the government onto his land.[6]

On the surface, then, Smock's argument that there were no lobbyists seems to have much merit. By many measures, there was less need for lobbyists in the 1790s than in later periods. Precious few *organized* special interests existed in the early days of the U.S. government—there were no national trade or professional associations or labor unions—and only a handful of lobbying's traditionally most important constituency, profit-making corporations. Perhaps even more importantly, the United States was simply a small place in the 1790s. The population at the beginning of the decade was a mere 3.9 million, about the size of present-day Alabama. The petition process described by several of the other essays in this volume seems to have worked well enough for most purposes on its own. The right to petition was a well-established prerogative by 1789, and the congressional workload was small enough in the 1790s that a mere paper petition often really was enough to get the government's attention. A brief glance through the records shows that Congress was willing to give serious consideration to all manner of petitioners, be they major business leaders or obscure citizens, from the merchants of Philadelphia at the high end, to the fishermen of Marblehead, Massachusetts, in the middle, and on down to a host of individual Revolutionary War soldiers and officers seeking pensions, back pay, or a settlement of their accounts.[7]

This kind of individual attention to petitions became less possible with the expansion of the government during the Civil War, and virtually impossible in the twentieth century, due mostly to the sheer size of the country and the ever-widening range of activities required to govern it. Thus growth alone was a major cause of the rise of the avowed,

---

[6]Raymond W. Smock, "The House of Representatives: First Branch of the New Government," *Prologue* 21 (1989):292; Kenneth R. Bowling, *The Creation of Washington, D.C.: The Idea and Location of the American Capital* (Fairfax, Va., 1991).

[7]U.S. Congress, House of Representatives, Committee on Energy and Commerce, *Petitions, Memorials and Other Documents Submitted for the Consideration of Congress, March 4, 1789, to December 1795* (Washington, D.C., 1986), pp. 103, 220, 331.

professional lobbyist in the mid-nineteenth century and the popular distaste for lobbyists that quickly appeared in response. The Gilded Age "lobby's" existence documented the fact that, as the government grew, one needed highly paid special representatives in order to truly have a voice at the capital. The paid representatives that one elected at the polls were no longer enough. Since only the wealthiest institutions and individuals could afford such extra representation, the polity seemed to be losing some of its democratic character. This was how the troubadour of American democracy, Walt Whitman, felt in the summer of 1856, when he included "lobbyers" (as he called them) in a list of the types of "politicians" and "nominating dictators" sapping the republic of its democratic vitality. Writing in a time when the party system was cracking apart under the stress of sectional crises and government corruption scandals, Whitman lumped "lobbyers" in with "bribers, compromisers . . . sponges . . . policy backers, monte-dealers . . . [who were all] men, scarred inside from the vile disorder, [but] gaudy outside with gold chains made from the people's money. . . . Crawling, serpentine men, the lousy combings and born freedom sellers of the earth." Such expressions of disgust against lobbyists would grow only stronger in later decades, when lobbying for the nation's first giant corporations involved the liberal distribution of money and high-class prostitutes to lawmakers.[8]

Clearly there was nothing like that going on in the 1790s, but perhaps it is a mistake to look for such brazen lobbying in this early period. It would certainly be a mistake to rely solely on the existing historical literature. If one goes beyond the literature into the sources, abundant evidence can be found of more subtle and limited forms of lobbying in the early Congress. For instance, the little-seen documents recently published in the petition histories volumes of the *Documentary History of the First Federal Congress* reveal that there was often much more to petitioning Congress than citizens putting their wishes on paper. However small the country and government was, Americans who had

---

[8]Schriftgiesser, *Lobbyists,* pp. 3–21; Walt Whitman, *The Eighteenth Presidency!* ed. Edward F. Grier (Lawrence, Kans., 1956), pp. 26–29; Edward Winslow Martin, *Behind the Scenes in Washington* (Philadelphia, 1873), pp. 215–47. On the scandals of the 1850s, see Mark W. Summers, *The Plundering Generation: Corruption and the Crisis of the Union, 1849–1861* (New York, 1987).

business before the government, or material interests affected by it, frequently felt the need to augment their written requests with what we would call lobbying.[9]

Most of the early petitions involved not large public policy questions but financial claims made by individuals or small groups ranging from veterans requesting pensions, or military contractors and tradesmen asking payment of old debts, to surveyors, printers, and others seeking new federal contracts. A significant number of these petitioners had their requests professionally drafted and/or personally presented by attorneys. For example, Josiah Simpson was hired by a group of Boston blacksmiths to appeal for back pay related to their wartime service, and former postmaster general Ebenezer Hazard filed a petition as attorney on behalf of some Orange County, New York, farmers who wanted compensation for wood taken from them during the war. Philadelphia printer Francis Bailey engaged Miers Fisher, one of the city's most eminent attorneys, to help him patent a method of type founding that could supposedly create documents that could not be counterfeited. Fisher seems to have been worth his doubtless exorbitant hire. With no patent procedures or policies yet established, a patent required an act of Congress, so Fisher duly drafted a private bill reflecting his client's desires and shepherded it to passage. A leader of Philadelphia's Quaker elite, Bailey's lawyer also lobbied successfully for at least one other petition, the Wilmington Academy's request to be compensated for damages sustained while the school was used as a Continental army barracks and hospital.[10] So the notable present-day Washington phenomenon of lawyers working as lobbyists can be traced back to the beginnings of the government. One major difference, however, is that these early lawyer-lobbyists mostly stayed away from policy questions, limiting themselves to individual claims needing congressional action to be settled.

Many other petitioners either believed that personal appeals would

---

[9]*Documentary History of the First Federal Congress of the United States of America, 1789–1791*, 14 vols. to date (Baltimore, 1971–), vols. 7–8 (Kenneth R. Bowling, William C. diGiacomantonio, and Charlene Bangs Bickford, eds.), hereafter cited as *DHFFC*.

[10]The specific examples mentioned can be found in *DHFFC*, 7:22, 107, 117–18, 8:73–84, but see also ibid., 7:21, 22, 31, 38, 75, 84, 98, 133, 171, 183, 273, 287, 316, 335, 356, 378, 380, 381, 392, 405n, 445, 446, 490, 599; 8:xxv, 40, 318, 555, 557, 558, 776.

increase their chances of success or could not afford a lawyer, and so traveled to New York and Philadelphia themselves to contact members and monitor the proceedings related to their cases. Several petitioners were urged to this step by one of their own representatives, or another friend on the scene. These temporary lobbyists came from a surprisingly wide cross section of white male American society (in addition to at least one widow), though most had a certain desperation in common. Numerous wounded veterans seeking pensions turned up at the seat of the federal government, including some reduced to rather marginal lives. One of the more pathetic cases was Robert Connelly of Maryland, a former prisoner of war who lost his sight from injuries sustained in the failed invasion of Canada and spent the rest of his life indigent, managing the trip to Philadelphia only through the charity of his neighbors.[11] At the other end of the spectrum, well-connected gentlemen came to lobby for a variety of petitions, most of them with a personal financial dimension even if they addressed a policy issue. Merchant, textile manufacturer, and future Massachusetts senator George Cabot went to New York soon after the new government's inception to lobby against a duty on foreign cotton and for a higher tax on imported cotton goods, and followed up the next year with a petition along the same lines. Cabot's fellow Massachusetts merchant-aristocrat Nathaniel Tracy, a close associate of several congressmen and Secretary of War Henry Knox, made the journey in 1790 to petition and lobby for a general bankruptcy bill, or, failing that, some personal relief for losses suffered supplying the armies and privateering during the Revolutionary War.[12]

Many of these temporary lobbyists came only to deliver their petitions, but some stayed on for extended periods. Disabled veteran David Cook of Westbrook, Maine, spent the entire two years of the First Congress trying to get his pension; he even followed Congress from New York to Philadelphia, only to have his relief bill killed by the Senate on the last day of the third and final session. Cook had to beg for the money to get back home. The exact nature of these petitioners' lobbying activities while visiting the seat of government is often unclear. One

[11]Ibid., 7:356–57, 8:53.
[12]Ibid., 8:365–71, 86–89.

suspects a good deal of loitering around taverns was involved, because in some cases (especially those of the less distinguished petitioners) there is little evidence of extensive or meaningful contact with members of Congress. Lobbying petitioner John Wilson, a Woodstock, Connecticut, farmer, managed to pack remarkably few activities into four months in New York. He first appeared there in March 1790, applied to various individual officials for a military pension, and, on their advice, petitioned Congress in April. Congress immediately referred Wilson's case to Knox, who reported on it unfavorably at the end of May, deeming Wilson insufficiently disabled to qualify for a pension. A month later, Wilson was still in town, writing letters to President Washington asking for a job and to Rep. James Madison seeking support for his doomed petition. Living expenses were high at the seat of government, exacerbating the financial problems that led to the petitions in the first place, but that does not seem to have deterred many of those who were determined to lobby.[13]

A few of the visiting petitioners came as the specially deputed emissaries of organized groups, performing functions much closer to lobbying as we know it than the individual claim seekers. The Providence town meeting appointed and paid Benjamin Bourn and James Manning, Rhode Island's soon-to-be first congressman and the president of Rhode Island College (later Brown University), respectively, to deliver petitions for relief from the federal impost and tonnage duties. A committee styling itself the "Public Creditors of Pennsylvania" sent Chief Justice Thomas McKean and other prominent citizens to New York to meet with the state delegation and present a petition calling for full payment of the Revolutionary War debt.[14]

By far the most elaborate petition and lobbying campaign in the First Congress (and probably for the rest of the 1790s as well) was that mounted against slavery by Philadelphia-area Quakers. Petitions were submitted by the Philadelphia and New York Yearly Meetings and the Quaker-dominated Pennsylvania Abolition Society. An "embassy" of eleven Philadelphia Quaker leaders spent several weeks at New York,

---

[13]Ibid., 7:395–99, 346–48, 460. Both Cook and Wilson did eventually get pensions from later congresses.

[14]Ibid., 8:389–90, 258–64.

employing every possible means of pressuring Congress to abolish or restrict slavery and the slave trade. The Quaker lobbyists wrote supplemental briefs for the committee considering their petition, accosted members outside the doors of Congress, visited them at their lodgings, and invited them for meals, all the while making themselves conspicuous in the House galleries, looming over the proceedings like the specters of a guilty national conscience. At the same time, their petitions were published in the newspapers, and New York seemed suddenly awash in antislavery pamphlets and broadsides. This onslaught of politicking by such a wealthy and well-connected group left southern congressmen infuriated and suspicious. They resented being pressured so intensely and incessantly by men who were not even their constituents, and they questioned the constitutionality of the whole procedure. The eventual House committee report declared that the federal government had no power to emancipate slaves or (for twenty more years) prevent their importation, and even mild committee resolutions affirming the right of Congress to lay taxes on imported slaves (along with the general principle that slaves should be treated well and educated) were struck down by southern votes.[15]

It is important not to stretch the evidence in the petition histories volumes too far and fully endorse the popular histories' view that lobbying—as we know it—is as old as the national legislature itself. Take away the various individual claims—for pensions, patents, damages, reimbursement of expenses, and settlement of official accounts—and relatively few examples of lobbying remain. Most of these individual claims were small and of a type that would not be handled by Congress in later decades as administrative bureaucracies developed. The connection of the bulk of this early petitioning to the later history of lobbying, then, may be rather weak. Even counting the claims, there is not enough evidence in the petition histories to conclude that much of the government's work or the general direction of public policy was being directed or even heavily influenced by avowed lobbyists.

The Quakers may have been an exception that proved and helped

[15]Ibid., 8:314–38; William C. diGiacomantonio, " 'For the Gratification of a Volunteering Society': Antislavery and Pressure Group Politics in the First Federal Congress," *Journal of the Early Republic* 15 (1995):169–97.

strengthen an unwritten rule against lobbying Congress. Striking as it was, the Quaker antislavery lobby failed. Moreover, it appears to have been unique in its openness, high degree of organization, and goal of effecting broad changes in government policy rather than merely settling claims or securing particular economic benefits. The evidence of other organized, policy-oriented lobbying campaigns is scant, and the Quaker example seems not to have found many immediate imitators, though various forms of antislavery agitation would continue. There are even some indications that the Quakers set the "cause" of lobbying back a few years. After the Quaker lobbying campaign ended, the editors of the *Documentary History of the First Federal Congress* wrote, "Congress took steps to prevent a repeat of the episode."[16]

The hostility to, and general absence of, open lobbying in the First Congress was entirely consistent with what we know about the political culture of the early United States. It would have been directly contrary to the hopes of the Federal Constitution's Framers if the new government had been immediately overrun by modern interest or pressure group politics. Most of the men we now know as the Founders disliked political parties and other forms of concerted, aggressive, competitive political action outside of the direst political emergencies.[17] James Madison, Alexander Hamilton, and many other leaders felt that the essence of good government, and virtuous leadership, was *dis*interestedness, and they had been profoundly disturbed by the self-interested, narrow-minded politics they saw dominating the newly democratized state governments during the 1780s. This was one of the chief ideas motivating the drive to replace the old confederation with a federal government that would not be under the states' control. While Madison and Hamilton knew that there inevitably would be competing interests in America that would selfishly seek benefits and advantages from the government, they hoped that their new national state would

---

[16]*DHFFC,* 8:314.

[17]Richard Hofstadter, *The Idea of a Party System: The Rise of Legitimate Opposition in the United States, 1780–1840* (Berkeley, 1969); Ralph Ketcham, *Presidents Above Party: The First American Presidency, 1789–1829* (Chapel Hill, 1984); William Nisbet Chambers and Walter Dean Burnham, eds., *The American Party Systems: Stages of Political Development* (New York, 1967), pp. 56–89.

be large, diverse, and distant enough to prevent any particular local interest from amassing the legislative majorities necessary to carry out their schemes.

Lodging supreme authority in a new layer of government above the states, Madison wrote in his famous *Federalist* No. 10, would result in the "substitution of representatives whose enlightened views and virtuous sentiments render them superior to local prejudices and schemes of injustice." Into this category, Madison lumped any efforts by one interest group to profit at the expense, or take the property, of another, even by such now commonly lobbied-for means as trying to shift a tax burden from one type of property to another.[18]

Should we conclude then that Madison's plan succeeded? Were private and particular interests unable to project their influence into Congress, leaving enlightened statesmen to choose wise policies for themselves? Our review of the petition histories suggests that they generally were, but what if we move beyond this particular set of documents? Unfortunately for Madison, there are suggestions that the most significant, expensive, and self-interested lobbying in the early Congress may have taken forms subtler and less readily identifiable than the petitioners and their attorneys. For instance, some of the most effective lobbying on behalf of private economic interests was conducted by the members of Congress themselves. House members and even most senators were elected by relatively small constituencies, places where the political, economic, and social leaders knew each other intimately—when they were not one and the same. Contrary to Madison's expectations, many of these enlightened statesmen showed little hesitation in aggressively promoting the local interests they knew so well.

Let's look at an example. One of the many popular accounts of lobbying mentions, without sources, that the first congressional debate over the tariff was the first time lobbying appeared in Congress. What the record shows, however, is that not lobbyists but petitions flooded

[18]This general interpretation of the constitutional movement appears in Gordon S. Wood, *The Creation of the American Republic, 1776–1787* (1969; reprint ed., New York, 1972). The Madison quotation can be found in Jacob E. Cooke, ed., *The Federalist* (Middletown, Conn., 1961), p. 64.

into Congress, asking high or low duties to protect this or that industry, and that congressmen promptly got up on the floor to plead for their local special interests: Pennsylvanians argued for duties high enough to protect the state's manufacturers, but not so high or so strict as to hurt Philadelphia merchants, and New Englanders fought against the proposed molasses duty because it would hurt Massachusetts rum distillers. These are only two of many examples. Several of the members making these arguments had personal connections to the industries they were speaking for, and their ability to defend local interests was greatly enhanced by Congress's incestuous tendency to appoint the members most interested in a particular measure to the committee charged with considering it. Merchants were the group most directly affected by import duties, so the House select committee appointed to draft the impost bill was made up of Philadelphia merchant Thomas Fitzsimons; Massachusetts merchant Elbridge Gerry, who was married to the daughter of a New York merchant; and attorney John Laurance of New York, described perhaps uncharitably by William Maclay as "a mere tool of British agents & factors."[19]

Maclay considered these three "very improper characters" for such a committee, but the rest of Congress must not have agreed because similar standards seemed to rule the selection of many if not most congressional committees. In Congress's defense, there was an important practical advantage to this committee selection practice. Members of Congress had to write their own legislation in those days, and merchant congressmen may have been the only members with the technical knowledge to tackle something as complex as a tariff bill.

Tariff legislation is not the only or even the most stark example in which congressmen acted as lobbyists. Territorial delegates to Congress, for instance, acted almost solely as lobbyists. They had no voting powers and were rarely called upon to do anything other than promote

[19]Margaret C. S. Christman, *The First Federal Congress, 1789–1791* (New York, 1989), pp. 119–25; Edward Stanwood, *American Tariff Controversies in the Nineteenth Century* (1903; reprint ed., New York, 1967), pp. 39–71; Kenneth R. Bowling and Helen E. Veit, eds., *The Diary of William Maclay and Other Notes on Senate Debates*, vol. 9 of *DHFFC*, p. 50. These trade petitions take up more than 80 pages of the "Petition Histories," the longest chunk of the volumes devoted to any single policy subject. See *DHFFC*, 8:339–421, 445–47.

legislation on behalf of local interests, usually those of whatever coterie of territorial officials and politicians had secured them election. Statehood, of course was the most typical issue they lobbied, but others came up as well, especially land. In 1799, for instance, twenty-seven-year-old future president William Henry Harrison was elected delegate to Congress from the Northwest Territory. Scion of one of Virginia's most aristocratic families and the sitting territorial secretary, Harrison was elected with the support of a group of rising young Republican politicians in the territorial legislature. They were dissatisfied with the existing public land laws, which favored large-scale, well-capitalized eastern speculators. The nearest place to buy public land was Pittsburgh, and the land was sold only in large tracts of at least 640 acres, for cash, with no credit extended. The future Ohioans wanted a smaller minimum tract, a lower price, branch land offices near the lands to be sold, and the chance to buy on credit. Though Harrison and his friends cast themselves as tribunes of the settlers, the practical effect of their proposals would be to allow ambitious westerners such as themselves to more easily become small-time land speculators. Almost upon his arrival in Philadelphia, Delegate Harrison broached the idea of changing the land law and was promptly made chairman of the committee to frame the bill. This was a congressional habit, as we will see. The Harrison Land Act of 1800 passed in May and, in its final form, embodied all the western speculators' demands, save for a lower minimum price.[20] While undoubtedly benefiting the special economic interests of himself and others, in this case William Henry Harrison had also probably fulfilled the genuine desires of many of his constituents.

Other examples of lobbying by congressmen seem less benign and less easy to explain away. In 1788, John Cleves Symmes of New Jersey, a delegate to the Confederation Congress in 1785 and 1786, had used his extensive congressional contacts to make himself a major land

---

[20]Malcolm Rohrbough, *The Land Office Business: The Settlement and Administration of the American Public Lands, 1789–1837,* 2d ed. (Belmont, Calif., 1990), pp. 16–22; Freeman Cleaves, *Old Tippecanoe: William Henry Harrison and His Time* (1939; reprint ed., Norwalk, Conn., 1986), pp. 22–32; Payson Jackson Treat, *The National Land System, 1785–1820* (New York, 1910), pp. 94–100; William Henry Harrison to Constituents, May 14, 1800, Logan Esarey, ed., *Messages and Letters of William Henry Harrison,* 2 vols. (Indianapolis, 1922), 1:12–13.

magnate, securing a contract to buy one million acres of land on the Great Miami River, the present Cincinnati, Ohio, area, for roughly 66⅔ cents an acre. This deal became known as the Miami Purchase. Symmes moved to the Northwest Territory himself (and was promptly appointed territorial judge), but this was not a colonization scheme. Instead, it was a straightforward land speculation, aimed at making money by selling land and town lots to migrants. Symmes's partner and agent in the venture was Jonathan Dayton, a sitting member of the New Jersey delegation to Congress who had also been the youngest member of the Constitutional Convention. Dayton went on to have an illustrious career in the new Congress, including a stint as a Speaker of the House in the late 1790s.[21]

The Miami Purchase was eventually doomed by many factors, including Indian wars, rising land prices, and the incompetence, greed, and personality of John Cleves Symmes. However, the efforts of Dayton and Elias Boudinot, a New Jersey House member who had invested in the project, kept it alive throughout the 1790s despite Symmes's best efforts to alienate congressional affections. Early on, Dayton and Boudinot defeated attempts to summarily retract the contract, and in ensuing years, Dayton especially warded off other threats to Symmes and his purchase. For the first two years of the new government, Dayton acted as an incredibly well-connected private lobbyist, one who lived near the capital in New Jersey near the seat of federal government and, because of his previous service in the Confederation Congress and Constitutional Convention, was on close personal terms with many of the most prominent members of the new Congress. In 1791, he continued this lobbying from within Congress itself, as a member of the House of Representatives. Dayton's exploits in the cause of the Miami Purchase were many. In 1789, he stopped an effort to take away Symmes's judgeship as part of the transition to the new government and then arranged for troops to protect the Miami settlement during

---

[21]Beverley W. Bond, Jr., ed., *The Correspondence of John Cleves Symmes, Founder of the Miami Purchase* (New York, 1926), pp. 1–16, 197 n. 1; A. M. Sakolski, *The Great American Land Bubble: The Amazing Story of Land-Grabbing, Speculations, and Booms from Colonial Days to the Present Time* (New York, 1932), pp. 100–119; Treat, *National Land System*, pp. 52, 54.

the flaring Indian wars. In 1790 and after, Dayton expended much effort "counteracting & frustrating" efforts to open a land office and begin selling federal lands in the Northwest Territory to individual settlers; he and Symmes feared the federal prices would be lower than what they were asking.[22]

Dayton's greatest service to Symmes and himself probably came in 1792. Out in the Northwest Territory, Symmes had been selling overlapping plots and land outside of his boundaries; at the same time, his title to the land itself was in question because of the poor state of his payments to the government. But not to worry—Dayton and Boudinot were on the case. In the midst of sabotaging yet another land office bill in the spring of 1792, they introduced resolutions in favor of Symmes's claims. Dayton himself was appointed chair of the committee to frame a bill and soon reported a measure confirming Symmes's title to his land (along with his own) and establishing a liberal interpretation of the purchase's disputed boundaries. He then muscled the bill through both houses of Congress. Dayton's personal stake in the Symmes purchase was well known to his fellow congressmen but caused little concern. In fact, Dayton claimed to have won some senators over with the assurance that he, rather than the erratic Symmes, would handle the final payment details.[23]

Still unsatisfied because he had not been granted the full million acres he had contracted for, Symmes pressed for yet more land and might have gotten it if he and Dayton had not fallen out with each other in the years after 1792. Without Dayton's help, future congressional action on the Miami Purchase, while frequent, was increasingly unfavorable to Symmes. Acts passed in 1797, 1801, 1802, 1803, and 1804 canceled most of Symmes's claims while granting some rights to innocent purchasers who had bought land he did not own. For a time around 1800, Symmes hoped that his son-in-law, the aforementioned

---

[22]John Cleves Symmes to Elias Boudinot, July 18, 1788; Symmes to Jonathan Dayton, Aug. 21, 1788; Dayton to Symmes, Sept. 12, 1788, Feb. 2 and Aug. 15, 1789, Mar. 16 and Sept. 13, 1790; Bond, *Correspondence of Symmes,* pp. 27, 37–38, 198–99, 210–11, 219, 225, 228, 248, 259.

[23]Beverley W. Bond, Jr., "John Cleves Symmes, Pioneer," Jonathan Dayton to John Cleves Symmes, May 6, 1792, Bond, *Correspondence of Symmes,* pp. 13–16, 267–69.

William Henry Harrison, would be able to help. Fresh from his land act triumph, Harrison got himself appointed chair of a committee to consider the Symmes matter and reported a bill giving his father-in-law one more chance to actually acquire the lands he had sold outside his boundaries, the purchasers of which were now suing him in droves. The Symmes relief bill passed the House but got postponed in the Senate, despite herculean efforts by Harrison that extended even to testifying before the committee on the bill. The loyal son-in-law admitted to his constituents that these activities placed him in a "most delicate situation," but assured them that his "whole conduct was meant to be guided by moral integrity."[24]

It is clear that there was much lobbying from outside Congress as well as inside, going far beyond what appears in the petition histories. This lobbying has been easy to miss, however, because it was nearly invisible, so deeply embedded was it in the social and political mores of the late eighteenth century.

One way to begin to see this is by tracing the origins of the term *lobbying*, and especially the extremely revealing circumstances in which the term developed. Though historians have generally treated lobbying as a Civil War era and Gilded Age phenomenon, the word emerged quite early. The origins can be dated back to sometime before 1808. In that year, Kentucky congressman Matthew Lyon made the first recorded political use of the word *lobby* in a debate on moving the seat of government back to Philadelphia,[25] where the antechambers of Congress had been popular places for upper-crust Philadelphians to congregate. This congregation had collectively been dubbed the *lobby*. This was not meant as a pejorative. The connotation was that this lobby was not so much a smoke-filled room as a glittering eighteenth-century drawing room. To understand what this could have meant requires some explanation of the setting in which Congress met in Philadelphia.

By all accounts, the Congresses of the 1790s were well integrated into polite Philadelphia society, considered the most sophisticated

---

[24]Bond, "Symmes, Pioneer," pp. 16–21; Treat, *National Land System*, pp. 60–62; Esarey, *Messages and Letters of Harrison*, 1:15–17.

[25]See the histories of "lobby" and related words in the works cited in note 4 above.

such scene anywhere in the United States.[26] This was no small matter in a period when, as Richard Bushman has shown in his brilliant book *The Refinement of America,* social refinement was almost a mania in the United States. George Washington and most of his colleagues among the early American elite were obsessed with perfecting and expressing their gentility. They and even relatively middle-class people studied, sweated, and spent to meet standards of behavior borrowed from the royal courts of Europe, standards that applied to every conceivable aspect of life: architecture, home furnishings, table manners, movement, cleanliness, conversation, penmanship, clothing, even bowel habits. Americans learned many of these rules from so-called courtesy books, how-to manuals for proper genteel living that were mostly adapted from advice written for European courtiers in earlier centuries. One of the most popular courtesy books in the English-speaking world was based on the letters written by Lord Chesterfield, a British courtier and politician, for the instruction of his illegitimate son. Bearing such titles as *The School of Good Manners and Youth's Behaviour, or Decency in Conversation among Men,* courtesy books explained how to behave in a life filled with formal entertainments and situations—balls, dinner parties, etc.—the kind of life that once only courtiers ever would have lived but that an ever widening circle of people were now trying to create for themselves. The books preached

[26]For an old but still useful account of Philadelphia high society in the 1790s, see Rufus Wilmot Griswold, *The Republican Court; or, American Society in the Days of Washington,* new ed. (1867; reprint ed., New York, 1971), pp. 365–412. For a modern history of Philadelphia's tenure as the nation's political, cultural, and economic metropolis, see Richard G. Miller, "The Federal City, 1783–1800," and Edgar P. Richardson, "The Athens of America, 1800–1825," in *Philadelphia: A 300-Year History,* ed. Russell F. Weigley (New York, 1982), pp. 155–205, 208–57. Several previous contributions to U.S. Capitol Historical Society volumes have dealt more specifically with the social setting of congressional life at Philadelphia and its political ramifications. See Fredrika J. Teute, "Roman Matron on the Banks of Tiber Creek: Margaret Bayard Smith and the Politicization of Spheres in the Nation's Capital," in *A Republic for the Ages: The United States Capitol and the Political Culture of the Early Republic,* ed. Donald R. Kennon (Charlottesville, 1999), pp. 95–98; Kenneth R. Bowling, "The Federal Government and the Republican Court Move to Philadelphia, November 1790–March 1791," and Anna Coxe Toogood, "Philadelphia as the Nation's Capital, 1790–1800," in *Neither Separate nor Equal: Congress in the 1790s,* ed. Kenneth R. Bowling and Donald R. Kennon (Athens, Ohio, 2000), pp. 3–33, 34–57.

the need to show elaborate respect for others and present a smooth, beautiful appearance by controlling your bodily movements, speech, and mind at all times. George Washington had to copy out a courtesy book as a schoolboy and listed rules against touching your private parts, rinsing your mouth, or humming in public, among other prohibitions. Americans who could afford it went beyond the self-help books, hiring writing masters to teach their children the fashionable round or Italian hand and dancing masters to teach them not only the complex group dances they were expected to navigate but also the genteel approach to the most basic movements of everyday life: how to stand, how to sit, how to walk, how to enter a room. As the courtesy books and dancing masters defined it, gentility involved living your whole life as if it were a public performance, as if one were playing the part of oneself on the stage of a theater. Members of the American gentry, a category that included most members of the early congresses, took this quite seriously, perpetually worrying about the figure they had cut in various situations and mercilessly reviewing the performances of themselves and others in their journals and letters. They greatly admired people who could perform well.[27]

Hence the impressive displays of gentility put on in Philadelphia seriously impressed the congressmen who served there. They not only attended the balls, dinner parties, and concerts of the Philadelphia elite but also apparently took some political guidance from the people they met in those circles. In many ways this made sense, since upper-class Philadelphia included some of the nation's leading scientists, artists, and businessmen, to name only three walks of life; the typical congressman doubtless had much to learn from these cosmopolitan, well-informed people. At any rate, members seem to have so relished hobnobbing with Philadelphia gentlemen and ladies, and been so eager to seek their insights into pending legislation, as to bring Philadelphia society to the very doorstep of their legislative chambers. It begins to look as if the large number of petitions that came to Congress

---

[27]Richard L. Bushman, *The Refinement of America: Persons, Houses, Cities* (New York, 1993). Washington's school exercise has been published as Charles Moore, ed., *George Washington's Rules of Civility and Decent Behaviour in Company and Conversation* (Cambridge, Mass., 1926). For a modern edition of one of the most popular courtesy books, see David Roberts, ed., *Lord Chesterfield's Letters* (Oxford, 1992).

from Philadelphia, New York, and other nearby urban business communities may well have had more extensive personal assistance than the records show.

The sponsors of the 1808 back-to-Philadelphia resolution held up the ease of access to "society" and the fund of well-informed opinion out in the lobby as advantages of meeting in Philadelphia. Matthew Lyon and several others denied it, citing that lobby scene as a baneful political influence. "We have heard . . . that if we move to Philadelphia we shall have a commanding lobby," he said, but to him this was exactly the problem. In Philadelphia, "Congress were almost overawed by that city; measures were dictated by that city" and especially by its polite society. A roughhewn Irish printer by background, Lyon himself had suffered there as a representative from Vermont. Blue-blooded Federalists had ostracized and taunted him, and one of them finally beat him savagely with a cane on the floor of Congress; even then it was Lyon who found himself facing censure, for having insulted his gentleman assailant.[28]

Other representatives were so taken with Lyon's redefinition of the word *lobby* as to employ it again and expand on his point. In the rustic setting of early Washington, Virginia's Joseph Lewis, Jr., argued, Congress had no dazzling lobby and they were better off for it. "If members of this House should ever become so dependent that they must be indebted to persons out of doors . . . as to the course of conduct that they should pursue, it will be time for the people to call us home, or . . . alter the Constitution and elect the whole representation of the Union from the city of Philadelphia, because Philadelphians alone are capable of directing legislation for the public good." Nathaniel Macon of North Carolina took the problem more seriously. Like Matthew Lyon, he recalled the 1790s but went further than Lyon in blaming the Philadelphia lobby not only for mistreating Republicans but also for helping push hated Federalist legislation through Congress. "We talk of our independence," chided Macon, "but every man in Congress, when at Philadelphia, knew that city had more than its proportional

---

[28] *Annals of Congress,* 10th Cong., 1st sess., House, pp. 1531–37. On Matthew Lyon's history, see Aleine Austin, *Matthew Lyon: "New Man" of the Democratic Revolution, 1749–1822* (University Park, Pa., 1981).

weight in the councils of the Union." He considered the proposed move back to Philadelphia as a plot to save Alexander Hamilton's Bank of the United States, whose charter expired in 1811. Move, Macon said, and there would be two years "to talk and be talked to about this bank" by the Philadelphia lobby. Other rural members saw even more generalized dangers. Otherwise "honorable and independent men," argued Maryland's Philip Barton Key, would be induced to "sacrifice agriculture at the shrine of . . . commerce." Key saw clearly how Philadelphia's high society lobbyists would go about their work: "The inhabitants would give us good dinners and handsome entertainments, operating on our prejudices and taking advantage of unguarded moments . . . [and] insensibly bias our better judgment."[29]

Key's fears were far from unfounded. Members of Congress do tend to be influenced by the social milieu in which they live, in ways that subtly change their personal sympathies and may in the long run shape their political decisions. By socializing frequently with wealthy Philadelphia merchants and financiers, many almost certainly came to share some of the concerns of wealthy merchants and financiers. At least in the early days, the atmosphere at the Capitol in Washington City was quite different, though Congress was still attended by throngs of people. Surveyor of Public Buildings Benjamin Henry Latrobe estimated that four to five hundred persons brought their business to

---

[29]*Annals of Congress,* 10th Cong., 1st sess., House, pp. 1538–48. There was a long history and many subtexts underlying these attacks on the Philadelphia "lobby." The corrupting influence of Philadelphia society had been complained of during and between the periods when it was the seat of government in the 1780s and 1790s. The animus that southern representatives such as Macon, Lewis, and Key felt against Philadelphia also stemmed from its status as the center of abolitionism in this period. Wealthy antislavery Quakers of the type who had lobbied Congress in New York doubtless had plenty of opportunities to proselytize congressmen amid the Philadelphia social whirl. See Bowling, *Creation of Washington, D.C.,* pp. 30, 159, 191, 198, 203, 211–12. Another issue was the powerful role that certain elite women enjoyed in the heyday of the Philadelphia "lobby," when the fashionable drawing room "salons" of society hostesses such as Anne Willing Bingham became important sites of intellectual and political exchange and of socialization into the ways of the would-be national elite. Jefferson and many other Republicans saw this salon culture as too European, monarchical, and corrupting for the American republic (as well as an inappropriate activity for women), and sought to end it once the government moved to Washington City. See Teute, "Roman Matron," pp. 95–98; and Rosemarie Zagarri, "Gender and the First Party System," in *Federalists Reconsidered,* ed. Doron Ben-Atar and Barbara B. Oberg (Charlottesville, 1998), pp. 118–34.

Washington during each session of Congress and for them and many Washington residents the Capitol's interior "afforded the only shelter during the severity of winter." It was impossible to tell who did and did not belong in the building, and the literal lobbies of the House chamber were often so loud and crowded with lobbyists, loiterers, and even food vendors that legislative business was sometimes interrupted. What was worse, from Latrobe's point of view, was that "idle and dissolute persons ranged the whole building," defacing the walls "with obscenity and . . . libels" and stealing "the public furniture and utensils." However, a majority of House members seem to have found these much more chaotic and democratic surroundings preferable to the lobby they knew in Philadelphia, with some members sharply criticizing Latrobe when he tried to regulate access to the House and its galleries. "In a speech of some length," David R. Williams of South Carolina condemned the "outrageous audacity" of the surveyor of public buildings "in lately altering the arrangement of the Representative Hall in respect to the entrance to the galleries."[30]

After this 1808 debate, references to the lobby and lobbying pop up more and more frequently, increasing in negativity all the time. The economic development schemes of the post–War of 1812 period, especially bank charters and transportation projects such as the Erie Canal, seem to have been particularly fertile ground for the development of lobbying as an activity and a term.[31] For present purposes, the most

---

[30]U.S. Congress, House of Representatives, *Documentary History of the Construction and Development of the United States Capitol,* Report No. 646 (Washington, D.C., 1904), pp. 129–30, 139.

[31]The term *lobbying* seems to have been decisively popularized by a widely read satirical poem published in 1819, "The State Triumvirate" by New York literary politician Gulian C. Verplanck. The lobby had seemingly become less subtle and more sinister than it had seemed to the participants in the 1808 debate. Verplanck attacked De Witt Clinton as "chief of all the lobby tribe" for the unseemly scramble that the Erie Canal and other development projects had generated around the state government. In a footnote to this line, Verplanck defined lobbyists as a distinct occupational category for the first time. There was a "class of men," he wrote, "whose profession and trade it is to attend at Albany during the sessions of the Legislature, with a view of soliciting or opposing the passing of bills, banks, insurance companies, &c. . . . They are generally known by the name of Lobby members. These men have been the principal agents in the scenes of corruption which for a few years past have disgraced this state" (Verplanck, *The State Triumvirate, A Political Tale* [New York, 1819], pp. 44, 67–68). From the New York state capital of 1819, "lobby members" and "lobby agents" fanned out (at least in political rhetoric) to stalk the nation.

important aspect of this early emergence of the idea of the lobby is the implication it carries that outside, special interest pressure on Congress began long before organized lobbying became infamous after 1865, and that the medium through which lobbyists operated was the society in which congressmen lived at the capital. The key to understanding that society in the 1790s is the culture of gentility. It turns out that genteel values and habits, especially the elaborate sociability that gentlepeople cultivated, could provide ample opportunity and even cover for rather aggressive lobbying efforts. The access to the powerful that modern lobbyists must fight tooth and nail for, an eighteenth-century gentleman could walk into noiselessly and almost automatically.[32]

To begin to see in more detail how this might have worked, let us turn now to an extended discussion of the one person referred to as a lobbyist in the literature of early American history, Rev. Manasseh Cutler of Massachusetts.[33] Cutler was not a professional lobbyist. For more than fifty years, he served as the Congregational pastor of Ipswich. It was in his spare time that he pulled off what is arguably the greatest

---

[32]Imposing gentility on the government was a major role of capital society, and particularly its elite female leaders. Political gentility included a moderation of partisanship that naturally pushed government officials toward more conservative and wealth-oriented views. This was especially true in Philadelphia, but it soon developed in Washington despite the efforts of many male Republicans and Democrats to counteract it, and the qualms of some Washington women. See Teute, "Roman Matron"; Jan Lewis, "Politics and the Ambivalence of the Private Sphere: Women in Early Washington, D.C.," in Kennon, *Republic for the Ages,* pp. 122–51; Barbara G. Carson, *Ambitious Appetites: Dining, Behavior, and Patterns of Consumption in Federal Washington* (Washington, D.C., 1990); E[lizabeth] F[ries] Ellet, *The Court Circles of the Republic; or, The Beauties and Celebrities of the Nation; Illustrating Life and Society under Eighteen Presidents; Describing the Social Features of the Successive Administrations from Washington to Grant* (Hartford, 1869); and Francis J. Grund, *Aristocracy in America* (1839; reprint ed., New York, 1959). Recent interpretations of the Peggy Eaton affair have depicted it as Andrew Jackson's partly victorious showdown with the forces of female-powered gentility that had come to dominate Washington society: see Teute, "Roman Matron," pp. 115–17; and Kirsten E. Wood, " 'One Woman So Dangerous to Public Morals': Gender and Power in the Eaton Affair," *Journal of the Early Republic* 17 (1997):237–75.

[33]The principal source on Cutler's life and career is William Parker Cutler and Julia Perkins Cutler, eds., *Life, Journals, and Correspondence of Rev. Manasseh Cutler, L. L. D.* (1888; reprint ed., Athens, Ohio, 1987), which reprints much material from the Manasseh Cutler Collection, Northwestern University. Secondary accounts include Louis W. Potts, "Manasseh Cutler, Lobbyist," *Ohio History* 96 (1987):101–23, and Janice Goldsmith Pulsifer, "The Cutlers of Hamilton," *Essex Institute Historical Collections* 107 (1971):335–408.

feat of lobbying in American history, the 1787 purchase of several million acres of public land on behalf of a group of New England Revolutionary War veterans and land speculators calling themselves the Ohio Company of Associates. It is not only the size of this purchase that has impressed its many historians. The deal required abandoning, without even a single trial, the land policy Congress had just established in the very slowly and painfully created Land Ordinance of 1785. The ordinance had envisioned selling relatively small plots of land to individuals for immediate cash or the return of various types of government debt securities from the Revolutionary War. By contrast, the Ohio Company purchase allowed a *corporation* to obtain a huge tract—an entire region of the Northwest Territory—on credit, and at a lower price than Congress planned to ask for lands that the government itself would sell. The terms of Cutler's deal called for eight payments: $500,000 when the contract was signed, $500,000 when the land had been surveyed, and the remainder in six installments spread out over three years. A deed would be issued for the first million dollars' worth once the two initial payments were made. The company would be able to pay in government debt certificates, which in that year of Shays's Rebellion could be had for a fraction of their face value.[34]

Another remarkable aspect of Cutler's feat was the speed with which he was able to induce the Confederation Congress to act, a trait for which that body was even less noted than its successors. The minister-lobbyist arrived in New York on July 5, 1787, presented Congress with his proposal the next day, and was able to leave town, mission accomplished, on July 27. Within that three-week span, he also had found time to make a jaunt to Philadelphia.[35] Massachusetts delegate Samuel Holten was agog at what Cutler had been able to do. "It was impossible for him to conceive," Cutler reported Holten as saying, "by what kind of address I had so soon and so warmly engaged the attention of Congress, for . . . he never knew so much attention paid to anyone who made application to them on any kind of business, nor did he ever

---

[34]Treat, *National Land System,* pp. 35–40, 48–49; Sakolski, *Great American Land Bubble,* pp. 101–4; Potts, "Cutler, Lobbyist."

[35]Cutler and Cutler, *Journals and Correspondence,* 1:225, 242–90, 309.

know them more pressing to bring it to a close." There were no *three* other men from New England, Holten opined, "even of the first character [who] could have accomplished so much in so short a time."[36]

Cutler and his associates spent the late summer and early fall of 1787 gathering up $500,000 in federal debt certificates, and in October the savvy cleric returned to New York to make the first payment to the board of Treasury. On the night this was accomplished, he celebrated with a large group of former Continental army officers, many of them Ohio Company investors and fellow land speculators, and noted in his journal that he had just completed "the greatest private contract ever made in America." This was not just a down payment. In a critical provision only implied in the original July agreement, the $500,000 bought the Ohio Company the right to actually occupy and improve 750,000 acres of the purchase, without need of a formal deed. This further testament to Cutler's lobbying skill went nearly unmentioned in his records, though it virtually guaranteed that the company would hold a very large chunk of land whether or not it made any other payments. The sweetness of the Ohio Company deal naturally caught the attention of other speculators, and soon new proposals from other large-scale speculators began to surface, including the already mentioned one from John Cleves Symmes.[37]

Cutler's lobbying for the Ohio Company continued into the 1790s. In the new Congress, the pastor faced a more typical type of lobbying problem, not engineering a massive transaction but instead quietly pressing for many small legislative adjustments in favor of his company. As the new government was forming in 1789, the company found its ability to make payments severely impaired by the increased value of the federal debt certificates that its shareholders intended to use as their currency.[38] It was widely expected that Congress would take immediate action to restore the nation's credit by paying off the

---

[36]Ibid., 1:302.

[37]Ibid., 1:320, 325–27. The July agreement and the October contract can be compared in Clarence Edwin Carter, ed., *The Territorial Papers of the United States,* 18 vols. (Washington, D.C., 1934–69), 2:61–63 and 2:80–81.

[38]A brief explanation may be in order here: the Ohio Company sold shares rather than land to settlers and speculators, with the idea that the ownership of the land would be distributed once the contract was completed. It was really an enlarged version of New England's traditional system of community migration.

debt at its face value, perhaps even with interest. Suddenly U.S. government securities became attractive investments again. This was good for the country, but it was bad for the Ohio Company. Its scheme would become totally unfeasible if the $500,000 in debt certificates they needed to make the next payment actually cost that much.[39]

At any rate, in the spring of 1789, with government securities becoming more expensive and harder to find, sale of Ohio Company shares declined and many earlier purchasers were not fulfilling their promises to pay. Cutler and the company directors determined to ask the new Congress for a reduction in the per-acre price agreed to in 1787 and an extension of the deadline for its next payment.[40] In 1790, Cutler's cohort Rufus Putnam came east from the Ohio Company settlement at Marietta to oversee the new push, but he soon realized that it was really a job for the company's master lobbyist. Believing that "our prospects are good if we are ready to strike when the Iron is hot," Putnam sent a breathless letter to Ipswich in early February calling Cutler into action: "Your presence here is very much wanted. I have not time to explain to you the necessity of your being on the spot as soon as possible, can only tell you that if you have any regard to your own interest" or the company's, "you will set out for New York without loss of time—I repeat it my dear friend come on without loss of time—Come my dear friend don't fail."[41]

Cutler swept into New York two weeks after Putnam's letter had been sent, but he soon found that his lobbying magic worked less swiftly on the new Congress, which was engaged in a lengthy debate on Secretary of the Treasury Alexander Hamilton's proposed financial program. Certain that their proposal would never get serious consideration on the floor of Congress in the midst of the Sturm und Drang over public finance, Cutler and Putnam delayed formally submitting it and focused on laying solid groundwork. For weeks, they visited members in their homes, quietly rounding up support for a rather cheeky

---

[39]Cutler explains the problem in Manasseh Cutler to Rufus Putnam, Apr. 9, 1789, Cutler and Cutler, *Journals and Correspondence,* 1:443–44. See also, Sakolski, *Great American Land Bubble,* pp. 105–6; Treat, *National Land System,* pp. 55–56.

[40]Cutler and Cutler, *Journals and Correspondence,* 1:443–46.

[41]Rufus Putnam to Manasseh Cutler, Feb. 3, 1790, Manasseh Cutler Collection, Northwestern University.

request that the contract price be knocked down to twenty cents per acre, "a saving to the Company," Cutler pointed out, "of more than $500,000."[42] The positive-minded cleric was still optimistic after a month of this effort. As winter turned to spring and his stay in New York approached two months, however, the tone of his letters turned to self-pity for those doomed to "adventure in this wild goose chase." He and Putnam had "been making every exertion to engage the interest of members in support of" the Company, but "[they] dare[d] not . . . promise anything." It now seemed "very doubtful whether Congress will act upon it in this session. The members to whom I have mentioned it, appear disposed to give it support," but there was no prospect of Congress having the "leisure to take it up."[43] In late April, Cutler gave up, settling some company accounts with the War Department and hopping a ship back to New England.[44]

Thanks to the Northwestern Indians, the Ohio Company's fortunes were about to get much worse. In 1790 and 1791, American military expeditions under Josiah Harmar and then Arthur St. Clair met humiliating defeats at the hands of Little Turtle and his force of Miami, Shawnee, and Delaware warriors. The fighting mostly took place hundreds of miles away from Marietta and the other settlements, but there were some murders of settlers in the countryside and much panic. Thousands had to be spent fortifying the company's settlements. All these events—especially St. Clair's defeat, by some measures the worst drubbing the United States received in the whole history of Indian warfare—gained wide publicity in the East, dampening the public's ardor for settling on or even speculating in western lands. In response, the market price of Ohio land dropped below what the company had contracted to pay for it, and this problem was exacerbated by Congress, where a land bill had passed the House (but then stalled in the Senate) setting the price of public land at twenty-five cents per acre, a fraction of what the Ohio Company was supposed to pay. The question for the company was no longer when its payments would be made—

---

42. Cutler and Cutler, *Journals and Correspondence,* 1:454–61.

43. Manasseh Cutler to Daniel Story, Apr. 7, 1790, Manasseh Cutler Collection, Northwestern University.

44. Cutler and Cutler, *Journals and Correspondence,* 1:457.

that was an impossibility—but whether it would ever get title to any land in return for the $500,000 already paid.[45]

Salvaging this situation was another stern lobbying challenge for Reverend Cutler. The company needed immediate relief to avoid ruin, and its chief lobbyist arrived at the seat of government, now Philadelphia, in early 1792. Cutler had burbled with praise for the leaders he met on his previous trips, but now he began to suffer from the jaundice felt by many a lobbyist under the stress of round-the-clock truckling to powerful men who knew all too well that desperate supplicants could be kept waiting indefinitely. It was tiresome, Cutler wrote, to spend every waking moment "trotting after their High Mightinesses" only to have them dawdle over one's important business. The slothful work habits of Congress were "intolerably provoking." One day, a committee meeting on his petition was suddenly suspended by the lack of quorum on the floor of Congress, leaving the good pastor fuming and helpless. "These idle, lazy, six dollars per day men," the usually sunny Cutler complained to his wife, "cannot rise in the morning, sip their coffee, and dismiss their barbers early enough to attend Congress at eleven o'clock." Didn't they know there were lobbyists who had work to do?

Of course, Cutler was well aware of one reason that some members of Congress had a hard time getting started in the morning. It was the strenuous nightlife they endured in various Philadelphia parlors and dining rooms. These were the venues in which Cutler had been doing much of his "trotting after," and he himself had found it rather taxing. "I am now pretty well," he wrote his wife, "but the constant routine of four and five o'clock dinners at the most sumptuous tables almost kills me. I had infinitely rather sit down with you to a piece of salt junk at one o'clock than be tormented with the parade and delay of Philadelphia entertainments."[46]

---

[45]Treat, *National Land System,* pp. 55–56; Sakolski, *Great American Land Bubble,* pp. 104–6; Beverley W. Bond, Jr., *The Civilization of the Old Northwest: A Study of Political, Social, and Economic Development, 1788–1812* (New York, 1934), pp. 242–54; Wiley Sword, *President Washington's Indian War: The Struggle for the Old Northwest, 1790–1795* (Norman, Okla., 1985).

[46]Manasseh Cutler to Mary Balch Cutler, Mar. 5, 1792, Cutler and Cutler, *Journals and Correspondence,* 1:482–86.

Despite these complaints, Cutler still managed to have his way with the legislators to an astonishing degree. The ease of it, in fact, left him feeling almost contemptuous. "However important" members of Congress "may appear abroad," he assured his wife, "they appear here, when you converse freely with them, as small as other people." Perhaps smaller, he seemed to imply, because, in their vanity, they were so easily manipulated by the attentions of a skilled lobbyist like himself. "It is not easy to conceive," he went on, "how much a very *little being* may, if disposed, work upon their caprice and whims." One high mightiness whom Cutler found especially vulnerable, apparently, was Senate President John Adams, who turned out to be a key to Cutler's success in this particular project.[47]

The legislative action began March 2, 1792, when Cutler and two other emissaries presented a memorial to the House reviewing their troubles and asking for relief. Among other favors, they asked that the company not be required to meet the terms of the original contract, and that it be granted title the full 1.5 million acres at the rate of twenty cents an acre. At that price the company had actually overpaid.[48] Though overloaded with work and rushing to adjourn by April 1, the House took up Cutler's memorial immediately and referred it, as per his wishes, to a special committee rather than to the secretary of the treasury. Cutler and friends were allowed to handpick the membership of this committee, which included Theodore Sedgwick from the Ohio Company's home state of Massachusetts and two other members (Amasa Learned and Abraham Baldwin) who, like Cutler, were Yale men from Connecticut (though Baldwin represented Georgia in Congress). Learned had even grown up in Cutler's own hometown of Killingly. (The other two members of the committee were William Findley of Pennsylvania and Egbert Benson of New York.) With Sedgwick, Learned, and Baldwin composing a majority of the committee, it acted favorably and expeditiously on Cutler's memorial. Sedgwick reported to the House only six days later, urging that action be taken in the present session of Congress and essentially endorsing the Company's position, except for a slightly higher per-acre price. Legislation

[47]Ibid., 1:484–86.
[48]Cutler and Cutler, *Journals and Correspondence,* 1:471–77.

was drafted that granted the Ohio Company 750,000 acres outright, and gave it various options to buy the rest: some for military bounty warrants and some for twenty-five cents per acre, if it could pay within six years. The bill passed, without enough opposition to even demand a roll-call vote, on April 6. There was more opposition in the Senate, but the process moved even more swiftly than it had in the House. The final section allowing the six-year option to buy more land was stripped out, but the Ohio Company relief bill was passed by April 16, barely six weeks after Cutler's arrival. The deciding vote in the Senate was cast by Vice President Adams.[49]

The Ohio Company's ace lobbyist was not entirely pleased with the outcome, having gone in believing he could save the whole 1.5 million acre grant, but it was in fact another remarkable victory. The other land companies who had received congressional grants in the late 1780s all came to nothing, but Cutler and friends walked away with nearly a million acres of land, at a cost of something on the order of twelve cents per acre, if the depreciated nature of the securities in which they had originally paid are taken into account. Since the government later set the price of the public lands at two dollars per acre, the Ohio Company Associates got more than a bargain, and the many would-be real estate magnates among them remained more than competitive with the government land offices.[50] Manasseh Cutler personally secured possession of many thousands of acres, including enough to give his eldest son, Ephraim, a large and potentially prosperous Ohio farm. Ephraim made money on the side as local agent for his father and other Massachusetts-based western land speculators. Later, he became a judge and prominent southern Ohio politician.[51]

The obvious question raised by this tale is: what was the secret of Manasseh Cutler's success? How do we account for his near mind control of both the old Congress in 1787 and the new one in 1792? It seems especially surprising in this period when politicians sincerely prided themselves on their intellectual independence and political

---

[49]*Annals of Congress,* 2d Cong., 1st sess., House, pp. 433–34, 437, 539, Senate, p. 123, appendix, pp. 1363–64; Cutler and Cutler, *Journals and Correspondence,* 1:477–79, 482.

[50]Treat, *National Land System,* p. 57.

[51]Pulsifer, "Cutlers of Hamilton," p. 335; Julia Perkins Cutler, ed., *Life and Times of Ephraim Cutler* (Cincinnati, 1890).

virtue, a word they used to mean something much closer to its Latin roots than our understanding of the term. The word implied virility, the manly quality (as they defined it) of being able to withstand whatever outside forces might try to bend a man's political will away from the common good, be they threats of violence, the temptation to join a party, or the blandishments of a lobbyist.[52]

In answer to this question, Walt Whitman and other detractors of lobbying would probably point to the weakness of human nature, often considered especially weak in politicians, and the inherent wickedness and perfidy of the lobbyist breed. And in all truth, if the Reverend Cutler did not go to the lengths of his Gilded Age descendants, he did occasionally enter some dark moral territory. In negotiating his original contract, Cutler had essentially bought the support of two key members of the Confederation government. A relatively innocent bit of logrolling was throwing the Ohio Company's support behind Gen. Arthur St. Clair, the sitting president of Congress, for governor of the new Northwest Territory. Much less innocent was the deal he made with the unscrupulous William Duer, who as secretary of the board of Treasury, was one of the principals in Cutler's negotiations. Duer would go on to be Alexander Hamilton's second in command at the Treasury Department and then the first U.S. government official to be forced to resign after the discovery of a vast insider-trading scheme involving government securities.[53] At a key point in the Ohio Company negotiations, Duer came to Cutler with a proposal, to be kept "a profound secret," that the Ohio Company join himself and "a number of the principal characters" in New York in forming another land company that would buy an even larger chunk of Northwest Territory land. This Scioto Company was highly leveraged to say the least, and close to an outright con game. It possessed no capital and was predicated financially on the dubious and devious proposition of selling western lands in Europe before said lands had even been bought, a practice

---

[52]On the evolution and many permutations of "virtue" in European and American thought, see J. G. A. Pocock, *The Machiavellian Moment: Florentine Political Thought and the Atlantic Republican Tradition* (Princeton, 1975). On the virile independence expected of virtuous republican statesmen, see Ketcham, *Presidents Above Party.*

[53]On William Duer, see Robert F. Jones, *"The King of the Alley": William Duer, Politician, Entrepreneur, and Speculator, 1768–1799* (Philadelphia, 1992).

known in the land business as "dodging." Cutler went along because he understood that giving Duer a piece of the action would "forward the negotiations." The Scioto Company never bought an acre of land, but its agents still sold some to a group of French settlers. The buyers only received any land through the charity of Congress in the 1790s.[54]

The Duer connection acknowledged, it would be wrong to attribute Cutler's success to simple corruption. Indeed, what is striking is that Cutler managed to commit such deeds as cutting key decision makers in on his business venture while fully retaining his standing as a gentleman and a clergyman. In fact, there was an almost complete lack of negative reaction (except years later among political opponents) to any aspect of his lobbying.

The explanation for both Cutler's success as a lobbyist and his ability to escape censure for it lies in his mastery of the culture of gentility in which the early Congresses were steeped. Many New England clergymen criticized gentility as it took hold in America during the eighteenth century, but Manasseh Cutler, resplendent in his black velvet suit and silver shoe buckles, was a thoroughgoing, self-conscious practitioner of it. The journals Cutler kept on his travels for the Ohio Company read like a series of reviews from one of the polite literary journals of the day, as Cutler measured everything and everybody he met according to genteel standards of taste. Little escaped the clergyman's keen eye as he ranged across the full breadth of lifestyle topics over which a gentleman was supposed to have command: the fashions worn by a genteel widow innkeeper and her "tasty" daughter; the draperies in the hall where Congress met; the hairstyle of Lucy Knox, the secretary of war's wife; the arrangement of William Bartram's formal gardens; Kitty (Mrs. William) Duer's table manners; a visiting French nobleman's conversational skills; and the quality of the food served everywhere he dined.[55]

The journal's highest praise was reserved for those people and

---

[54]Cutler and Cutler, *Journals and Correspondence,* 1:295–98; Treat, *National Land System,* pp. 58–60; Sakolski, *Great American Land Bubble,* pp. 106–10; Theodore Thomas Belote, *The Scioto Speculation and the French Settlement at Gallipolis: A Study in Ohio Valley History* (1907; reprint ed., New York, 1971).

[55]Cutler and Cutler, *Journals and Correspondence,* 1:225, 231, 238, 240, 273, and passim.

places who clearly qualified as genteel. For instance, there was a riding companion on the way into New York whom Cutler suspected of being a Tory but enthused over in any case as "perfectly intelligent and well informed, much of a gentleman, and of most pleasing address." By contrast, Cutler found many of the numerous fellow clergymen he met on his travels rather dull. One he rather liked was Rev. John Rogers of New York's Wall Street Presbyterian Church, whom he found "certainly the most accomplished gentleman, for a clergyman, I have ever been acquainted with. He lives in elegant style and entertains company as genteelly as the first gentleman in this city." For sheer excellence in the arts of gentility, however, Cutler found no one to top William Duer. Duer made a strong first impression on Cutler by inviting him to an impossibly sumptuous dinner. Afterwards, the cleric gushed that his host "lives in the style of a nobleman. . . . I presume he had not less than 15 different sorts of wine at dinner . . . besides most excellent cider, porter, and several other kinds of strong beer." Over time, Cutler discovered even more sterling qualities in Duer. The night after signing the Ohio Company contract, Cutler bid his new friend an affectionate farewell and rhapsodized about Duer in his journal: "He is a gentleman of the most sprightly abilities, and has a soul filled with the warmest benevolence and generosity. He is made both for business and the enjoyment of life, his attachments [are] strong and sincere, and [he] diffuses happiness among his friends, while he enjoys a full share of it himself."[56]

As Cutler saw him, Duer was the embodiment of "complaisance," one of gentility's, and, Cutler's, favorite qualities. This was the ability to please other people, not necessarily by flattery or servility, but by making them feel at ease with themselves and with whatever others happened to be present. Complaisance was at the heart of genteel culture because it served what Richard Bushman calls the ultimate purpose of gentility, besides elevating the gentry above everyone else. This was the promotion of "harmonious and easy intercourse" in a society prone to irritation, misunderstanding, and conflict.[57]

By all accounts, Manasseh Cutler was an especially complaisant man.

---

[56]Ibid., 1:237, 240–41, 306.

[57]Bushman, *Refinement of America,* pp. 44–45.

His particular strength as a gentleman was his skill at conversation. One of his grandchildren remembered him as "a man of consummate prudence in speech and conduct; of courtly manners, a favorite in [the] drawing room" and a noted dining table raconteur.[58] Conversation was the central activity of genteel life. Along with dancing, card playing, and eating and drinking, it was what one did on those very frequent occasions when gentry gathered to perform for and acknowledge each other. People built parlors in their houses as arenas for conversation, went on country outings to hold conversations, and read books, patronized museums, and bought curios to provide material for conversations. Conversation allowed gentry to show each other their parts: their cultivated tastes, their extensive information, their quickness of intellect.[59] One source of Cutler's strength as a conversationalist was that he himself was a man of many parts: besides his work in religion, land speculation, and politics, he, like so many eighteenth-century gentlemen, was a dedicated amateur scientist. A member of several scientific societies, his particular interest was botany. Like Thomas Jefferson, he kept a demonstration garden at his house and collected plant samples wherever he traveled. He worked on a natural history of New England for much of his life and had classified some 350 species before the manuscript of his book was consumed in a fire. Science was a sure-fire conversation starter among the eighteenth-century gentry, and Cutler found many of his contacts with powerful men greatly facilitated by their interest in his scientific activities.[60]

Courtesy book authors stressed the paramount importance of conversation, describing it in such terms as "the Cement and Soul of Society," because conversation was the primary means by which complaisance could be exercised and social ease and harmony promoted.[61] It may be more accurate to say that polite conversation was the cement of gentry society, that it created cohesion and a sense of distinctness among the particular stratum of society that had the money and knowledge to be genteel. Of course, this excluded the vast majority of

---

58Pulsifer, "Cutlers of Hamilton," pp. 361, 363.

59Bushman, *Refinement of America,* pp. 83–89.

60Cutler's scientific activities are covered at many points in Cutler and Cutler, *Journals and Correspondence;* and Pulsifer, "Cutlers of Hamilton."

61Bushman, *Refinement of America,* p. 84.

Americans, but what is more relevant to the subject of lobbying is the way that polite conversation, and gentility generally, were also *in*clusive. They created a national and even international community of gentry who could recognize and easily interact with each other even across thick barriers of nationality, region, language, and occupation. Cutler found this an invaluable asset on his lobbying tours. After a day in Philadelphia, pleasantly and productively spent with powerful politicians he barely knew, Cutler sang hosannas to gentility in his journal: "What advantages are derived from a finished education and the best of company! How does it banish that awkward stiffness when strangers meet . . . ! How does it engage the most perfect strangers in all the freedom of an easy and pleasing sociability, common only to the most intimate friends."[62]

Thus we come to the major advantage gentility gave Cutler in his lobbying. It provided him what all lobbyists and other political supplicants need most, even today: access to key legislators and policymakers. In the 1790s, a lobbyist whose manners, appearance, and knowledge seemed to mark him as a gentleman had virtually unlimited access to any member of Congress he chose. Gentility created a kind of imaginary club, and one of the key benefits of membership was the right to be treated hospitably, as a friend, an equal and honored guest, by other gentry wherever you happened to go.[63] Once acknowledged as a fellow gentleman, a lobbyist could not only see congressmen but join fully in their social life at the seat of government, providing all sorts of nonofficial settings where contacts could be built and sensitive business matters could be discussed discreetly and effectively.

---

[62]Cutler and Cutler, *Journals and Correspondence,* 1:263.

[63]For examples of this principle in action, see Hunter Dickinson Farish, ed., *The Journal and Letters of Philip Vickers Fithian, 1773–1774: A Plantation Tutor of the Old Dominion* (Charlottesville, 1957), p. 161; and Nicholas Cresswell, *The Journal of Nicholas Cresswell, 1774–1777* (1924; reprint ed., Port Washington, N.Y., 1968), p. 270. Traveling in status-conscious Virginia, Cresswell found that a genteel exterior was his passport and meal ticket: "If a stranger went among them, no matter of what country, if he behaved decently, had a good face, a good coat and a tolerable share of good-nature, would dance with the women and drink with the men . . . with these qualifications he would be entertained amongst them with the greatest friendship as long as he pleased to stay. If he is a traveller he is recommended from one Gentleman's house to another to his journey. I believe it is possible to travel through both the Carolinas, Virginia and Maryland without a single shilling."

Gaining access was not always quite so simple as walking the walk and talking the talk. It helped to have evidence of gentility beyond one's personal qualities, such as a noble title, a well-known family name, or recommendations from other members of the club. Cutler took the latter route, bringing so many letters of introduction with him to New York that it takes an entire page of the published edition of his journal just to list them all.[64]

Admitted to the club, Cutler used his membership privileges to the hilt. Almost all of his lobbying took place at private homes or social gatherings. On his first lobbying trip to New York in 1787, he ate virtually every meal with members of Congress and/or key officials of the Confederation government. He ate with Treasury Board President Samuel Osgood two nights in a row, once by himself, to talk and perhaps eat turkey. On another night, British Consul-General Sir John Temple had him to dinner and "was so complaisant" as to also invite the Massachusetts congressional delegation, at least one of whom was wavering on the deal. Then there were social outings. On one occasion, Duer took the lobbyist and some others over to Brooklyn to see the sights and enjoy an elegant oyster dinner. Cutler also made valuable contacts on a side trip to Philadelphia when, among other star-studded encounters, he took an outing to see William Bartram's gardens with a platoon of delegates to the Constitutional Convention, including both Madison and Hamilton. On the same trip, he made lengthy social visits to Benjamin Franklin and Benjamin Rush, who were both eager to meet a fellow man of science. Summing up his 1787 trip, Cutler had to admit that "I passed away my time, notwithstanding all my labor and fatigue, in a constant round of pleasure."[65] His later lobbying trips were longer, less enjoyable, and less well documented, but they were no less full of social gatherings where subtle but effective lobbying might occur. In fact, Cutler turned his earlier luck into a settled strategy. Trying to get the Ohio Company's contract altered in 1790, he wrote to a cohort that his time had been spent "securing the interest of the members . . . at their private lodgings."[66]

---

[64]Cutler and Cutler, *Journals and Correspondence,* 1:228–30.
[65]Ibid., 1:305–6.
[66]Ibid., 1:461.

That brings us to the other advantage that gentility provided for lobbyists and those they lobbied: wide latitude, even cover, for dealings that in retrospect were shot through with conflict of interest and even corruption. The basic reason for this is that, while gentlemen often evaluated one another's characters, genteel culture was fundamentally superficial in its standards of character judgment. Its standards were almost exclusively external. Gentry were judged by how successfully they projected the qualities of gentility in their speech, dress, manners, and tastes. When they referred to someone's character, they meant something much closer to our term *reputation*. Sometimes they talked about a person's character in the same manner we might speak of a character played by an actor in a drama. But that was just it. Gentlepeople *were* actors, on stage before the rest of the society. Genteel characters were not made up or false—the way to ruin a character was to commit some deed that revealed the public self to be hiding a more sordid reality inconsistent with the character played—but they were quite explicitly taken at face value. Gentlepeople really were what they ate and wore, in addition to how well they danced and wrote and spoke. In a sense, the generation of American gentlemen who founded the United States were especially superficial. Having rejected objective and inflexible standards of gentility such as membership in a titled nobility—you either were the Earl of Shaftesbury or not, no matter how you behaved—American gentry were left to rely exclusively on outward, learned characteristics.[67]

The most serious problem with this in terms of government was that the members of the American gentry did not know that they were superficial. Their assumption was that the genteel mask really did reflect the inner person, or else that the beast within had been effectively repressed. Genteel standards of taste and beauty were all about imposing smoothness, order, and harmony on rough nature, about putting an overlay of beautiful serenity on the harsh, chaotic realties of human life, about valuing and believing in those exteriors rather than the things they covered. Richard Bushman writes that "the attempt to control nature and society for the sake of a beautiful appearance made

[67]Gordon S. Wood, *The Radicalism of the American Revolution* (New York, 1992), pp. 189–212.

denial and repression essential traits of gentility. . . . Gentility hid what it could not countenance and denied whatever caused discomfort."[68] Gentility assumed integrity, but it did not necessarily teach honesty, which, as we all know, is often not very complaisant. Samuel Johnson growled that Lord Chesterfield's letters, one of the bibles of gentility, taught "the morals of a whore, and the manners of a dancing master."[69]

It is easy to see how this type of thinking could cause problems when employed by men in power and those who wanted things from them: if a man had been accepted by society as a gentleman, he was assumed to be a man of honor and integrity, and therefore was safe to put in office. There was no need for close oversight or regulation of such a man's official conduct, because his gentlemanly regard for his own character would automatically preclude any misbehavior.[70] To question an official gentleman's integrity or even appear to doubt it, was to question his gentility, along with that of everyone who had acknowledged it. That was the kind of insult that duels were fought over. Therefore, a gentleman's official integrity was rarely questioned, safeguards or even taboos against conflict of interest were rare, and the Manasseh Cutlers and William Duers and Jonathan Daytons could wheel and deal and lobby with near carte blanche. It took overwhelming, absolutely incontrovertible evidence of a legislator's or official's criminality before the genteel world would admit that its standards of character judgment had failed. The dazzling gentility of William Duer covered up his chicanery for years, allowing him to remain outwardly respectable even after he was forced from office. Things did finally fall apart for Duer until his speculations finally caused a national economic crisis that sent him to debtor's prison. Jonathan Dayton's ethically

---

[68]Bushman, *Refinement of America,* p. 99.

[69]James Boswell, *Life of Johnson,* ed. R. W. Chapman (Oxford, 1980), p. 188.

[70]Federal statutes prohibited, and prescribed condign punishments, for many different kinds of official malfeasance, but there was no apparatus for detecting such crimes other than the cumbersome process of auditing and settling official accounts. Even when there was a discrepancy in the accounts of a gentleman official, government managers often preferred to deal with the problem privately rather than through legal action. The assumption of official integrity shows in the fact that Washington removed only seventeen officials during his eight years as president, many of them diplomats who were recalled for various policy reasons. See Leonard D. White, *The Federalists: A Study in Administrative History* (New York, 1956), pp. 284–90, 341–47, 424–33.

challenged behavior would go nearly unchecked until he was caught up in the Aaron Burr conspiracy in 1807. A gentleman lobbyist who avoided those extremes, like Manasseh Cutler, could expect no problems at all, and it is likely that there were many others whose activities escaped even detection, much less disapproval. We would probably never have known about Cutler's lobbying if his family had not saved and published his journals and letters.

The results could be very different for those who tried to lobby without benefit of gentility. In 1795, two men showed up in Philadelphia with a proposition not unlike Cutler's Ohio Company deal. Robert Randall and Charles Whitney appeared on behalf of some British fur traders in Detroit who offered to extinguish the Indian title to "all the Western lands lying between Lakes Michigan, Erie, and Huron" (the present lower peninsula of Michigan) if Congress would grant them much of the land. Like Cutler, Randall and Whitney made their pitch at congressmen's private lodgings and offered to let sympathetic members share in the profits of the project. However, Randall and Whitney could not get admittance to the gentlemen's club. They knew no one, had no letters of recommendation, and distinctly lacked Cutler's knack for genteel socializing. Instead of his easy conversation, Randall came to members' homes (without benefit of dinner invitations) and spoke of Michigan "in the terms that he might have employed from a pulpit," one member sniffed. This was too much. Such clownish behavior afforded Randall and Whitney no cover for their activities and earned them instant disgrace and even a trial on the floor of Congress.[71] Lobbying without gentility could be given the

[71]*Annals of Congress,* 4th Cong., 1st sess., House, pp. 166–95, 200–229, 232–33, 243–45, quotations on pp. 165–67; *Proceedings of the House . . . in the Case of Robert Randall and Charles Whitney, Published by Order of the House* (Philadelphia, 1796). Brief secondary accounts of the Randall-Whitney case can be found in William T. Hutchinson and William M. E. Rachal, eds., *The Papers of James Madison,* 17 vols. (Chicago and Charlottesville, 1962–91), 16:175; and Treat, *National Land System,* pp. 77–78. The congressional reaction to Randall and Whitney was also probably influenced by contemporaneous exposure of the Yazoo land frauds, in which the Georgia legislature had been bribed en masse by land speculators. Significantly, the involvement of numerous prominent political figures in purchasing the corruptly obtained Yazoo lands eventually led to a federal bailout of the buyers, a much more sympathetic reaction than that received by the friendless schemes of Randall and Whitney. See C. Peter Magrath, *Yazoo: Law and Politics in the New Republic—The Case of "Fletcher V. Peck"* (New York, 1967).

different labels of bribery and corruption. It was in bad taste, because it allowed self-interest to come into Congress without the mask that had made its presence bearable so many times before.

Even in those cases of lobbying where there was no question of corruption, gentility clearly made a difference. Gentlepeople who wanted or needed something from Congress simply seem to have been more likely to get it than those less well versed in the codes and practices of gentility. No scientific survey has been attempted but some suggestively contrasting examples can be offered. Though neither got everything they wanted, both Baron Frederick William von Steuben and Catharine Greene, the widow of Gen. Nathanael Greene, were compensated by Congress for massive private debts incurred during the Revolutionary War. Steuben and especially Nathanael Greene suffered financially in the course of their wartime duties, but it was also clear that in compensating them, Congress was going beyond what it legally was obligated to do, and far beyond what had been done for the thousands of less prominent Americans who also sacrificed for the cause. Major lobbying campaigns were mounted on behalf of both claims, with numerous sitting members of Congress and cabinet secretaries involved; correspondingly lavish amounts of congressional time and energy were expended in considering the petitions. Steuben's claim was aided immeasurably by his status as one of America's few resident titled aristocrats and as a leader of both high New York society and the Society of the Cincinnati. These impeccable social credentials allowed Steuben to maintain his retinue of prominent supporters despite criticism of his claim and to counteract the many nonmitigating factors surrounding his case. These included the uncertain nature and origins of the "contract" Steuben claimed to have made with the Continental Congress, the petulant sense of entitlement with which he pursued his claim, and the fact that his dire financial situation obviously stemmed more from failed land speculations and an unrepentantly luxurious lifestyle than wartime sacrifices. The Greene petition was less controversial and better founded—Nathanael had used his private credit to supply the southern Continental army—but it benefited no less from the good offices of important people who were also social peers and friends of the petitioner. Connecticut Rep. Jeremiah Wadsworth was an executor of Greene's estate and his wife's chief advocate in Congress. Secretaries Hamilton and Knox helped draw up her petition and (as they did for Steuben) issued political guidance as the document made its way to passage.[72]

The success of Steuben and Greene can be contrasted with the fate of John Fitch, self-proclaimed inventor of the steamboat. An uneducated man who had grown up poor in Connecticut and worked variously as a surveyor, gunmaker, and all-purpose metalsmith, Fitch spent the late 1780s investing all his hopes, energies, and money in an attempt to perfect a method of steam-driven navigation. He produced several working steamboats and even ran a steam-driven packet service on the Delaware River for a time, but he never managed to make his steamboat design economically viable. While Fitch was partly doomed by technology (his steamboat never went fast enough to outstrip horse-drawn stages), politics and gentility also played important roles, for the inventor was highly unskilled in both of those areas.[73]

Hard-drinking, blunt, and given to openly expressing his often intensely negative emotions, Fitch was far from a complaisant man. Moreover, although he was mechanically brilliant, Fitch's lack of education and breeding left him (by his own admission) so "unfortunate that I am not able to communicate my Ideas by word of mouth," and his written communication skills were only a little better.[74] These social deficits proved to be insuperable barriers to the success of his steamboat project. Needing to finance construction of his steamboat, Fitch first submitted his ideas to the American Philosophical Society, a gentleman's club as well as a scientific organization, but was rejected. Benjamin Franklin received Fitch politely but brushed him off, though the inventor went away erroneously convinced that he had the great man's support. Similar encounters followed with George Washington,

---

[72]*DHFFC,* 7:201–46, 493–542.

[73]The general information on John Fitch, James Rumsey, and their battle to patent the steamboat in this and the following paragraphs is based on *DHFFC,* xxi–xxii, xxv, 8:39–43, 48–55, 60–65, 68–73; Frank D. Prager, ed., *The Autobiography of John Fitch, Memoirs of the American Philosophical Society,* vol. 113 (Philadelphia, 1976); Thompson Westcott, *The Life of John Fitch, The Inventor of the Steamboat* (Philadelphia, 1857); Thomas Boyd, *Poor John Fitch, Inventor of the Steamboat* (1935; reprint ed., Freeport, N.Y., 1971); "Fitch, John," and "Rumsey, James," *American National Biography,* ed. John A. Garraty and Mark C. Carnes, 24 vols. (New York, 1999).

[74]Prager, *Autobiography of Fitch,* p. 181.

James Madison, and other prominent men. Fitch had to move forward with only a handful of middle-class Philadelphia businessmen (including grocers and tavern keepers) as his backers, and by 1788 his resources had begun to run dry. Fitch had unsuccessfully petitioned the Confederation Congress four times for support, but with the new government organizing, his best hope of attracting major investment seemed to be obtaining a federal patent that would guarantee him exclusive rights to steam navigation nationwide. He would submit four petitions to the First Congress asking for such a patent.

Meanwhile, a Virginia tavern keeper named James Rumsey (who had no more formal education than Fitch but had clearly mastered the basics of genteel social interaction) emerged to make a competing claim on the steamboat patent and quickly gathered the kind of high-level support that always eluded Fitch. Rumsey gained the sponsorship of Washington while working on the latter's pet project to open the upper Potomac River to navigation. He picked up the endorsement of Benjamin Franklin by complaisantly adopting Franklin's idea of a jet-propelled steamboat. While his boats were considerably less successful than Fitch's, technologically and commercially, Rumsey was elected to the American Philosophical Society in 1788. Several APS members then organized the Rumseian Society to back his steamboat project, with Franklin as chair and such other Philadelphia social leaders as Miers Fisher, Levi Hollingsworth, William Bingham, and Benjamin Rush among the membership. Rumsey, who also managed to win Thomas Jefferson over to his cause, published a pamphlet taking credit for the steamboat idea himself and labeling Fitch a plagiarist.

Fitch defended himself fiercely, writing pamphlets (with some editing and rewriting from a better-educated investor) and lobbying Congress in favor of his petitions, but he was politically and socially outclassed by his myriad opponents. Financially, he had no possibility of hiring an expensive lawyer, as his fellow patent seeker Francis Bailey did, and, personally, he had few powerful friends to help. Rumsey went to England to negotiate a steamboat monopoly there and still defeated Fitch in absentia. Though Fitch was by now a longtime Philadelphia area resident, the eastern Pennsylvania congressional delegation was against him, a situation to which the inventor responded by uncomplaisantly naming Reps. George Clymer and Thomas Fitzsimons in the newspapers "as my avowed enemies." This ham-fisted tactic seems to have been characteristic of Fitch the politician, whose surviving letters to the public officials whose support he needed are full of a thoroughly off-putting form of belligerent self-pity, roughly but luridly expressed. A smooth gentleman lobbyist such as Cutler would never have written, to his chief congressional supporter, that "if my just Rights must be taken from me . . . may I not as well be delivered over to the Rude Savage . . . to sport with and put an end to my wretched Existence to quench their thirst for blood." Fitch ended a later lobbying letter by wailing that "it is too evident that my Country hates and despises me for what I have done," a fact which would "demand the serious Pity and Censure of future Generations."[75]

Hectoring when he should have hobnobbed, Fitch's campaign failed miserably. Increasingly destitute, dependent on the charity of his landlady, his clothing going to pieces, the inventor saw Congress frame a patent law partly the result of his requests, then table all of his own petitions. Finally, a patents commission made up of cabinet members Secretary of State Jefferson, Secretary of War Knox, and Atty. Gen. Edmund Randolph settled the steamboat dispute by issuing patents to both Fitch and Rumsey, dated on the same day, effectively crushing Fitch's hopes of ever finding investors or profiting from his invention. Fitch argued loudly with the commission and later tried to appeal to Jefferson, but in effect he was finished.[76] His steamboat company ceased business; construction of a new, large boat intended to navigate the Mississippi River (a plan that would have revolutionized the western economy and surely made Fitch's fortune) was abandoned. Never well respected, Fitch became a more pathetic figure than ever in genteel eyes. "Often I have seen him stalking about like a troubled spectre," remembered Philadelphia merchant Thomas P. Cope, evaluating Fitch according to the typically external standards of gentility, "with downcast eye and lowering countenance, his coarse, soiled linen, peeping through the elbows of a tattered garment."[77]

---

[75]Ibid., pp. 180–89; John Fitch to William Samuel Johnson, May 30, 1789, Fitch to [unknown], Feb. 16, 1791, *DHFFC,* 8:54, 68.

[76]Prager, *Autobiography of Fitch,* pp. 197–99; Westcott, *Life of Fitch,* pp. 340–41; Boyd, *Poor John Fitch,* p. 241.

[77]Westcott, *Life of Fitch,* p. 338.

Applying desperately for government jobs in this state, Fitch was, not surprisingly, turned down. After failed efforts to renew his steamboat dreams in Europe and then Kentucky, Fitch settled in a Bardstown, Kentucky, tavern and decided to implement perhaps long-entertained thoughts of taking his own life. (A frequent thought from the period when Fitch was battling Rumsey and lobbying Congress was the wish "that Heaven had rather put it in my mind to have cut my own throat, than to have put me in mind of building Steam Boats.") When drinking himself to death seemed to be moving too slowly in 1798, Fitch finished the job by collecting twelve opium pills, prescribed by a physician for an illness, and then swallowing them all at once.[78]

The "buying" of Congress by highly organized special interest lobbies is often lamented in our time, and not without cause. However, Fitch's bitter experience should alert us to the fact that the less tawdry-seeming, relatively unorganized lobbying culture of two centuries ago had its costs and injustices as well. Gentility was a club to which only some belonged, yet the access of all citizens to the favor of their government was structured by it. It concealed some forms of influence and excluded others, and did it all without much necessary reference to the real merits of any particular case or person. We should not romanticize or whitewash the political culture of the Founding Era any more than we should assume that politics and government were always conducted as they are today.

---

[78]Ibid., pp. 356–70; Prager, *Autobiography of Fitch,* p. 184.

Richard R. John and Christopher J. Young

Rites of Passage

Postal Petitioning as a Tool of Governance in the Age of Federalism

In July 1793, a group of South Carolinians requested that the Federal Congress extend mail delivery to the extreme western corner of the state. Their request took the form of a petition, a customary device for publicizing grievances that the government was presumed to have the authority to redress. "We recommend that a post be established to our district and county towns," the South Carolinians declared, since such facilities were the "soul of commerce!" Lacking such a direct, regular, and immediate means of communication, they were "kept in ignorance" and "know not anything which concerns us, either as men or planters."[1] The following year, Congress established three new routes to link this remote hinterland district with the nascent postal network.[2]

One cannot know for certain whether the South Carolinians' plea prompted Congress to extend them the desired facilities. Neverthe-

[1]Lemuel L. Alston et al. to Judge Thomas Waties, in *State Gazette of South Carolina*, July 1, 1793. This unusual item was brought to our attention by Robert J. Stets. It is one of the earliest requests for the designation of a post route that we have been able to locate and the oldest known post route petition.

[2]All information in this essay on the establishment of post offices and the designation of post routes is derived from Robert J. Stets, *Postmasters and Post Offices of the United States, 1782–1811* (Lake Oswego, Ore., 1994). This invaluable reference tool is an authoritative compendium of information on the American postal network in the early republic that deserves to find a wide audience among specialists in the period.

less, the possibility that a relationship existed between the drafting of a petition and the passage of legislation is suggestive and furnishes this essay with one of its principal themes.

The opening years of the federal republic witnessed the founding of a new and more powerful national government, the beginning of popular involvement in national politics, and the ascendancy of the Federalists — the political leaders who, having drafted the Federal Constitution in 1787, oversaw its implementation during the next fourteen years.

While these developments have long intrigued historians, their significance is subtly diminished by the frequent assertion that the defeat of the Federalists in the election of 1800 hastened the demise of the values and practices that they had worked so hard to sustain. The 1790s, as Gordon S. Wood has declared in an unusually forthright statement of this widely held position, were for this reason the "most awkward decade in American history, bearing little relation to what went on immediately before or after."[3] From Wood's standpoint, and that of the many historians who hold similar views, the Federalists were anachronistic holdovers from a soon-to-be repudiated aristocratic past. The true heralds of the future, these scholars contend, were the Federalists' political antagonists, the Republicans. With the victory of Thomas Jefferson in the election of 1800 — and not before — the electorate embraced popular politics, rejected governmental activism, and forged the peculiar alliance between antistatism and democracy that has been a hallmark of American public life ever since.[4]

The Woodsian thesis is grounded in a careful analysis of the policy pronouncements of the Federalists and their Republican antagonists. Only rarely, however, does it expand its ambit to embrace what the government actually did. As a consequence, it tends to obscure the distinction between ideological commitments and institutional outcomes. In so doing, it minimizes the institutional momentum set in motion with the establishment of the federal government in 1789 and

[3]Gordon S. Wood, "Framing the Republic, 1760–1820," in Bernard Bailyn et al., *The Great Republic: A History of the American People* (Lexington, Mass., 1977), 1:341.

[4]Gordon S. Wood, *The Radicalism of the American Revolution* (New York, 1992). For a survey and analysis of historical writing on the role of governmental institutions in the early republic, see Richard R. John, "Governmental Institutions as Agents of Change: Rethinking American Political Development in the Early Republic, 1787–1835," *Studies in American Political Development* 11 (1997):347–80.

understates the extent to which administrative mechanisms originating in the Federalist era continued to shape public policy long after Jefferson's victory in the election of 1800. Even more basically, it exaggerates the extent to which antistatism became in the early republic a pillar of the democratic creed.

This dismissive view of the Federalists' legacy has not gone uncontested. More than twenty years ago, Noble E. Cunningham, Jr., challenged the notion that the federal government in the early republic was isolated from the citizenry. By highlighting the significance of certain frequently overlooked forms of civic engagement—including the petition process—he pointed us toward a new way of thinking about public life in the Federalist era.[5] More recently, several historians of popular politics have highlighted linkages in the 1790s between national politics and the public-at-large.[6] Still others have underscored the enduring character of the Federalists' contribution to politics, public administration, and law.[7]

This essay contributes to this revisionist project by exploring one intriguing, yet oft-neglected, chapter in the history of public life during the Federalist era. Specifically, it analyzes those petitions that the Federal Congress received in the period between March 1789 and March 1801 that dealt with the post office and mail delivery. It is not our intention to contend that these petitions were representative of all the petitions that Americans sent to the Federal Congress during these tumultuous years. Rather, we use them to gauge the effectiveness of the petition process as a tool of governance and the extent to which practices begun during the Federalist era survived the Federalists' demise.

---

[5]Noble E. Cunningham, Jr., *The Process of Government under Jefferson* (Princeton, 1978), esp. p. 303; idem, *The United States in 1800: Henry Adams Revisited* (Charlottesville, 1988), esp. pp. 54–56.

[6]Alan Taylor, *William Cooper's Town: Power and Persuasion on the Frontier of the Early American Republic* (New York, 1995); Simon P. Newman, *Parades and the Politics of the Street: Festive Culture in the Early American Republic* (Philadelphia, 1997); David Waldstreicher, *In the Midst of Perpetual Fetes: The Making of American Nationalism, 1776–1820* (Chapel Hill, 1997).

[7]Stanley Elkins and Eric McKitrick, *The Age of Federalism: The Early American Republic, 1788–1800* (New York, 1993); Doron Ben-Atar and Barbara B. Oberg, eds., *Federalists Reconsidered* (Charlottesville, 1998). For a related critique of scholarship on the 1780s, see Peter S. Onuf, "Reflections on the Founding: Constitutional Historiography in Bicentennial Perspective," *William and Mary Quarterly*, 3d ser. 46 (1989):341–75.

In the late eighteenth century, Edmund S. Morgan has observed, the petition process was one of the rituals of popular government.[8] Our case study elaborates on Morgan's insight by showing how, in the Federalist era, some—but by no means all—petitions also became tools of governance. In so doing, we highlight some often overlooked continuities between the Federalist era and the nineteenth century and provide a vantage point from which to evaluate the Federalists' contribution to the subsequent course of American public life.

In the Federalist era, the right to petition was relatively noncontroversial—enjoying, as it did, an honored place in English constitutional law. While petitions took many forms, most combined two basic elements: an appeal to a superior political authority and a request to this authority that a particular grievance be redressed. By the mid-eighteenth century, their drafting was routine not only in Great Britain but also in Britain's North American possessions. Colonial legislatures in British North America were actually more likely than the British Parliament to permit the receipt of petitions on controversial topics such as taxation. Colonial legislatures also were more willing to act on the petitions they received. In colonial Virginia, petitions spurred the passage of more legislation than any other legal device.[9] In colonial Pennsylvania, fully one-half of all legislation originated in this way.[10] In fact, the effectiveness of the petition process as a tool of governance in colonial British North America may go far toward explaining why—as is sometimes contended—colonial legislatures enacted a significantly larger body of law than the British Parliament itself.

The Framers of the Federal Constitution were mindful of this heritage, and, in the First Amendment, guaranteed the citizenry the right

---

[8]Edmund S. Morgan, *Inventing the People: The Rise of Popular Sovereignty in England and America* (New York, 1988), p. 230.

[9]Raymond C. Bailey, *Popular Influence upon Public Policy: Petitioning in Eighteenth-Century Virginia* (Westport, Conn., 1979), p. 166. For the text of selected Virginia petitions from the 1780s, see Frederika Teute Schmidt and Barbara Ripel Wilhelm, "Early Proslavery Petitions in Virginia," *William and Mary Quarterly,* 3d ser. 30 (1973): 133–46.

[10]Alan Tully, "Constituent-Representative Relationships in Early America: The Case of Pre-Revolutionary Pennsylvania," *Canadian Journal of History* 11 (1976):145. See also Tully, *Forming American Politics: Ideals, Interests, and Institutions in Colonial New York and Pennsylvania* (Baltimore, 1994).

to petition the government for a "redress of grievances." Throughout the 1790s—and, indeed, for well into the nineteenth century—Congress invested this constitutional guarantee with an almost sacred solemnity.[11]

It would be misleading to treat the petition process in the Federalist era as a transparent expression of unalloyed grassroots sentiment, unmediated by elites. Many if not most petitions were drafted by members of the local gentry and boasted the signatures of an impressive array of local notables, with merchants or lawyers often heading the list. However, their presentation was by no means mere cynical "acts of ventriloquism" orchestrated by political leaders, as was often the case in Great Britain.[12] Few petitions originated with legislators, while many included the signatures of a wide array of people, including, in some instances, women and free blacks.

In theory, the petition process might seem to undermine the principle of representation upon which the federal republic was based. After all, it provided virtually anyone with a technique for appealing directly to the federal government, circumventing the elaborate filters that the Founders had established to separate this institution from the public-at-large. In practice, however, the petition process was far less subversive. By adopting the deferential pose of respectful supplicants, petitioners buttressed the authority of the existing regime. The intrinsic conservatism of petition etiquette was nicely revealed by the deferential pose two petitioners assumed in a letter to their congressman in 1793. We have "taken the liberty to send forward the enclosed petition

---

[11]Useful discussions of petitioning in the 1790s include "Introduction," in *Documentary History of the First Federal Congress* (Baltimore, 1997–), vol. 7 (eds. Kenneth R. Bowling, William C. diGiacomantonio, and Charlene B. Bickford), pp. xi–xvi; vol. 8, pp. xi–xxviii, hereafter cited as *DHFFC;* William C. diGiacomantonio, " 'For the Gratification of a Volunteering Society': Antislavery and Pressure Group Politics in the First Federal Congress," *Journal of the Early Republic* 15 (1995):169–97; and David P. Currie, *The Constitution in Congress: The Federalist Period, 1789–1801* (Chicago, 1997), pp. 229–32. See also *Petitions, Memorials, and other Documents Submitted for the Consideration of Congress: March 4, 1789 to December 14, 1795*, 99th Cong., 2d sess., committee print 99-AA. This document, which was compiled by Rebecca Rogers, includes a catalog of all of the petitions submitted to the federal Congress during the first six and a half years of its existence. On petitioning in the states, see Ruth Bogin, "Petitioning and the New Moral Economy of Post-Revolutionary America," *William and Mary Quarterly*, 3d ser. 45 (1988):391–425.

[12]Morgan, *Inventing the People*, p. 230.

to your Honor," the constituents declared, "and at the same time must presume so far upon your goodness as to ask the favor of your attention in preferring the same to that honorable body."[13]

Sometimes the petitioners' deference to established authority prompted what might well seem to be an excessive regard for propriety. In the petition discussed at the opening of this essay, for example, the petitioners directed their appeal not to the Federal Congress, but, rather, to a local notable. This notable, in turn, was—or so the petitioners assumed—to present their appeal to the state legislature, which, in turn, would "impress" on the Federal Congress the need for the sought-after change.[14]

Petitioners almost invariably framed their appeals as polite suggestions rather than imperative demands. For political leaders fearful of direct democracy, this made the petition process a superior alternative to the direct instruction of representatives, a practice that it in some ways resembled. With the gradual decline of direct instruction as a popular device, the petition process became—after voting—the primary mechanism for popular involvement in national politics.[15] Similar to participation in a festival or parade, membership in a voluntary association, or attendance at a political rally, it helped to create and sustain a distinctive realm of civic engagement.

The physical appearance of the petition reinforced its cultural authority. Like the parchment version of the Declaration of Independence, many were artfully drafted and elegantly inscribed.[16] This remained true, significantly, as late as the 1830s, when it became popular to copy petitions verbatim from a printed text. In effect, printers deliberately designed mass-produced documents to appear as if they had been composed by hand.

The traditionalism of the petition process invested it with an aura of legitimacy that other techniques for mobilizing public sentiment had yet to acquire. When George Washington assumed the presidency in

---

[13]Stephen Waite and Abner Bagley to George Thatcher, Jan. 15, 1793, Thatcher Family Papers, Massachusetts Historical Society, Boston, Mass.

[14]*State Gazette of South Carolina,* July 1, 1793.

[15]"Introduction," *DHFFC,* 8:xi.

[16]For a related discussion, see Pauline Maier, *American Scripture: Making the Declaration of Independence* (New York, 1997).

1789, political communications remained limited, politically oriented voluntary associations suspect, and political parties reviled. Indeed, it had yet to be decided even if Congress, as a representative body, had an obligation to broadcast its ongoing deliberations to the public-at-large. In such a setting, the petition process emerged, almost by default, as a mobilizing technique.

Petitions reached the seat of government in various ways. Some came in the mail, a practice that was greatly facilitated by the congressionally mandated franking privilege, which enabled legislators to send or receive an unlimited number of documents free of charge. Should Congress abolish the franking privilege—one legislator warned in 1791, in defending its continuation—the "privilege of petitioning the House would be in a great measure destroyed."[17] Critics of the franking privilege demurred. Far fewer petitions had been sent to him in the mail—declared Congressman Jeremiah Wadsworth of Connecticut, in rebutting his colleague's assertion—than had been handed him by constituents he met face to face during his trips back home.[18]

Wadsworth's rejoinder testifies, if inadvertently, to the limited facilities that the postal system at this time provided. Only in the following year, with the passage of the Post Office Act of 1792, would the federal government begin to extend even a rudimentary level of service to the vast majority of the general population. Following this expansion, it became easier for petitioners to send off their appeals—free of charge—to the seat of power. The volume of petitions multiplied accordingly, until, by the 1820s, it had become a veritable deluge.

When a petition reached Congress, it was presented to the legislature as a regular part of its proceedings, typically by the petitioner's representative. When the petitioner's grievance was read aloud, the voice of the people entered, both figuratively and literally, into the legislative chamber. During the Federalist era, this ritual was scrupulously observed. "Much depends on public opinion in matters relating to government," explained one editorialist in 1790. If the government were "to gain the confidence of the people," the people must be "fully

---

[17] *Annals of Congress,* Dec., 20, 1791, p. 276.

[18] *Annals of Congress,* Dec. 28, 1791, p. 289.

convinced that their memorials and petitions will be duly attended to when they are not directly repugnant to the interest and welfare of the community."[19]

The presentation of petitions significantly shaped the flow of business within the national legislature. At the beginning of each new Congress, legislators dutifully acknowledged the receipt of every petition that had arrived since the body had last convened. Because no petitions were rejected, and the topic of each read aloud, this took a good deal of time. "Congress has now been in session more than two weeks"—remarked one government insider in 1795—and "the principal part of the time has been taken up in reading & referring petitions—the number of which is great."[20] Following their initial presentation, some petitions were set aside. Others were referred to an executive department, while still others were assigned to a legislative committee—which, at this time, generally meant a specific, ad hoc body, since few permanent congressional committees had yet been established.

One index of the significance of the petition process is quantitative. In its first twelve years, the House of Representatives received 2,924 petitions: 567 in the First Congress, 585 in the Second, 575 in the Third, 535 in the Fourth, 382 in the Fifth, and 280 in the Sixth. During the same period, the Senate received an additional 316 petitions: 68 in the First Congress, 95 in the Second, 49 in the Third, 33 in the Fourth, 40 in the Fifth, and 31 in the Sixth.[21]

Whether or not these totals were large or small, of course, is a matter of perspective. One way to approach this issue is to compare the number of petitions the Federal Congress received with the number of petitions that found their way to the legislatures of the colonies and

---

[19]"Candidus," *Gazette of the United States,* June 5, 1790, cited in *DHFFC,* 8:xii.

[20]John Fenno to Joseph Ward, Dec. 25, 1795, in John B. Hench, ed., "Letters of John Fenno and John Ward Fenno, 1779–1800," *Proceedings of the American Antiquarian Society* 90 pt. 1 (1980):208.

[21]The petition totals in this essay were derived by Christopher J. Young from the printed journals of the House and the Senate. Young's tally of 634 petitions for the First Federal Congress (68 for the Senate and 566 for the House) is quite close to the estimate—more than 600—of the editors of the First Federal Congress project. See *DHFFC,* 8:xi.

states during a roughly similar period of time. While this comparison is open to various objections, it does provide a relatively simple way to measure the extent to which Americans had grown accustomed to petitioning the Federal Congress during its earliest years.

Such a comparison reveals that, during the Federalist era, the Federal Congress received more petitions than the legislatures of even the largest and most expansion-minded colonies and states. Consider Pennsylvania, one of the most geographically extended and rapidly growing of Britain's overseas possessions. In the fifty-two-year period between 1717 and 1775, the Pennsylvania legislature received 1,922 petitions. While this total might appear to be large, it was, in fact, considerably smaller than the total number of petitions that the federal House received in the twelve-year period between 1789 and 1801.[22] Even the Virginia House of Burgesses—the popular assembly in the largest, oldest, and most populous of the colonies—did not exceed the volume of petitions that the early Federal Congresses received. In the period between 1752 and 1799, the House of Burgesses received an average of 239 petitions per year. In the federal House, in contrast, the annual average for the period between 1789 and 1801 was 244.[23] The federal petition totals are particularly impressive when one remembers that under the Federal Constitution the mandate of the federal government remained quite limited in comparison to that of the states.

The significance of these comparisons should not be exaggerated. In this period, constituents were more likely to maintain a personal relationship with their colonial or state legislators than with their national representative. As a consequence, if they had a grievance to redress, they would have had less reason to prepare a petition. Still, it remains suggestive that, in an era in which so many historians have assumed the federal government to have been isolated from the public at large, the Federal Congress received such a relatively large number of appeals.

In the Federalist era, Americans petitioned Congress for a variety of reasons. Some sought financial compensation for services performed

---

[22] Tully, "Constituent-Representative Relationships," p. 140.

[23] Bailey, *Popular Influence*, p. 62.

or losses suffered in the War of Independence. Others protested the Jay Treaty, the government's financial policies, or the expansion of the military. Still others urged the suspension of the slave trade—and, in at least one instance, the abolition of the institution of slavery.[24]

One revealing class of petitions concerned the administration of the postal system. In contrast to the treasury, the military, or the other parts of the executive branch, the postal system provided a specific benefit that was of considerable grassroots concern. In no sense were postal petitions representative of all the petitions that the early Federal Congresses received. Postal petitions made up but a small fraction of the total number of petitions that found their way to the federal legislature and—in contrast to petitions dealing with slavery, commerce, or military affairs—rarely proved controversial. Nonetheless, their reception does provide a window on the possibilities—and the limitations—of the petition process as a tool of governance.[25] Postal petitions originated with one of three groups—postal officers, mail contractors, and postal patrons. Each provides insight into the relationship of petitioning and governance in the Federalist era.

Perhaps the most intriguing postal petition to find its way to Congress during the Federalist era was penned by Mary Katherine Goddard, the former postmaster of Baltimore and one of the few women to hold public office in the federal government during the eighteenth century.[26] Goddard's petition had been occasioned by her peremptory dismissal in the fall of 1789. As such, it was one of a relatively small number of petitions from this period to have originated in the grievance of a disaffected public servant. Within the annals of the Post Office Department, it was unique. Though many postal officers would

---

[24]Currie, *Constitution in Congress,* p. 272; petition of the Pennsylvania Abolition Society, Feb. 15, 1790, *DHFFC,* 8:324–26.

[25]For a more general discussion of the postal system in the early republic, see Richard R. John, *Spreading the News: The American Postal System from Franklin to Morse* (rev. paperback ed., 1998, Cambridge, Mass., 1995), chaps. 1, 2.

[26]On Mary Goddard, see Carol Sue Humphrey, "Mary Katherine Goddard," in *American National Biography,* ed. John Arthur Garraty and Mark C. Carnes (New York, 1999), 19:136–37; Martha King, "Making an Impression: Women Printers in the Southern Colonies in the Revolutionary Era," Ph.D. diss., College of William and Mary, 1992; and Ward L. Miner, *William Goddard: Newspaperman* (Durham, N.C., 1961).

petition Congress in the early republic for improvements in their pay or working conditions, Goddard was the only one to protest her dismissal. Thus, though her petition was extremely unusual, the circumstances that led to its preparation provide a good deal of insight into the workings of the petition process during the Federalist era.

Goddard had initially been appointed Baltimore postmaster—or, as she styled herself, "postmistress"—in 1775; she would remain in this position for the next fourteen years. Her tenure in office spanned the War of Independence and coincided with Baltimore's emergence as a booming port. No woman served with greater distinction in the federal government during its formative era. Few have been more neglected by historians interested in women's contribution to public life in the Revolutionary era.[27]

Goddard's petition challenged the rationale for her dismissal and called for her immediate reinstatement. It had been "universally understood," Goddard lectured the Senate (the body to whom her petition was addressed), that, under the new regime, "no person should be removed from office . . . unless manifest misconduct appeared." Since none of her superiors had accused her of any such dereliction of duty, she presumed herself "happy in the idea" that her office was secure.[28] To lend authority to her appeal, Goddard accompanied her petition with a testimonial to her character and official conduct that had been signed by the governor of Maryland and two hundred of the leading inhabitants of Baltimore.[29]

Goddard's plea, like that of her supporters, highlighted aspects of public life during the early republic that are sometimes overlooked. At no point, for example, did either Goddard or her backers contend—as would, for example, many a British placeman—that her office was a species of property to which she possessed a vested right. On the contrary, everyone assumed her continuation in office to be contingent upon her good behavior. "We wish her to be continued no longer in

---

[27]Mary Goddard's public service goes unmentioned, for example, in Linda K. Kerber's justly praised *Women of the Republic: Intellect and Ideology in Revolutionary America* (New York, 1980).

[28]Petition of Mary Katherine Goddard, Jan. 29, 1790, *DHFFC,* 8:234.

[29]Inhabitants of Baltimore to Osgood, Nov. 12, 1789, *DHFFC,* 8:236–37.

office" — declared her supporters, in supporting her reinstatement—"than her conduct is consistent with the duties & interest of the establishment."[30]

Goddard may not have regarded her office as a form of property, yet she remained insistent that her dismissal could not possibly have been justified by mere partisan wrangling. In the "old countries" of monarchical Europe, Goddard conceded, it was customary to appoint and dismiss officeholders on political grounds. In the republican United States, in contrast, she "never could suppose" that any minister, party, or individual would "deign to cast a wishful eye" upon "so small an object" while it was "in the hands of such a possessor."[31]

Historians have sometimes assumed that Goddard was being disingenuous, and that, in fact, her dismissal had in fact been politically motivated. Though Goddard heaped praise on the "federal cause," it was widely known that her brother, William Goddard, had close ties with the Federalists' political foes. However, such partisan considerations are easily exaggerated. Goddard and her brother had long been estranged, while at no point did either Goddard and her supporters or her antagonists so much as allude to Goddard's politics in explaining her dismissal. For each, instead, the deciding factor was Goddard's inability, as a woman, to supervise in person the various post offices that were located south of Baltimore on the main north-south post route.

Neither Goddard nor her supporters denied the contention that, as an elderly matron, she lacked the physical stamina to travel about. This was unsurprising. In this period, transportation facilities remained rudimentary, and few women of any age embarked on extended journeys.[32] However, Goddard found it unrealistic for her superiors to demand that she maintain such a heavy travel schedule. No Baltimore postmaster, Goddard explained, could fulfill such a charge without putting at risk the large number of letters containing money and other valuable enclosures that postal patrons had entrusted to the mail. The

---

[30]Ibid., 8:237.

[31]Mary Goddard petition, ibid., 8:234.

[32]Patricia Cline Cohen, "Safety and Danger: Women on American Public Transport, 1750–1850," in *Gendered Domains: Beyond the Public-Private Dichotomy in Women's History,* ed. Susan Reverby and Dorothy Helly (Ithaca, N.Y., 1992), pp. 109–22.

supervision of such delicate transactions, Goddard declared, had to devolve upon the "principal" of the office, if this officer were to "give satisfaction" to the merchants who frequently made large remittances by post.[33]

If Goddard had genuinely hoped that her petition might bring about her reinstatement—and it is by no means self-evident that she did—her effort failed. President Washington remained silent, Postmaster General Samuel Osgood backed his subordinate, Jonathan Burrall—the officer who had ordered Goddard's dismissal—and the Senate declined to issue a report or even to convene a committee. The government's refusal to reinstate Goddard is understandable. Had it bowed to popular pressure, it would have established a precedent that would have rendered all federal appointments vulnerable to local interference. Goddard was, after all, by no means the only officeholder whom an incoming administration might wish to dismiss. By rejecting her petition, her official superiors buttressed the autonomy of the executive branch and established a precedent that discouraged other ex-officeholders from pursuing a similar course.

Why Burrall dismissed Goddard in the first place is somewhat harder to explain. Part of the answer can be traced to Goddard's gender. As a woman, Goddard's continuation in office posed a problem for the new regime. In 1789, the future of the Founders' bold experiment in republican government remained highly uncertain, and every public figure had a vested interest in rendering it more secure. The Baltimore postmastership was a visible, prestigious, and lucrative public office. The fact that it was held by a woman challenged the patriarchal presumption that, in a republic, such positions were an exclusively male prerogative.

A mock petition published in a Philadelphia newspaper in 1791 evoked the distinctive mix of incredulity and scorn with which political leaders contemplated the prospect of female involvement in the public sphere. Supposedly prepared by a group of "federal maids," the petition humorously implored Congress to grant women the right to serve in the military, hold public office, and exercise an "absolute

---

[33]Mary Goddard petition, *DHFFC,* 8:235.

command" over their husbands.[34] The patriarchal premises that underlay this gentle satire would be articulated more bluntly a few years later by Thomas Jefferson. "The appointment of a woman to office," Jefferson observed, "is an innovation for which the public is not prepared, nor am I."[35] Had Goddard not been dismissed, such a categorical pronouncement would have been harder to sustain.

Goddard was by no means the only postmaster in the early republic to regard her dismissal as manifestly unjust, but she *was* the only postmaster to petition Congress for redress. At approximately the same time she lost her position, the postmasters in New York and Philadelphia also were dismissed. Though the New York postmaster wrote President Washington to protest his dismissal, neither petitioned Congress to be reinstated.[36] To what extent, then, might her gender have predisposed her to adopt this highly unusual course? For a woman, the petition process had certain indisputable attractions. By throwing herself on the mercy of her superiors, Goddard acknowledged the authority of the patriarchs to whom she appealed. Significantly, at one point Goddard went so far as to advert to her dependent station, styling her office "small" and protesting that the government ought not to dislodge "such a possessor."

To ascribe Goddard's decision to her status as woman, however, leaves a good deal unexplained. To begin with, neither Goddard nor her supporters drew attention to her gender, preferring instead to let her record stand for itself. In addition, such an explanation cannot account for the nonpostal male ex-officeholders who mounted analogous appeals. During the same congressional session, for example, Sen. Robert Morris also petitioned the Senate to exonerate himself

---

[34]*Gazette of the United States,* Jan. 27, 1791, cited in *DHFFC,* 8:xxvi. Mary Goddard petition, ibid., 8:235.

[35]Thomas Jefferson to Albert Gallatin, Jan. 13, 1807, Paul Leicester Ford, ed., *The Works of Thomas Jefferson,* 12 vols. (New York, 1905), 10:339.

[36]William Bedlow to George Washington, Sept. 27, 1789, Papers of the Continental Congress, Record Group 360, National Archives and Records Administration, Washington, D.C. "Above all," Bedlow wrote, he deplored his dismissal, since "it may leave a stigma on my character by persons who do not 'feel another's woe.' . . . Could Mr. Osgood have known my peculiar situation, sure I am he could never have thought of dismissing of me to provide for another, without some misdemeanor of mine."

from the charge that as superintendent of finance under the Articles of Confederation he had mishandled public funds.[37] Morris was, of course, a far more prominent public figure than Goddard. That he, too, had petitioned Congress on a job-related matter suggests that Goddard's decision was by no means entirely out of line with prevailing conventions.

Perhaps the most straightforward explanation for Goddard's decision to petition Congress can be traced to the simple fact that—at this time—there existed few alternative mechanisms for ex-officeholders to clear themselves from the inevitable calumnies that their dismissal could be expected to spawn. In 1789, an organized political opposition had yet to emerge; as a consequence, it was difficult for Goddard to rally the disaffected to her cause. Under the circumstances, the drafting of a petition was one of the few options at Goddard's disposal. At the very least, it furnished her with a blunt but serviceable weapon to defend her honor, castigate her political foes, and avenge her public humiliation: "defense pamphlets," as historian Joanne B. Freeman has aptly labeled such often hyperbolic productions. In time, they would evolve into a somewhat less overheated (yet still emphatically masculine) literary form: the ex-officeholder's lament.[38] Goddard's petition, in short, may well have been intended less to countermand her superiors' judgment than to hasten her public vindication. For her, the right to petition was less a tool of governance than what a later, more irreverent generation would call a public relations ploy. Whether or not her effort succeeded is, therefore, a matter to be decided not only by Goddard's peers but also by posterity.

Though Goddard had prepared her petition with care, it occasioned no congressional action. More effective were the various mail

---

[37]Petition of Robert Morris, Feb. 8, 1790, *DHFFC,* 8:667–69.

[38]Joanne B. Freeman, "Slander, Poison, Whispers, and Fame: Jefferson's 'Anas' and Political Gossip in the Early Republic," *Journal of the Early Republic* 15 (1995):52.

One artful example of an ex-officeholder's lament was Nathaniel Hawthorne's "Custom House," a memoir of his years as a federal customs collector. Hawthorne's contribution to this genre was particularly ingenious, since he excised from it even the merest hint of partisan bile. Herman Melville's "Bartleby the Scrivener" can also be profitably read with these literary conventions in mind. For an elaboration of this theme, see Richard R. John, "The Lost World of Bartleby the Ex-Officeholder: Variations on a Venerable Literary Form," *New England Quarterly* 70 (1997): 631–41.

contractors who used the petition process as a lobbying technique. Here, too, the right to petition posed as many problems as it resolved. As a consequence, by the end of the Federalist era, mail contractors had largely abandoned the petition process in favor of more flexible, less formal techniques. The rise and fall of this kind of petition effort is illustrated by the brief public career of Nathaniel Twining, a Virginia stagecoach promoter who in the 1780s oversaw a stagecoach empire that stretched from Pennsylvania to Georgia.

Twining's foray into mail contracting began in April 1785, when he petitioned the Confederation Congress to transport the mail by stagecoach between New York City and Norfolk, Virginia. Should the government award him an appropriate contract, Twining boasted, he could convey the mails "to the southward . . . quicker than it has ever been done."[39] Congress endorsed Twining's proposal and instructed Postmaster General Ebenezer Hazard to recruit stagecoach proprietors to transport the mail, but Congress refused to give Hazard a free hand. In addition to mandating stagecoach service between New York and Norfolk, as Twining had proposed, Congress also required Hazard to establish stagecoach service along the entire length of the north-south post route—an enormous expanse, that, at the time, stretched from Portsmouth, New Hampshire, to Savannah, Georgia.[40]

This directive marked something of a milestone in transportation history. Never before had the government entered into a contract with a stagecoach firm to carry the mail. No less important, in the three southernmost states that the mandate embraced—namely, North Carolina, South Carolina, and Georgia—never before had regular stagecoach service been even attempted.

To fulfill this congressional mandate, Hazard turned to Twining. Accordingly, in late 1785, Hazard hired Twining to carry the mail by stagecoach between Philadelphia and Savannah. Twining's venture

---

[39]Memorial of Nathaniel Twining, April 1785, Papers of the Continental Congress, RG 360, NARA. On Twining's staging operations, see Oliver W. Holmes, "Shall Stagecoaches Carry the Mail? A Debate of the Confederation Period," *William and Mary Quarterly,* 3d ser. 29 (1963):555–73, and Oliver W. Holmes and Peter T. Rohrbach, *Stagecoach East: Stagecoach Days in the East from the Colonial Period to the Civil War* (Washington, D.C., 1983), pp. 17–18, 24–26, 82–83.

[40]Worthington C. Ford et al., eds., *Journals of the Continental Congress, 1774–1789,* 34 vols. (Washington, D.C., 1904–37), 29:684.

was difficult, bold, and risky. For much of the six-hundred mile route, roads were poor, bridges nonexistent, and ferry crossings wide. In the absence of a substantial government outlay, such a staging operation could not possibly succeed. North of Philadelphia, Twining observed, it was at least conceivable that a stagecoach line might be able to support itself, "independent of the advantages of the mail."[41] To the southward, however, public support was indispensable. Hazard recognized the magnitude of the challenge that Twining confronted and agreed to pay him a generous sum. For the year 1786, Twining was to receive just more than $10,000 for the Petersburg-Savannah run alone. This worked out to fully one-third of all the postal revenue that the government received in that year for a route that could not possibly return more than a tiny fraction of its cost.[42]

Twining's reliance on government support was highlighted by a second petition that he submitted in September 1787. Hazard, Twining complained, had unjustly reduced the size of Twining's contract, while unfairly fining him for shifting the mail on a part of his route from stagecoach to post rider. Accordingly, Twining petitioned Congress to restore his contract to its former level and to remit the fine.[43] Congress granted Twining's request, securing him some much-needed fiscal relief.[44] It did nothing, however, to solve his more basic problem, which stemmed less from the postmaster general's parsimony than from the limited demand for passenger travel and the deplorable state of the roads.

Twining's problems persisted, and, in late 1787, Hazard once again penalized him for switching the mail from stagecoach to post rider on a part of his route. Though Twining soon suspended his stagecoach ventures in the Lower South, he remembered this fine, and, shortly after the establishment of the federal government in 1789, petitioned the First Federal Congress to secure its remission.

Twining's resubmission led to the appointment of special committees in both the Senate and House and the preparation by each committee of a written report. The House committee ruled in Twining's

---

[41]Petition of Nathaniel Twining, Sept. 18, 1787, *DHFFC,* 8:243.

[42]Holmes, "Stagecoaches," p. 566; Ford, *Journals of the Continental Congress,* 34:463.

[43]*DHFFC,* 8:244.

[44]Ford, *Journals of the Continental Congress,* 33:531–34, 536–37, 593; 34:463–64.

favor and prepared a bill for Twining's relief. "Inasmuch as no injury has happened to the public," the House committee explained, "it would be reasonable and just to remit the . . . penalty."[45] The Senate committee, in contrast, found the House bill unmerited and recommended that it be rejected.[46] The bill for Twining's relief, one Pennsylvania senator indignantly declared, was "contrary in my opinion to every idea of justice."[47] Eventually the House prevailed, and Congress once again remitted Twining's fine.

Twining's petitions exposed one of the most conspicuous anomalies in postal policy during the Federalist era. Though the transportation of the mail was an undisputed federal prerogative, the rights of way over which it was conveyed fell within the domain of the states. To put it somewhat differently, though Congress had the authority to establish stagecoach service, it lacked the jurisdiction to improve the route over which the stagecoaches would run. In an age in which many parts of the country lacked suitable roads, bridges, and ferries, this circumstance raised a host of thorny issues that were not easily resolved. A new stagecoach route, after all, might well foist expensive new public works projects upon states or localities that they were unwilling or unable to undertake.[48]

Twining tried to solve this problem by lobbying Congress to remit the fines that poorly maintained rights of way had forced him to incur. Stagecoach proprietor Isaac Trowbridge took a somewhat different tack. Publicly conceding that he had made a bad bargain, Trowbridge petitioned Congress in 1790 to relieve him of a mail contract that he had entered into without having sufficiently investigated the deplorable state of the roads.[49]

45"House Committee Report," May 20, 1790, *DHFFC*, 8:245.

46"Senate Committee Report," June 23, 1790, ibid., 8:245.

47June 24, 1790, Kenneth R. Bowling and Helen E. Veit, eds., *The Diary of William Maclay and Other Notes on the Senate Debates*, vol. 9 of *DHFFC*, pp. 297, 302, quote on p. 302.

48This divided mandate helps explain why so many travelers in the early republic complained about the bumpiness of their stagecoach rides. In effect, the federal government had mandated the establishment of stagecoach service on routes in advance of the establishment of a suitable right-of-way. Here was one instance in which improvements in transportation followed improvements in communications—rather than preceding them, as is often assumed.

49Petition of Isaac Trowbridge, Mar. 28, 1788, *DHFFC*, 8:230.

Certain expedients provided mail contractors with a measure of relief. In the First Federal Congress, for example, stagecoach proprietors successfully secured legislation penalizing local authorities for interfering with the passage of the mail.[50] However, as long as the states retained jurisdiction over the rights of way, it was hard to envision how the federal government could get at the root of the problem. We seem to be "getting into a maze," declared one exasperated congressman in January 1792, in reflecting upon one particularly difficult jurisdictional conundrum: the post office bill had been "long under consideration, and we seem to make no progress." Would it not be better, he added, if the whole bill were "buried" and the legislature spared from ever again having to contemplate such a complicated array of concerns?[51] Many contractors agreed. As the 1790s progressed, fewer and fewer petitioned the federal legislature. As an alternative, they turned their attention to the states, where they tried to goad state and local authorities into improving the rights of way over which they transported the mail.[52]

Some public figures hoped that the federal government might soon increase its involvement in the construction and maintenance of the country's transportation infrastructure. In 1790, for example, engineer Christopher Colles unsuccessfully petitioned Congress for funds to conduct a major road survey.[53] Two years later, the House briefly contemplated the prospect of using federal funds to turnpike the main north-south post road.[54] In 1796, another road survey proposal received the endorsement of James Madison.[55] And, in 1801, Maryland Sen. Robert Goodloe Harper recommended that Congress transform the postal surplus into a permanent road construction fund.[56] In the end, all of these proposals failed, stymied by fears that they would

---

[50]Petition of mail contractors on the route between Philadelphia and New York, Feb. 9, 1790, *DHFFC,* 8:229; *Statutes at Large,* 1:234.

[51]*Annals of Congress,* Jan. 5, 1792, p. 310.

[52]*Public Records of the State of Connecticut* (Hartford, 1953), 9:269–70.

[53]Christopher Colles petition, Mar. 29, 1790, *DHFFC,* 8:13–14. See also Walter W. Ristow, *A Survey of the Roads of the United States of America* (Cambridge, Mass., 1961), pp. 50–52.

[54]*Annals of Congress,* Jan. 3, 1792, p. 306.

[55]Ibid., Feb. 11, 1796, pp. 314–15.

[56]Robert Goodloe Harper, "Mr. Harper's Motion," Mar. 10, 1800, in *National State Papers of the United States, 1789–1817,* ed. Michael Glazier (Washington, D.C., 1985).

dangerously augment the political patronage at the disposal of the existing regime. Not until after the Federalist era had come to a close would Congress embark on its first major road-building project by approving federal funding for an ambitious east-west thoroughfare that would come to be known as the National Road.

The mixed outcome of these Federalist-era proposals serves as a reminder that, at least for mail contractors, the petition process was a clumsy device. It was awkward, and potentially embarrassing, to list as a grievance an appeal that was, in fact, a request for additional funds. Compounding the contractors' problem was the visibility of the process. In addition to rendering their requests susceptible to partisan maneuvering, it exposed their business practices to a potentially devastating degree of public scrutiny. During the next half-century, few mail contractors would emulate Twining and petition Congress for redress. This circumstance helps explain why, in this period, stagecoach policy only rarely found its way onto the national political agenda. In one sense, this outcome was paradoxical: after all, in the 1810s and 1820s, the federal government actually increased its financial commitment to the stagecoach industry. Indeed, by the Jacksonian era, postal subsidies accounted for as much as 33 percent of all the revenue the stagecoach industry received.[57]

In fact, this paradox was easily explained. Though stagecoach lobbyists were becoming increasingly adept at negotiating advantageous mail contracts, almost all of the pivotal negotiations took place in secret, generating little in the way of a paper trail. Not until the 1830s would a congressional investigation subject the stagecoach industry to the glare of publicity. And not until 1845 would Congress take decisive action to scale back its subsidies for stagecoach service, crippling almost overnight an industry that had been benefiting from public largesse for more than fifty years.[58]

For mail contractors, then, the significance of the petition process was somewhat greater than Twining's experience might lead one to conclude. Though it only temporarily served as a tool of governance, it

---

[57]John F. Stover, "Canals and Turnpikes: America's Early Nineteenth-Century Transportation Network," in *An Emerging Independent American Economy, 1815–1875,* ed. Joseph R. Frese and Jacob Judd (Tarrytown, N.Y., 1980), esp. p. 75.

[58]John, *Spreading the News,* esp. chap. 6.

helped establish precedents that would long shape federal transportation policy in the United States. Subsequent contract negotiations with mail contractors were informal and almost always private. As a consequence, they rarely occasioned public discussion or historical scrutiny. To this day, Nathaniel Twining remains one of the best-documented mail contractors of the early republic; in large measure, this was because he had the temerity to petition the federal government to remit a fine.

In Article I, section 8, of the Federal Constitution, Congress is granted the power to establish post offices and post roads. Between 1789 and 1792, congressmen, government administrators, and even a few ordinary citizens struggled to interpret the meaning of this clause. Few Americans assumed that it gave the federal government the authority to build or improve the roads over which the mail was conveyed—a power that, in most instances, remained within the domain of the states. A growing number of citizens were no longer content to leave control over the designation of these routes to the executive, as had previously been the norm. Here, then, was one indisputable realm in which the petition process would emerge as a rite of passage for legislation that was destined to have far-reaching implications for American public life.

The idea that the petition process might be deployed to expand the mail facilities provided by the government first emerged in the months immediately after the establishment of the federal government in 1789. For the next three years, this possibility was a subject of extensive and sometimes intense public debate. Not until the first session of the Second Federal Congress would Congress settle the issue with the passage of the Post Office Act of 1792. In this law, Congress reserved to itself the authority to designate every post route in the country. In so doing, it established an institutional mechanism that enabled ordinary Americans to petition Congress to determine the routes over which the mails were to be conveyed.

Congressional control over the designation of post routes was by no means noncontroversial. Contemporaries complained endlessly about its cost, capriciousness, and administrative complexity. As recently as 1997, such concerns were echoed by a prominent constitutional scholar.[59] Notwithstanding this critique, congressional control would remain a cornerstone of postal policy for the next ninety years. Not until 1884 would it come to an end.[60] As a consequence, for almost a century, every major piece of postal legislation included a detailed description of every new post route that Congress had approved.[61] Many, if not most, of these routes had been established in response to, and as the result of, the preparation of a petition by interested parties. Here, in the designation of post routes—far more than in the protestations of postal officers or the lobbying of mail contractors—the petition process became a tool of governance for important legislation.

During the Federalist era, route petitions constituted the vast majority of all the postal petitions that Congress received. Indeed, route petitions would remain the largest class of postal petitions to find their way to Congress during the first half of the nineteenth century. Thousands, mostly from the period after 1815, can be found today in the National Archives. As recently as the 1980s, many remained tri-folded, like a business letter, just as they had been when originally filed away by a congressional clerk. Their existence testifies to the confidence with which ordinary Americans looked to the federal government to provide a public service that they increasingly came to view as less of a privilege than a right.

Prior to 1792, the designation of new post routes remained the responsibility of the postmaster general and his staff.[62] In January

---

[59]Currie, *Constitution in Congress,* p. 149.

[60]In that year, Congress eliminated the rationale for route petitions by designating as post routes "all public roads and highways, while kept up and maintained" (*Statutes at Large,* 23:3). For the rationale for this legislation, see *Congressional Record,* Feb. 14, 1884, pp. 1113–14. In a certain sense, this law anticipated the declaration of census officials following the census of 1890 that the western frontier had finally closed.

[61]For a more detailed discussion of the Post Office Act of 1792, see John, *Spreading the News,* chap. 2.

[62]See, for example, Samuel Holton to Richard Bache, May 18, 1780, Paul H. Smith, ed., *Letters of Delegates to Congress, 1774–1789,* 25 vols. (Washington, D.C., 1976–2000), 15:151. The published and manuscript records of the various congresses that met prior to the establishment of the federal government in 1789 contain few references to congressional involvement in the designation of post routes. One exception occurred in May 1788, when the Confederation Congress authorized the designation of a post route in Delaware. Postmaster General Hazard took care to specify, however, that the route had to cover its costs. Hazard to Congress, May 22, 1788, Ford, *Journals of the Continental Congress,* 34:174.

1790, Postmaster General Osgood articulated the conventional understanding of this policy in a letter to Treasury Secretary Alexander Hamilton. "The application for new post offices and new post roads are numerous," Osgood informed Hamilton. "Cross posts must be established, and of very considerable extent."[63] In keeping with convention, the postmaster general chose the course of those post routes that crossed state lines. If, however, a route began and ended within a state, it was the responsibility of the postmasters within the immediate vicinity to determine the roads it would traverse and the towns it would pass. Predictably, this arrangement discouraged innovation, since few postmasters could be expected to support alterations that might oblige them to move. In states like Connecticut—where the post route was long, and the mix of interests complex—this deference to local postmasters greatly frustrated political leaders, since it limited their ability to bring the facilities of communication into alignment with public demand.[64] In such an informational ancien régime, any alterations in the location of the post route were bound to prove contentious. After all, with every shift in the chain, some localities won and some lost.

Prior to 1792, the expansion of mail facilities was further constrained by the expectation that the postal system, like the customs, should provide a steady stream of revenue to the general treasury.[65] This assumption persisted even after the adoption of the Federal Constitution in 1788. The post office, declared one congressman, in May 1789, in a typical statement of this common view, was one institution "which the ingenuity of government can devise and is entitled to, for the purpose of revenue."[66] Though a few expansion-minded legisla-

---

[63]Osgood to Hamilton, Jan. 20, 1790, Harold C. Syrett and Jacob E. Cooke, eds., *Papers of Alexander Hamilton,* 27 vols. (New York, 1961–87), 6:197. Though Osgood believed in executive control over the designation of new post routes, he conceded that Congress had the ultimate authority to determine whether the postal system should be a source of general revenue. Ibid., 6:202.

[64]Jeremiah Wadsworth to William Samuel Johnson, Mar. 13, 1785, in Edmund C. Burnett, ed., *Letters of Members of the Continental Congress,* 8 vols. (Washington, D.C., 1921–36), 8:73–74 n. 2. Wadsworth wrote in part: "If the matter of the Post Office should undergo any alteration, the regulations respecting the coming and g[oing] out of the posts in the different States as well as their route should be regulated by Congress and not left to the postmasters."

[65]To be sure, pre-1792 critiques of the fiscal rationale for postal policy were by no means unknown. For an early example, see North Carolina delegates to Alexander Martin, Jan. 28, 1783, Smith, *Letters of Delegates to Congress,* 19:633–34.

[66]*DHFFC,* 10:566.

tors questioned this premise, before 1792 no postal administrator felt emboldened to follow their lead. Rather, like Hamilton, they looked to the postal system to help generate the revenue upon which the national credit was based. In keeping with this fiscal rationale for postal policy, postal administrators opposed ambitious schemes that were likely to prove financially burdensome, such as the subsidization of stagecoach service or the establishment of cross posts between the Atlantic seaboard and trans-Appalachian hinterland. Instead, they preoccupied themselves with maintaining a single chain of posts along the Atlantic seaboard, the route that would eventually become known as the "Old Post Road." Since merchants in these localities generated all but a tiny fraction of postal revenue, it seemed only reasonable that the institution should cater to their needs.

While the vast majority of Americans at this time lacked access to mail facilities, few found in this circumstance a cause for concern. In the "late Congress," reported one legislator in 1790, the designation of new post routes had been left to the executive, and few had complained.[67] Had the Confederation Congress publicized its ongoing proceedings—or, at the very least, permitted newspapers to report its debates—more Americans might well have lobbied it to improve their access to information about its ongoing activities. Instead, Congress had deliberated behind closed doors, and few seemed to care.[68]

With the establishment of the federal government in 1789, each of these assumptions would come under assault. To understand the nature of this challenge, and the character of the obstacles to be overcome, it is helpful to consider how, in the period between 1789 and 1792, Americans went about securing improvements in mail delivery. The experience of three individuals—Nathaniel Rochester of

---

[67] *Gazette of the United States,* July 10, 1790, in *DHFFC,* 13:169. For a different interpretation, see Currie, *Constitution in Congress,* p. 147. Currie relies on this quotation to contend—incorrectly in our view—that, in the period after 1789, executive control over the designation of new post routes worked well and aroused little popular opposition. While Currie's conclusion holds for the years preceding 1789, it overlooks the more complex situation that emerged between 1789 and 1792.

[68] J. R. Pole, *The Gift of Government: Political Responsibility from the English Restoration to American Independence* (Athens, Ga., 1983), pp. 133–34; Jack N. Rakove, *The Beginnings of National Politics: An Interpretive History of the Continental Congress* (New York, 1979), p. 355.

Maryland; Oliver Wolcott, Sr., of Connecticut; and Samuel Henshaw of Massachusetts—is illustrative of the general pattern.

Nathaniel Rochester was a Virginia-born merchant and landowner who had served with distinction in the War of Independence. Intent on boosting the fortunes of Hagerstown, Maryland, where Rochester had settled after the war, he petitioned the postmaster general in late 1789 to reroute through this locality the "continental post." Should the postmaster general oblige—or so Rochester hoped—this would transform a struggling settlement into a bustling crossroads astride a major east-west commercial corridor.

Though Rochester's petition has not survived, its contents can be reconstructed from a letter that he wrote in November 1789 to the former Revolutionary War general Horatio Gates. In this letter, Rochester informed Gates that he had circulated his petition not only in Hagerstown, but also in Shepardstown and Martinsburg, Virginia. Its goal was to persuade the postmaster general to reroute through Hagerstown the existing east-west post routes between Philadelphia and Pittsburgh and between Pittsburgh and Alexandria, Virginia. The petition also proposed, almost incidentally, that the federal government establish a new post route between Baltimore and Hagerstown.

While Rochester's request might seem straightforward, it in fact raised a thorny issue that at the time remained unresolved: did the federal government possess the power to establish a post route that fell entirely within the boundary of one state? Rochester seemed aware of the complexities that this issue raised, and, in his letter, stressed that he sought these facilities less to accommodate the inhabitants of Hagerstown than to improve the flow of information on the preexisting *inter*state routes.[69]

Rochester's letter revealed unmistakable misgivings about the appropriateness of the petition process to secure the sought-after change.

[69]Rochester to [Horatio Gates], Nov. 18, 1789, Stauffer Collection, New York Public Library. Rochester's efforts to designate a post route between Baltimore and Hagerstown were complicated by the existence in Maryland at this time of a skeletal statewide postal system that was administered by the Maryland state government. This system had been established around 1786 on the understanding that the jurisdiction of the Confederation Congress did not extend to the designation of post routes that ran entirely within the boundaries of a single state. Hazard to Congress, Oct. 30, 1786, Ford, *Journals of the Continental Congress,* 31:918 n. 1; Frederick Green to James Bryson, Oct. 23, 1786, Papers of the Continental Congress, RG 360, NARA.

Rochester assumed that Gates, who himself owned an estate near Martinsburg, would support the effort. Moreover, Rochester also hoped that Gates would do more than merely lend his name to the cause. In addition, he urged Gates to write a letter to Rochester's business partner, Thomas Hart, supporting the scheme. Such an appeal, Rochester explained, would "have more weight" than Gates's mere signature on a petition.[70]

Rochester's petition highlighted the constraints that limited the expansion of mail facilities in the years preceding the passage of the Post Office Act of 1792. Because intrastate post routes remained under the jurisdiction of the state, Rochester had no choice but to propose a radical alteration in the existing line of communication. Had the government seriously considered Rochester's proposal—and there is no evidence that it did—it would almost certainly have raised howls of protest from the towns whose mail facilities it would have disrupted.

With the passage of the Post Office Act of 1792, Rochester secured at least part of his goal. Though Congress refused to reroute the continental post, it did extend a basic level of mail facilities to Hagerstown, Shepardstown, and Martinsburg. Shortly thereafter, the postmaster general established a post office in Hagerstown and appointed Rochester the first postmaster, a position that he and his nephew would hold almost continuously until 1804.[71]

If Rochester's petition illustrates the constraints upon the expansion of mail facilities in the period prior to 1792, Oliver Wolcott, Sr.'s, request highlights some of the advantages of congressional control. As a signer of the Declaration of Independence and the lieutenant governor of Connecticut, Wolcott was one of the most prominent public figures of the day. It was perhaps for this reason that when, in December 1789, Wolcott sought an improvement in mail facilities, he couched his request in the form of an open letter to his representative, Jeremiah Wadsworth.

Wolcott's goal was the establishment of a post route embracing

---

[70]Rochester to [Gates],Stauffer Collection, NYPL.

[71]Nathaniel Rochester, "A Brief Sketch of the Life of Nathaniel Rochester, Written by Himself for the Information of his Children," *Rochester Historical Society Publication Fund Series,* ed. Edward R. Foreman (Rochester, N.Y., 1924), 3:311. Six years later, in 1810, Rochester left Maryland for the Genesee Valley in western New York, where he would help found the thriving commercial center that today bears his name.

Litchfield, Connecticut, a prosperous market town in the western section of the state. Like Rochester, Wolcott assumed that the improvements he desired were most easily attained by associating it with a project that crossed state lines: in Wolcott's case, the establishment of an inland post route from New York City to Hartford. To dignify his appeal, Wolcott appended to his letter the signatures of several of the most prominent men of Litchfield, including—in addition to Wolcott himself—the jurist Tapping Reeve and the Revolutionary War officers Benjamin Tallmadge and Uriah Tracy. While the presence of these signatures lent credibility to Wolcott's proposal, they did not transform it into a petition. Wolcott made no reference to a specific grievance; he addressed an individual legislator rather than a collective body; and he adopted an informal—and, indeed, almost conversational—tone. At no point did Wolcott indicate that a petition would be forthcoming; there is no evidence that one was ever prepared.

Wolcott recognized that, as a congressman, Wadsworth lacked the authority to extend to Litchfield the desired level of service. Accordingly, Wolcott urged Wadsworth to lobby the postmaster general to secure the sought-after change. Wolcott took it for granted that Wadsworth supported his proposal and reminded him that it had also received the endorsement of Connecticut Sen. William Samuel Johnson. Wolcott understood that the designation of those post routes that fell entirely within the states remained under the jurisdiction of the postmasters along the route. So, too, did Wadsworth. Indeed, a few years earlier Wadsworth had drawn attention to just this fact in a letter to Johnson.[72] Such jurisdictional issues may help explain why, in his letter to Wadsworth, Wolcott took care to stress that the proposed route would link two states—New York and Connecticut—even though the core of his proposal involved an extension of mail facilities within Connecticut alone.

Wolcott declined to specify the towns that he hoped the proposed post route would pass through—provided, of course, that they included Litchfield. This was prudent, since Wolcott and Johnson had different ideas as to which route would be best. Wolcott favored a

---

[72]Wadsworth to Johnson, in Burnett, *Letters of Members of the Continental Congress,* 8:73–74 n. 2.

northerly route from Danbury to Litchfield through New Milford and Woodville; Johnson a southerly route via Newtown and Woodbury. By settling this issue, federal officials far from the scene could help resolve this impasse.

Wolcott did not, of course, anticipate that the federal government would build or upgrade the road over which the mail was to be conveyed. After all, in this period such alterations remained the responsibility of the states. Rather, he assumed that, once federal officials had designated the route, state and local authorities would oversee the necessary improvements in the right of way. To minimize local opposition to what was, in effect, an unfunded federal mandate, Wolcott hoped that Congress would wrest from the postmaster general and his staff the designation of new post routes. "So forcible" were the prejudices that local leaders confronted in improving the roads, Wolcott declared, that he hoped that the designation of post routes throughout the United States would soon be taken from the executive and "made subjects of the supreme legislative consideration." Such a seemingly minor jurisdictional shift, Wolcott added, was imperative to surmount the formidable local obstacles—rooted in inertia, local rivalries, and even personal animosities—that would otherwise stymie the construction and maintenance of suitable roads. "The business," Wolcott concluded, "will never be thoroughly done in any other way."[73]

Wolcott's strategy succeeded. Shortly after he wrote his letter, Litchfield became a designated stop on a private post route that was paid for by the postage it generated. Such routes—unlike regular post routes—had, by definition, to cover their costs. Two years later, Litchfield secured its first federal post office, yet another beneficiary of the expansion in mail facilities mandated by the Post Office Act of 1792.

It is sometimes contended that the failure of Congress to pass a comprehensive postal law until the first session of the Second Federal Congress demonstrates the relative insignificance of mail delivery to the political leaders of the day. This conclusion is mistaken. As the previous discussion suggests, it would make more sense to conclude that the establishment of regular procedures for the designation of post

---

[73]Oliver Wolcott, Sr., and nine others to Jeremiah Wadsworth, Dec. 7, 1789, Wadsworth Papers, Connecticut Historical Society, Hartford, Conn.

routes was one of the thorniest and most intractable problems that the new regime confronted. In fact, the issue proved to be so contentious that it took Congress almost three full years to work out a solution.

Few insiders doubted that, should Congress set up a regular mechanism to evaluate post route petitions, such appeals would rapidly multiply. The consensus on this point was particularly notable, because in the First and Second Congresses only a small number of post route petitions found their way to the seat of government.[74] In the second session of the First Federal Congress, legislators found themselves deluged with a flood of petitions asserting claims for compensation that had been occasioned by the petitioner's participation in the Revolutionary War. Given this fact, it did not take a great deal of imagination to envision the coming avalanche of petitions requesting improvements in mail facilities. In July 1790, one congressman addressed the matter directly. If the House wished to avoid a "great deal of unnecessary business" that would almost certainly come before it in the shape of petitions to abolish old post routes and designate new ones, he declared, it should leave the designation of post routes to the postmaster general.[75]

Opposition to congressional control received much of its impetus from public figures troubled by its probable cost. Congressional representation was geographically based and settlers were moving rapidly into the backcountry. Should Congress prove responsive to popular demand, it seemed self-evident that the chain of posts along the Atlantic seaboard would rapidly expand into a full-fledged network that would penetrate far into the interior. Few of these interior routes could be expected, at least for the foreseeable future, to break even. As a consequence, their designation would significantly reduce the surplus that the postmaster general returned to the general treasury, and, conceivably, eliminate it altogether. Should, in contrast, the postmaster general retain control over the designation of new post routes, popular involvement would be more limited, expansion slower, and the surplus larger.

Recognition of the desirability of the anticipated expansion in mail

---

[74]Unfortunately, none of these petitions have survived.

[75]*Gazette of the United States*, June 19, 1790, in *DHFFC*, 13:1571.

facilities was by no means confined to legislators. In January 1791, for example, Samuel Henshaw of Northampton, Massachusetts, drew attention to some of these potential benefits in a letter to his congressman, Theodore Sedgwick. Prior to the relocation of the federal seat of government from New York to Philadelphia, Henshaw observed, it had been easy to stay abreast of political news. Located as the residents of Northampton, a short boat ride up the Connecticut River from Long Island Sound, they "seemed almost to hear your debates" to "understand all that was doing." Now, however, that Congress sat to the southward, "we scarce know you are in session." The lesson seemed unmistakable: "This in my mind proves the necessity of post roads through all parts of the Union—people would then have early information & be influenced by it." Was it not possible, Henshaw wondered, for Congress to designate a post road that would pass through Northampton and continue all the way up the Connecticut River to Coos County in the northernmost corner of New Hampshire? The advantages of such an improvement seemed unassailable: "Business up the river is rapidly increasing and would be greatly facilitated by such an establishment. Should you effect it, your constituents would thank you."[76] Though Henshaw's request did not take the form of a petition, its import was plain: the founding of the federal government had greatly increased popular expectations with regard to public access to information, and legislators would be wise to respond. And so they did. Northampton secured its first post office in 1792, another beneficiary of the Post Office Act of 1792; the first post office in remote Coos County would be established a mere thirteen years later in 1805.

Congressional control over the designation of new post routes hastened the rapid expansion of mail facilities from the seaboard to the hinterland, just as its supporters had hoped and its critics had feared. Once a post route acquired a statutory designation, it required another law to effect its abolition. Such a step was at once time consuming and risky—because the affected parties might well orchestrate a public discussion and possibly even a congressional debate. Routes established by the postmaster general, in contrast, could be

---

[76]Samuel Henshaw to Theodore Sedgwick, Jan. 10, 1791, Sedgwick Papers, Massachusetts Historical Society, Boston, Mass.

readily abandoned, because, as mere administrative contrivances, they lacked the imprimatur of statutory law.

The practical consequences of congressional control were illustrated by the efforts of Postmaster General Joseph Habersham in 1798 to extend mail facilities to Kaskaskia, a tiny fortified hamlet on the Mississippi River in the Northwest Territory in what is today southwestern Illinois. Habersham's efforts were particularly notable because Kaskaskia was located far from the centers of population on what was then the western frontier. Habersham, the ablest of the Federalist postmasters general, fully supported the new expansionist rationale for postal policy that Congress had mandated with the passage of the Post Office Act of 1792. As a consequence, he was undeterred by the financial scruples that precluded his predecessors from initiating such ambitious and costly schemes. Habersham lobbied Congress to establish regular mail delivery to Kaskaskia from Louisville, Kentucky, by way of Vincennes. When Congress demurred—objecting, presumably, to the expense—Habersham contracted with Illinois merchant John Rice Jones to carry the mail on Jones's private account.[77] Because Congress had refused to designate the Kaskaskia route a "public post road," Habersham explained, it would be Jones's personal responsibility to "make good any deficiency in the postages arising on the route below the expense of carrying the mail."[78] The route, in short, would be a private post road that, under law, had to pay its own way. The following year, Congress rewarded Habersham's persistence and Jones's risk-taking by formally extending mail facilities to Kaskaskia and appointing Jones the first postmaster in Illinois. Henceforth, the

---

[77]Habersham to John Edgar, Nov. 29, 1799, Clarence Edwin Carter, ed., *Territorial Papers of the United States,* 18 vols. (Washington, D.C., 1934–69), 3:70. "Having repeatedly applied to Congress to extend the post road from Louisville to Kaskaskias without accomplishing that very desirable object," Habersham explained, he had "finally determined" to send the mail once a month on that route on the "personal engagements of the inhabitants of Vincennes and Kaskaskias."

[78]Habersham to John Rice Jones, Nov. 28, 1799, ibid., 3:70; Habersham to Jones, Mar. 22, 1800, ibid., p. 79. Throughout his tenure as postmaster general, Habersham remained committed to improving mail delivery between the Atlantic seaboard and what was then the country's westernmost settlements. Characteristically, during his final days in office, Habersham informed the chairman of the House post office committee, George Thatcher, that he had "taken the liberty" of inserting six routes into the post office bill—including a route from Vincennes to Kaskaskia (Habersham to Thatcher, Feb. 10, 1801, ibid., 3:121).

cost of the Kaskaskia route would be paid for out of general postal revenue. This meant that, like most routes in the South and West, its maintenance would be derived, at least in part, from postal revenue that had been generated hundreds—and, in some instances, thousands—of miles away in the North and East.

Congressional control obliged legislators to preoccupy themselves with a multitude of detailed matters of often purely local concern. By necessity, the congressional committees that drafted the post route legislation became highly knowledgeable about the vagaries of local geography. In 1798, for example, Congress enacted legislation specifying that a new post route in North Carolina was to pass by the house of either John Anders or William H. Beaty.[79] Constituents appreciated this attention to detail and were quick to respond. The following year, for example, a group of inhabitants of Cecil County, Maryland, and Lancaster County, Pennsylvania, petitioned Congress to designate a post route that would pass by the house of John Mifflin, in West Nottingham, and the house of William White, in Lancaster County.[80] Such scrupulous solicitude for local interests helped buttress the legitimacy of the federal government, even as it provided ordinary Americans with the mail facilities that they earnestly sought.

Not everyone, of course, secured the level of service that they desired. Some postal petitioners were rebuffed, sometimes by Congress and sometimes by the postmaster general, with whom Congress regularly consulted in evaluating the post route petitions that came its way.[81] In addition, at least in the 1790s, Congress actually designated more post routes than petitioners sought. Nevertheless, the trajectory was plain. The advent of congressional control over the designation of new post routes established a set of procedures that, in conjunction with the petition process, would transform the informational environment of the United States. By 1801, the north-south chain of posts—the "Old Post Road"—had been transformed into a dense and interlocking network of intersecting routes.

To an extent that has rarely been appreciated, this development was

---

[79] *Statutes at Large,* 2:43.
[80] *Journal of the House,* Jan. 10, 1798, 2:117.
[81] *Annals of Congress,* Dec. 24, 1798, p. 2488.

a product less of happenstance than of deliberate design. In 1790, the postal system consisted of a mere 1,875 miles of post routes; by 1792, this total had more than doubled to 5,642 miles. Two years later, in 1794, it would almost double again to 11,984 miles. By 1801, the total reached 22,309 miles—almost a twelvefold increase for the decade. Particularly impressive was the extension of mail facilities to thinly settled areas of the South and West, where the income that these routes generated could not possibly cover their cost. The balance, of course, was paid for by postal revenue generated in the North and East. Lacking a statutory imprimatur, such an elaborate system of interregional transfers—inconceivable before 1792—would have been far more difficult, if not impossible, to sustain.

As the postal network expanded, support for the once-unchallenged fiscal rationale for postal policy receded. Henceforth, it would be taken for granted that, virtually without regard for cost, the federal government would provide the citizenry with uninterrupted access to up-to-date information on commerce and public affairs. By 1795, the merits of this new, educational rationale for postal policy were conceded even by stalwart champions of fiscal propriety, such as outgoing Treasury Secretary Hamilton.[82] Two years later, even congressional critics of the rapid proliferation of post routes now conceded it to be a "settled principle" that "profits arising from one part of the Union should go to the establishment of post routes in other parts."[83] Accompanying this explicit endorsement of interregional cross-subsidization was the recommendation that Congress abandon every post route that, within three years of its establishment, failed to return a mere one-fifth of its expense. Even this minor concession to fiscal propriety was rejected by congressmen unwilling to risk any check on the headlong expansion of the burgeoning postal network.

Once the floodgates had been opened, few congressmen were bold enough to swim against the current. Before long, it became a popular cliché that no post route petition was ever turned down. During the past twenty-five years, reported one congressman in the 1850s, he could not remember a single instance when a petition for a new post

[82]Hamilton to Washington, Jan. 31, 1795, in Syrett and Cooke, *Papers of Alexander Hamilton,* 18:239.

[83]*Annals of Congress,* February 1797, p. 2062.

route had been refused.[84] Predictably enough, the annual postal surplus had by this time become transformed into an annual postal deficit—a situation that would persist, with a few notable exceptions, well into the twentieth century.[85]

The distinctiveness of the American experience is highlighted by a comparison with Great Britain. In Great Britain, the designation of post routes never came under the jurisdiction of Parliament. As a consequence, popular involvement in routing decisions remained limited, the network expanded slowly, and postal administrators generated a substantial annual surplus for the treasury. In the United States, in contrast, petitioning was encouraged, expansion occurred at a rapid pace, and the postal surplus remained small. Funded largely by merchants and traders in the principal seaboard ports in New England and the Middle Atlantic states, the postal network provided a basic level of service—including, in time, a rudimentary system of public transportation—throughout the South and West. As such, it deserves to be remembered as one of the first major experiments in national planning to have been undertaken in the United States.

While most contemporaries recognized the benefits of congressional control, some scholars take a more jaundiced view. According to the eminent constitutional historian David P. Currie, it was "absurd" for Congress to arrogate to itself the responsibility for designating new post routes—because, among other things, this saddled it with a variety of onerous tasks that it was ill-suited to perform.[86] Congressional

---

[84]*Congressional Globe,* 32d Cong., 1st sess., July 6, 1852, p. 1664.

[85]Wayne E. Fuller, *The American Mail: Enlarger of the Common Life* (Chicago, 1972), p. 45. Congressional control over the designation of post routes, Fuller perceptively observes, would have "far-reaching effects" on the nation's communications grid, and, "more than any other single factor," guarantee that the American people—both collectively and as special interests—would shape its expansion.

[86]Currie, *Constitution in Congress,* p. 149. Currie is correct to contend that the Framers of the Federal Constitution did not intend Congress to administer the postal system directly, yet he fails to recognize the extent to which the premises undergirding postal policy changed during the course of the congressional debates over postal policy that took place between 1789 and 1792. Currie's neglect of this shift is curious, since the theme of his study is the extent to which the "original understanding" of the Constitution had been forged in Congress rather than in the courts or the executive branch. Currie is similarly mistaken to contend that the designation of post routes was less important than the establishment of post offices (p. 149). Contemporaries almost always regarded the former as the main point of contention and rarely made the latter a focus of debate.

control, Currie added disapprovingly, was a product of narrow congressional self-interest—a "taste for pork"—rather than a "principled concern" for the virtues of representative government.[87] Such an assessment has a certain theoretical cogency, because, after all, the expansion of the postal route network had been hastened by a multitude of local interests. However, it is misleading on at least three counts. Not only does Currie overlook the rough yet unmistakable egalitarian logic that underlay this jurisdictional shift, but also, and no less importantly, he subtly discounts the genuine popular sentiment that hastened this shift and ignores the remarkable expansion in mail facilities that it did so much to encourage.

Congressional control over the route network would remain a cornerstone of American postal policy long after 1801. Indeed, if anything, this principle became even more firmly entrenched as the postal network expanded, because, by an increasingly frenzied and self-intensifying logic, each improvement in mail facilities ratcheted up expectations among those inhabitants who suddenly found themselves left behind. In addition, of course, every such improvement in mail facilities made it easier for ever more remote petitioners to send off their appeals to the federal legislature. Here, then, was one realm in which the petition process became—in practice as well as in theory—a rite of passage for legislation that Americans energetically sought and enthusiastically embraced.

The growing confidence of the general population in the petition process as a tool of governance is illustrated by the increasingly expansive arguments that petitioners advanced to justify the designation of new post routes. The earliest post route petitions focused narrowly on the specific grievances that the petitioners suffered as a result of a want of adequate mail facilities. Though the South Carolinians whose 1793 petition was featured at the beginning of this essay found the "language of complaint" to be "disagreeable," they lamented nonetheless their isolation from the wider world.[88] Equally particularistic concerns surfaced repeatedly in the years to come. The recent relocation of the main north-south post route from the seaboard to the interior, de-

[87] Currie, *Constitution in Congress,* p. 149.
[88] *State Gazette of South Carolina,* July 1, 1793.

clared another group of South Carolinian petitioners in 1796, deprived them of mail facilities that they had formerly enjoyed.[89]

By the end of the decade, petitioners began to invest their grievances with a more universalistic gloss. In 1800, for example, petitioners in Wayne County in the Northwest Territory—then a tiny backwoods settlement near present-day Detroit—complained that, in the absence of a public mail, they were "wholly barred from the enjoyment of this privilege common to the citizens in all other parts of the Union."[90] In the following year, a group of petitioners from New Hampshire and Massachusetts struck a similar note. The establishment of a post route from Brookfield, Massachusetts, to Bethel, Maine, the petitioners declared, would be of "great public utility," because it would "facilitate the means of communication" and "diffuse information" among a "large number of people who now labor under many inconveniences which might be thereby removed."[91]

In the ensuing years, route petitions continued to mingle highly specific grievances with more general considerations of public policy. The overall trend was unmistakable. A legal device that had been intended originally to permit individuals to seek restitution for a specific wrong had rapidly been transformed into a vehicle for claiming a collective right—or what a later age would term an entitlement. It was "incalculably advantageous," declared a group of petitioners from Connecticut in 1809, for "every well-regulated government" to keep its citizenry well informed by "disseminating every species of useful information among them."[92] Though this vision of governance was

---

[89]Petition of Abraham Cohen and inhabitants of Georgetown, South Carolina, Feb. 29, 1796, Senate Records, RG 46, NARA.

[90]Petition of inhabitants of Wayne County, Northwest Territory, Sept. 2, 1800, Carter, *Territorial Papers,* 3:105.

[91]Petition of inhabitants of the state of New Hampshire and Massachusetts, Jan. 13, 1801, House Records, RG 233, NARA. A diligent search for postal petitions in the manuscript records of the House and Senate for the period between 1789 and 1801 proved disappointing. A few turned up in the papers of the Senate; the largest number can be found in the House records for the Sixth Congress. The paucity of surviving petitions for the first four federal congresses testifies to the industry of the House clerk, John Beckley, who, in an early exercise of what today would be called records management, destroyed many documents that he had assumed to have become obsolete. For a related discussion, see "Introduction," *DHFFC,* 8:xxix–xxx.

[92]Petition of inhabitants of Reading, Connecticut, Dec. 22, 1809, House Records, Committee on the Post Office and Post Roads, RG 233, NARA.

remarkably bold and open-ended, it was one that, after almost two decades of unprecedented expansion in the postal route network, many Americans had come wholeheartedly to endorse.

This case study of postal petitioning in the Federalist era highlights one realm in which institutional innovations originating in the 1790s continued to shape American public life long after the Republicans had come to power with Jefferson's victory in the election of 1800. For postal patrons—though not for postal officers or mail contractors—the petition process was not only a ritual of popular government but also a tool of governance. A generation before the triumph of universal male suffrage, and long *before* the victory of Thomas Jefferson in the election of 1800, large numbers of Americans had found it an effective instrument for participating in the work of the nation.

To an extent that has often been overlooked, popular involvement in national politics was self-intensifying: as the mandate of the federal government expanded, so, too, did popular expectations regarding the appropriate scope of federal power. In no sense was this Federalist legacy repudiated following the Federalists' political demise. Though Thomas Jefferson briefly tinkered with the idea of abolishing the post office, his administration continued to support the rapid expansion of post routes linking the Atlantic seaboard and the trans-Appalachian hinterland.[93] If anything, after 1801 the pace of expansion actually accelerated, hastening the elaboration of a postal network that, by the time of its completion in the 1820s, was far larger and more geographically extensive than any similar institution in the world.

Before long, Americans began to petition Congress for even more ambitious projects, such as roads and canals. Now that Americans had grown accustomed to petitioning Congress to designate post routes, it was but a short step for them to petition it to build the rights of way on which the mails would be conveyed. That such projects enjoyed such an impressive measure of public support testifies not only to the effectiveness of earlier government-run enterprise, such as

---

[93]John, *Spreading the News,* p. 110.

the postal system, but also to popular confidence in the utility of the petition process as a policy tool.[94]

Some kind of backlash, perhaps, was unavoidable. In the 1830s, President Andrew Jackson checked federal involvement in internal improvements by vetoing federal funding for a major road project in Kentucky—the Maysville Road—while southern Congressmen enacted the so-called gag rule to block the presentation of petitions on the slavery issue.

Scholars sometimes contend that the institution of the gag rule in 1836 eviscerated the petition process as a tool of governance.[95] While this conclusion may well hold true for the slavery issue, it overlooks the extent to which, long after 1836, the petition process remained a valued instrument for influencing other, less controversial, kinds of legislation, such as the designation of new post routes. And even the gag rule did not last indefinitely: after all, the ban on slavery petitions was lifted in 1842. The architect of its repeal was John Quincy Adams—who, among his many other accomplishments, deserves to be remembered for his tireless advocacy of this basic constitutional guarantee.[96] Thanks in no small part to Adams, and his congressional allies, Congress would continue to treat the petition process with respectful concern for the next seventy-five years.

For the period between the 1830s and the 1910s, the papers of the

---

[94]For a related discussion, see John Lauritz Larson, "Liberty by Design: Freedom, Planning, and John Quincy Adams's American System," in *The State and Economic Knowledge: The American and British Experience*, ed. Mary O. Furner and Barry Supple (Cambridge, 1990), pp. 73–102. See also John Lauritz Larson, *Internal Improvement: National Public Works and the Promise of Popular Government in the Early United States* (Chapel Hill, 2001). Larson's long-awaited study should greatly expand our understanding of this important topic.

[95]For a different view, see David C. Frederick, "John Quincy Adams, Slavery, and the Disappearance of the Right to Petition," *Law and History Review* 9 (1991):113–55, and Stephen A. Higginson, "A Short History of the Right to Petition Government for the Redress of Grievances," *Yale Law Journal* 96 (1986):142–66. Frederick mistakenly contends that the right to petition was "little exercised" following the gag rule controversy (p. 141). Higginson is similarly wrong to assert that the gag rule had "effectively abolished" the right to petition (p. 144).

[96]On the gag rule controversy, see William Lee Miller, *Arguing about Slavery: The Great Battle in the United States Congress* (New York, 1996); William W. Freehling, *The Road to Disunion: Secessionists at Bay, 1776–1854* (New York, 1990); and Leonard L. Richards, *The Life and Times of Congressman John Quincy Adams* (New York, 1986).

House and Senate contain hundreds of thousands of petitions on an extraordinary range of topics. To a degree that scholars have yet to appreciate, this archival treasure-trove furnishes eloquent testimony to continuing vitality of the right to petition. Had the gag rule truly destroyed the effectiveness of the petition process—as several legal scholars have contended—it is hard to understand why Congress would have continued to debate the issues that petitioners raised, or, for that matter, why Americans would have persisted for so long in organizing large-scale petition campaigns. Petitioning remained an important, and often surprisingly effective, form of collective action until the era of the First World War, when it was supplanted—and largely superceded—by more systematic techniques for registering public sentiment, such as public opinion polls and social scientific surveys. Though Americans continue even today to send off petitions to the national capital, Congress has long since abandoned the custom of formally acknowledging their receipt.[97] This seeming indifference to a basic constitutional guarantee, however, should not lead us to overlook the gravity with which the right to petition had once been regarded, or to underrate the role it long played in helping ordinary Americans to secure improved access to information about the wider world.

---

[97] *Petitions, Memorials, and Other Documents Submitted for the Consideration of Congress*, p. 9.

Marion Nelson Winship

The "Practicable Sphere" of a Republic

Western Ways of Connecting to Congress

IN A TIME BEFORE steam power and electricity, before rapid and reliable long-distance communications, how could the vast and expansive new American nation actually function? This question certainly concerned the men who created the republic, but it did not puzzle them (as it puzzles us).

"The Practicable Sphere"

Writing for the first time as "Publius" in November 1787, James Madison set his pen to one of the greatest challenges facing the new United States—"the experiment of an extended republic." The results were published later that month as *Federalist* Nos. 10 and 14. In *Federalist* No. 10, Madison worked out a crucial problem of political theory, and it is on this level of abstraction that the essay has been considered and celebrated ever since.[1] But we can more fully appreciate Madison's mind-set—one held in common with all political men of his

[1]For a superb discussion of *Federalist* No. 10 and a critique of the earlier literature, see Lance Banning, *The Sacred Fire of Liberty: James Madison and the Founding of the Federal Republic* (Ithaca, N.Y., 1995), pp. 195–233. And for stimulating consideration of contemporary "spatial assumptions about government," see Rosemary Zagarri, *The Politics of Size: Representation in the United States, 1776–1850* (Ithaca, N.Y., 1987), quote on pp. 84–85.

generation, including his fellow Founders—if we take *Federalist* No. 14 as an integral part of his thinking on the challenge of the extended republic. There, Madison was concerned to demonstrate just how it was that, while a democracy must be "confined to a small spot," a republic could be "extended over a large region." In *Federalist* No. 14, Madison considered the "practicable sphere" of the republic.[2]

Madison and his peers seem to have liked the word *practicable*, and their use of it suggests a fresh way to grasp the political workings of the early republic. For them, practicability was never solely about nuts and bolts. But their choice of the word nevertheless reminds us that however lofty and universal the political questions these men addressed, their thinking remained grounded in the actual possibilities and limitations of the world in which they operated. Thus, as he considered the extended sphere of republican government, Madison turned in *Federalist* No. 14 to the most practical considerations. "As the natural limit of a democracy is that distance from the central point, which will just permit the remote citizens to assemble as often as their public functions demand," he wrote, "so the natural limit of a republic is that distance from the center, which will barely allow the representatives of the people to meet as often as may be necessary for the administration of public affairs." How was this critical distance to be determined? Madison pointed out that for thirteen years representatives from the most distant states had attended the Continental and Confederation congressional sessions. Just how far had these representatives managed to travel? To give some idea, he calculated the mean dimensions of the union. The "north-south Atlantic distance" was 863¾ miles, and the "distance from the Atlantic to the Mississippi" (Madison was hazier here) did "not probably exceed 750 miles." Of course, the Mississippi boundary might prove temporary. Madison may have had that open-ended future in mind when he clinched this part of his argument by turning hopefully to the "new improvements" that would soon be facilitating representatives' journeys to and from the seat of government: roads "every where . . . shortened and kept in better

---

[2][James Madison], "The Federalist No. 10" and "The Federalist No. 14" (published in *Daily Advertiser, New York Packet,* and the *Independent Journal,* Nov. 22–24 and Nov. 30–Dec. 1, 1787), *The Federalist,* Jacob E. Cooke, ed. (Middletown, Conn., 1961), pp. 56–65 and 83–89; quotes from pp. 83, 84, 88.

order," travel accommodations "multiplied and meliorated," river travel "rendered more and more easy" by improvements and canals.[3]

Taverns to be enjoyed or endured; roads, rivers, canals, and actual miles to be traveled. But the crux of the "practicable sphere of republican administration," as Madison explicated it in *Federalist* No. 14, was the men—the people's "representatives and agents," as he called them—who would be doing the traveling. Madison knew all about such men and the power-in-motion which they habitually achieved: in many ways, he was himself one of them. Perhaps that is why, in *Federalist* No. 14, he felt no need to explain in detail exactly how and why such men could make representative government work across a vast republic, even while his argument both took for granted and depended upon their skills and willingness to negotiate the distance.[4]

What if we elaborated what Madison assumed but did not elaborate? Following his own logic, we might examine the problem of the practicable sphere of government by focusing on its extreme limits. Through the 1790s (and beyond), western distances would be the farthest from the seat of the general government—and by far the most difficult to traverse. We might consider how western "representatives and agents" of the people managed their connections to Congress during the first decade of the experiment of the extended republic.[5]

"Western Men"

Who were these western political men? No doubt there were as many hundred variations on the type as there were individuals who fit it, but its most common and essential elements can readily be delineated. The

---

[3]Ibid., pp. 85–87. For Madison's own more abstract use of *practicable,* see *Federalist* No. 51, where, discussing the separation of powers, he concluded that the "practicable sphere may be carried to a very great extent, by a judicious modification and mixture of the *federal principle*" (ibid., p. 353). The *Oxford English Dictionary* (2d edition, 1989) confirms the range of Madison's usage, from the abstract "capable of being put into practice, carried out in action, effected, accomplished, or done," to the earthbound "capable of being actually used or traversed, as a road, passage, ford, etc."

[4]Cooke, *Federalist,* pp. 83, 84.

[5]This is one aspect of the phenomenon explored in Marion Nelson Winship, "Power in Motion: Western Success Stories of the Jeffersonian Republic," Ph.D. diss., University of Pennsylvania, forthcoming.

future western political man was born and raised east of the Appalachian Mountains (though probably west of the tidewater) in a colony, then state, that stretched to the Mississippi River. His family farmed, but the more enterprising of his elders also threw themselves into buying and selling land and were soon deeply involved in western land speculation. Typically, the western man did have the good fortune to be endowed with at least one able and outstandingly enterprising elder—an uncle or guardian if not his own father. Such an elder had been successful enough in his land dealings that he held the highest civil and military offices in his home county—and quite likely the county surveyorship, too. This home power base was not permanent, however; the elder had already moved his family at least once (usually westward) and might do so again if an attractive opportunity offered.

As the future western man grew up, he would accompany his older kin on western land-scouting and surveying expeditions and might himself work for a while as a licensed surveyor. Because of his family's position, he was better educated than most of his neighbors (he also had been a more apt pupil than most of his brothers and cousins). He might go on to study law. His family were patriots and he may have seen some Revolutionary War service, though he was too young for any significant role in the war or in the other great national event of his lifetime, the creation of the new republic. As a youth observing his elders, he had learned the inner workings of local politics but did not find them inspiring—he would never become a county magistrate! He was more likely while still a very young man to go straight to the state legislature, where he could better exercise his talents—and where issues relating to western lands would be decided. During the decade after the Revolution, as the disposition and security of western lands passed increasingly to the federal government, he followed with growing interest the proceedings of Congress. He thought he might run for a seat in the House of Representatives. He could even imagine himself a senator.

By the time he married and established his own family, the future western man had not only land but also interests, opportunities, and connections west of the mountains. But would he actually migrate? The decision would turn on a complex calculation of the basic factors of land for settling and speculating, of lucrative professional and business opportunities and scope for his political ambitions, and of the tug of friends and family (especially his wife's family) from either side of the mountains. If enough of the factors were favorable, he would move, but the decision could easily have gone the other way. It is crucial to note that, when he did move, this western man would be supremely well connected. He would have migrating family and friends to form an instant western network of power, but he would also have brothers and sisters, cousins, and old friends who had stayed put. This last circumstance would prove advantageous to both movers and stayers: the movers would serve as agents and informants on western lands, while the stayers provided inside links to legislatures and land offices back in the mother state.[6]

By nature and nurture, the western man was a land speculator. Equally by nature and nurture, he was a political creature. (In fact, the term *Western Man*—often capitalized—was not just a geographical designation, but rather a way that these men identified themselves in a national, often adversarial and always political, context.)[7] Land speculator and political creature—these twinned and intertwined identities, of course, raised ethical questions whose exact boundaries would have to be worked out in Congress beginning in the 1790s—questions which continue to exercise historians of both the trans-Appalachian and the trans-Mississippi West. There is no doubt that western men have always pursued politics in part to make the West safe for land speculation.[8] While investigating how such men managed to

---

[6]This dynamic of movers and stayers is examined in Marion Nelson Winship, "The Land of Connected Men: A New Migration Story from the Early American Republic," in *Empire, Society, and Labor: Essays in Honor of Richard S. Dunn,* ed. Nicholas Canny, Joseph E. Illick, and Gary B. Nash, *Pennsylvania History* 64 (1997):88–104.

[7]For example, see James Brown to John Breckinridge, Oct. 31, 1805, Breckinridge Family Papers, Manuscript Division, Library of Congress.

[8]Thomas Perkins Abernethy set an early and high standard for sardonic treatment of land-speculating trans-Appalachian western men (Abernethy, *From Frontier to Plantation in Tennessee: A Study in Frontier Democracy* [Chapel Hill, 1932]; and *Western Lands and the American Revolution* [New York, 1937]). "To make the West safe for land speculation," paraphrases Abernethy, ed., "Journal of the Kentucky Convention," *Journal of Southern History* 1 (1935):69. For fine recent studies in similar spirit, see Ellen Eslinger, "The Great Revival in Bourbon County, Kentucky," Ph.D. diss., University of Chicago, 1988, vol. 1; and Fredrika Johanna Teute, "Land, Liberty, and Labor in the Post-revolutionary Era: Kentucky as the Promised Land," Ph.D. diss., Johns Hopkins University, 1988. Stephen Aron has persuasively claimed a middle ground, arguing that

achieve this end across the extended new republic, I take their private interest in public service as a given.

Contemporaries did the same, and, once again, we can turn to James Madison to articulate their understanding. In the spring of 1788, preparing for the Virginia ratifying convention and anticipating Antifederalist votes from the Kentucky delegates, Madison rehearsed how the proposed new Constitution would benefit the West. "The protection and security which the new Government promises to purchasers of the foederal lands," he wrote, would encourage the migration of "adventurers of character and talents" who would add to the "weight" of the West in the "general scale." These new western migrants would "leave behind them friends and connections" who would then "stand up for whatever concerns the Western Country." The new government's promised protection of federal lands would also "induce many who will remain at home to speculate in that field with a view of selling out afterwards, or of providing for their children, who with all their friends will form a new class of advocates for their Western brethren." Again, Madison knew his subject intimately. He himself was one who had "remained at home" while kin and connections moved. He understood and supported western interests. And he might easily have been a mover himself.[9]

Madison's entire argument was keyed to the interests of the purchasers of western lands. Surely those "adventurers of character and talents" on whom he counted to give weight to the West in the national scale were men of means—speculators in other words. And at the same time, surely they were the very same men who (Madison had

---

virtually any western man, rich or not, would naturally speculate if he could. See Aron, "Pioneers and Profiteers: Land Speculation and the Homestead Ethic in Frontier Kentucky." *Western Historical Quarterly* 23 (1992):179–98; and *How the West Was Lost: The Transformation of Kentucky from Daniel Boone to Henry Clay* (Baltimore, 1996). For the trans-Mississippi West, see Paul W. Gates, "The Role of the Land Speculator in Western Development," *Pennsylvania Magazine of History and Biography* 66 (1942):314–33; and, more recently, Patricia Nelson Limerick, *The Legacy of Conquest: The Unbroken Past of the American West* (New York, 1987), pp. 78–96; and Richard White, *It's Your Misfortune and None of My Own: A History of the American West* (Norman, 1991), pp. 57–59, 353–63.

[9]James Madison to George Nicholas, May 17, 1788, William T. Hutchinson et al., eds., *The Papers of James Madison,* 17 vols. (Chicago and Charlottesville, 1962–91), 11:45–46. For a vivid sketch of Madison's speculative side and his thoughts of moving west, see Drew R. McCoy, *The Last of the Fathers: James Madison and the Republican Legacy* (Cambridge, 1989), pp. 230–33.

assumed in *Federalist* No. 14) could and willingly would serve as the "representatives and agents" of the western people across the extended sphere of the republic. Such men would never be isolated or out of touch with national affairs. They would, as Madison pointed out, maintain their personal, private, and political ties with "eastern friends and connections" (men who were, after all, just "adventurers of character and talents" who happened to have stayed "at home"—where they would quite likely represent the people of their eastern states in Congress!). Western political men, Madison and his peers knew, would be able to negotiate the distance between the farthest reaches of the republic and the federal government seated at Philadelphia—or the new City of Washington.[10]

For these practical men and their "practicable sphere" of government, the truth was and is in the details. What follows focuses in on one of them, John Breckinridge, and then ratchets up the magnification a bit further to examine some of the ways that Breckinridge connected himself and his adopted western country of Kentucky to the U.S. Congress.

To "Acquire Honor & Be of Real Service"

John Breckinridge was one of the most prominent of Kentucky's Republicans, and, until his younger legal associate Henry Clay came on the scene, by far the best-known Kentuckian in national politics. Breckinridge could be taken as a special case—or as emblematic of the western man of the early republic. There is something to each of these seemingly incompatible positions; it is as a result of both that his experience illuminates the dynamic of western ways of connecting to Congress.

Born and raised in Virginia counties west of the Blue Ridge but east

[10]The choice of a permanent seat for the general government involved the same mix of high theory and practical thinking discussed above, a fact that is reflected in the subtitle of the best book on the subject (Kenneth R. Bowling, *The Creation of Washington, D.C.: The Idea and Location of the American Capital* [Fairfax, Va., 1991]). In contrast, it is an anachronistic blindness to the actual "practicable sphere" that fatally undermines James Sterling Young's elegant essay, "Government at a Distance and Out of Sight," *The Washington Community, 1800–1828* (New York, 1966), pp. 1–37.

of the Appalachians, Breckinridge was the son of a moderately successful farmer and land dealer—and the nephew and protégé of the most important leader in an expansive southwestern Virginia, William Preston.[11] As a very young man, Breckinridge became a deputy surveyor, studied law at William and Mary, and served in the Virginia House of Delegates. Before moving west, he married well, farmed, and practiced law throughout piedmont and western Virginia. And all the while, in cooperation with his brothers who were surveying in Kentucky, Breckinridge was wheeling and dealing in Virginia's western lands.

The development of Breckinridge's interest in national politics was at once very special and entirely typical. It was special because he happened to be in Williamsburg and Richmond in 1783–85, a unique and exhilarating time when the political philosophy of the academy, the concerns of the Commonwealth of Virginia, and the most basic issues of the new nation strikingly converged. In Williamsburg, Breckinridge and his peers studied under men who had the fate of the new United States on their minds; George Wythe's law students were encouraged in their mock legislature to debate the urgent issues of the Confederation. Their course of law, as its chief architect Thomas Jefferson had intended and would later recall, was truly "the nursery of our Congress." In Richmond, Breckinridge rubbed elbows with men who were, and who would be, prominent national statesmen; in 1784, for example, he first made the acquaintance of James Madison and became an enthusiastic follower.[12]

Aside from his extraordinary Williamsburg-Richmond experience, Breckinridge's growth into national-mindedness was altogether typical of ambitious speculating Virginians. Through the 1780s, as Breckinridge bought up Virginia land warrants and took care of land office

---

[11]The assessment is from Abernethy, *Western Lands,* p. 80.

[12]Thomas Jefferson to James Madison, Feb. 17, 1826, James Morton Smith, ed., *The Republic of Letters: The Correspondence between Thomas Jefferson and James Madison, 1776–1826,* 3 vols. (New York, 1995), 3:1965. For his first acquaintance with Madison, see James Madison (cousin of the statesman) to John Breckinridge (hereafter JB in these notes), May 24, 1784, Breckinridge Family Papers, Manuscript Division, Library of Congress (hereafter BFP); and Archibald Stuart to JB, Nov. 24, 1786, BFP. See, for example, the list of JB's companions at the meeting of a political society formed in June 1784 ("Rules of the Constitutional Society of Virginia," [ca. June 14, 1784], *Madison Papers,* 8:71–75).

business in Richmond, he and his surveying brothers began to find the land northwest of the Ohio River particularly enticing. Neither Virginia's 1784 cession of most of that land to the United States nor the continuing threat from Indians on that side of the Ohio nor even the long delay in opening the first northwest territory land office seems to have dampened their enthusiasm. Each of these factors did, however, cause Breckinridge's interest naturally to shift from Richmond to the seat of the federal government. In the 1790s, it became not uncommon for men like him to make a winter visit to Philadelphia to "superintend for a while the proceedings of Congress." Breckinridge made such a trip in 1791 when he and some friends developed a "scheme" of "purchasing from Congress a quantity of land"—and of finding some men with "the command of money" to back the purchase.[13]

Though his visit to Philadelphia was motivated by the speculating Virginian's interest in western land, Breckinridge was also quickly drawn there into national politics, which meant, during that heated period, partisan politics. He attended congressional debates and made every possible political contact in the capital, including Sen. James Monroe and Rep. James Madison. Monroe promised to keep Breckinridge informed should Congress act on northwestern lands; Breckinridge offered to lobby in Virginia against some pending Federalist measure.[14] As soon as Breckinridge got home, and in spite of his plan to migrate to Kentucky within the year, he ran for one of Virginia's new post-census congressional seats. As he prepared to migrate, he was advised, probably unnecessarily, that Kentucky's faction-rent politics ought to be avoided, but if he were "called to federal councils, well enough," since there he could "acquire honor & be of real service."[15]

[13]Quote from John Marshall to Archibald Stuart, Mar. 27, 1794, Herbert A. Johnson et al., eds., *The Papers of John Marshall,* 10 vols. (Chapel Hill, 1974–2000), 2:261; and on JB's Philadelphia journey, see Wilson Cary Nicholas to JB, Nov. 17, 1791 (quoted); Robert Rives to JB, Sept. 25, 1791, BFP; and Robert Smith to Wilson Cary Nicholas, Jan. 10, 1792, Wilson Cary Nicholas Papers, Manuscript Division, Library of Congress.

[14]This essay takes *party* as its subjects did. In letters to JB, for example, Monroe indulged in the most common usage—as a dig at political opponents, e.g., "the monarchy party." But he could also report on a presidential veto that had given "a ray of hope to the desponding mind of the republican party" (James Monroe to JB, Aug. 23, 1793, Stanislaus Murray Hamilton, ed., *The Writings of James Monroe,* 7 vols. [New York, 1898–1903], 1:272–73; and Apr. 8, 1792, BFP).

[15]Undoubtedly, it was in the interests of Virginia's "republican party" that JB offered

Breckinridge's western migration was arguably more about connection than about separation.[16] He had, for example, hardly arrived in Kentucky before he got involved in a western land scheme much like the one that had taken him to Philadelphia two years earlier.[17] And the arc of his political ambitions also spanned the mountains. In fact, even as he and his household embarked on their migration journey in April 1793, Breckinridge declared to Madison his intention as a loyal Republican to try for a Kentucky seat in the House of Representatives.[18]

"This Distant and Dangerous Desart"

But there is a twist to this story of connection and smoothly arching ambition. Within a very few months of his arrival in Kentucky, Breckinridge was elected the founding president of the Lexington Democratic Society and became the chief draftsman of the society's papers. And so it happened that, in the early days of December 1793—the very days when the newly numerous and Republican Virginia delegation were taking their seats in Congress without him—Breckinridge was seated

---

himself as a candidate. He won the election, but, as he had suspected at the time, it would turn out that the commonwealth had jumped the gun in calling the 1792 elections, and the winners would not claim their seats (JB to Archibald Stuart, Feb. 14, 1792, BFP; printed in "Papers of Archibald Stuart," *William and Mary Quarterly,* 2d ser. 5 [1925]: 294–96. Quote from Archibald Stuart to JB, Feb. 25, 1792, BFP).

[16]I have argued this in Winship, "Land of Connected Men," pp. 88–104.

[17]It was another attempt to get a head start on federal land sales northwest of the Ohio. This time JB's partner, an old Virginia-Kentucky connection named Robert McAfee, made the trip to Philadelphia, "attending Congress several weeks," and obtaining promises "of support from many of the members," including Sen. John Brown of Kentucky (Robert B. McAfee, "Life and Times of Robert B. McAfee and His Family and Connections," *Register of the Kentucky Historical Society* 25 [1927]:124; and Robert McAfee to JB, Oct. 12, 1793, BFP). Meanwhile, JB had been in correspondence with a Virginia friend who, as he set off to Philadelphia to take his new seat in the Third Congress, wrote that he wished JB to tell him the "extent" of the land "scheme" he had in mind, and who promised, "if anything shall be done in Congress respecting it, you shall be advised of it" (Francis Walker to JB, Nov. 6, 1793, BFP). One of the ethical limits to such schemes became apparent on the floor of Congress when, in 1795, a couple of hopeful speculators attempted to bolster the chances of their "memorial . . . applying for a large tract of Western territory" by privately offering shares in the scheme to a number of representatives (*Annals of Congress,* 4th Cong., 1st sess., pp. 166–70).

[18]For Madison's chance encounter with "Mr. Brackenridge on his way to Kentucky," see James Madison to Thomas Jefferson, Apr. 12, 1793, *Madison Papers,* 15:7.

in his law office seven hundred miles from Philadelphia, drafting an angry remonstrance to that very Congress.

Peeking over his shoulder, we can appreciate the sea change: he began on the issue of the federal excise tax, which, "if carried into effect in this state, will be unjust and oppressive." It was oppressive because the government that enacted it gave the citizens no means to pay it. The citizens of Kentucky, he wrote, were "surrounded by a rugged desart" — no, worse than "rugged" — "surrounded by a *tractless* desart, which is infested by savages dispersed over an extensive country whose stream we durst not navigate." Kentuckians dared not navigate the streams because the general government would not demand from Spain the right of Mississippi navigation.[19] It is true, Breckinridge archly conceded, that Kentuckians were not without alternatives: "we may cease to distill and not incur the tax and may go naked and lighten the import duties." For Kentuckians, however, ceasing to distill would be "as difficult as" going naked.[20]

Perhaps Breckinridge got a bit carried away in his first exercise as a western man; at any rate, this first petition was not adopted by the

---

[19]Honesty subsequently led JB to modify his satisfying declaration of distance to "an *almost* tractless desart" (emphasis mine). See "Petition of the Inhabitants of the State of Kentucky to the Congress of the United States of America," Dec. 4, 1793, draft in JB's hand, BFP). The indispensable background sources on Mississippi navigation are still Arthur Preston Whitaker, *The Spanish-American Frontier, 1783–1795: The Westward Movement and the Spanish Retreat in the Mississippi Valley* (Boston, 1927); and idem, *The Mississippi Question, 1795–1803: A Study in Trade, Politics, and Diplomacy* (New York, 1934). E. Merton Coulter correctly emphasized Mississippi navigation as the motivating goal of Kentucky's political action at this time (Coulter, "The Efforts of the Democratic Societies of the West to Open the Navigation of the Mississippi River," *Mississippi Valley Historical Review* 11 [1924]:379–89).

[20]JB added his own rhetorical flourishes, but his argument against the excise merely reiterated the reasoning of earlier Kentucky political men (as, for example, the "Petition from sundry inhabitants of the district of Kentucky, praying to be relieved from the operation of the excise law, until they shall have obtained free navigation of the Mississippi," presented by Rep. John Brown, Nov. 16, 1791 [*Annals of Congress,* 2d Cong., 1st sess., p. 192]). For Kentucky's resistance to the federal excise tax, see Mary K. Bonsteel Tachau's elegant essay, "The Whiskey Rebellion in Kentucky: A Forgotten Episode of Civil Disobedience," *Journal of the Early Republic* 2 (1982):239–59. Tachau, however, neglected Kentucky's resistance through connection to Congress, including the remonstrances and the activities of the well-connected leadership behind them, which are my focus here. For a useful digest of petitions, see U.S. House of Representatives, Committee on Energy and Commerce, *Petitions, Memorials, and Other Documents Submitted for the Consideration of Congress, March 4, 1789, to December 14, 1795,* 99th Congress, 2d sess., Committee Print 99-AA (1986).

Democratic Society (probably never presented to it), was not printed in the *Kentucky Gazette,* and was not circulated around the republic. But the next week, Breckinridge tried again, this time producing a document that did reach the halls of Congress and that did reverberate through the nation. He began with the ancient salutation, the "Remonstrance of the Citizens West of the Allegany Mountains Respectfully sheweth," and continued in the time-honored language of supplication. That humble mode, of course, has always set the stage for a grievance, and within the dramatic expression of that grievance has always lain a powerful censure of authority.[21]

Breckinridge would adapt the old form to the purposes of the moment in particular and revealing ways. The grievance was that, for almost a decade, Spain had effectively prohibited American trade down the Mississippi River. As Breckinridge put it, "In colonizing this distant and dangerous desart, they [the western remonstrants] always contemplated the free enjoyment of this right, and considered it an inseparable appendage to the country they had sought out, had fought for, and acquired." The censure inherent in this grievance was of course aimed at the general government. As Breckinridge framed the narrative, in earlier years the (Confederation) government had excused its failure to secure the right to Mississippi navigation on grounds of weakness. Now that the government was strong, however, its continued failure must be attributed to other causes. The western citizens' plight, he stressed, had "not been concealed from, or unknown to Congress": "We have, without ceasing, deplored to you our degraded situation, and burdened you with our humble petitions and requests." But, "alas!" the "strong nerved government of America" had protected everyone but the westerners, had proved itself "competent to every end" except securing western rights. In fact, Breckinridge added, "Your Remonstrants are constrained to be of the opinion, that the

---

[21]For subtle discussions of petitioning, I am indebted to Edmund S. Morgan, *Inventing the People: The Rise of Popular Sovereignty in England and America* (New York, 1988), pp. 209–33; Richard L. Bushman, *King and People in Provincial Massachusetts* (Chapel Hill, 1985), pp. 46–53; Noble E. Cunningham, Jr., *The Process of Government under Jefferson* (Princeton, 1978), pp. 272–315; P. D. G. Thomas, *The House of Commons in the Eighteenth Century* (Oxford, 1971), pp. 18–19; and *Documentary History of the First Federal Congress, 1789–1791,* 14 vols. to date (Baltimore, 1972–), vol. 8 (Kenneth R. Bowling, William C. diGiacomantonio, and Charlene Bangs Bickford, eds.) pp. xi–xxxi.

neglect or local policy of American councils, has never produced one single real effort to procure this right." Now, it was "high time that we should be thoroughly informed of the situation on which your negotiations, if any, have left this right."

Western citizens, Breckinridge insisted, "yield not in patriotism to any of their fellow-citizens: but patriotism, like every other thing, has its bounds. . . . To be subjected to all the burthens, and enjoy none of the benefits, is what we will never submit to." Finally, the demand—"From the General Government of America . . . protection, in the free enjoyment of the navigation of the river Mississippi"; and the declaration—"that if the General Government will not procure it for us, we shall hold ourselves not answerable for any consequences that may result from our procurement of it."[22]

"In colonizing this distant and dangerous desart," this "(almost) tractless desart which is infested by savages," was written by a supremely well-connected man who had just arrived uneventfully by river and taken up his choice eight-hundred-acre piece of the Kentucky Bluegrass! Such images were endemic to western rhetoric, and, in an important sense, Breckinridge came by them honestly enough. He had grown up among Virginia movers and shakers who were masters of such language; he was acquainted with (and kin to) several of the political men at early Kentucky's "articulate center," men who had for a full decade already been ringing the changes on distance, danger, and difficulty as they protested eastern blindness to western needs.[23]

How this national-minded man came suddenly to be penning

---

[22]"Remonstrance of the Citizens West of the Allegany Mountains to the President and Congress of the United States," December 1793, not in JB's hand but annotated, "a remonstrance which I drew for the committee of the Democratic Society," vol. 10, following no. 1592, BFP; reprinted in Philip S. Foner, ed., *The Democratic-Republican Societies, 1790–1800: A Documentary Sourcebook of Constitutions, Declarations, Addresses, Resolutions, and Toasts* (Westport, Conn., 1976), pp. 366–68.

[23]See the voluminous archive of petitions from western counties (including Augusta, Botetourt, and Montgomery, in which JB grew up) to the Virginia legislature (Archives Branch, Library of Virginia); and, for missives from the country that would become Kentucky, see James Rood Robertson, ed., *Petitions of the Early Inhabitants of Kentucky to the General Assembly of Virginia, 1769–1792* (Louisville, 1914); and John Frederick Dorman, ed., *Petitions from Kentucky to the Virginia Legislature, 1776 to 1791* (Easley, S.C., 1981). For the west-east dynamics of Kentucky's first decade, see Patricia Watlington, *The Partisan Spirit: Kentucky Politics, 1779–1792* (Chapel Hill, 1972), Watlington's apt phrase is on page 43.

threats of disobedience and even defection from the federal government—also a Kentucky tradition by the time Breckinridge arrived there—is less clear. What real peril these western threats, conspiracies, and filibusters presented to the republic is also very difficult for historians to see clearly. It was surely obvious to any political man at the time that both the threats themselves and the administration's alarmed responses to them could be used to great effect in partisan wrangles, and, because of the polemics, it is in many cases now impossible to know what in the way of western defiance really happened or really might have happened.[24] In spite of the polemical storm clouds, however, it is clear that the activities of the Democratic Society, including the fiery declarations that Breckinridge drafted for it, were meant not for separation but for connection. It is clear that, in the hands of western men like Breckinridge, they aimed for far-reaching, even national effect.

The mechanisms of the democratic societies in general and the Democratic Society of Kentucky in particular had been used in this large way from the start. The impetus to the Kentucky society's formation, to begin with, had come from seven hundred miles away, in the form of a copy of the "Principles, Articles, and Regulations" of the Democratic Society of Pennsylvania. A group of Lexington men then met, resolving to form their own society and also to request *Kentucky Gazette* editor John Bradford (an energetic one of their number) to print the Philadelphia society's proceedings in the *Gazette.* News of that first Lexington meeting appeared in the *Gazette* on August 24, 1793, along with the complete Pennsylvania document. Through the medium of a politicized press, with its widespread practice of papers exchanged among editors, the Kentuckians were sending ripples out across the republic even before they had actually organized themselves. The next week they did organize, adopting the Philadelphia statement virtually unchanged, electing Breckinridge as their presi-

[24]The fullest discussion of western threats and their effects at the seat of the general government remains Julian P. Boyd, ed., "Editorial Note: The Threat of Disunion in the West," *The Papers of Thomas Jefferson,* 28 vols. (Princeton, 1950–2000), 19:429–518. The rhetorical uses of western threats are also suggestively explored in John K. Alexander, *The Selling of the Constitutional Convention: A History of News Coverage* (Madison, Wis., 1990).

dent, and, of course, sending another item to the *Kentucky Gazette*—and around the nation.[25]

Because of this reverberation through the press, the society's proceedings were themselves political documents. Thus, when Breckinridge sat down early in October to draft a "resolution to be offered to the democratic society today," he took as much care as if he were drafting an official remonstrance to Congress. And, tellingly, he designed his draft for striking appearance in newsprint: the citizens of Kentucky had for a series of years been hoping for free use of that "all important right, which they received from NATURE," Breckinridge wrote. The free and undisturbed use of the river Mississippi was the "NATURAL RIGHT of the inhabitants." Breckinridge's "draft" was printed, complete with the intended eye-catching typography, on October 12 and again, with additional resolutions from a meeting that month, on November 16.[26]

The November meeting resolved that a committee be appointed to prepare two documents; first, an address calling for the united efforts of "the inhabitants of the western country," and, second, a "remonstrance to the President and Congress" (the document at which Breckinridge would be working during the coming weeks). Again, this last resolution not only called for political documents to be drawn up, but also was itself a political polemic. The proposed remonstrance should state, "in the bold, decent and determined language, proper to

---

[25] *Kentucky Gazette,* Aug. 24, 31, 1793; reprinted in Foner, *Democratic-Republican Societies,* pp. 357–59. Much of the Democratic Society material also appears in Thomas D. Clark, ed., *The Voice of the Frontier: Bradford's Notes on Kentucky* (Lexington, 1993), pp. 197–201, 205–8, 213–24. However, this entertaining volume consists of John Bradford's own much editorialized 1828 *Kentucky Gazette* reprintings and cannot be relied on for accuracy or completeness of the original documents.

[26] "Rough draft of resolution to be offered to the democratic society today," Oct. 7, 1793, in JB's hand, placed following no. 1531 in vol. 9, BFP; *Kentucky Gazette,* Oct. 12, 1793; and Clark, *Bradford's Notes,* p. 205. For the role of newspapers in the political life of this tumultuous decade, see Richard R. John, *Spreading the Word: The American Postal System from Franklin to Morse* (Cambridge, Mass., 1996), pp. 31–42; Richard B. Kielbowicz, *News in the Mail: The Press, Post Office, and Public Information, 1700–1860s* (New York, 1989); John Paul Nord, "Newspapers and American Nationhood, 1776–1826," *Proceedings of the American Antiquarian Society* 100 (1990):391–405; Donald H. Stewart, *The Opposition Press of the Federalist Period* (Albany, 1969), pp. 3–32; and David Waldstreicher, *In the Midst of Perpetual Fetes: The Making of American Nationalism, 1776–1820* (Chapel Hill, 1997), pp. 10–12, 109–12.

be used by injured freemen, when they address the servants of the people," that "we consider the feeble attempts which have been made by the executive under the present government, and the total silence of Congress on this important subject, as strong proof that most of our brethren in the eastern parts of America, are totally regardless whether this, our just right, is kept from us or not."[27]

The proceedings of the November meeting of the Kentucky Democratic Society then themselves loudly and publicly remonstrated, rehearsing the history of the Jay Treaty and setting out the western grievance against "the present government." And just a month after these proceedings were printed in the *Kentucky Gazette*—but before the proposed address to western citizens and remonstrance were composed, printed, or dispatched—Lexington's Democratic Society was already making waves in Philadelphia.

The society's November meeting had also delivered the western threat of unilateral action in the form of a resolution to float an American vessel "in a peaceable manner" down the Mississippi. The express purpose was to provoke a reaction from the Spaniards, so "that we may be able to lay before the Federal Government, such unequivocal proofs . . . that they will be compelled to say whether they will abandon or protect the inhabitants of the western country."[28] We do not know whether it was Breckinridge himself who articulated this motivation, or one of his fellow western political men. Either way, it likely brings us as close as we will get to understanding the spirit in which a superbly connected, national-minded man such as Breckinridge issued his western threats against the federal government.

During this stressful season, the men at Kentucky's "articulate center" went so far as to justify the threats of Kentucky filibustering expeditions and even to formulate threats of their own, on the grounds that it would take such extreme measures to get through to the seat of government. Early in 1794, for example, the Washington administration directed Gov. Isaac Shelby's resistance to administration directives to clamp down on western Revolutionary War hero Gen. George Rogers

---

[27]Foner, *Democratic-Republican Societies,* pp. 362–63.

[28]*Kentucky Gazette,* Nov. 16, 1793; and Foner, *Democratic-Republican Societies,* pp. 360–62.

Clark, who was recruiting for an unauthorized campaign against the Spaniards. Kentucky secretary of state and western man James Brown encouraged the governor to resist the directive from Philadelphia, urging that "Congress . . . *ought to know through every possible channel,* that we are convinced of our wrongs, and conscious of our ability to address them. Such information might *call their attention to our situation, and give our interests a place in their political deliberations.*" It was, Brown judged, "a favorable juncture" for doing this, since Congress might "be alarmed at the idea of our detaching ourselves from the Union at so critical a period."[29] Were these men disloyal? Were they secessionists? Were they (as General Clark seems to have been) loose cannons? It is true that during the first decades of the republic, not a few prominent western men were implicated in filibustering and separatist activity, but, tellingly, the men who joined in such efforts were *not* those who drafted and disseminated the blustering rhetoric of western threats.[30] However the conspiracies and expeditions may have been intended by their organizers, it is clear that, in the hands of a man like Breckinridge, these western threats against Spain were aimed straight at Philadelphia.

In this case, in addition to the persistent reports that General Clark was attempting to raise an armed force against the Spaniards, Philadelphians also soon heard that the Democratic Society planned intentionally to aggravate the situation with their Mississippi trial boat.

---

[29]James Brown to Isaac Shelby, Feb. 16, 1794, "Selections from the Draper Collection . . . to Elucidate the Proposed French Expedition under George Rogers Clark against Louisiana, in the Years 1793–94," *Annual Report of the American Historical Association for the Year 1896* (Washington, D.C., 1897), 1:1041 (emphasis mine); and for a similar treatment of Kentucky filibusters, see Harry Innes to Thomas Jefferson, Jan. 21, 1794, Thomas Jefferson Papers, Library of Congress, Manuscript Division.

[30]JB's cousin (and James Brown's older brother) John Brown, for example, had been involved in the "Spanish Conspiracy" of the late 1780s, a circumstance that was brought up again for partisan purposes in 1806 (Watlington, *Partisan Spirit,* pp. 253–60). JB himself was twice implicated, though apparently innocent of such charges. Historians have sometimes listed him as one of the subscribers who in March 1794 pledged money for the Clark expedition. This error appears to be based on a slip by Richard Lowitt, "Activities of Citizen Genet in Kentucky," p. 264 (contrast "Proposed French Expedition against Louisiana," pp. 1073–74). JB was also briefly implicated in the Burr Conspiracy in 1806, when a Kentucky informant included him on a list sent to Jefferson. However, the Kentuckian soon wrote again exonerating both JB and Henry Clay (Thomas Perkins Abernethy, *The Burr Conspiracy* [New York, 1954], pp. 90–91).

And, although neither expedition would actually be carried out, the news had effects at the seat of government. As Kentucky Sen. John Brown, just arrived in Philadelphia for the legislative session, reported in December 1793 to a Kentucky friend, "Some resolutions of the Democratic Society of Kentucky" had been reprinted there, which, combined with the reports of Clark's expedition, had "excited some attention & perhaps some apprehension" that impatient Kentucky might precipitate in an undesired clash with Spain.[31]

Perhaps it would be pushing this still-partial example too far to suggest that western ways of connecting to Congress during the 1790s had little to do with connecting to Congress. But certainly the efforts of men like Breckinridge through the Democratic Society show that the text of any given petition with its actual reception on the floor of Congress—whether positive, negative, or perhaps some passive-aggressive stance in between—was only a very small part of the political effect desired. In this case, the proposed remonstrance to the president and Congress was never intended to stand alone; it had been preceded, as we have just seen, by half a dozen well-publicized political efforts. And, once drafted by Breckinridge and approved by the society, the remonstrance would be sent out across the West and the nation, not alone, but as part of a package that sheds further light on its purpose.

Three printed documents made up the package: a cover letter and the address and remonstrance as projected by the November meeting. The cover letter introduced the other two documents and was addressed in the singular to "Fellow Citizen." "We flatter ourselves that the measures recommended in the Address will meet your approbation, and that you will use your influence to induce your neighboring fellow-citizens to give their sanction to the Remonstrance," the Lexingtonians wrote. And, with an eye to the practicable, they included instructions: "The Remonstrance, when signed, may be transmitted to the representative in Congress from your district, or to any other mem-

[31]John Brown to Harry Innes, Dec. 31, 1793, container 1, Harry Innes Collection, DLC. John Brown was JB's once much admired older first cousin, but the two (to historians' loss) had become estranged over a lawsuit in 1789 and afterward virtually never corresponded. The background of Clark's proposed campaign and the waves it made in Philadelphia are detailed in Richard Lowitt, "Activities of Citizen Genet in Kentucky, 1793–1794," *Filson Club Historical Quarterly* 22 (1948):252–67; and for an astute and concise assessment of the Clark episode, see James Roger Sharp, *American Politics in the Early Republic: The New Nation in Crisis* (New Haven, 1993), pp. 105–9.

ber of that body, delegated from the Western Country." This should be done as soon as possible, they reminded, since it was "intended that a decision should be obtained during the present session of Congress." This cover letter was a communication from Lexington's political men to their western peers, without whom, apparently, Breckinridge and his colleagues expected no organized, coordinated, effective action.[32]

In the address "To the Inhabitants of the United States West of the Allegany and Appalachian Mountains," the Democratic Society rehearsed the history of the closure of the Mississippi and the general government's failure to open it (western men evidently thought this narrative could not be repeated too often), before urging a new kind of action:

> We have found prayers and supplications of no avail, and should we continue to load the Table of Congress with Memorials, from a part, only of the Western Country, it is too probable, they would meet with a fate similar to those which have been formerly presented. Let us, then, all unite our endeavors in the common cause. Let all join, in a firm and manly remonstrance to the President and Congress of the United States, stating our just and Undoubted right to the Navigation of the Mississippi, remonstrating against the conduct of Government with regard to that right which must have been occasioned by local policy or neglect and demanding of them speedy and effectual exertions for its attainment.

Then the dramatic peroration:

> The obstacles are great, and so ought to be our efforts; Adverse fortune may attend us, but it shall never dispirit us. We may for awhile exhaust our Wealth and Strength, but until the all important object is procured, we pledge ourselves to you, and let us all pledge ourselves to each other, that our Perserverance and our firmness will be inexhaustible.[33]

---

[32]Foner, *Democratic-Republican Societies,* pp. 362–63. For one of these printed cover letters, addressed to Andrew Jackson, see James A. Padgett, ed., "Letters of James Brown to Presidents of the United States," *Louisiana Historical Quarterly* 20 (1937): 61–62.

[33]Foner, *Democratic-Republican Societies,* pp. 363–66, quotes on 365–66. I join JB's biographers in hedging on his authorship of this document. JB did not annotate his own copy of the address ("To the Inhabitants of the United States West of the Allegany and Appalachian Mountains," Dec. 13, 1793, printed broadside, vol. 10, following no. 1583, BFP; and Lowell H. Harrison and James C. Klotter, *A New History of Kentucky* [Lexington, 1997], p. 73). The Breckinridge biographies are Harrison, *John*

The three documents prepared by the Kentucky Democratic Society made up a complete and handy kit for political action. Any western man who received it need only get together with some like-minded peers and call a meeting. There, with the aid of the ready-to-declaim "Address to the Inhabitants," he would remind the assembled crowd of the context and nature of the current grievance and exhort them to sign the "Remonstrance," which would also be ready at hand. It would only remain for someone to write up the meeting and deliver the account, along with the Kentucky address and remonstrance, to the editor of the "local" paper.

In the spring, the seeds from Kentucky's year-end address and remonstrance began to sprout. It was, for example, the arrival of the Kentucky packet that inspired the organization of the Washington County, Pennsylvania, Democratic Society. At a March meeting, they resolved to adopt the Lexington remonstrance, ordered it to be published in the *Pittsburgh Gazette,* and forwarded it to the President and Congress.[34] "Amongst other persons" of Pittsburgh who received the Kentucky packet was the author and western man Hugh Henry Brackenridge (no recognized relation to John Breckinridge). Brackenridge called for a meeting to form a Pittsburgh Society, which then took the same measures as their Washington County countrymen, joining with their "brethren of Kentucky in their complaint," drawing up resolves, publishing them and sending them to the parent and grandparent societies of Kentucky and Philadelphia, and to "the members of Congress from this side of the Mountain."[35] In both the Washington and Pittsburgh meetings, there was some discussion of whether simply to adopt the Kentucky remonstrance or to alter it to include their own specific local grievances. The Pittsburgh Society did draft a customized remonstrance, but the Washington County Society, as they explained

---

Breckinridge, Jeffersonian Republican, Filson Club Publications Second Series, No. 2. (Louisville, 1969); and Klotter, *The Breckinridges of Kentucky, 1760–1981* (Lexington, 1986), pp. 3–35.

[34]"Democratic Society of the County of Washington, Pennsylvania, Remonstrance to the President and Congress on Opening Navigation of the Mississippi River, March 24, 1794," Foner, *Democratic-Republican Societies,* pp. 127–29, printed in the *Pittsburgh Gazette,* Apr. 5, 1794.

[35]"H. H. Brackenridge to the *Pittsburgh Gazette,* April 4, 1794," and "Response to an Address from the Democratic Society of Kentucky, April 26, 1794," Foner, *Democratic-Republican Societies,* pp. 129, 131–33, printed in the *Pittsburgh Gazette* on Apr. 5 and May 17, 1794.

in a letter to Breckinridge, decided that in order to "remonstrate before the present session of Congress should rise," they would sign, publish, and circulate the Kentucky remonstrance as it stood.[36]

This last example drives home a point about this particular species of connecting to Congress. Historians have preferred to view the democratic societies as vehicles for popular expression of local grassroots issues, but it has always required some fancy footwork to support the preference. An individual meeting of a certain democratic society might reasonably enough be labeled *local,* and its texts taken at their word as *democratic.* But this requires ignoring the activities of an entire network of canny, well-connected, and national-minded political men — some (like Breckinridge) working to create and disseminate the message, others (like Brackenridge) to manage its application to the local scene and to send the results spinning out to Philadelphia and around the republic.[37]

"The Petition of the Good People West of the Allegany Mountains *Humbly Sheweth* &c."

Drafted, published, packaged, circulated, republished, and recirculated around the republic, Breckinridge's Kentucky Remonstrance would reach the floor of Congress before the end of the session (which fortunately for that purpose would stretch into June 1794), but there the storm of energetic western motion would become stalled. The first

[36]Washington (Pennsylvania) Democratic Society to "Citizen Brakinridge," Apr. 8, 1794, Foner, *Democratic-Republican Societies,* pp. 129–30. Foner apparently mistook this letter for one to H. H. Brackenridge.

[37]On the question of democracy, the necessity for this fancy footwork dogged Eugene P. Link, for example, throughout his classic study (Link, *Democratic-Republican Societies, 1790–1800* [Morningside Heights, N.Y., 1942]). And on "local" protests, a particularly unfortunate example: Thomas P. Slaughter, writing about the Washington County, Pennsylvania, society discussed above, found himself arguing that, "Some of the grievances that led militiamen in Washington County to establish the society are contained in its remonstrance to the President and Congress. At the top of their list was the unsettled matter of free navigation of the Mississippi," and so on, point by point through a very familiar document. It could be, as Slaughter emphasized, that "the settlers perceived" their grievances just as articulated in this remonstrance, but the inescapable fact remains that it is, word for word, the December 1793 remonstrance that John Breckinridge drafted and the Lexington Democratic Society circulated to democratic societies around the republic (Slaughter, *The Whiskey Rebellion: Frontier Epilogue to the American Revolution* [New York, 1986], pp. 163–64).

session of the Third Congress found the Federalists rather desperately focused on reaching some accommodation to a provocative Great Britain. Congressional Republicans fumed at this, and the relative disregard for the Mississippi question made the situation all the more maddening.[38] In mid-April, "several remonstrances from citizens of the United States West of the Allegheny Mountains" were "presented to the House," "read," and referred to committee. That committee, reporting their "full confidence that the desired object will be speedily and vigilantly pursued by the proper constitutional authority [the executive]," recommended that the remonstrances be sent on to the president. At the wrap-up of their session, the House, after "some time spent" on the question, concurred with the committee report: since "communications from the Executive" indicated that negotiations with Spain were then going on and since it was "in the interest of the United States and every part thereof, to come to an amicable adjustment" in the diplomatic mode, the House should proceed no further on the "the said remonstrance."

Meanwhile in the Senate, two resolutions on Mississippi navigation were presented by the Kentucky members and referred to a committee that came to the same basic conclusion as its House counterpart. But while the Senate committee expressed confidence in the administration's good faith efforts, it also urged action to "satisfy" the disaffected westerners. The Senate accordingly resolved that the president be requested to communicate to the governor of Kentucky "such part of the existing negotiations between the United States and Spain, relative to this subject, as he may deem advisable and consistent with the course of negotiations." The president responded quickly, but in ways designed more to cover himself than to reassure the westerners. He sent a message informing Congress of "the present state of certain hostile threats against those territories of Spain in our neighborhood," and, to show that his responses to those threats had been vigorous and timely, he submitted a sheaf of correspondence between the administration and Kentucky Governor Shelby. This correspondence was, of course, also meant to establish that the Kentuckians had been all along

---

[38]The disparity of Federalist interest between diplomatic-commercial relations affecting easterners and westerners is nicely mirrored in Stanley Elkins and Eric McKitrick's masterful 754-page volume on the period: Mississippi navigation rates only nine brief mentions (Elkins and McKitrick, *Age of Federalism* [New York, 1993]).

receiving adequate information and assurance of the administration's good faith efforts in the Spanish negotiations—and therefore that their actions were doubly indefensible. In a March 1794 letter from new Secretary of State Edmund Randolph to Governor Shelby, we can see the Federalist stance in a nutshell. To the customary praise of the executive's diplomatic efforts, Randolph added that if the evidence were published, anyone reading it would agree. He closed with a pointed warning: "Let not unfounded suspicions of a tardiness in Government prompt individuals to rash efforts."[39]

Beyond that somewhat ambiguous flurry of attention, it would be another six months before the administration took any action to assuage western disaffection, and another eighteen months before Spain conceded American free navigation of the Mississippi. What light does this response—or lack of response—from Philadelphia shed on western ways of connecting to Congress? We can consider the question by checking in again with Kentucky's political men.

As the congressional session frustratingly unfolded, western Republicans, whether in Philadelphia or at home, encouraged each other to make themselves heard in Congress. Kentucky Sen. John Edwards, for example, wrote in March to Breckinridge. Edwards reported on the session and gave his suggestions for "improving our country," one of which was "by all opportunities remonstrate Congress for their [exer]tions towards securing our trade down the river." Actually, Breckinridge needed no reminders that spring to make sure (as his cousin James Brown had put it) that Congress heard "through every possible channel" that Kentuckians were convinced of their wrongs and conscious of their ability to address them. President Washington's opening message to Congress gave Breckinridge an early impetus to begin.[40]

---

[39]*Annals of Congress,* 3d Cong., 1st sess., pp. 99, 594, 603–4, 607–9, 769; and Report of "Mr. Lee, to whom were referred several remonstrances from the citizens west of the Alleghany mountains, respecting the navigation of the river Mississippi," Apr. 23, 1794, *American State Papers, Class 1: Foreign Relations,* CIS US serial set, microfiche (Washington, D.C., n.d.), p. 448, quotes on pp. 454, 456–57. The fact that at one point the *Annals* referred to the western "remonstrance" in the singular perhaps reflects the fact that the "several remonstrances" were identical, i.e., copies of JB's Kentucky document (p. 769).

[40]John Edwards to JB, Mar. 16, 1794, BFP; and James Brown to Isaac Shelby, Feb. 16, 1794, "Selections from the Draper Collection," 1:1041.

The president had concluded his message: "On the subjects of mutual interest between this country and Spain, negotiations and conferences are now depending. The public good requiring that the present state of these should be made known to the Legislature *in confidence* only, they shall be the subject of a separate and subsequent communication." Though Washington could hardly have intended this explanation to rile the westerners, any western man could see it was bound to do so. Senator Brown, for example, wrote apprehensively home late in December: he expected *Kentucky Gazette* editor John Bradford would by then have reprinted the president's speech and he dreaded the reaction in Kentucky. Bradford would not actually print the speech until February, but it was circulating among Kentucky's political leaders long before then. Breckinridge, for example, had quickly received his own special delivery copy of the speech from Kentucky Rep. Christopher Greenup, who had taken advantage of a Lexington merchant's departure from Philadelphia to write to his Kentucky compeers. The letter took care of what was routine business for congressmen: arranging subscriptions to the national-Philadelphia newspapers for a politically minded constituent. And, just two days after Washington had delivered his message to Congress, Greenup enclosed a copy of it for Breckinridge. When the president's message did appear in the *Kentucky Gazette,* then, Breckinridge would be ready with his editorial blast.[41]

Taking Washington's words as his text, Breckinridge set himself to rework an old familiar story, that of the betrayal of the western country from 1785 onward, around the new theme of the "veil of secrecy" between the government and the western people. In 1785, Breckinridge wrote, John Jay had been instructed by a wise Congress to make no treaty that endangered the American right to the navigation of the Mississippi. Jay had eventually reported that "*great difficulties* had arisen between himself and the Spanish Minister, but it was necessary those difficulties should be kept a *secret.*" In truth, according to Breckin-

[41]George Washington to Congress, Dec. 5, 1793, James D. Richardson, ed., *A Compilation of the Messages and Papers of the Presidents, 1789–1897,* 9 vols. (Washington, D.C., 1896–99), 1:145–47, quote on p. 147; John Brown to Harry Innes, Dec. 31, 1793, container 1, Harry Innes Collection, DLC; and Christopher Greenup to JB, Dec. 7, 1793, BFP.

ridge, the secret was that Jay "thought it beneficial to the commercial interest of America" to "yield the navigation of the Mississippi for twenty-five or thirty years."

Under the "new government," Breckinridge continued, an American ambassador had once again been sent out, the right to free navigation again asserted, "and (as we were told) real negociations opened." And what had four years of diplomatic discussions produced? "Another *secret!*!!" A secret "communicated in whispers to a body, whose very whispers are not intrusted to Plebeian ears." "After contemplating the history of this business," Breckinridge asked, who "could any longer have any faith in the friendly intentions of Congress?" He finished with a western threat wrapped in a patriot flag: one right would always remain, which could "never be rendered equivocal or be whispered into a secret, the right of expatriation." "To those remaining veteran Patriots, therefore, whose footsteps we followed to this distant desart, and who by their blood and toil have converted it into a smiling and delightful country, we now look up. Under your guidance we fought we bled and acquired this country, and under your guidance we still wish to fight and bleed, while any appendage to its complete enjoyment remains to be procured."[42]

A few months later, Washington's words again sent Breckinridge into action. The president, as part of his effort to keep political, if not actual, control over the persistent reports of George Rogers Clark's efforts, had issued a "solemn warning to any one levying troops or assembling persons, or to anyone enlisting enrolling or assembling themselves," "under color of a foreign authority [meaning France, who had offered aid to the filibusters] . . . for the purpose of invading and plundering the territories of a nation [meaning Spain] at peace with the said United States."[43]

Breckinridge responded with a letter for the *Kentucky Gazette,* which

---

[42]"An Old Fashioned Republican," "The Crisis" (annotated in JB's hand), "February 1794 for Mr. Bradford vs. secrecy in government"; also "copy of my original sent Mr. Bradford, February, 1794" (annotated in JB's hand), vol. 11, nos. 1848–1849b, BFP. The main body of this text, though without JB's western threat and stirring conclusion, can be found in Clark, *Bradford's Notes,* pp. 219–23.

[43]George Washington, "A Proclamation," Mar. 24, 1794, Richardson, *Messages and Papers of the Presidents,* 1:157–58, quotes on p. 157. The proclamation was published in the *Kentucky Gazette,* May 4, 1794 (Clark, *Bradford's Notes,* pp. 227–28).

historian Arthur Preston Whitaker once labeled "the key to Breckinridge's conduct in national affairs." What sparked off the editorial was the president's characterization of Spain as being "at peace" with the United States. To try to obtain free navigation of the Mississippi "by attacking these *peaceable* people," Breckinridge began sarcastically, "is going the wrong way to work."

> The way, is to *petition* Congress; altho it may not at first appear so *direct,* as to force passage down the actual *channel.* "The Petition of the good people west of the Allegany Mountains *humbly sheweth* &c." This method cannot fail of success. State your Situation truly & appeal to their *Justice* & *public spirit.* State that you inhabit one of the most delightful Countries in the world, natured with fine navigable streams . . . this delightful country, if not crushed by unwarrantable policy, will soon be the Eden of America & will draw from the barren & inhospitable parts of eastern America all its enterprising & industrious Inhabitants.

Continuing in a sarcastic mode, Breckinridge then recounted the familiar narrative of Mississippi navigation in terms of what the federal government, "labouring incessantly for us since the year 1783," had accomplished. If the western "people have got it into their heads that they have a right" to Mississippi navigation, he concluded, "let them only send forth petitions to Congress in the way I have directed . . . and I assure them, that Congress will most certainly, on their petitions being presented, order them to be—read."[44]

Historians have understandably preferred not to deal with the element of sarcasm in the polemical productions of the early republic's political men. We are too far removed to judge how the sarcasm may have hit or missed the mark among the newspaper-reading populace of the time, and, in any case, to modern readers (to this modern reader at least) it seems more embarrassing than effective. Best to leave it alone. Still, it is partly because of the sarcasm that this piece is so revealing, not only of Breckinridge's conduct as a political man, but also as a guide to the nature of western ways of connecting to Congress.

We have already seen that petitions of the sort that contemporaries labeled memorials and remonstrances were intricate documents in

---

[44]"To Mr. Bradford, May 6, 1794, draft in JB's hand, annotated, "written for the paper on seeing the President's proclamation in last Saturday's paper," BFP.

which the ancient form of written supplication was manipulated with skill and finesse for rhetorical effect. This essay also advances the less verifiable proposition that political men at the time, Republican and Federalist, and eastern and western men alike, took these rhetorical manipulations for granted and routinely dealt with them in kind. Thus, for example, Breckinridge would have composed his classic 1793 Democratic Society petition with confidence not only in his own skills as a draftsman but also in the sophistication of his audience. The western inhabitants of "this dangerous and distant desart" had, "without ceasing," burdened the president and Congress with their "humble petitions and requests," but, "alas!" the federal government had "never produced one single real effort" to procure their right to Mississippi trade.[45] Breckinridge wrote knowing that the political-minded citizenry who encountered such texts, whether in a tavern, at a court-day meeting, or on the floor of the U.S. Congress, understood them to be less about pioneer hardship or participatory democracy than about politics, which in this context meant passionate partisan politics. He wrote confident that it literally went without saying that such political missiles were aimed straight at the Federalist administration in Philadelphia.

The full-blown sarcasm of Breckinridge's May 1794 editorial demonstrates in dramatic form the extent to which he assumed a sophisticated understanding between author and audience. His sarcasm on the subject of petitioning is particularly telling, since it shows that readers, in Kentucky as well as around the republic, were presumed to share his own highly developed appreciation of the petitioning process as politics. If the western people wished to gain free navigation of the Mississippi, they need only "*petition* Congress. . . . 'The Petition of the good people west of the Allegany Mountains *humbly sheweth* &c.' This method cannot fail of success. State your Situation truly & appeal to their *Justice* & *public spirit.*" Let the people "only send forth petitions to Congress in the way I have directed . . . and I assure them, that Congress will most certainly, on their petitions being presented, order them to be — read."

---

[45] [JB], "Remonstrance," December 1793, Foner, *Democratic-Republican Societies,* pp. 366–68.

Breckinridge, indefatigable draftsman, wrote for a readership he assumed, during this tumultuous political season of 1793–94, had been following the activities of the Kentucky Democratic Society, had been watching the proceedings of the Third Congress for signs of response to the December remonstrance and its clones, and therefore knew that no positive action had yet been taken on them — *and expected that none was likely to be taken.* This last point (unfortunately not easily verifiable in any specific sense) reinforces appreciation for Whitaker's insight that what Breckinridge urged in this document (which Whitaker called the "key" to his "conduct in national affairs") was "not the secession of Kentucky but the overthrow of the Federalists."[46] For that purpose, it would not help if Congress proved responsive to every barb and remonstrance hurled its way. Breckinridge and his fellow western Jeffersonians were evidently convinced that, for the overarching purpose of bringing down the Federalists, disappointment, disaffection, outrage, even sarcasm about the federal governmental process—all broadcast through the republic as loudly and widely as possible—would be the most effective western way of connecting to Congress.

"The Eden of America" vs. "The Barren & Inhospitable Parts of Eastern America"

The Federalist administration and the Third Congress together would continue to produce a bountiful supply of fuel for Jeffersonian fires. Given the incessant circulation of political texts and of correspondence among political men around the republic, it is no surprise that Kentucky's fiery responses had much in common with those elsewhere—a congruence that of course was no accident either. But Kentucky's Jeffersonian activism, even in the hands of newcomer Breckinridge, also carried a distinctive western punch. This section takes special note of the character and utility of the westernness of one western man's political efforts, following Breckinridge through the heat of Kentucky's politics in the summer of 1794.

Imagine, for example, the delicious outrage of Kentucky Jeffersonians on hearing that President Washington had selected none other

[46]Whitaker, *Mississippi Question,* p. 9.

than John Jay as minister extraordinary to Great Britain. As soon as the news of Jay's April appointment reached Lexington, the Democratic Society held several meetings to plot strategy (and to have their "Democratic Publications" printed and disseminated). Those meetings were of course reported in the newspaper, along with an invitation to a general citizen's meeting to be held at the State House on May 24.[47] For that occasion, Breckinridge sat down to draft a resolution detailing this new affront to western citizens. His pen must hardly have needed to pause over the first few points. They recited the old familiar litany of the federal government's decade-long failure to insist on the right to Mississippi River navigation, and they incorporated the already well-practiced new theme of government secrecy: "That the General Government whose duty it was to have put us in possession of this right have, either through design or mistaken policy, adopted no effectual measures for its attainment, and even those measures have been obstinately and uniformly concealed from us" [no, make that "veiled in secrecy"]. And Breckinridge must have made quick work of the familiar conclusion, too: "That we have a right to expect and demand, that Spain should be compelled immediately to acknowledge our right." But at that point, Breckinridge moved into new territory, from the old western grievance against Spain, the federal government and John Jay to the *new* western grievance—against Great Britain, the federal government, and John Jay.

The "voice of all Eastern America" had now called for redress against Great Britain's "insults and injuries," but "Western America," Breckinridge wrote, had an even "stronger claim to satisfaction" against Great Britain, in terms both of "atrocity and continuance." The "recent appointment of the *enemy* of the western country [Jay], to negotiate with that nation, and the tame submission of the General Government when *we* alone were injured by Great Britain" therefore made it necessary for the "Western people" to communicate their demands to the president and Congress. Breckinridge's long draft was broken up into fourteen resolutions passed at the May 24 meeting. The accompanying remonstrance also followed his draft, though it stated more explicitly the western grievances. It targeted the king of Great Britain (in Declaration of Independence style), charging him

---

[47] *Kentucky Gazette,* May 17, 1794.

with a list of "injuries and insults," among which were that he still held "posts fortified and garrisoned" within United States territory and that he had, "by his agents, supplied arms, ammunition, clothing, and provisions to those merciless savages, who have so long ravaged the Western frontier of these States."[48]

Just after the May 24 citizen's meeting, an effigy of Jay was guillotined and incinerated on the streets of Lexington. Though politics out-of-doors hardly seems to fit the modus operandi of a man like Breckinridge, there are sure signs in this case that some western man, if not Breckinridge himself, could be found behind the curtain busily working the controls. The "likeness of this evil genius of Western America" went to the stake not only "dressed in a *courtly* manner," but also bedecked with classical tags and political texts. Around his neck on "a *hempen* string" (a reference to Kentucky's thwarted hopes for an export trade) hung a copy of John Adams's "Defence of the American Constitution," its cover inscribed with a quote from Ovid, translated as "Gold bade me write." In the effigy's hand was a copy of "Swift's late speech in Congress on the subject of British depredations." This speech by Connecticut Federalist Congressman Zephaniah Swift, conciliatory toward Great Britain, also was annotated with Latin tags: one from Juvenal, translated as "No man e'er reached the heights of vice at first," and the other from Virgil, "A *second* is not wanting" (referring to Jay's new chance to reach the "heights of vice"). And what enables the historian to describe so circumstantially how "John Jay" was fitted out? Just like the citizens of Kentucky and around the republic in 1794, she can read all about it in the newspapers.[49]

It was Breckinridge who with evident relish wrote the newspaper account of the burning of the effigy. It was Breckinridge who identified

---

[48]"Resolution to be offered at a meeting of the citizens of Lexington the 24th of this instant respecting the Mississippi," May 20, 1794, draft in JB's hand, vol. 10, no. 1695 (quoted); and broadside version, May 28, 1794, no. 1697, BFP; and "On Saturday the 24th instant a numerous meeting of respectable Citizens from different parts of the State assembled in Lexington, May 28, 1794," broadside, Evans, *Early American Imprints,* microfiche 131, no. 27219; and Clark, *Bradford's Notes,* pp. 262–64.

[49]*Kentucky Gazette,* May 31, 1794; reprinted in Clark, *Bradford's Notes,* pp. 265–66; and (lacking JB's account of the effigy burning) in Foner, *Democratic-Republican Societies,* pp. 271–73. "Swift's late speech in Congress" could be either of two that Zephaniah Swift delivered in the spring of 1794 (Mar. 28 and Apr. 14), both protesting proposed hard-line measures against Great Britain (*Annals of Congress,* 3d Cong., 1st sess., pp. 552–56, 576–81).

the texts that "John Jay" carried, Breckinridge who quoted the Latin tags and helpfully supplied the translations. (Was it also Breckinridge who literally supplied the texts and saw that the effigy was decked out in them? Quite possibly.) In addition to these obvious signs of gentry-politico involvement, Breckinridge perhaps hinted at the role of men like himself when he wrote, in a phrase commonly used to describe citizens' meetings, that "a number of respectable citizens" had ordered the effigy to be fashioned. Nevertheless, Breckinridge worked to present this event as an effusion of what historians today would call "popular political culture." He stressed that Jay's appointment had brought his earlier treachery "so strongly to the recollection of the *people*" that "*they* could not refrain from testifying their abhorrence of the man" (emphasis added). As for the demonstration itself, he wrote that the effigy was brought to the street from a local barbershop "amidst the shouts of the people," and he made it clear that the subsequent proceedings were a people-pleasing spectacle—the guillotine and then the torch, "which finding its way to a quantity of powder which was lodged in his body produced such an explosion" that "scarcely . . . a particle" of Jay was afterward to be found.

In his account "for the press," Breckinridge was able to construct the ideal political event, in which popular politics powerfully combined with reasoned and responsible republican leadership. And his account *was* a construction rather than a reconstruction. Surely the "people" on the scene could hardly have read or appreciated the texts on "Jay's" person, however aptly chosen. In fact, it could be that when the effigy was sent out from the barber's shop, the pamphlets got left behind or someone rescued them as too precious to burn; maybe the guillotining was not quite so "dexterously executed," as Breckinridge reported, or the powder stuffed inside the effigy was too damp to ignite. Perhaps the "respectable citizens" were not entirely able to orchestrate the "people's" behavior. But none of this really mattered. Spectators who had failed to notice the effigy's "courtly" dress or the texts attached could read about them in the paper. And, most important from the western Jeffersonian point of view, the event became, for national political purposes, precisely what Breckinridge said it was.[50]

---

[50]"An account of the burning in effigy of John Jay on May 24 for the press," May 29, 1794, in JB's hand, BFP; *Kentucky Gazette,* May 31, 1794. For illumination (pun intended)

What is notable about these activities as western politics? Taking care to consider this subject purely from the point of view of contemporary possibilities and expectations, we cannot help but be impressed by the dispatch and timeliness of Breckinridge's Kentucky efforts.[51] He was quick to recognize a new opportunity in this national political moment and to use it to promote western interests. As he explained to a Virginia connection, the "people" had "for some time considered themselves as being deluded by government and sacraficed for the narrow local policy of the eastern states," and now, "the appointment of Jay (whom they consider the evil Genius of this country)" had "brought the business to issue." It took only three weeks for Breckinridge's report of this meeting, along with the text of the thirteen resolutions and the remonstrance approved there, to reach the Philadelphia press, whence it quickly circulated through the eastern papers. And, as for the street demonstration, Kentuckians were far in the vanguard; it would be another year before burnings of Jay in effigy became a common occurrence around the republic.[52]

Kentucky's Jeffersonians (with John Breckinridge again behind the curtain) also had assembled yet another complete kit for political action, and sent it around the nation, conveniently contained in a single issue of the *Kentucky Gazette.* Included were useful instructions:

---

of the "politics of the street" or the "politics of celebration" of the early republic, see Simon P. Newman, *Parades and the Politics of the Street: Festive Culture in the Early American Republic* (Philadelphia, 1997); and Waldstreicher, *In the Midst of Perpetual Fetes* (second quoted phrase on p. 3 and passim).

[51]Communications in the early republic will always seem slow by our standards, and western communications especially so; it is best, therefore, to refrain from thinking about speed in the abstract. The shortcomings of such analysis are illustrated in a frequently consulted study by Allan R. Pred: "In absolute terms, the entire nation was still in a pronounced state of public-information isolation in 1790." Perhaps recognizing the logical absurdity of this statement, Pred moved quickly from the "absolute" to a "comparative" analysis, but here he stressed "the extreme informational isolation of the sparsely populated wilderness to the west of the Alleghenies, as in [for example] the time lag from Lexington, Kentucky, to Philadelphia." In spite of their frequent complaints about the unreliability of the mails, western men like JB would not have recognized such a description of the western world in which they operated (Pred, *Urban Growth and the Circulation of Information: The United States System of Cities, 1790–1840* [Cambridge, Mass., 1973], quotes on pp. 36, 39).

[52]JB to Samuel Hopkins, Sept. 15, 1794, BFP; and "Lexington Resolutions," as reprinted in the *Maryland Journal,* June 25, 1794, datelined "Philadelphia, June 23," in "Selections from the Draper Collection," 1:1056–60. For an example of Jay in effigy, see Waldstreicher, *In the Midst of Perpetual Fetes,* pp. 138–39.

one resolution recommended that each county "appoint a committee, to give and receive communications on these subjects," to call meetings, and to elect representatives for a convention to discuss western rights. And the packet contained something for every taste along the spectrum of political passion. The remonstrance (which Breckinridge organized but may not have drafted) was remarkably restrained: excoriating the general government only in passing and forbearing to mention Jay at all, it concentrated instead on the western grievances against Great Britain and Spain. But the resolutions were more vehement—reading them in Philadelphia, Gen. Anthony Wayne would soon be condemning their "most inflammatory & invective language." And the account of Jay's incineration would set any western or republican pulse racing. Considering that they emanated from a political hotbed seven hundred miles from Philadelphia, these activities (including of course their publication) were notable for their timeliness and initiative. Far from being the products of isolation or narrow local vision, they managed to be national and partisan while expressing regional concerns.[53]

Democratic societies continued in 1794 to circulate texts and tactics around the democratic-republican world of the young nation. The Lexington Society, as we have seen, had from the start often taken the initiative in opposition politics while also deriving inspiration from other societies. Now, at an early August meeting, the Kentucky Society read letters from the Washington County, Pennsylvania, and Prince

[53]Gen. Anthony Wayne to Henry Knox, June 11, 1794, quoted in Tachau, "Whiskey Rebellion in Kentucky," p. 248. Breckinridge would continue to use Jay and, in due course, Jay's Treaty, as a focus for western protests against the federalist administration. In August 1795, for example, only nine days after President Washington signed the treaty, Breckinridge would prepare resolutions against a treaty "shameful to the American name" and he would venture into the composition of political toasts, again sounding national and partisan alarms alongside the old western firebells ("The free use of the Mississippi by constitutional means, if shortly; if not, by *any means*" [Drafts in JB's hand], "Resolution at a meeting of the Inhabitants of Fayette County, Aug. 28, 1795"; "To the Honorable General Assembly of Kentucky," Nov. 1794, vol. 11, #1, 27; and Petition to the Kentucky General Assembly, requesting that Senator Humphrey Marshall be instructed to vote against the Jay Treaty, Nov. 1795, vol. 13, #40, BFP. And see David Walker to JB, Nov. 8, 1794, BFP. For the subsequent course of protests against the Jay Treaty, see Thomas J. Farnham, "The Virginia Amendments of 1795: An Episode in the Opposition to Jay's Treaty," *Virginia Magazine of History and Biography* 75 [1967]:75–88; and Elkins and McKitrick, *Age of Federalism*, pp. 431–49).

William County, Virginia, societies, and they approved a set of resolutions that the Virginians had generated and shared. It was one of these that inspired new Kentucky action: the Virginia Society had declared that the "System of Politicks" of their congressman, Richard Bland Lee, "ought to meet the most pointed disapprobation of his constituents and that said Richard Bland Lee as a public character is altogether unworthy of the future confidence of Good Republicans." The Kentucky Society resolved to invite their congressmen to their next meeting, and they included the provision that "such of our Members of Congress who ~~are not now within this State~~ cannot attend the next stated meeting of this society" would "be requested by the said committee to give such information to them as they possess on the abovementioned subjects."[54]

When Senator Edwards accepted the Democratic Society's invitation to take part in a public question-and-answer session, he must have had some hopes of explaining exactly what had gone on during the previous Congress and of justifying his own role in the proceedings. This would require at the best of times a tricky balance between sympathy with constituents' concerns and his own insiders' appreciation of the workings of the federal government. An incumbent congressman in 1793–94, Edwards had to deal not simply with his countrymen's *concerns,* but also with their well-publicized rage, rhetorical and otherwise. Just a few months earlier, for example, Edwards's fellow senator, John Brown, had communicated his own sense of this predicament in a letter to a Kentucky friend. Brown admitted that diplomatic efforts with Spain had been "ineffectual" and asked sympathetically (and rhetorically), "How will the inhabitants bear this disappointment . . . in a matter which so nearly concerns their present Interest & future Prosperity?" But then, perhaps hoping to discourage further explosions from his state that he knew to be detri-

[54]Resolutions adopted by the Democratic Republican Society of Prince William County, Va., June 7, 1794, and letter to the Democratic Society of Kentucky, June 9, 1794, Foner, *Democratic-Republican Societies,* pp. 350–52; "Proceedings of the Democratic Society at a stated meeting held at the State House, Monday the 11th of Aug 1794 (Col. Edwards)," vol. 11, #1741, BFP; and draft (apparently of the resolution from the August 4 meeting) on a scrap of paper, n.d., Harry Innes Papers, Box 11, DLC.

mental to diplomatic progress, he also stressed the "extremely critical" situation of American diplomacy.[55]

Edwards was no doubt doing his best, but perhaps was not up to this daunting task.[56] And so his mediating turned quickly to something that would (according to Breckinridge's notes) inevitably be read by some as stonewalling: "I am forbid to go into that business"; "That would be communicating everything which I cannot"; and (asked if he had ever seen the official papers on the last decade of relations with Spain) "I have not been in the habit of begging a sight of old confidential papers that have never been admitted to the press." But, for Breckinridge, Edwards's weaknesses may have been exactly the point: in 1792, when Kentucky's new senators had arrived in Philadelphia to be seated, Edwards had drawn the short straw. His seat would be up for grabs when the legislature met in November, and Breckinridge had his eye on it.

Besides the politicking that was surely embedded in these proceedings, they also gave Breckinridge and his colleagues a great opportunity to display their regional passions. Question: "Do you believe it to be the earnest wish and desire of the Northern & Eastern politicians in Congress, that we should be invested with this right?" (Edwards's answer: "Some do & some I believe do not.") Question: "Would they be perfectly satisfied to see the subject forever languish, under the most hopeless and unavailing negociations?" (Edwards replied that a majority of the senators did not harbor those feelings.) Among the queries prepared for Edwards, the most ornery and the most pugnaciously *western* were contributed by John Breckinridge: "Have they, or any of them in your hearing ever expressed a wish or hope that western

---

[55]John Brown to Harry Innes, Dec. 31, 1793, container 1, Harry Innes Collection, DLC.

[56]A leading Kentucky lawyer-politician reported to Madison in 1792 that, except for John Brown, the new state of Kentucky's representatives to Congress were "made of very soft materials and may be moulded into any form by a workman who will take the trouble to handle them." Edwards, he warned, was "particularly well adapted to this kind of business. I wish I could see him in the hands of Sherman &c., I am much deceived if they do not make him change his opinions as often as an actor ever did his dress." He urged Madison to see that his Jeffersonian colleagues hurried to beat the Federalists to the casting (George Nicholas to James Madison, Sept. 5, 1792, *Madison Papers,* 14:359).

America might continue under its present embarrassment and distress that its superior natural advantages might not too quickly & strongly allure its inhabitants & weaken the strength of the impoverished and frozen northern and Eastern states? Do they in short view the rising importance of Western America with the eye of patriotic liberality, or with the squint of Jealousy & disaffection?"[57]

The westernness of Breckinridge's questions is obvious. Their most fundamental characteristic, however, is not merely that they were so blaringly, boisterously western, but that they were so fundamentally western *and* national, and, further, that by 1793 (just the time when Breckinridge arrived in Kentucky), being national meant being partisan. And what of the regional and local dimensions in which western political behavior has so often been characterized? In all the remonstrances, editorials, and private letters to influential friends and connections that western men like Breckinridge would write during this time, grievances that had for a decade been expressed in terms of regional rivalry took on another layer of meaning. Breckinridge carried on the western tradition, but when from his 1793 migration to Jefferson's 1801 election he or other western Jeffersonians complained of the "local policy of American councils," of the "interest of Eastern America," or, more vividly, of the interest of "Cod-fish and Molasses," they were not simply adopting the old language of western disaffection from eastern governments. They were transforming it into a new rhetoric of national partisan politics.[58]

---

[57]"Queries put to Col. Edwards, Aug. 11, 1794" (last three questions in JB's hand), BFP. The work of the August 11 meeting soon appeared in the *Kentucky Gazette*, and the Democratic Society also circulated queries in writing to western congressmen, including Edwards (*Kentucky Gazette*, Aug. 23, 1794; "Notes of meeting of the Aug. 11, 1794, meeting"; John Edwards, Answers to queries and cover letter for same, n.d., Vol. 11, #1745; and Edwards to JB, Sept. 3, 1794; and John Rhea [congressman from Tennessee] to JB, Sept. 10, 1794, BFP).

[58]JB's December 1793, "Remonstrance," BFP; and Foner, *Democratic-Republican Societies*, p. 367; and "Cod-fish and Molasses" ([JB] as an Old Fashioned Republican, Feb. 1794, vol. 11, #1848–1849b, BFP and Clark, *Bradford's Notes*, p. 222). For an article that has been formative of recent thinking on early national regionalism and nationalism, see Drew R. McCoy, "James Madison and Visions of National Identity in the Confederation Period: A Regional Perspective," in *Beyond Confederation: Origins of the Constitution and the Making of National Identity*, ed. Richard R. Beeman et al. (Chapel Hill, 1987), pp. 226–58. Peter S. Onuf has worked wonderfully at the western knot of nation, party, and region (Onuf, "Federalism, Republicanism, and the Origins of American Sectional-

Like the political action that western men like Breckinridge generated, his own personal political ambitions were simultaneously western, national, and partisan. It was a nice convergence, since Breckinridge took up his western pen at a time when the most pressing problems of his new country (Kentucky) were national problems—in the sense that both frontier defense and, above all, free navigation of the Mississippi River involved questions of international relations, the most obvious business of the new national government.[59] And that he was on a national trajectory of ambition was obvious to his Virginia connections: on hearing of his Democratic Society leadership, one archly expressed pleasure that "we might soon promise ourselves the pleasure of seeing you [in Virginia] once more without travelling to Kentucky."[60] When Breckinridge ran for Edwards's Senate seat, his national aspirations were certainly clear to fellow Kentuckians as well.

Breckinridge did not win the Senate seat in 1794, though he was a strong contender while Edwards trailed last.[61] Probably with his national ambitions in mind, he plunged into Kentucky politics, serving in the legislature and as Speaker in 1799. Meanwhile, he would work the western-national-partisan convergence ever more powerfully through the 1790s, culminating in the historical episode known as the "Kentucky Resolutions," in which he was the key Kentucky player. For Breckinridge, that episode functioned precisely as it has sometimes been described—as a prelude to the "Revolution of 1800."[62] As part of that Jeffersonian "revolution," Breckinridge was easily elected as a U.S. senator from Kentucky, and traveled (also easily) back and forth to Washington, D.C., until his early death in 1806.

---

ism," in *All Over the Map: Rethinking American Regions,* ed. Edward L. Ayers et al. [Baltimore, 1996], pp. 27–36; for a more culturally oriented analysis, Waldstreicher, *In the Midst of Perpetual Fetes,* esp. pp. 108–73, 246–93).

[59]Over sixty-five years ago, Arthur Preston Whitaker wrote the best last word on this convergence in a wonderful passage that begins: "The West had its grievances, and resentment was aggravated by the fact that the national government was in Federalist hands while most of the frontiersmen were Republicans. Or perhaps most of the frontiersmen were Republicans because the national government was in Federalist hands" (Whitaker, *The Mississippi Question,* pp. 22–23).

[60]John Nicholas, the Glebe, to JB, July 15, 1794, BFP.

[61]Kentucky's leading Federalist, Humphrey Marshall, captured the Senate seat, an aberration that historians have tried not very certainly to explain. (See, for example, Harrison, *JB,* pp. 63–64.)

[62]Elkins and McKitrick, *Age of Federalism,* p. 721.

The "Practicable Sphere" of a Republic

"We may be wrong, for we are too distant from the grand seat of information," Breckinridge wrote to a Virginia confederate. Encountering such a clause in such a man's papers, one must note the sarcasm, read the distance and isolation rhetorically, and look, always, for the hook. One also must, however, not only see the sentence from which the quotable phrase has been lifted, but also consider what the drafter was up to within a specific political context.[63] But if every contemporary declaration of distance, difficulty, and disaffection must be prodded and probed for its political purpose, how can we ever get any reliable sense of the "practicable sphere" of the "extended republic"?

Luckily, some texts seem more trustworthy than others as guides to the practicable limits of distance and connection. We are fortunate to have a very suggestive one, for example, in a 1794 letter from Englishman Harry Toulmin. Toulmin had arrived in Lexington supremely well connected; he carried letters of introduction from both Jefferson and Madison to the leading men of Kentucky, including Breckinridge. In that way, his migration mirrored that of Breckinridge, who was one of his Kentucky informants. Here is what Toulmin had to say about the practicable sphere of the early republic:

> But why are we to calculate the distance of every place on the continent of America from the town of Philadelphia? It is true, we are seven hundred miles from the people of Philadelphia, but it is only seven hundred miles from men like ourselves. We are as much in the busy scenes of life as the people of Philadelphia are. The settlements of Kentucky are but one hundred miles from the settlements of Virginia and North

---

[63]JB to Gen. Samuel Hopkins, Sept. 15, 1794, copy not in JB's hand, BFP. The complete sentence: "But we may be wrong; for we are too distant from the grand seat of information, and are much too hackneyed in the old-fashioned principles of 1776, to receive much light from the banking, funding & other new fashioned systems & schemes of policy, which are the offspring and ornament of the present system." The political context: JB was excoriating the federal government's past diplomacy and Jay's new mission to Great Britain. What he was up to: JB took the step, most unusual for him, of having a copy of this letter made for himself. It is likely that he wrote it with an eye to publication, perhaps even in pamphlet form, as yet another channel of communication with Congress and the republic at large. For extensive quotation and a face-value analysis of this letter, see E. Merton Coulter, "The Efforts of the Democratic Societies of the West to Open the Navigation of the Mississippi River," *Mississippi Valley Historical Review* 11 (1924):376–89.

> Carolina; and ere long it is probable that the roads from Kentucky to the new Federal City will be no more than four hundred miles. As to intelligence, we have a regular post, which comes and returns once a fortnight, and brings a multitude of newspapers from all parts of the continent. I have had frequent opportunities of observing as great a want of information respecting the public affairs of America and Europe within fifty or a hundred miles of Philadelphia as in Kentucky.[64]

That, in a nutshell, is how a man like Breckinridge must have viewed the distance from Philadelphia. But in the end, it is not the words of texts but rather their voluminous existence that tells the historian what Madison and his political contemporaries took for granted. The newspaper editorials, the remonstrances, the resolutions, and their everyday correspondence chart the practicable sphere of the republic by showing the practice of the men who made it work. Like Breckinridge, these men were far from ordinary citizens. As Madison made clear in *Federalist* No. 14 and as contemporaries perfectly understood, the potential geographical scope of the republic would be measured not by the activities of its ordinary citizens but by the capabilities and willingness of the people's "representatives and agents" to manage the distances. Breckinridge (a self-styled "agent" of the people until he finally became a representative in 1801) and western men like him were the ideal characters to keep the republic (or, soon, the Jeffersonian empire)[65] connected—from the farthest western expanses to the seat of the general government at Philadelphia or Washington, D.C.

---

[64]Harry Toulmin to James Leigh, May 19, 1794, in *The Western Country in 1793: Reports on Kentucky and Virginia,* ed. Marion Tinling and Godfrey Davies (San Marino, Calif., 1948), p. 134. Toulmin, of course, wrote with his own agenda in mind: convinced that Kentucky was an ideal country, he hoped to convince friends (all followers of Joseph Priestly) to join him there.

[65]On this subject, the essential new study is Peter S. Onuf, *Jefferson's Empire: The Language of American Nationhood* (Charlottesville, 2000).

Christine A. Desan

Contesting the Character of the Political Economy in the Early Republic

Rights and Remedies in Chisholm *v.* Georgia

The United States Constitution, as ratified in 1788, contained an odd ambiguity. It did not specify the remedy that an individual could use if a state violated his or her rights.[1] The silence in the Constitution mattered greatly: within a few years of ratification, a contract dispute between the state of Georgia and a man who sold it supplies during the Revolution had created a constitutional crisis. Then, as now, the very definition of a right depended on the kind of remedy used to secure it. If the nature of the remedy was contested, so, too, was the meaning of the right. And if the meaning of a right was contested, so, too, was the shape of popular sovereignty—for rights against the state implicated, at a basic level, the relationship of individuals to the communities they inhabited.

The crisis caused by the Constitution's silence left several land-

I am grateful for the comments and suggestions of David Barron, Ken Bowling, Robert Clark, Jerry Frug, Duncan Kennedy, Donald Kennon, Roy Kreitner, Maeva Marcus, Matt Seccombe, David Shapiro, and Natalie Wexler, and to research support from the American Philosophical Society. This essay is dedicated to the memory of a profound philosopher and planetary man, Wilfrid Desan (1908–2001).

[1]Article III of the Constitution extended "the judicial Power" of the United States to "Controversies . . . between a State and Citizens of another State . . . and between a State, or the Citizens thereof, and foreign States, Citizens, or Subjects." It did not clarify whether federal jurisdiction depended on the existence in state law of a right enforceable in court against the state.

marks, including a famous Supreme Court case, *Chisholm* v. *Georgia,* and the country's first addition to the Constitution after the Bill of Rights: the Eleventh Amendment. Despite the intense attention paid those monuments in the centuries since, two aspects of the constitutional controversy have so far escaped sufficient notice.

First, the question that created contention was not, as later commentators often assumed, whether a remedy should exist for a breach by a state government, but what kind of remedy was appropriate. All agreed that there should be some redress; they disagreed over its nature. The contest posed a judicial against a legislative alternative: should an individual wronged by a state sue the state in a federal court or petition the state's assembly to do justice?[2] Knowledge of the existence and depth of that contest was gradually lost over the course of the nineteenth century as changes in the constitutional structure of society weakened the connection between legislative remedy, economic authority, and political self-determination. Over time, judicial redress alone seemed real and meaningful.

The second neglected aspect of the early crisis over remedies concerns the kind of claim that was at issue. *Contract* was the cause of dispute that broke the surface of popular compliance with state authority again and again. The phenomenon was not accidental. Contract delimited the rights that an individual could claim and the duties that a government had to observe in economic exchange. That was true at the generic level of public finance, where contract as a commitment to pay gave government notes and securities their value, and at the level of individual dealings, where government encountered the many people who had sold to it, worked, or soldiered for it. In their frequency, contract claims against the government overwhelmed other categories of cause urged against it.

Both of these aspects are critical to understanding *Chisholm* v. *Georgia,* the Eleventh Amendment, and the events that produced them. The controversy over contract rights and remedy in the early republic laid bare a society in transition: Americans were moving from a

[2]Suit against a state in its own courts was not a possible remedy; none of the original states had waived their immunity from such suit at the time. See *Chisholm* v. *Georgia,* 2 U.S. (2 Dall.) 419, 434–35 (1793).

constitutional tradition that cast the monetary role of the state as a part of politics to one that articulated it as a concern outside of politics, from a constitutional order that made economic relations with government a matter for legislatures to a constitutional order that made such relations a matter for the judiciary. The transition would eventually reorganize the relationship between politics and the economy, creating a recognizably modern liberal market-based state out of its early American alternative, a set of quasi-populist regimes based on mercantilist precepts that had been adapted for colonial circumstances.[3] It was a dramatic shift, one that affected the way individuals conceived their own agency and their place in the polity. The new model would be based on individual action in a world of separated powers and an independent economy. It replaced one based on a more organic connection, both hierarchically structured and popularly exposed, between people and their political representatives in an order considered to compound the political and the economic.

The transformation from an older form of political economy to a modern, market-based liberalism warrants more attention as a matter of constitutional study than it has received. That is true whether one recognizes only how penetrating was the change and how powerful became the new paradigm, or whether one is also skeptical of the development of liberalism as the foundation for a beneficent constitutional tradition. The turn away from the legislatures to the courts in cases of public contract corresponded to a reconceptualization of economic obligation from a socially relative matter into a matter of individual dealing and choice. Judicial institutionalization of such relations, which represented a reform in many real senses, has at the same time obscured the selective and intensely controversial nature of

---

[3]British officials conceived and, so far as possible, managed the American colonies to fit within the mercantilist organization of empire. See, e.g., John J. McCusker and Russell R. Menard, *The Economy of British America, 1607–1789* (Chapel Hill, 1991), pp. 35–50. My label is meant to flag a further characteristic, however, of colonial political economies. The character of colonial economies at the provincial level was nonliberal, insofar as those regimes clearly placed the monetary system within political control and made it susceptible to popular influence. See, e.g., Richard B. Morris, "Labor and Mercantilism in the Revolutionary Era," in *The Era of the American Revolution,* ed. Richard B. Morris (New York, 1939); Claire Priest, "Currency Policies and Legal Development in Colonial New England," *Yale Law Journal* 110 (2001):101–205. For an account arguing a dilution of mercantilism in practice in Massachusetts, see Stephen Innes, *Creating the Commonwealth: The Economic Culture of Puritan New England* (New York, 1995).

the regime that resulted. We are left with a constitutionalism that notably proclaims its own boundaries. Within that model, the economic realm appears illusively distinct from the political postulates that structured it and continue to sustain it. Granted that the new regime has brought tremendous advantages: it replaced a system of local political economies ill-suited to the transnational arena that Americans entered, and it facilitated great material development, including growth in individual and societal well-being. Liberal constitutionalism also has brought, however, destructive effects with its denial of public obligation as a unique force in regulating matters of economic right.

Legislative remedy remained vital in the new republic because early Americans attributed to their political representatives a very different authority to define the political economy of the state than the one we now assume. In the early part of the eighteenth century, colonial legislators had struggled to take power over revenues away from imperial officials by asserting control of all provincial expenditures.[4] Simultaneously, legislators in several colonies began emitting and managing paper currency, the kind of money predominantly used in everyday life.[5] The authority that legislators claimed over paper money and public spending rested on the responsibility they claimed to make and manage public contracts. *Contract* was the doctrinal device that, by distributing rights and duties to public and private actors alike, underlay most public spending and gave value to paper currency. And, the terms of the public contract were safely within legislative control: representatives had effective power to support paper money and to control government spending because they alone could provide the remedy for contract claims made against the government.

The regime that resulted gave political representatives an enormous amount of power over the course of their communities. That power—which had pried local life loose from imperial authority—came to be identified by many Americans as their source of popular

---

[4]See, e.g., Christine A. Desan, "The Constitutional Commitment to Legislative Adjudication in the Early American Tradition," *Harvard Law Review* 111 (1998):1383–503.

[5]See, e.g., Leslie V. Brock, *The Currency of the American Colonies, 1700–1764* (New York, 1975). Money was often first emitted at the moment that a colonial assembly gained the power to pay off public claims; the new bills of credit functioned as a kind of cash on hand. See, e.g., John Hickcox, *History of the Bills of Credit or Paper Money Issued in New York from 1709 to 1789* (Albany, N.Y., 1866).

sovereignty. Those in the provincial assemblies had succeeded in transferring control over the common resources of the colonies from imperial to American hands. Legislative power then, not executive or judicial, over public debts and financial obligations held the key to government by the people. And so it continued into the new republic: committed by a century of struggle to acquire legislative authority over money, Americans did not quickly surrender that approach.

The ordinary individuals caught in the contract dispute that became *Chisholm* v. *Georgia* put into practice these abstractions about where to find remedy. Again and again, the claimants turned for relief to the legislatures, both state and federal. The legislatures themselves, in their reception and management of claims, confirmed their expansive control over public money. Indeed, the financial and political crisis produced by the Revolutionary War and exacerbated by the uncertain relations between federal and state authorities made many Americans especially sensitive to threats against the old order.

The moment was, however, faced like Janus: the *Chisholm* drama attests not only to the power of the traditional approach but also to the strength of the challenge posed it. That challenge grew out of a new way of conceiving public obligation and latitude in economic relations. Although the process took another century, the courts eventually displaced the political branch as the appropriate forum for contract claims against the state. Abstractions about rights, like abstractions about remedies, depend for their content on institutional practice, and *contract* was not a static category. In the moment at issue here, the notion of public contract was moving from one politically mediated to one judicially defined. That shift underlay, indeed facilitated, the larger shift identified above in the political economy of America from one centered in legislative orchestration, intervention, and regulation to one assumed to be independent of legislative manipulation — from a kind of mercantilism to modern economic liberalism.

The essay invites further inquiry into the nature of the relationship between the political and the economic that existed before the détente they currently enjoy as separate spheres within the liberal order. Exploring the roots of political power in control of the economic, the essay in fact suggests the inherent presence of that relation: the transition toward a more judicialized ethic resulted from a particular political process that redefined the public approach to the economy. The role of the courts today remains dependent on that politically structured equilibrium.

Laid out below is the story of the dispute between Georgia and the man, Robert Farquhar, who sold it war supplies. The narrative begins with the contract that started the controversy and highlights the depth of disagreement over the remedy that resulted. The account then follows the parties to the contract, considering the avenues—both legislative and judicial—they took or resisted. The constitutional regimes mapped by those routes differed dramatically on a number of dimensions, including the way each defined popular sovereignty, another abstraction made real by the practices employed to assert it. Those practices specifically articulated contrasting regimes of power for public authorities, and therefore different approaches to the political economic relations that linked members of the community.

The drama that began in 1777 finally ended more than a century later. Tracing very briefly its denouement in the nineteenth century serves to indicate the direction of change that took place in the American system. In closing, the essay suggests that recent scholarly approaches to the *Chisholm* controversy define rights, remedies, and popular sovereignty in ways that assume—largely without articulation or attention—a particular relationship between the political and the economic. That relationship is, however, itself the product of a constitutional transformation over the past two centuries. We should consider, rather than assume, the character and content of that change in order to understand liberalism and its limits.

The Chisholm Claim and the Contest over Remedies

In the fall of 1777, a South Carolina citizen, the merchant Robert Farquhar, agreed to sell the state of Georgia supplies for the use of its militia. According to an official account produced years afterward, the army, then quartered near Savannah, was in a state of "great destitution."[6] As the son of one of the executive officials who authorized

[6]Memorial of William M. Varnum, Agent of the State of Georgia to U.S. Senate, March 8, 1858, Record Group 46, Senate 36A-H17, National Archives and Records Administration (NARA). As an earlier legislative report puts it, "It was in the day of need and sore distress that the State contracted with Robert Farquhar. By the

the contract with Farquhar later testified, "[his] father [often] mention[ed] the purchase of a cargo of goods from Captain Farquhar for the use of the State during the Revolutionary War. He always alluded to the transaction as one of the most fortunate incidents of the times, and to the end of his life regarded it as the principal means by which this State was enabled to perform a part worthy of the great cause of the Revolution."[7]

The state agreed to pay Farquhar £63,605 in South Carolina currency or approximately $39,141 "in Continental money."[8] Thomas Stone and Edward Davis of Savannah were expressly authorized as "Commissioners" to make the deal and to draw on the state treasury for the requisite amount.[9] Farquhar supplied the state militia with a great quantity of dry goods, including "26 great coats, @ £30 each, 47 jackets, @ £28 each, 21 lbs. fine thread, @ 35s. per oz," and "379 blankets, @ £30 each."[10] He delivered the goods before December 1, 1777, fully performing his part of the contract.[11] Stone and Davis did not reciprocate, however, ushering in a century (or more accurately two centuries) of controversy over the case.

A special state commission that struggled to reconstruct the facts of the claim some sixty years later could not ascertain what steps Farquhar initially took to demand payment for his claim. "It must, indeed,

---

reasonable aid obtained from him, her men were clothed and her soldiers armed for the battle of freedom" (Report of Joint Select Committee, Georgia Legislature, Nov. 29, 1838, reprinted in U.S. House of Representatives, *Money Due the State of Georgia*, 46th Cong., 2d sess., 1880, H. Rep. 115, pp. 19–21).

[7]Affidavit from Tomlinson Fort to Ambrose Baber, Nov. 26, 1838, reprinted in U.S. House, *Money Due the State of Georgia,* p. 10. Arthur Fort, a member of the Georgia council, was present with the governor when the contract was authorized. See Minutes of Executive Department, Oct. 31, 1777, reprinted in U.S. House, *Money Due the State of Georgia,* p. 4.

[8]The executive document authorizing the contract with Farquhar carefully set out a conversion scale. Account of Robert Farquhar, see Minutes of Executive Department, Oct. 31, 1777, reprinted in U.S. House, *Money Due the State of Georgia,* p. 4.

[9]Minutes of Executive Department, Oct. 31, 1777, and Report of Committee, Georgia House, Nov. 25, 1789, reprinted in U.S. House, *Money Due the State of Georgia,* pp. 4, 5.

[10]The supplies also included cloth, coarse thread, sewing silk, handkerchiefs, linen, and other goods. Account of Robert Farquhar, as sworn by Colin Cambell and Lawrence Campbell, Feb. 10, 1794, reprinted in U.S. House, *Money Due the State of Georgia,* p. 4.

[11]Report of Committee, Georgia House, Nov. 25, 1789, reprinted in U.S. House, *Money Due the State of Georgia,* p. 5.

be acknowledged as strange," the commission reported, "that no demand should have been made upon the State (and no evidence can be found that any was made), from 1777, the date of the delivery of the goods, till 1789," when Alexander Chisholm, one of Farquhar's executors, presented his petition to the legislature.[12] "It may perhaps, be accounted for in the state of things then existing in the country," the commission concluded, "and in the death of Farquhar which intervened."[13]

It is not clear whether Farquhar filed any petitions with the legislature, as the special commission evidently expected, or whether he worked purely through less formal channels. Nor is it clear what happened to the Continental Loan Office certificates that the state apparently did issue to Stone and Davis in order to pay for the supplies.[14] On the latter point, Thomas Stone swore, after the death of his co-commissioner, Davis, that Davis alone had received the certificates.[15] In any case, no certificates reached Farquhar, whose misfortunes only deepened during the attempts he did make to collect. According to his future son-in-law, Peter Trezevant, "in the Year One Thousand Seven Hundred and Eighty Four, the said Robert Farquhar was lost at sea going from Charleston to Savannah in order to endeavor to get payment of this debt."[16] Farquhar's death left his only child, Elizabeth,

[12]Report of Special Commissioners, Nov. 6, 1839, reprinted in U.S. House, *Money Due the State of Georgia,* p. 12.

[13]Ibid.

[14]See Report of Committee, Georgia House, Nov. 25, 1789, reprinted in U.S. House, *Money Due the State of Georgia,* p. 5. Loan office certificates were interest-bearing preferred securities issued by the Continental government. Those issued before March 1778 were especially valuable because they bore interest payable in bills of exchange drawn on France, a specie-equivalent commitment of paper. Designed to be used for procuring specie, they were increasingly given out as payment for supplies. See E. James Ferguson, "State Assumption of the Federal Debt during the Confederation," *Mississippi Valley Historical Review* 38 (1951):403, 411. Their use in 1777 is, however, early and somewhat surprising. See note 28 below.

[15]Some legislators in the Georgia House agreed soon after that it was "notorious that Edward Davis did receive a very considerable sum in loan office certificates of the United States for the payment of said goods" (Motion, Georgia House, Dec. 6, 1794, reprinted in U.S. House, *Money Due the State of Georgia,* p. 7).

[16]Peter Trezevant, petition to Congress, Feb. 8, 1794, in Maeva Marcus et al., eds., *Documentary History of the Supreme Court of the United States, 1789–1800,* 6 vols. to date (New York, 1985–), 5:261, hereafter *DHSC.* According to the *South Carolina Weekly Gazette,* Jan. 30, 1784, as quoted in A. S. Salley, Jr., "Daniel Trezevant, Huguenot,

orphaned and dependent on the efforts of executor Alexander Chisholm to get satisfaction from the state of Georgia.

For James Wilson, who encountered the case in 1793 as an associate justice of the Supreme Court, the route that Chisholm could take to attain redress was relatively straightforward. It was an ordinary contract, and when a state made such an "engagement," it could be sued in court just as an individual could be sued:

> If justice is not done; if engagements are not fulfilled; is it upon general principles of right, less proper, in the case of a great number, than in the case of an individual, to secure, by compulsion, that, which will not be voluntarily performed? Less proper it surely cannot be. The only reason, I believe, why a free man is bound by human laws, is, *that he binds himself.* Upon the same principles, upon which he becomes bound *by the laws,* he becomes amenable to the *Courts of Justice,* which are formed and authorised by those laws. If one free man, an original sovereign, may do all this; why may not an aggregate of free men, a collection of original sovereigns, do this likewise? If the dignity of each *singly* is undiminished; the dignity of all *jointly* must be unimpaired.

As Wilson concluded, a state, "like a merchant," could make a contract; a "dishonest state," "like a dishonest merchant," could refuse to discharge it. A state at that point could not "be permitted, proteus-like, to assume a new appearance," able to "insult [its creditor] and justice," claiming immunity from suit "by declaring *I am a sovereign State[.]*" Just as a man, a state was "amenable to a Court of Justice," just as a man, it was subject to "general principles of right."[17]

Wilson's logic seemed to later commentators virtually unimpeachable—the individual was, after all, the basis of government and the source of sovereignty itself. The state was merely an aggregation of such men, a derivative sovereignty. It was, therefore, clearly amenable to law. And the law was, just as clearly, the product of the courts.[18] Finally, market transactions were matters of private right; just as the

---

and Some of His Descendants," *South Carolina Historical and Genealogical Magazine* 3 (1902):39 n. rrr: "A few days ago Mr. Robert Farquhar, of this City on his passage from hence to Georgia, was knocked overboard by the boom of the vessel, and unfortunately drowned, notwithstanding every possible assistance was given. His body was carried to Savannah, and decently interred."

[17] *Chisholm,* 2 U.S. 456 (italics and punctuation as in original).

[18] See, e.g., Akil R. Amar, "Of Sovereignty and Federalism," *Yale Law Journal* 96 (1987):1425–520.

common law courts resolved disputes between individuals over economic matters, so also should they resolve disputes between individuals and the public.

The drama of the early republic was the vehemence, the conviction, of the contrary view. James Iredell, Wilson's colleague on the bench, expressed his disagreement in tones more sober, and perhaps for that reason more striking, than many louder men. After an opinion carefully restricted to statutory interpretation,[19] he broached the constitutional question with very few words. "So much, however, has been said on the Constitution," he wrote, "that it may not be improper to intimate that my present opinion is strongly against any construction of it, which will admit, under any circumstances, a compulsive suit against a state for recovery of money." "I pray to God," he continued, "that if [the contrary view argued by the attorney general of the United States] be established by the judgment of this Court, all the good he predicts from it may take place, and none of the evils with which, I have the concern to say, it appears to me to be pregnant."[20]

Others made very clear what they believed were the evils that threatened. The alarm went to the very core of politics as it had been practiced. As one writer in Massachusetts put it, "Legislators! . . . If you acquiesce [by allowing suits against the state], you will seal your own *extinction,* as a legislative body—and become merely a Court of Sessions of a county, and a body of Electors of the Senators of the Union. . . . your acts [will be] those of an unimportant subordinate corporation."[21] The governor of Georgia made his northern neighbor seem circumspect. "Were [such a suit in court against Georgia allowed]," he warned the legislature, "an annihilation of her political existence must follow."[22]

Wilson's view would come to prevail by the end of the nineteenth century; its structure of supporting assumptions about institutional roles and the meaning of abstractions is therefore more evidently coherent to us than the alternative. That alternative, now a more obscure

[19]John V. Orth, "The Truth About Justice Iredell's Dissent in *Chisholm* v. *Georgia* (1793)," *North Carolina Law Review* 73 (1994):255–70.

[20]*Chisholm,* 2 U.S. 449, 450.

[21]"Brutus," *Independent Chronicle,* July 18, 1793, *DHSC,* 5:392.

[22]Extracts from the Message of Gov. Edward Telfair, *Augusta Chronicle and Gazette of the State,* Nov. 9, 1793, in Herman V. Ames, ed., *State Documents on Federal Relations: The States and the United States* (Philadelphia, 1906), p. 9.

approach, and the logic that once animated it, is illuminated by the practices of the people around Robert Farquhar.

The Regime of Legislative Remedy

Robert Farquhar's claim against the state of Georgia was first and repeatedly pressed in the Georgia legislature, was settled in the state legislature, and was considered in the federal Congress—all in the 1780s and 1790s—because Farquhar's heir petitioned those forums to get his money. Recourse to the legislature was not, however, the sole prerogative of individuals: representatives of the state of Georgia sought indemnification from Congress in 1795 after the state had settled the claim with the heir. And it is worth noting, if only to understand their behavior, that none of these claimants was weak at heart. The Chisholm claim was revived by petition in the state legislature in the 1830s and 1840s where payment, long due on the settlement, was finally obtained. Only after that point did the regime of legislative recourse clearly erode. In the following decades, federal and state governments negotiated their own adjustment of the claim. Their use of venues both legislative and judicial choreographed a slow passage of change, arriving ultimately at a new era of remedy—recourse to the courts—in a modern liberal order.

When Alexander Chisholm acquired the problem of Robert Farquhar's outstanding claim on the state of Georgia, then, he did what any responsible executor at the time would have done: He petitioned the state legislature for the money due. According to Elizabeth Farquhar's husband, Chisholm filed his first petition in 1787. He received no response during that session of the legislature.[23] Chisholm either filed a new petition in 1789 or pressed for an answer to his earlier submission. Persistence, it seems, was the key to bring to conclusion the mysterious workings of a state legislature. Peter Trezevant, who married Elizabeth Farquhar on September 13, 1789, quickly assumed responsibility for this role. As he later put the matter: "[I] was per-

[23]See Peter Trezevant, petition to Congress, Feb. 8, 1794, *DHSC,* 5:260, for reference to a Chisholm petition filed in 1787. I have been unable to confirm through any other source that Chisholm petitioned the state legislature in 1787.

sonally engaged from one thousand seven hundred and eighty-nine to one thousand seven hundred and ninety-four in the prosecution of [Captain Farquhar's] claims, and attended every meeting of the legislative body of the said State, till [I] received [in settlement] the audited certificates now in [my] possession."[24] Trezevant's tenacity in this instance was apparently characteristic; it is likely his determination that drove the claim bearing Alexander Chisholm's name to such notoriety.

A broker or bank clerk of modest fortunes,[25] Peter Trezevant apparently entered the case unwittingly. "Prior to his marriage," he later recalled, "he knew nothing of Captain Farquhar's claims on the State of Georgia."[26] If so, he became the innocent victim as well as the central figure in a half century of petitioning. He quickly "took the management of the business of the recovery of [Captain Farquhar's] claims into his own hands, under a power of attorney from Mr. Chisholm, the executor," and personally presented the series of petitions made to the state legislature in the following decade.[27]

Trezevant received his first response from the state legislature—a sharp rebuff from the House committee on petitions—in late November 1789. The committee did not indicate that Trezevant's application to a legislative forum was in any way odd; to the contrary, it acted on the merits of the case. The committee reviewed the details of Farquhar's contract with the state, carefully recording the rather intricate authorization that the governor and his council had given Stone and Davis.[28] The committee agreed that the goods had been received,

---

[24]Peter Trezevant, affidavit, June 15, 1840, reprinted in U.S. House, *Money Due the State of Georgia,* p. 22.

[25]Salley, "*Daniel Trezevant,*" p. 38.

[26]Peter Trezevant, affidavit, June 15, 1840, reprinted in U.S. House, *Money Due the State of Georgia,* p. 22.

[27]Ibid.

[28]According to the report: "It appears by a resolution of the honorable, the executive, dated the 31st day of October, 1777, that the said Thomas Stone, and Edward Davis, were empowered to purchase from Captain Farquhar, a quantity of goods, and that they were authorized to pay in Continental money, on or before the 1st day of December following; and if the same should not arrive by that time, they were authorized to pay for said goods in indigo, at the Carolina prices, and that they were empowered to draw on the treasury for a sum sufficient to discharge the same" (Report of Committee, Georgia House, Nov. 25, 1789, U.S. House, *Money Due the State of Georgia,* p. 5).

although noting that "how they were applied," it could not "from the distance of time that has intervened . . . receive [any] information."[29]

What set the Farquhar claim apart from others that were acknowledged and ordered paid by the legislature was a circumstance that, according to the House committee, exonerated the state from further liability. The "honorable executive" had, in fact, issued Continental Loan Office certificates to the state commissioners "for the special and particular purpose of discharging the said Farquhar's demand."[30] Admittedly, the commissioners, Stone and Davis, had failed to pass on the money. For that, however, concluded the committee, Georgia "is by no means accountable."[31] Farquhar's executors were on their own in trying to get their money; the committee suggested that they go to court against Stone and Davis.[32] The House accepted the committee's report,[33] and on December 12, 1789, the state Senate agreed to reject Trezevant's petition.[34]

Several aspects of the episode are clear on the basis of the scant record, even two centuries later. One is that the 1789 state legislature made a mistake when it concluded that the state was no longer responsible for the Farquhar debt. Admittedly, one could argue as a matter of logic that when the state paid the commissioners, it had dispatched its duty in the case; that position did not mesh, however, with long-established practice. More speculatively, perhaps, there were other circumstances—collusion in the disappearance of the funds, delinquency in the attempt to collect, or as later representatives implied, private dealing by Davis—that colored the case. But according to the consensus of state legislators who subsequently reviewed the claim, their predecessors' conclusion was wrong: the state could not dis-

[29]Ibid.

[30]Ibid.

[31]Ibid.

[32]Ibid. Five years later, a group of legislators elaborated on the reasoning of the 1789 committee, suggesting that Davis had acted in a private capacity in his dealings with Farquhar or, perhaps, for the United States. See Motion to amend resolution, Georgia House, Dec. 6, 1794, reprinted in U.S. House, *Money Due the State of Georgia,* pp. 7–8; see also Letter from Commissioners to Attorney General of Georgia, Nov. 6, 1839, ibid., pp. 12–13 (reviewing theories under which state could escape liability).

[33]Committee Report agreed to by Georgia House of Representatives, Nov. 25, 1789, reprinted in U.S. House, *Money Due the State of Georgia,* p. 5.

[34]Senate Proceedings, Dec. 12, 1789, Journal of Georgia State Senate.

charge a public debt simply by releasing the appropriate funds to its own officials. Additionally, no circumstances impugned Farquhar or suggested that Davis had not acted for the state. Standard agency law dictated that a principal remained liable for obligations still owed because of the misfeasance by its agents. That doctrine applied to governments as well, declared later generations of Georgia legislative committee reports.[35] Like the fact that the legislature had made a mistake, a second aspect of the episode is clear: the mistake was theirs to make. As the many generations of legislative reports also indicate, the body that had generally ensured that the state fulfilled its obligations under a contract was the legislature.

Settlement and Strategies of Self-Government

The legislature's authority over contract claims drew heavily on the American experience of self-government from the earliest days of settlement. That experience identified local or provincial authority with collective political control over the common wealth of members. In particular, legislative control over public money and finance—"the power of the purse"—was indispensable to the growth of American political power. Provincial elites moved early to take control of public spending. At the same time, in many colonies, they created and supported the paper currency that largely supplied the money for their economies. Both strategies depended on legislative control of public contract. Together, they combined to produce provincial political authority that subverted imperial control.

The political chronology of the movement to gain control of public money is recounted in the classic institutional histories of the colonial era.[36] Those histories document how legislatures up and down the continent gained control over an increasing number of provincial

---

[35]See, e.g., Report of Committee, Dec. 11, 1793, reprinted in U.S. House, *Money Due the State of Georgia,* pp. 5–6. Joint Resolution, Georgia legislature, Dec. 13, 1793, ibid., p. 6. Report of Special Commissioners, Nov. 6, 1839, ibid., pp. 12–13; see also David E. Engdahl, "Immunity and Accountability for Positive Governmental Wrongs," *University of Colorado Law Review* 44 (1972):15–16.

[36]See, e.g., Jack P. Greene, *The Quest for Power: The Lower Houses of Assembly in the Southern Royal Colonies, 1689–1776* (Chapel Hill, 1963); Herbert L. Osgood, *The American Colonies in the Eighteenth Century,* 4 vols. (New York, 1924–25); Evarts B. Greene, *The Provincial Governor in the English Colonies of North America* (Cambridge, Mass., 1898), pp. 12–22.

funds and then used their control as leverage to pry other rights and powers from imperial officials. Part of the story is familiar: American assemblies early and successfully claimed the authority to levy taxes. Because royal officials depended on provincial tax revenues to pay for everything, from their own salaries to frontier defenses, colonial legislators could negotiate the terms upon which they would grant the levies. American assemblies withheld permission to levy taxes until they received the concessions they sought from imperial officials. A complementary piece of the American strategy is less well known. If the legislatures had the authority to collect public money, they also needed the authority to control that money once they got it. The pledges of imperial officials were only so useful. Instead, provincial representatives maneuvered to add the authority to control public expenditures to their authority to tax.

In particular, legislators in most colonies over the course of the eighteenth century asserted the right, nominally justified as one of overseeing the spending practices of imperial actors, to approve every grant of money made from the provincial treasuries. In practice, the assemblies assumed jurisdiction over claims against the government, including legal claims—those of contract, taking, and compensation for service.[37] In other words, the legislatures became sites for determining claims of individual right against the government.

Their procedures evolved correspondingly. To resolve cases, legislatures set up select or standing committees that dealt with claims and similar petitions, like the committee on petitions established by the Georgia House.[38] Claimants generally submitted their accounts or requests for payment by petition to the elected branch of their assemblies. That phenomenon, which drew on English models, helps explain why petitioning figured so prominently as an institutional channel between citizens and their governments during the eigh-

---

[37]For a case study of the development of legislative adjudication in colonial New York, see Christine A. Desan, "Remaking Constitutional Tradition on the Margin of the Empire: The Creation of Legislative Adjudication in Colonial New York," *Law and History Review* 16 (1998):257–317.

[38]See generally Ralph V. Harlow, *The History of Legislative Methods in the Period before 1825* (New Haven, 1917), pp. 8 (North Carolina), 11 (Virginia), 20 (Massachusetts), 21 (New Hampshire). Assumedly, most claimants were paid by administrative or legislative agents, leaving only contested cases to come to the legislatures.

teenth century.[39] The petitions were often thus private, not public, and they were routinely granted, not disputed.[40] The accountability of the legislature to individual claimants likely rested on conditions that ranged from the franchise to, perhaps more importantly, the capacity of claimants to disrupt or otherwise undermine the fragile governments of their day.[41] By the end of the colonial era, most Americans apparently assumed routinely, like Alexander Chisholm, that they should petition their legislatures, rather than sue in the courts, for money due them by the government.[42]

But the reorganization of economic life effectuated by the colonial assemblies extended far beyond individualized dealing with the government. Legislatures in a number of colonies created paper money to pay the public claims they now controlled. The currency responded to a powerful popular need: gold and silver (specie) were generally scarce on the continent—Americans typically had an unfavorable balance of trade with England, and their hard money went to pay for imports from the mother country.[43] Paper money filled the void left by the outflow of gold and silver specie; it supplied a transferable medium of exchange. Not coincidentally, it alone made many public

---

[39]See, e.g., Greene, *Quest for Power,* pp. 51–71; S. M. Pargellis, "The Procedure of the Virginia House of Burgessess," *William and Mary Quarterly Historical Magazine,* 2d ser. 7 (1927):73–86, 143–57; *cf.* Edmund S. Morgan, *Inventing the People: The Rise of Popular Sovereignty in England and America* (New York, 1988), pp. 223–33.

[40]Greene, *Quest for Power,* pp. 51–71; Pargellis, *House of Burgesses,* pp. 142–46; Raymond C. Bailey, *Popular Influence on Public Policy: Petitioning in Eighteenth Century Virginia* (Westport, Conn., 1979), pp. 129–30.

[41]See Desan, "Constitutional Commitment to Legislative Adjudication," pp. 1481–94.

[42]As originally understood, the "right to petition" was thus a guarantee that protected private as much as public or political rights. The most significant debate in the First Federal Congress over the right to petition arose when Quaker abolitionists attempted to petition for an end to slavery. Southern representatives argued that Quakers had no *right* to petition on matters in which they were not personally interested. See *Documentary History of the First Federal Congress, 1789–1791,* 14 vols. to date (1978–), vols. 12 and 13 (Helen E. Veit, Charlene Bangs Bickford, Kenneth R. Bowling, and William C. diGiacomantonio, eds.) entries for Jan. 6–Aug. 12, 1790, esp. Feb. 11 and 12, 1790, hereafter *DHFFC.* The southerners were rather sharply understating the scope of the petition right; the point here is simply that they could even make such an assertion.

[43]See, e.g., Brock, *Currency of the American Colonies,* pp. 4–7; Curtis P. Nettels, *The Money Supply of the American Colonies before 1720* (1934; reprint ed., New York, 1964), pp. 59, 68–69.

expenditures possible, especially during wartime. The colonial governments themselves had limited specie available. By contrast, armed with a printing press and a promise to tax in the paper currency they created, they could issue as much money as they could credibly circulate and support in a provincial economy.

In a variety of ways, the advent of paper money further expanded the economic authority of the American assemblies. Most obviously, it allowed them to increase public spending. In turn, the money launched through government expenditures entered, indeed pervaded, the world of private exchange, as those who took paper notes from the colony passed them on as currency.[44] Money returned to the government in the form of taxes; the levies imposed by assemblies generally could be satisfied in paper. Indeed, the paper had value because it could be used to pay taxes, fines, and other fees. In effect, the American legislatures ran a kind of supplemental, quasi-independent cash economy for their provinces. Their power penetrated that economy: both public creditors who were paid in notes and private individuals who took the notes afterward as tender depended on the legislatures to maintain the value of the currency and the economic system built upon it.[45]

The responsibility of the legislatures was mediated through, or defined by reference to, contract. Specifically, the governments' responsibility to satisfy individual claims for money and to support the value of paper money—that is, the duty of the assemblies at both the level of individual dealings and the level of public finance—depended on a commitment to pay (or to do its equivalent, by accepting outstanding notes for value); that commitment was articulated as a contractual obligation that was the legislatures' to fulfill. In the case of individual claims, legislators imported the vocabulary of legal duty and debt, one inherited from English ministerial, parliamentary, and judicial sources. Just as those decision makers had molded their approach to contract in manners specific to their institutional locations, so, too, did

---

[44]See, e.g., John J. McCusker, "Colonial Paper Money," in *Studies on Money in Early America,* ed. Eric P. Newman and Richard G. Doty (New York, 1976), pp. 97–100.

[45]See, e.g., Priest, "Currency Policies," pp. 150–57.

provincial representatives. In particular, the representatives shaped their responses to claimants in ways injected with their political capacity, including the ability to redefine categories of entitlement, to delay payment in order to pressure imperial officials, to extend remedies to late but deserving applicants, and to intervene in other manners we know little about.

Legislative obligation was again elaborated through the rubric of contract in the case of public finance. Paper currency itself was a kind of promissory note: It had value because of the government's agreement to receive the note for a public payment due. That agreement, which contemporaries expressed as a *contract,* had to be maintained despite the fluctuating social circumstances of colonial life. Economically literate Americans believed in a quantity theory of money, according to which a community required a certain amount of currency to serve as a means of economic exchange: too little hampered exchange and too much depreciated. That is, society required the right volume of money to support trade and production; at such a level, the value of the currency would remain stable, while an oversupply would cause the notes to lose value and prices to rise.[46] Unlike their monetarist successors, many of these thinkers, as well as the bulk of American legislators, concluded that political actors—legislators—bore the responsibility of modulating the money supply. Indeed, a political commitment to maintain the value of money alone could protect the public contract it represented.[47]

The political role in this system was a complicated one in which judicial interference was, for practical purposes, inconceivable. Modulating the money supply required that assemblies take stock of their

---

[46]See, e.g., Benjamin Franklin, "Of the Paper Money of the United States of America" (1784), in *The Writings of Benjamin Franklin,* 10 vols., ed. Albert Henry Smyth (New York, 1905–7), 9:232; John Adams to the Comte de Vergennes, June 22, 1780, in *The Revolutionary Diplomatic Correspondence of the United States,* 6 vols., ed. Francis Wharton (Washington, D.C., 1889), 3:809–16.

[47]Not all advocates of publicly issued money agreed that the legislatures should determine the amount supplied. See, e.g., John Webbe, *A Discourse Concerning Paper Money* (Philadelphia, [1742 or 1743]), pp. 8–10, who suggested a loan scheme intended to link the amount of money in circulation to the amount desired by landowners, whom Webbe took to reflect more accurately than merchants the pace of economic activity in a community.

communities and, as necessary to maintain stable values of money, issue more currency or, less frequently, hasten the retiring of excess currency. That task could conflict with the nominal commitments, made at the time of issuing paper notes, to draw in money at a preordained rate. But the task became even more intricate. Legislators considered it legitimate, given their responsibilities to the larger society, to add to currency supplies at times to stimulate an economic recovery—another act that could be claimed to violate the rights of those holding existing notes. American populations themselves had power to influence the amount of currency in circulation. Most notably, they could refuse to pay taxes or to comply with price regulations.[48] Finally, exigencies like war brought spending demands that upset the stability of currencies. Those phenomena could dramatically affect the circumstances in which governments and individuals exchanged money.[49]

In such conditions, Americans experienced the management of their paper economies to be an urgent and constant political task, one that centrally concerned legislators, not courts, as the communities' representatives. The contract underlying paper money, in particular, represented the relationship between the public and its members, a pact that rested on a commitment by all parties in "public faith" to maintain the value of money in changing situations. The approach to paper economies that the Americans developed, one that included periods of depreciation, episodes of official devaluation, price and wage controls, revisions in the periods during which paper money was valid or due for retirement, and the constant adjustment of the money supply through other means encompassed to a significant degree the challenges of their circumstances. The system was fraught with risk, including imperial interference, political ineptitude or corruption, and exposure to popular pressure—but in a majority of colonies it met the needs of the community.[50]

---

[48]Roger H. Brown, *Redeeming the Republic: Federalists, Taxation, and the Origins of the Constitution* (Baltimore, 1993); Morris, "Labor and Mercantilism," pp. 103–10.

[49]See, e.g., Morris, "Labor and Mercantilism," pp. 92–139.

[50]See, e.g., Brock, *Currency of the American Colonies,* pp. 20, 73–74 (New York), 77–78, 82–84 (Pennsylvania), 93–95 (New Jersey), 96–99 (Delaware), 104–6 (Maryland),

Revolution and Continuity

The power of the legislatures informed the Revolutionary conflict and remained central throughout it. The decade that followed the Revolutionary War brought both challenge and adamant adherence to the model of legislative centrality that Americans had earlier established in their approach to sovereignty.

The Revolutionary War flowed, in part, from the expansion of political economic power that the American legislatures had achieved. Threats to their control of financial revenues and to their ability to support provincial paper economies catalyzed the discord that became rebellion.[51] Financing that revolt in turn confirmed the Americans' dependence on the financial systems they had developed in the colonial period. Absent either hard money or sufficient foreign loans, Americans fell back on paper money: the Continental Congress and every American state financed its Revolutionary War activity largely through printed currency. The money was paid out to participants who would, in the future, become individual claimants on the public fisc. In the end, the debts left behind were huge—the national government alone had issued some $226 million in Continental currency (approximately $45.5 million specie value) and perhaps an equal amount of noninterest bearing certificates that eventually ceased circulating because of depreciation. Remaining federal obligations to creditors were estimated after final settlement to reach approximately $42.5 million specie value.[52]

Management of those obligations formed the very core of political life throughout the war and the decade afterward. E. James Ferguson has demonstrated, with particular power, how the controversy over

---

129 (reviewing performance of middle colonies); E. James Ferguson, *Power of the Purse: A History of American Public Finance, 1776–1790* (Chapel Hill, 1961), pp. 8–24; Richard Lester, "Currency Issues to Overcome Depression," *Journal of Political Economy* 46 (1938):324–25; James R. Morrill, *The Practice and Politics of Fiat Finance: North Carolina in the Confederation, 1783–1789* (Chapel Hill, 1969).

[51]Edmund S. Morgan and Helen M. Morgan, *The Stamp Act Crisis: Prologue to Revolution* (Chapel Hill, 1995); Greene, *Quest for Power;* Joseph Ernst and Marc Egnal, "An Economic Interpretation of the American Revolution," *William and Mary Quarterly,* 3d ser. 29 (1972):3–32.

[52]Ferguson, *Power of the Purse,* pp. 30, 43, 63, 341.

funding the war monopolized American attention during the conflict and permeated society in the following years.[53] Contention focused on how to support the value of money during the war and how to pay off the obligations that remained afterward.

In each of its aspects, the debate implicated the power of the American legislatures as representatives of the larger community. Although Americans took an almost infinite variety of positions on the financial crisis generated by the war, the poles of the conflict were relatively clear. On one hand, some Americans favored expansive legislative management of the Revolutionary economy and the debt it generated. This group, which dominated the Continental Congress during the first half of the war, readily employed paper money as an instrument of public finance and to some extent identified economic behavior with Revolutionary commitment: complying with currency supports and price supports was a matter of patriotism.[54] These Americans recognized the cruelties of currency depreciation but emphasized its advantages in sinking public debts. And they articulated the payment of remaining debts as a complex matter requiring the calibration of diverse needs: creditors could be paid in the manner, at the time, and in the currency—land, paper, tax relief—that satisfied claims understood in a social context in which demands from many others who had contributed to the war effort also required attention.[55] Each of these commitments directly affected the practical circumstances of economic life, including the distribution of public resources and the behavior of private parties.

Others preferred legislative action disciplined along new lines. This group, more deeply steeped in the approach to public finance that the

---

[53]Ibid.

[54]For examples of the way Congress articulated the economic demands of the war, see, e.g., "To the Inhabitants of the United States of America" and "A Circular Letter from the Congress of the United States to their Constituents," Sept. 13, 1779, *DHFFC*, vol. 5 (Charlene Bangs Bickford and Helen E. Veit, eds.), pp. 824–39. See generally, Ferguson, *Power of the Purse*, pp. 8–26, 109–13; Morris, "Labor and Mercantilism," pp. 92–118. Some scholars do not consider the power shift in Congress to have been so sharp. See, e.g., Jack Rakove, *The Beginnings of National Politics* (New York, 1979).

[55]For suggestive material, see Morrill, *Practice and Politics of Fiat Finance*, pp. 15–99; Ferguson, *Power of the Purse*, pp. 68, 221–50; E. James Ferguson, "Currency Finance, An Interpretation of Colonial Monetary Policies," *William and Mary Quarterly*, 3d ser. 10 (1953):153–80.

English had developed over the course of the eighteenth century, denounced paper money as an evil, although one that had been minimally necessary during the war. Supporters of this view advocated the use of gold and silver as money that would have value impervious to political manipulation; additional funds could be generated by issuing securities that represented interest-bearing loans. For these Americans, who dominated the management of Revolutionary finances during the war's latter years, the war debt had to be repaid in hard money and punctually serviced with interest until that was accomplished. Absent public emergencies, contract claims were matters of individual right independently understood, not matters of individual right relative to other social demands.[56]

The debate between those committed to traditional currency and those attracted to the English model brought challenges to the old system. Perhaps most importantly, the Constitution of 1787 limited Americans to using only silver and gold as legal tender and prohibited the states from emitting paper currency.[57] The changes represented a clear victory for those advocating specie-based finance, gained at a moment when the tumults of the paper system seemed to them particularly threatening and the advantages of the alternative particularly powerful. Indeed, the shift constituted the beginning of a substantially new approach to the monetary system and to matters of the market, one in which the power of the legislatures would be radically reduced. In many ways, Peter Trezevant and Alexander Chisholm's efforts to attain a remedy from the state of Georgia would experiment with the logic of the new approach.

But that approach would take years to establish itself. Until then, the traditional powers of the political assemblies remained apparently intact; despite their differences, most Americans assumed that their legislatures continued to hold critical power over the political economy. Thus, a population famously concerned with curbing legislative abuses

---

[56]For contemporary expositions, see Robert Morris, Report on the Public Debt, July 29, 1782, Worthington C. Ford, ed., *Journals of the Continental Congress,* 34 vols. (Washington, D.C., 1904–37), 22:429–45, hereafter *JCC;* Alexander Hamilton, Report of the Secretary of the Treasury on the Public Credit, Jan. 14, 1790, *DHFFC,* 5:743–77; Ferguson, *Power of the Purse,* pp. 109–24, 292–96.

[57]See Art. I, sec. 10. A paper currency note was a *bill of credit* in the legal terminology of the time.

took no action to relocate either the legislatures' core power over levying taxes or their ultimate authority to approve all government expenditures; it was evidently unimaginable to limit so soon after the Revolutionary War the powers that had made the break with Britain necessary.

Likewise, state legislatures throughout the Confederation and into the new republic continued to manage the sinking of the Revolutionary debt, using methods, including official devaluations and payment in paper or confiscated property, that were inherited from paper currency days.[58]

Americans continued the routines of interaction that had long connected them to political assemblies endowed with such powers. During the 1780s and 1790s, claimants still assumed that they should petition their legislatures, not sue in the courts, to get money owed them by the government. Thus, committees on petitions and accounts like that of Georgia's legislature operated in other states.[59] Several court cases from the period suggest that institutional understandings like that of the earlier eighteenth century prevailed; movement to experiment with the delegation of claims to the courts was limited.[60] Petitioning continued in the Confederation Congress, which, given its restricted powers, referred many petitions to state legislatures for action.[61]

---

[58]For the articulation of legislative power to tax and spend at the federal level, see U.S. Constitution, Art. I, sec. 7, 8, cl. 1; sec. 9, cl. 7. For the activity of state legislatures, see, e.g., Lemuel Molovinsky, "Pennsylvania's Legislative Efforts to Finance the War for Independence: A Study of the Continuity of Colonial Finance," Ph.D. diss., Temple University, 1975; Morrill, *Practice and Politics of Fiat Finance;* Ferguson, "State Assumption of the Federal Debt," p. 408.

[59]Research about the daily pattern of legislative work in the 1780s and 1790s remains necessary to confirm their load and management of claims. See, e.g., Harlow, *Legislative Methods,* pp. 63–69; Gregory A. Mark, "The Vestigal Constitution: The History and Significance of the Right to Petition," *Fordham Law Review* 66 (1998):2199–203 (reviewing state constitutional protection of petitioning).

[60]See, e.g., *Respublica* v. *Sparhawk,* 1 U.S. (Dall.) 357 (Pennsylvania 1788); *Nathan* v. *Virginia,* 1 U.S. (Dall.) 77 (Pennsylvania Court of Common Pleas, 1781); cf., *Newbold* v. *Republicam,* 1 Yeates 140 (PA, 1792); "An act for methodizing the department of accounts of this commonwealth," Apr. 13, 1782, and "An act to give the benefit of trial by jury to the public officers of this state, and to other persons, who shall be proceeded against in a summary manner by the Comptroller-General of this state," Feb. 18, 1785, *The Statutes at Large of Pennsylvania from 1682 to 1801* (Harrisburg, 1896–1906), 11: 435, 441.

[61]U.S. Congress, House Committee on Energy and Commerce, *Petitions, Memorials and Other Documents Submitted for the Consideration of Congress, March 4, 1789, to December 14, 1795,* 99th Cong., 2d Sess., Committee Print 99-AA, 1986, p. 5.

The congresses after 1789, which inherited huge numbers of claims from those who had contributed to the Continental Revolutionary effort, adopted similar procedures as those in the states, retaining ultimate authority to settle claims appealed from executive branch resolution or arising outside the authority of that branch.[62] It is clear that the early congresses considered responding to petitions to be obligatory. Journalist John Fenno asserted in 1795 that, along with "arranging and committing the business of the session," the "principal part of [Congress's] time has been taken up in reading and referring petitions—the number of which is great."[63] In fact, according to the best available record, there were at least seven hundred to one thousand petitions submitted to each of the early congresses on both private and public matters.[64] From the beginning, the federal legislature struggled to manage the workload generated by private claims. It delegated significant investigatory and reporting duty to the executive branch and designed its committee structure to deal with the remaining petitions. By 1794, the House had moved beyond appointing select committees to deal with particular claims; it established the House Committee on Claims, second as a standing committee only to the Committee on Elections.[65] Consonant with these practices, the "right to petition" was apparently originally understood as a guarantee that protected private as much as public or political rights.[66]

Finally, the great majority of individuals left holding paper notes or claims for service, supplies, or property impressed from them during the Revolutionary War did not, in fact, sue in either state or federal court for redress. There remained a well-entrenched expectation that "sovereigns"—both state and federal—were "immune" from judicial suit by individuals in the early republic. The shell of the English practice had served eighteenth-century Americans interested in local

---

[62]Ibid., pp. 1–14.

[63]Ibid., p. 6 (quoting John Fenno).

[64]Ibid., p. 362; see also Report of Committee on Claims, Mar. 2, 1795, U.S. House of Representative, M1267, Roll 1, p. 42, NARA. A much smaller number of the petitions survive today.

[65]Congress did initially attempt to delegate reporting duties to the federal courts; it abandoned that possibility for more than sixty years once the federal circuit judges made clear that they could only act as courts if they had final decision-making authority. See *Hayburn's Case,* 1 U.S. (Dall.) 409 (1792).

[66]See note 42 above.

power well: sovereign immunity doctrine guaranteed that the courts had only as much authority to hear claims against the government as delegated to them by the king in Parliament—in America, the political assemblies. Leaving aside for the moment the hot issue of suits against states in the new federal system, the rule clearly remained in place for governments within their own court systems, for everything from garden variety contract claims to constitutional violations. Justice James Iredell could report that neither Georgia nor any other state had, by 1790, passed an act authorizing suit against it.[67] Although he referred to a subsequently passed waiver of some kind enacted by the Georgia legislature, the act must not have delegated significant amounts of authority to the courts; nineteenth-century advocates of enlarged judicial power found no substantial waivers in any of the original states, nor indeed in many of the rest of them.[68] The federal Congress also long retained its exclusive authority over claims, finally establishing a special legislative court, the Court of Claims, and delegating contract claims to it in 1866.[69]

The Farquhar Claim

The claims committee in Georgia that received the Farquhar claim acted, then, from a tradition critical to American understanding of

---

[67] *Chisholm,* 2 U.S. (Dall.) 434–35. While Iredell referred to a subsequently passed waiver of some kind enacted by the Georgia legislature, the act must not have delegated significant amounts of authority to the courts; nor do Georgia's judiciary acts make mention of any delegation to the court. Ibid., 435; An act to revise, amend, or consolidate the several judiciary acts of this state, Dec. 18, 1792; An act for regulating the judiciary departments of this state, Dec. 23, 1789, *Acts of the General Assembly of the State of Georgia.*

[68] See generally Charles Martindale, "The State and Its Creditors," *Southern Law Review* 7 (1882):544–48, 545 (suits authorized in Alabama and Arkansas); George M. Davie, "Suing the State," *American Law Review* 18 (1884):814–30 (suits authorized in Mississippi; describing legislative lobbying occurring over claims). The scope of sovereign immunity was judicially mitigated in part by the fact that government officials could be sued in certain cases, preeminently for allegations of tortuous conduct that could not be "immunized" as proper governmental activity. See Engdahl, "Immunity and Accountability," pp. 16–21.

[69] The Court of Claims was first established as an advisory court in 1855. Over the next decade, Congress reorganized the court and, in 1866, strengthened its authority effectively to order payments from the treasury. Floyd Shimomura, "The History of Claims Against the United States: The Evolution from a Legislative Toward a Judicial Model of Payment," *Louisiana Law Review* 45 (1985):626, 651–60. The Court of Claims was rechristened an Article III court in 1961. See ibid., pp. 687–90.

self-government. Local elites had fashioned political authority by using the legislatures to take control of public money and to affect the economy it animated. The result was a system that bound those elements together: in the American experience, a community's sovereignty lay in its collective management of its public wealth, as orchestrated by its political representatives. That wealth consisted both in public revenues collected and spent as the legislature directed and in the creation and support of a currency (soft or hard) that supported exchange in both governmental and private relations. Over the decades, the institutions that related lay Americans to those with official authority had been configured in ways reflecting those roles.

At the moment that Georgia's legislature confronted Chisholm's claim in 1789, circumstances had raised the stakes for the traditional system. On the one hand, the federal Union represented a threat to the sources of state sovereignty insofar as they were rooted in state legislative control of money and finance. The changes effected by the Constitution—the turn to specie money and the prohibition of state paper emissions—reduced the control that state representatives had over the resources of their communities. Those convinced of the importance of local authority had reason to guard against further invasions of state legislative power. With a flamboyance that was as remarkable as his energy, Rep. James Jackson of Georgia spent most of the First Federal Congress attacking measures in the House that reduced federal, and especially state, legislative power to settle the war debt.

On the other hand, the financial crisis of the war had placed tremendous pressure on state legislators to use, as fully as possible, every bit of their power in the economic sphere. The circumstances were demanding: tied to distressed populations disparately ravaged by the war and accustomed to extralegal action, tax resistance, and, increasingly, political mobilization, representatives had to devise general methods of defining, servicing, and paying the debt, and to find ways to manage individual demands for redress.

Throughout the 1780s, those tasks had been shouldered largely by the state assemblies; to the dismay of those promoting a more powerful central authority, the Confederation Congress remained without its own tax power and thus without revenues. The fragility of government constantly confronted state legislators, pervading their calculations of the right, the possible, and the necessary; critics concluded that they were captive to the populist demands of citizens.[70] For a number of reasons, retirement of the war debt went especially far in Georgia and the rest of the South, where the legislatures used the means of paper finance, including levying taxes payable in securities, to sink both state and federal debts.[71]

Despite their efforts, many in the southern states felt little assurance in 1789 that the war burdens would ever be equally spread. Convinced that they had outspent and outsacrificed their neighbors, they nevertheless had no confidence that a federal settlement of accounts, which was supposed to tally total spending, charge debtor states, and compensate creditor states for wartime expenditures, would ever be fairly accomplished. The disarray in their own records undermined their claims; Georgia never did fare particularly well under the settlement, although its claims may well have been too large for even an increasingly expansive federal commission to credit.[72]

In this context, the Farquhar claim was shunted aside by a Georgia assembly exhausted by debt management and anxious to be rid of a large claim that they could not expect the federal government would help shoulder, especially given their own agents' misconduct. It may have seemed enough to a majority that they had already, in the straitened circumstances of the times, paid for the claim once; the Farquhar claimants could track down the money themselves and save the people of Georgia more expense. Later legislators would conclude that the 1789 decision had been a breach of the "public faith," as the responsibility of the legislatures to keep public contracts was called in the vernacular of the period. The decision was not, however, one that could be categorized as faulty according to abstractions about "popular sovereignty." The step was taken by an assembly acting with dramatic exposure to its constituent population and according to the very practices that had created local power.

---

[70]See, e.g., Brown, *Redeeming the Republic;* Merrill Jensen, *The Articles of Confederation: An Interpretation of the Social-constitutional History of the American Revolution, 1774–1781* (Madison, Wis., 1940); Gary B. Nash, *The Urban Crucible: Social Change, Political Consciousness, and the Origins of the American Revolution* (Cambridge, Mass., 1979).

[71]See Ferguson, *Power of the Purse,* pp. 307, 309, 311 (Georgia); idem, "State Assumption," pp. 406–9 (Virginia, special tax); Morrill, *Practice and Politics of Fiat Finance,* pp. 132–37 (North Carolina).

[72]Ferguson, *Power of the Purse,* pp. 212, 214–15, 309–10, 322–24.

The irony of the moment was that the Georgia legislature added a note to its 1789 report that seemed designed, in retrospect at least, to add to its problems. Without offering any clear reason that would make the affair between Farquhar and the commissioners a private matter, the House committee nevertheless expressly introduced the logic of private relations into the case. It noted that the executors should "seek redress in a court of law against the said [Thomas] Stone and the representatives of the said [Edward] Davis."[73] Georgia legislators here exhibited the fascinating complexity of the period: mainly Federalists, they would vociferously defend state power; committed to legislative authority over public funds, they invited a private initiative in the courts to get the money; unaware that a new constitutional order approached, they launched the case that would promote it.

The particular judicial remedy that the legislature recommended was, in fact, almost sure to fail. There was obviously no guarantee that either Stone, the surviving commissioner, or the heirs of Davis any longer had the money owed the Farquhar family.[74] But the committee's own recommendations apparently compounded the hazards of a lawsuit. The committee noted that the expense of the Farquhar contract, which had after all gone to defend the Revolutionary cause, appeared to ground "a proper charge against the Union, for which the State ought to be credited."[75] According to the committee, the governor should therefore demand "an account and vouchers" from its former agents (or their executors). In case they could not account for the funds to his satisfaction "within three months after demand made," the governor should "direct the attorney-general to prosecute."[76] The problem that legislators sitting in the 1793 session of the Georgia House identified with the advice of their earlier colleagues was that "the said executor could not, with safety, commence an action against the said executor of Davis and Thomas Stone, because the attorney-general was directed to prosecute them, and if both actions had been pending at the same time one must have fallen to the ground;

---

[73]Report of Committee, Georgia House, Nov. 25, 1789, reprinted in U.S. House, *Money Due the State of Georgia,* p. 5.

[74]Davis in fact became insolvent after the Revolution. See *DHSC,* 5:128 n. 11.

[75]Report of Committee, Georgia House, Nov. 25, 1789, reprinted in U.S. House, *Money Due the State of Georgia,* p. 5.

[76]Ibid.

whereby the said executor would have risked a total loss of his demand, as the suit of the State would have had the preference to that of an individual."[77]

Whether or not the 1789 legislature laid a procedural trap for Peter Trezevant is lost in the murkiness of Georgia's common law. But it seems quite possible that by its dismissive treatment of a claimant who was following the well-established mode for obtaining payment from the state, the committee invited not only Trezevant's renewed claim on the state, but also the angry expansion of his efforts into a very different forum.

Judicial Initiative, Legislative Defense, and the Controversy over Popular Sovereignty

While Trezevant continued after 1789 to press the state legislature for payment, he and Alexander Chisholm attempted as well a radically new approach to remedy. By his own word, Trezevant became the moving force behind their initiative in the federal courts.[78] Sometime early in the spring of 1791, the Farquhar claimants filed suit in the U.S. Circuit Court for the District of Georgia. The case was heard and dismissed for lack of jurisdiction the following fall.[79] The Farquhar claimants persevered. The next spring, 1792, they filed suit under Alexander Chisholm's name in the U.S. Supreme Court.[80]

The court cases were so unprecedented that neither Georgia officials nor the judges themselves were sure who should be served with the summons or who should appear for the state—governor, attorney-general, legislators?[81] Despite their novelty at the time, however, the suits would be highly scrutinized later: *Chisholm* v. *Georgia,* the Supreme Court's eventual decision that the court had jurisdiction over the suit, would become the compulsory starting point for both judges

---

[77]Report of Committee, Georgia House, Dec. 11, 1793, reprinted in U.S. House, *Money Due the State of Georgia,* pp. 5–6.

[78]Trezevant, while leaving the conduct of the case in court to counsel, demonstrated his tenacity again in the judicial realm, attending "at every suit, till a verdict was given in his favor" (Affidavit of Peter Trezevant, June 15, 1840, reprinted in U.S. House, *Money Due the State of Georgia,* p. 22).

[79]*DHSC,* 5:128, 129–30.

[80]Ibid., 5:131.

[81]Ibid., 5:128–30.

and scholars concerned with state suability for the next two centuries. The details of the litigation in *Chisholm* and the cluster of similar cases in the early republic have been definitively documented by Maeva Marcus and her colleagues; the substance of the case has been dissected by countless lawyers and academics.[82] While that territory is well known, the conditions that made the courts a conceivable recourse are less familiar.

The Attempt at Judicial Remedy

Throughout the turmoil of the 1780s, many remained convinced that legislative management of finance, with its susceptibility to demonstrations of social need and the latitude it offered for the calibration of those demands, represented the fairest approach possible in a constitutional regime.[83] During that decade and for some time afterward, representatives devised funding schemes that devalued debts across the board, treated mediums of repayment flexibly (substituting land or tax relief, for example, for values promised in cash or specie), or, occasionally on the state level, differentially paid holders of government debt on the basis of need or desert. The inability of individuals to sue states in court for payment protected such arrangements.[84]

Those politically gauged arrangements appeared increasingly problematic to the men attracted to the British approach to public finance

---

[82]Ibid. See, e.g., Amar, "Of Sovereignty and Federalism"; William A. Fletcher, "A Historical Interpretation of the Eleventh Amendment: A Narrow Construction of an Affirmative Grant of Jurisdiction Rather than a Prohibition against Jurisdiction," *Stanford Law Review* 35 (1983):1033–131; John J. Gibbons, "The Eleventh Amendment and State Sovereign Immunity," *Columbia Law Review* 83 (1983):1889–2005.

[83]See, e.g., William Manning, "Some Proposals for Making Restitution to the Original Creditors of Government," in *The Key of Liberty: The Life and Democratic Writings of William Manning, "A Laborer," 1747–1814*, ed. Sean Wilentz and Michael Merrill (Cambridge, Mass., 1993), pp. 95–116; Ferguson, *Power of the Purse*, pp. 222–23, 228–30.

[84]Federal devaluation of the Continental dollar furnished the most famous such episode. See *JCC*, 16:262–67 (Mar. 18, 1790). For a similar instance in which a state legislature determined that depreciation, which had gutted the value of funds available for redeeming bills of credit, diluted the requirement that the state pay back holders ("the public [have not] made themselves answerable to aid the pledge if it should prove inadequate"), see Maryland House of Delegates, committee report, Nov. 25, 1791, *Votes and Proceedings of the Maryland House of Delegates* (Annapolis, 1792), p. 50 (also differentially treating various holders). For an example of a state determination to pay interest only on state debt held by the original holders, see "An Act to Appropriate Certain Moneys Arising from the Excise," Mar. 21, 1783, chap. 1024, *Statutes at Large of Pennsylvania*, 11:100–101. Georgia engaged in similar strategies when funding the certificates held by claimants like the Farquhar heirs. See text accompanying note 131.

that was developing across the Atlantic. Over the course of a century and a half, the English had dismantled a system built on specie, impressments, and highly concentrated large loans; they reconstructed a funding method based on specie and widely subscribed long-term government borrowing. Proponents articulated the new arrangement as one rooted in individual choice, ex ante commitment, and constancy.[85]

Indirectly, if not directly, the new British funding system invited recalibration of the institutional roles imputed to legislatures and courts. In England, change took a route distinctively affected by the presence of a strong ministry and the early development of the Bank of England. Parliamentary cooperation with those institutions apparently deflected, to some degree, movement expressly to limit legislative authority.[86] The course of events in America was quite different; the dramatic uses of power made by the legislatures during the war and postwar period marked them as objectionable in the eyes of those who, like Robert Morris, appointed federal superintendent of finance in 1781, were committed to developing a system of public finance along English lines.

To men like Morris and those associated with him, the modes of authority exercised by the common law courts were frequently superior to the practices of the legislatures as a means of supervising matters of economic exchange. Those most vocal about the advantages of the English system were disproportionately merchants or lawyers attached to the commercial community; men such as Gouverneur Mor-

---

[85]See generally Henry Roseveare, *The Treasury, 1660–1870* (London, 1973); P. G. M. Dickson, *The Financial Revolution in England: A Study in the Development of Public Credit, 1688–1756* (London, 1967). For the shift in terminology, see Robert Morris, Report on the Public Credit, July 29, 1782, *JCC,* 22:429–46 (Aug. 5, 1782).

[86]The first dramatic judicial intervention explicitly to enforce a public contract was thus directed against ministerial, not parliamentary, authority to pay the debts. See *The Case of the Bankers,* in *A Complete Collection of State Trials,* ed. Thomas Bayly Howell, 33 vols. (London, 1809–26), 14:1–114. Similarly, Parliament almost from the start used the Bank of England to develop methods of long-term government borrowing. That device allowed private rules of liability to apply in certain parts of the process, without exposing Parliament directly to suit. The development of regime of modern public contract in England remains to be explored. Among others, Douglass North and Barry Weingast have flagged the importance of the transition. See Douglass C. North and Barry R. Weingast, "Constitutions and Commitment: The Evolution of Institutions Governing Public Choice in Seventeenth-Century England," *Journal of Economic History* 49 (1989):803–32.

ris, William Duer, Alexander Hamilton, and James Wilson, were accustomed to the practice of the courts and to the law produced by them in matters of private contract.[87] That community influenced, in ways that remain to be explored, the movement during the 1780s to enlarge generally the institutional power of the courts. At the same time, Morris and others began to realign public funding practices, especially at the federal level, so that they followed private common law analogues more closely.

The transition toward the British fiscal model was, then, a move calculated from the outset to reduce the ability of legislatures to use inflationary means beyond the power of individuals to sink public debts, such as issuing more currency. Morris and like-minded Americans also disavowed other techniques that legislatures had conventionally used flexibly to retire public debts. Assemblies had, for example, imposed restraints on the alienability of government securities in order to privilege repayment to the creditors who had earned public compensation over the speculating purchasers who appeared less deserving. More generally, those advocating the new approach to public finance rejected legislative strategies that interfered with the negotiability of notes, advocating the liberty of parties to contract as they individually judged appropriate to their interests.[88] Their thinking drew support from models of individual economic behavior suggested by free trade theorists in the seventeenth century and powerfully developed by Adam Smith.[89]

Arguments in favor of the new approach were publicly aired—and conspicuously endorsed by federal officials—shortly before the Farquhar claimants filed suit in Georgia's federal circuit court. The debates in the First Federal Congress over funding the public debt

---

[87]See Ferguson, *Power of the Purse,* pp. 70–81, 109, 110–14, 117–24, for the predominant role of merchants in directing the funding system adopted by the Continental Congress toward English forms during certain periods of the 1780s.

[88]See Morris, Report on the Public Debt, July 29, 1782, *JCC,* 22:443–45; Alexander Hamilton, Report of the Secretary of the Treasury on the Public Credit, Jan. 14, 1790, *DHFFC,* 5:750–51.

[89]See generally Albert O. Hirschman, *The Passions and the Interests: Political Arguments for Capitalism before Its Triumph* (Princeton, 1977); Joyce O. Appleby, *Economic Thought and Ideology in Seventeenth Century England* (Princeton, 1978); idem, *Liberalism and Republicanism in the Historical Imagination* (Cambridge, Mass., 1992).

furnished the platform; newspapers in the spring of 1790 were filled with information and commentary on the progress of the congressional debates.[90] Time and again, the issue that divided congressmen was the scope of legislative authority over public contract. While James Madison of Virginia, James Jackson of Georgia, and a small group of others staunchly defended the legislature's latitude, indeed obligation, to adopt ways of paying the debt that attended to goals of social equity, need, and desert, they were substantially outnumbered. Congress was dominated by Federalists eager to support the proposals of Secretary of the Treasury Alexander Hamilton, proposals similar to those of Robert Morris a decade earlier. In matters of contract, they argued, the legislature had to act as if it were a common law court, applying the same rules to obtain the same results. As William Smith of South Carolina put it: "[The payment of the face value of a contract] is law and justice between man and man: is there another sort of law and justice for the government? by what rule is the government to square its conduct, if not by those sacred rules which form the basis of civil society, and are the safeguard of private property?"[91]

For these men, proper servicing of the debt both met past obligations and ensured future progress. There was no conflict: A regime of choice and unmodifiable commitment could alone provide the structure that the United States needed in order to grow into a powerful nation.

The logic propounded so publicly by the Federalist majority made conceivable, perhaps even evoked, Chisholm's suit against the state of Georgia. With scant exception, the congressmen debating how to fund the federal debt had not themselves taken the position that an individual could claim any payment from a government in court. Habituated to the legislative control of finance, they had instead assumed that

[90]As one observer reported on the eve of congressional debates, New York City was "all in a flame about funding, nothing else heard even among the women and children." See William Neilson to John Chaloner, Feb. 17, 1790, as quoted in Charlene B. Bickford and Kenneth R. Bowling, *Birth of the Nation: The First Federal Congress, 1789–1791* (Washington, D.C., 1989), p. 64; see also the Feb. 16, 1790, speech of Rep. James Jackson, *DHFFC,* 12:358. William Manning, the author of "Some Proposals for Making Restitution to the Original Creditors of Government," was one of many Americans who closely attended the debate.

[91]William Smith, Feb. 15, 1790, *DHFFC,* 12:328.

restraints on federal legislative action would be self-imposed.[92] But it was not such a long step to the position that limits on the legislatures had to be externally enforced. Indeed, in this view, *sovereignty* could only belong to the people if the power and activity of government were carefully restrained. No branch of the government, least of all the legislature with its generative and destructive potential, should be allowed special prerogatives; the public must be answerable to the same extent and in the same way as an individual in a court of law. Indeed, if economic relations were matters of free choice between bargaining parties, there was no need for legislative adjustment for changing social circumstances or for balancing multiple demands. A court could do as well, in fact better, than a political forum in enforcing established contracts.[93]

The ambiguity of the Constitution as ratified left these individuals—as well as those still committed to the earlier model of self-government—free to consider that their own views had prevailed. To those Americans who were moving to a more judicialized understanding of the relationship between citizen and government, the extension of federal judicial power in Article III to controversies "between a State and Citizens of another State" wrote into the Constitution the recognition that a state was suable. To those who remained committed to a legislatively centered vision of popular sovereignty, the phrase allowed judicial suit only where a state legislature permitted it: a federal court could exercise jurisdiction if and when a state had waived its immunity to a cause of action against it.[94] The Judiciary Act of 1789 carried

[92]Elias Boudinot (N.J.) was the only representative who may have favored accepting court enforcement of public contracts. See Feb. 9, 1790, *DHFFC,* 12:227.

[93]See, e.g., Solon, "Domestic Miscellany," *Independent Chronicle,* Sept. 19, 1793, *DHSC,* 5:421–23.

[94]That would occur in two circumstances: either the state had initiated the suit under existing law, or the state legislature had agreed to delegate resolution of the dispute to the courts. For example, Pennsylvania had waived its immunity to certain claims against it. See "An act for methodizing the department of accounts of this commonwealth," Apr. 13, 1782, and "An act to give the benefit of trial by jury to the public officers of this state, and to other persons, who shall be proceeded against in a summary manner by the Comptroller-General of this state," Feb. 18, 1785, *Statutes at Large of Pennsylvania,* 10:448–57, 11:435–41. Although the state legislature may have believed it would need to expand that waiver in order to subject itself to suit in a federal forum, there was certainly nothing to keep the legislature from making that additional delegation.

forward the same ambiguity, with its provision for suits "where a state is a party": that provision could be read by individuals with radically different premises to be consistent with their own understandings.[95]

Resort to higher theory did nothing to rid the Constitution of ambiguity. For Americans committed to older ideas of the political economy, the legislature remained the institution most effectively designed to express the popular will. Legislative power over the purse continued to be a critical safeguard of a republican system. The courts could not be given the power to impose binding money damage awards against the government because that would delegate power over the treasury to the judiciary; the action was unthinkable to those who identified popular control of the purse with liberty and equity. To this group, the obligation of legislators to keep the "public faith" was vitalized by both internal conscience and popular action.[96] A suit against the government, by contrast, would arrest the political pulse of the community and destroy its spirit.

Opposed to this view was a conception of popular sovereignty richly articulated by James Wilson in one of the opinions that the Chisholm claim elicited from the Supreme Court in 1793. The driving force of Wilson's idea abstracted the notion of "the People" from its previous institutional home in the legislatures. As it had became clear that "the People" could act extra-legislatively in the 1770s and 1780s, it became desirable to a significant group that "the People" *should* act extra-legislatively in ratifying the Constitution in order to curb potential excesses of the state assemblies. "The People," who once acted solely through their legislative representatives, were now identified as the

[95]The same is not true, of course, where the United States was concerned. The federal government figured only as a plaintiff in the Judiciary Act, see Sec. 9, 11. As I note below, however, the divergent treatment of the United States is, if anything, more consistent with an assumption of legislative than judicial responsibility for redress of private grievances. The federal Congress had, in the Judiciary Act or other legislation, control over a waiver of "immunity" or, put another way, the prerogative to delegate its conventional role to a judicial forum. The federal Congress could not, of course, be similarly specific with regard to that same decision on the part of various state legislatures. Conversely, if a majority of the federal legislature had been convinced that popular sovereignty demanded a judicially administered model of remedy, that majority could have arranged for the suability of the United States in the Judiciary Act.

[96]These issues were debated in the House of Representatives by Jackson, Madison, Page, Scott, and Stone in February 1790. See *DHFFC,* 12:202, 213–14, 242, 248–49, 280, 281, 357, 360–61.

principals of each of the legislative, executive, and judicial branches equally. Given this evolution of thought, the judiciary would come to occupy its now familiar place as the protector of individual rights against governmental abuse.[97]

For those willing to follow the logic of judicialized protection of individual rights as far as it went, Peter Trezevant's case was an easy call. He had the best on the merits of the contract claim, and the misfeasance of Davis and Stone did nothing to exonerate their principal, Georgia. Finally, it was well within the power of a common law court to recognize that a cause of action existed against a state just as a cause of action existed against an individual, if states had the same status as did individuals in the law. This logic would, of course, have supported suit against the federal government itself. But for those still leery of that conclusion, this was a halfway point: those oriented toward federal authority could find this incursion into state legislative power by federal judicial power easier to stomach.

The Vibrancy of Legislative Commitment

Even nationally oriented Americans, however, did not fall neatly into the "judicialized protection" camp. Trezevant's suit reached the limits of its effectiveness when it repulsed all those who continued at some level of commitment, even if vague or conflicted, to adhere to a legislatively centered model of remedy. The reaction swept up Americans of many different persuasions. It was, to be sure, even more bitterly refracted through a commitment to state authority for those who had been leery of federal union.

---

[97]See *Chisholm,* 2 U.S. (Dall.) 555–57; Gordon S. Wood, *The Creation of the American Republic, 1776–1787* (Chapel Hill, 1969), pp. 446–53. Wood has elaborated both the development and the power of this Wilsonian notion of popular sovereignty; I do not dispute either the character of this notion or its ultimate predominance. It is the speed of its ascendancy that is belied by the institutional practices I have studied. There is no doubt that reforms in the structure of assemblies (preeminently the move to bicameralism), the institution of the convention as a form of ratification, and the fact of "constitutions" themselves were powerful limits (among others adopted in the 1780s) on legislative power. They do not, however, amount to the rejection or displacement of the legislatures as the central institution of governance in the early republic. On this point, compare M. Horwitz, *Separation of Powers and Judicial Review: The Development of Post-Revolutionary Constitutional Theory,* Thomas M. Cooley Lecture, Michigan Law School (n.d.), pp. 19–20.

By 1792, Trezevant and Chisholm had advanced their judicial initiative, filing a motion for default against the state of Georgia in the Supreme Court during its August term. Moving cautiously, the Court held the motion to give the state time to appear in the February term of 1793. Georgia officials refused to cooperate. Its legislature debated denouncing the case while the state's governor submitted a written remonstrance against federal jurisdiction at the Court's February term.[98]

Georgia's resistance met its well-known fate on February 18, 1793, when the Court determined by a 4–1 decision that an individual could sue a state in federal court.[99] The Court's judgment catalyzed proposals in Congress to amend the Constitution that would resurface the following year: The Eleventh Amendment provided that "the Judicial power of the United States shall not be construed to extend to any suit in law or equity, commenced or prosecuted against one of the United States by Citizens of another State, or by Citizens or Subjects of any Foreign State."[100] The amendment was ratified and went into effect in 1798; applied retroactively, it barred *Chisholm* and the handful of suits like it that had been filed in the Court.

The drama over the Farquhar claim, however, moved back to the legislatures. On November 19, 1793, the House of Representatives of the state of Georgia passed a bill responding to the Supreme Court's

---

[98]On December 14, 1792, a resolution introduced into the Georgia House of Representatives linked power over the treasury and the ability of state government to function. The resolution did not pass, perhaps because of its inflammatory description of the court threat as one that could "annihilate the very shadow of State government, and . . . render them but tributary corporations to the government of the United States" (House resolution of Dec. 14, 1792, *Augusta Chronicle*, in *DHSC*, 5:161–62). The resolution was apparently introduced at the request of the governor (Ames, *State Documents on Federal Relations*, pp. 7–9). The remonstrance was presented by court reporters Jared Ingersoll and Alexander Dallas, who acted on behalf of the state but were instructed not to participate in the argument. *Chisholm* v. *Georgia*, 2 U.S. (Dall.) 419.

[99]Justices voting in favor of jurisdiction were Blair, Wilson, Jay, and Cushing. Justice Iredell dissented. The Court determined only the jurisdictional question; it did not consider the merits of the case.

[100]The Eleventh Amendment expressly addressed, and prohibited, the kind of federal court jurisdiction found to exist by the Court in *Chisholm*—diversity suits, or suits against a state by a citizen of another state. It was silent about suits based on federal law brought against states; those suits would have been permissible under the federal courts' federal question jurisdiction, barring state sovereign immunity. In *Hans* v. *Louisiana*, 134 U.S. 1 (1890), the Court determined that federal question suits were, implicitly, prohibited by the Eleventh Amendment.

decision in *Chisholm* v. *Georgia.* One section of the bill provided that anyone who attempted to levy state property or funds "under any execution from or by the authority of the Supreme Court, for or in behalf of . . . Alexander Chisholm, executor, . . . or for or in behalf of any other person or persons whatsoever, for the payment or recovery of any debt or pretended debt, or claim against the said State of Georgia, shall be and are hereby declared to be guilty of felony and shall suffer death, without the benefit of clergy, by being hanged."[101] Observers, both then and now, have repeatedly cited the House bill; violent and extreme, it seems to them to discredit the rationality of the Georgians' response to the *Chisholm* decision.[102]

However, less than a month later, a committee of the same House of Representatives responded to a petition from Trezevant by issuing a report recommending that Georgia pay the Chisholm claim.[103] The committee recounted evidence indicating that the state clearly owed the money claimed by Chisholm; it did so without any mention of the *Chisholm* decision and without any apparent concern that its recital of these facts could affect the "merits" stage of the case, in which the Supreme Court had yet to determine the liability of the state.[104] Concluding that "the State is now liable, and ought to pay the said debt to the petitioner," the committee resolved that the auditor of the state "examine the account of the said Robert Farquhar," that he "depreciate the same" agreeably to the correct scale of depreciation, and that

---

[101]House resolution, Nov. 19, 1793, *Augusta Chronicle,* Nov. 23, 1793, in *DHSC,* 5:236–37. The Georgia Senate took no action on the bill; ibid., 5:237 n. 2.

[102]See, e.g., Clyde E. Jacobs, *The Eleventh Amendment and Sovereign Immunity* (Westport, Conn., 1972), pp. 56–57; "An Intemperate Resolution of Georgia," *American Minerva* (New York), Jan. 15, 1794, *DHSC,* 5:237–38.

[103]Trezevant had returned to the Georgia legislature in the fall of 1793, even as that body and its counterparts in states north and south mobilized to resist the *Chisholm* decision. Trezevant, petition to Congress, Feb. 8, 1794, *DHSC,* 5:260–61. Report of Committee, Georgia House, Dec. 11, 1793, reprinted in U.S. House, *Money Due the State of Georgia,* pp. 5–6.

[104]The committee noted that "the original entry of the said goods in the handwriting of the said Robert Farquhar, corroborated by the evidence of Arthur Fort, Esq., who was at the time one of the honorable the council, prove the delivery of the goods." The committee criticized its 1789 predecessor for both its conclusion that the state was not liable and its relegation of Trezevant to a judicial remedy (Report of Committee, Georgia House, Dec. 11, 1793, reprinted in U.S. House, *Money Due the State of Georgia,* pp. 5–6).

he "give the aforesaid Peter Trezevant, heir and attorney as aforesaid, a certificate for the sterling amount of the same, expressing in the body of said certificate, that the same was given in payment for army supplies."[105] The Georgia Senate had apparently come to a similar conclusion. Two days after the committee issued its report, the Georgia legislature passed a joint resolution as reasonable and evenhanded in tone as the earlier House bill had been violent and extreme. The joint resolution first identified the general responsibility of the government: "That it is the duty of the State, in justice and good faith, to settle and finally adjust, all claims brought against the government thereof, in such manner as may be most beneficial to the same."[106]

On the Farquhar claim, specifically, the joint resolution continued: "That the honor and interest of this government is bound for the payment of all just debts that have been contracted for the defence of this State, during the late revolution; and if the said claim of the executor of Farquhar should come under this description, it is the duty of the legislature to settle the same in the manner most accommodating and beneficial to both parties; and that the necessary vouchers being produced to substantiate such claim, the general assembly will provide for payment thereof."[107]

Juxtaposing Georgia's legislative actions—the hanging bill and the process of claim consideration culminating in the joint resolution—reveals their rationale, as well as the depth of feeling that animated it. Consistent with their history, political representatives articulated the state's responsibility to "settle and finally adjust" claims against the state "in justice and good faith." It was, however, "the duty of the legislature" alone to resolve such claims, not any federal court. As the House had demonstrated, it had the means and procedures to consider claims. And it was the "general assembly," and only the general assembly, that had access to the treasury and could therefore "provide for payment thereof."

The Georgia legislature acted with vehemence because underlying the apparently simple power over contract it claimed was the complex

[105]Ibid., p. 6.

[106]Joint Resolution, Georgia Legislature, Dec. 13, 1793, reprinted in U.S. House, *Money Due the State of Georgia,* p. 6.

[107]Ibid., p. 6.

constitutional regime it defended. That regime rooted political power in control over public expenditures and, even more basically, the value of money. When Georgia's governor addressed a joint session of the state legislature on November 4, 1793, he explicitly identified the threat represented by state suability in court as one that would fundamentally subvert the state's system of finance and funding. According to Governor Telfair, state suability in court was "replete with danger." The state had emitted "upwards of one hundred and fifty thousand pounds since the close of the last war, a considerable part of which is yet outstanding."[108] If actions against the state to recover paper money emitted by it were allowed, "an annihilation of her political existence must follow."[109]

A 1792 resolution debated by the Georgia House put the matter similarly. It noted: "If acquiesced in by this State [the suit] would not only involve the same in numberless law-suits for papers issued from the Treasury thereof to supply the armies of the United States, and perplex the citizens of Georgia with perpetual taxes, in addition to those the injustice of the funding system of the United States hath already imposed upon them, but would effectually destroy the retained sovereignty of the states, and would actually tend in its operation to annihilate the very shadow of state government, and to render them but tributary corporations to the government of the United States."[110]

The 1792 resolution exposed another, intimately related dimension of the controversy. Insofar as Americans believed that the political viability of a government depended on its power over public finance, they assumed that the state legislatures would inevitably surrender their identity to the federal government when they lost the ability to control their own economic systems. The move to hard money and the prohibition on paper emissions had reduced state power in significant

---

[108]The paper was apparently used in frontier defense. As Telfair put it, the state had been "reduced by savage inroads" to a "singular predicament." See extracts from the message of Gov. Edward Telfair, *Augusta Chronicle,* Nov. 9, 1793, Ames, *State Documents on Federal Relations,* p. 7.

[109]Ibid., p. 9. The governor therefore urged the legislature to direct its representatives in Congress to seek a constitutional amendment and to press for its ratification in order to guard against "civil discord and impending danger."

[110]Resolution of Dec. 14, 1792, *Augusta Chronicle,* Dec. 22, 1792, *DHSC,* 5:161–62. The Senate postponed consideration of the resolution; ibid., 5:162 n. 4.

ways. But the threat went further. On August 5, 1790, Congress had assumed the bulk of the debt that the states still owed from the Revolutionary era.[111] The initiative was an important part of Hamilton's strategy to realign toward the national government the loyalty of public creditors—the class he considered most critical to the economic development of the new country, given their resources, entrepreneurialism, and energy.[112] The same advantages that Hamilton coveted now flowed away from the states. For Georgia, as for several of her sister states in the South, the pill was especially bitter, since inhabitants considered that they had largely sunk their own debts and would now have to bear the taxes it took to pay off the liabilities of others. It was, for many, a return to the years of the British empire and the indignities of a regime in which the only local role was to tax at the behest of a distant power.

In this context, state liability to suit in federal court was the final blow, a slap delivered by men, James Wilson and John Jay in particular, who had been highly visible and controversial nationalists.[113] In Massachusetts, an editorial writer tied together people and self-governance, his commonwealth, its representatives, and its power, and exhorted resistance: "Citizens, rouse! Let us before [the legislature] comes together, call Town Meetings and County Conventions on this business to take the sense of the PEOPLE on a question as *big* with the fate of our *interest* and *liberties* as any one that has agitated the public mind since [the end of the Revolutionary War]." For the writer, the danger was clear: suits against the state "would *destroy the sovereignty* of this commonwealth, and with it, the liberties of the PEOPLE."[114]

---

[111]See "An Act to Provide More Effectually for the Settlement of the Accounts between the United States and the Individual States," Aug. 5, 1790, ch. 38, 1 Stat. 178.

[112]See Stanley Elkins and Eric McKitrick, *The Age of Federalism: The Early American Republic, 1788–1800* (New York, 1993), pp. 114–18. Compare the threat perceived by nationalists when the states had moved to service federal debt in the 1780s. Ferguson, "State Assumption of the Federal Debt," pp. 421–24.

[113]On Wilson, see John K. Alexander, "The Fort Wilson Incident of 1779: A Case Study of the Revolutionary Crowd," *William and Mary Quarterly,* 3d ser. 31 (1974):589–612. Jay's allegiances had long been clear; he had co-authored *The Federalist* letters and, more recently, had run against Republican-identified George Clinton in the 1792 gubernatorial election. See Elkins and McKitrick, *Age of Federalism,* p. 288.

[114]"Marcus," *Massachusetts Mercury,* July 13, 1793, *DHSC,* 5:389–90. A report of the Georgia House of Representatives, issued Nov. 9, 1793, recommended that the legisla-

The Mechanics of Legislative Remedy

In a world in which legislative responsibility for claims like Trezevant's was the norm, one might expect its logic would extend to the federal sphere. That is in fact where the drama leads. By early 1794, Trezevant was ready to try that venue. On the one hand, he responded to the state legislature's invitation to submit materials demonstrating his claim to them.[115] On the other hand, he now approached the federal Congress. It had, after all, assumed the bulk of the states' debts, a fact of which Trezevant was aware.[116] The act may have invited Trezevant to conceive of federal responsibility for his claim, and he was as ready as ever to read an invitation expansively. The petition he wrote to Congress was straightforward and, in its own way, quite eloquent.[117] Trezevant recounted the facts of the Farquhar claim and the acquiescence of the state in the merits of the claim, carefully noting that he could document each step with affidavits. His theory as to the basis of federal liability was simple: "All the Articles charged in the Account against the State of Georgia, tho' purchased by that State, were bought for the Benefit of the Union, because they were for the use of the Army and Navy; your Petitioner therefore humbly conceives that as the State of Georgia would undoubtedly have charged to the United States the

---

ture pass a bill declaratory of state's retained sovereignty, and that it request the concurrence of other state legislatures in the "explanatory amendment" to the Constitution being debated. *Augusta Chronicle,* Nov. 16, 1793, ibid., 5:235–36.

[115]In February 1794, two men personally acquainted with Robert Farquhar and his business, his late copartner and his former clerk, appeared before a justice of the peace in Charleston. They swore that copies of the charges made in Farquhar's book accounts in October, 1777 to the state of Georgia were authentic, and that "the original entry in the said books is made in the proper handwriting of the said Robert Farquhar, deceased" (Affidavit of Colin Campbell and Lawrence Campbell, Feb. 10, 1794, reprinted in U.S. House, *Money Due the State of Georgia,* pp. 4–5). The state special commission that assembled evidence supporting the Trezevant claim in 1839 treated this affidavit as a document submitted to the legislature rather than the court. See Report of Special Commissioners, Nov. 6, 1939, reprinted in U.S. House, *Money Due the State of Georgia,* p. 3.

[116]Peter Trezevant, petition to Congress, Feb. 8, 1794, *DHSC,* 5:258–62.

[117]Trezevant explained his authorship of the petition as follows: "The Petition [is that of] Peter Trezevant of the city of Charleston in the State of South Carolina who has intermarried with Eliza Willoughby Farquhar, the only child and sole Legatee and Devisee of Robert Farquhar late of Charleston aforesaid deceased, and is also the Attorney (lawfully authorized, constituted and appointed) of Alexander Chisholm of Charleston aforesaid, the surviving Executor of the last Will and Testament of the said Robert Farquhar deceased" (ibid., 5:259).

Amount of this debt and the Interest thereon if they had paid it he may with Justice apply to your Honorable House[s] for Relief."[118] The claimant's need for federal relief was just as simply stated: "This Demand is almost all [Robert Farquhar] left for the Support of his Daughter . . . and since his marriage, your Petitioner has necessarily lost a vast deal of time and expended large Sums of Money in striving to obtain payment for this Debt, and it will be ruinous to him and his Family if he is kept out of it much longer."[119] In fact, only the federal legislature could help him; the federal judicial route had backfired since he knew not "how he should get his [federal court] Judgement satisfied whenever he obtains it, and if he should ever attempt to have an Execution levied upon the State of Georgia, it might occasion some unhappy civil Commotion, as the Inhabitants of that State conceiving [the *Chisholm* ruling] a degradation are resolved not to submit to it."[120]

Trezevant concluded his application to Congress with a general appeal for relief but added some specific suggestions to ease the way to agreement. First, he "humbly pray[ed]" that the legislature take into account "the particular hardship of his case and provide for the Payment of his Debt with Interest." But if Congress did not think it appropriate to assume payment of the debt, it should "secure the Amount to him out of the balance due to Georgia by the United States" given its assumption of the states' debts.[121] Finally, as a fallback, Georgia had clearly billed Congress for a small fraction of the goods; Congress should pay at least that amount.[122]

It is only in retrospect that Trezevant's petition to Congress seems a hopeless or quixotic, as opposed to a totally natural, step. Indeed, the House of Representatives, which received Trezevant's petition on March 4, 1794, apparently handled the petition through its usual

[118]Ibid., 5:261.

[119]Ibid.

[120]Ibid.

[121]Ibid.

[122]Trezevant had been able, he said, to trace a portion of the Farquhar goods up until their delivery to the "Clothier General" of Georgia, Raymond Demere. The state had charged the United States for this portion (slightly over a tenth) of the contract price as part of the settlement reached under the assumption act. The United States should secure that portion of the money to Trezevant out of the amount still due to Georgia under the terms of the settlement. Ibid., 5:261.

claims procedure even as it debated and passed the Eleventh Amendment.[123] While Congress ultimately rejected Trezevant's claim, it did not note any institutional impropriety in Trezevant's effort to reach the legislature.[124]

To the contrary, the move that would have been truly surprising—and apparently remained inconceivable—was a suit against the U.S. government in federal court. Potential claimants were everywhere; soldiers, suppliers, government officials, and, predominantly, investors, all held evidence of federal government debt that were far more direct than Trezevant's claim on the federal government as the state's virtual surety. Justice John Jay, in his *Chisholm* decision, had suggested that such suits would be possible; the opinions of others had adverted more nervously on the applicability of a logic that leveled state and federal authorities. The language of right, remedy, and popular sovereignty made no relevant distinctions between governments: the United States surely should have been answerable for its debts in court, as was any individual. The language of Article III would not have been a problem, since it extended "to Controversies to which the United States shall be a Party." Congress, had it wished, could have drafted legislation clearly to implement the constitutional provision by waiving any immunity.

However, very few Americans, even those staunchly Federalist, could imagine such an arrangement. Their most notable spokesmen had conducted the entire debate on funding the national debt in the First Congress on the premise that economic arrangements remained a political matter. To be sure, the Hamiltonian funding system advanced a new kind of legislative strategy, one that modeled management of public contract on private common law analogs. That, however, was only one early step in a process that would eventually make conceivable external constraint on political power over the economic relations of the state.

From 1794 on, the drama wove from state to federal legislatures. Both played characteristic roles, drawn from the delicate transitional

---

[123]See U.S. House of Representatives, Mar. 4, 1794, *Journal of the House of Representatives,* 3d Cong., 1st sess. (1793–94), p. 164.

[124]Report of Committee on Claims, Apr. 25, 1798, U.S. House of Representatives, M1267, Roll No. 1, p. 505, NARA.

moment in which the controversy arose. Legislators in Georgia, for their part, managed the Farquhar claim in a manner consistent with traditional understandings. At the same time, they sought help from the federal Congress, the body that in many ways most threatened the old regime of locally controlled political economies. By contrast, those in the federal Congress exercised their own legislative authority: they defended its most recent product, the funding system that itself diminished the power of political representatives.

So Peter Trezevant returned to the Georgia legislature in the fall of 1794. On November 28, the Georgia Senate overwhelmingly passed a resolution (17 yeas, 1 nay) adopting the report of their "committee, No. 2" on the Trezevant petition.[125] The committee report recommended payment of the whole contract price, without interest, a sum of 7,586 pounds, 10 shillings, and 1 penny, in return for which Trezevant was to "give a full and ample discharge of all claims against this State."[126] The House quickly concurred, affirming that "the book of the said Robert Farquhar, containing the entry of the late claim against the State of Georgia, [had been] corroborated by the affidavits of many respectable citizens of this State, as well as by the orders of the executive council" that had authorized the contract.[127] Trezevant received audited certificates from the state totaling the stipulated amount, although the certificates did not grant him the payment in specie.[128] Rather, they documented the state's debt to him and pro-

125Proceedings of Georgia Senate, Nov. 28, 1794, reprinted in U.S. House, *Money Due the State of Georgia,* p. 6.

126Ibid., p. 6.

127Proceedings of Georgia House, Dec. 6, 1794, reprinted in U.S. House, *Money Due the State of Georgia,* p. 8. A minority in the House objected on grounds that returned to the theme of commissioner Davis's receipt of funds, added the suggestion that any material purchased was for the "use of the United States," and rested with the contention that the "petty ledger" produced to substantiate the Farquhar claim was insufficient— "the book of original entries and other sufficient vouchers" should be required. See motions made Dec. 6, 1794, Georgia House, reprinted in ibid., pp. 7, 8. The Senate concurred on December 8, 1794, to an amendment to the resolution made by the House. Concurrence, Dec. 8, 1794, reprinted in ibid., pp. 8–9.

128The certificates documented that the "said sum is in full of the demand of Alexander Chisholm against the said State, as executor of the last will and testament of Robert Farquhar" (receipt for certificates received Dec. 9, 1794, as sworn by Peter Trezevant, Aug. 16, 1838, reprinted in U.S. House, *Money Due the State of Georgia,* pp. 9–10; see also Affidavits of Seaborn and John Jones, Nov. 24, 1838, reprinted in ibid., p. 10).

vided that such a sum would be "received in payment of any purchases made by him, of confiscated property, that may have been sold pursuant to the act of attainder." If Trezevant did not choose to use this kind of credit, his payment would be "otherwise provided for by the legislature."[129]

When the state legislature paid Trezevant in value receivable in confiscated property (or as "otherwise provided") instead of silver or gold, it acted according to the norms that had long regulated public obligation. According to those norms, one could hardly have expected payment in hard money, a relatively recent demand by public creditors after the war. In the colonial era, provinces had paid their debts in currency that held value because it was receivable for taxes; the scarcity of currency left governments with few other options. Nor did practice change quickly after the war, when the states were heavily indebted and strapped for money. While the most ambitious creditors had lobbied for a funding plan (state or, increasingly, federal) that would pay their principal in specie and service it with interest, many and perhaps most Americans approved or at least accommodated state funding systems that devalued currency, sank debts by imposing new taxes, or paid off public creditors in confiscated goods, western lands, or other options.[130] Constructing fair resolution of the public debts had great salience as a political matter: if the payment of such debts was a responsibility that required balancing the obligations due to a wide number of people who had sacrificed for the cause in different ways, popular representatives were the appropriate ones to fashion diverse methods of funding. In the decades that followed the settlement of the Farquhar claim, the Georgia legislature did modify its contracts with state creditors several times, once calling in notes for renewal and once reducing the value of audited certificates, apparently because the legislature believed that they were held mainly by speculators. Such strategies were risky—they had to be accepted popularly as

---

[129]Certificates issued by Abram Jones, Georgia auditor, Dec. 9, 1794, reprinted in U.S. House, *Money Due the State of Georgia,* p. 9.

[130]See, e.g., Manning, "Some Proposals for Making Restitution to the Original Creditors of Government"; see generally Ferguson, *Power of the Purse,* pp. 220–50, 292–96; Morrill, *Practice and Politics of Fiat Finance,* pp. 15–99 (analyzing strategies of paying public debt adopted in North Carolina).

adjustments consistent with the public faith—but they were coherent initiatives within the conventions of the time.[131]

The records left by the Georgia legislature discuss only the merits of the Farquhar claim and record only the selected settlement; they do not reveal why the representatives reversed themselves when nothing about the claim had changed. The *Chisholm* litigation had brought public scrutiny; shame and embarrassment presumably goaded action, although no judicial action directly threatened the state by November 1794.[132] Perhaps as important, state legislators at this point realized that help in paying the debt might be available. They determined that the state should "urge the justice and propriety of the United States assuming the [expense of the claim] as a debt chargeable to the general government."[133]

That, of course, would be done *legislatively*. The Georgia general assembly had concluded in its 1791 and 1793 sessions that "a further assumption by the United States of the debt incurred in prosecution of the late war" was warranted.[134] Now, the state legislature resolved that "the proceedings in this case be transmitted by his excellency the governor to our Senators and Representatives in Congress," requiring them to urge that the Trezevant claim be assumed.[135] Thus Georgia turned to the federal Congress, the body leading the movement away from traditional modes of funding, for aid on an old debt; Peter Trezevant followed closely.

---

[131]See Report of Commissioners, Georgia, 1839, reprinted in U.S. House, *Money Due the State of Georgia,* pp. 13–15. By contrast, the renewal requirement and devaluation were rejected by the state legislature of 1839, with its standards of private law contract, ibid., pp. 15–16.

[132]Popular reaction to the Supreme Court's decision in *Chisholm* had already crystallized; the Eleventh Amendment had been proposed, passed, and sent out to the states; seven states had already ratified the amendment, as would Georgia by the end of November 1794. Georgia's legislators could conceivably have wished to settle in order to avoid the possibility that the Eleventh Amendment, assuming its ratification, would be construed to have prospective effect only, which would leave the state open to a damages assessment that included interest on the contract price. But such an outcome probably did not seem likely under the political circumstances as they had developed by late 1794 or indeed dispositive to a state legislature well-accustomed to defiance.

[133]Resolution and amendment, Georgia House, Dec. 5, 1794, reprinted in U.S. House, *Money Due the State of Georgia,* p. 7.

[134]Ibid.

[135]Ibid.; Concurrence, Georgia Senate, Dec. 8, 1794, reprinted in U.S. House, *Money Due the State of Georgia,* pp. 8–9.

On January 26, 1795, Georgia raised its claim by a motion in the U.S. House of Representatives.[136] The motion, which may have been supported by written material from the state, requested reimbursement for the Farquhar claim; Congress referred it to its Committee on Claims.[137] On February 17, 1795, Trezevant petitioned Congress once again, "praying compensation for supplies furnished by [Robert Farquhar] for the use of the Army and Navy of the United States, pursuant to an order of the Governor and Executive Council of the State of Georgia, during the late war."[138] The petition does not survive, but the House committee's report—made three years later—reviews the petition's contents:

> That the petitioner states that the said Robert Farquhar, in the year 1777, sold to the State of Georgia, a large quantity of dry goods, and that no payment having been made for them, the petitioner commenced an action against the said State, in the supreme court of the United States, to recover payment for said goods, but before he could obtain final judgment and execution thereon, an alteration was made in the constitution of the United States, by which it is declared, that no action in favour of an individual shall be sustained against a state, in any court of the United States, in consequence of which he was induced to accept from the said State in satisfaction of the said demand, certain certificates, acknowledging that the said State was indebted to him for supplies furnished for the continental army in the sum of seven

136U.S. House, Jan. 26, 1795, *Journal of the House of Representatives,* 3d Cong., 2d sess. (1794–95), p. 182.

137Ibid., p. 182. The summary of the motion's subject matter, as recorded in the House Journal, interestingly links the state's application and the suit against it. Thus the House referred the following resolution to its committee: "That the State of Georgia be reimbursed the amount of a suit of the executors of Robert Farquahar [*sic*] against the said State, for sundry good sold to the said State, for the use of the troops of the United States, which suit was depending before the Supreme Court at the time of settlement of the accounts between the United States and individual States, and had been since discharged by the said State giving its obligation for the principal sum of the said suit."

It is not clear if the claim made, presumably by Georgia's representatives, was similarly stated. The House Journal reference to settlement may be to the Report of the Commissioners of the Public Debt, issued June 29, 1793, that apportioned the amounts due and from states for common costs of the war. See Ferguson, *Power of the Purse,* p. 333 and n. 19.

138U.S. House, Feb. 17, 1795, *Journal of the House of Representatives,* 3d Cong., 2d sess. (1794–95), p. 242.

thousand five hundred and eighty-six pounds, ten shillings and one penny, receivable in payment of any purchases made by him, of confiscated property, or to be otherwise provided for by the legislature;—being only the amount of the principal of the said debt, without any interest. The petitioner prays he may be permitted to fund the said certificates.[139]

The report issued by Congress on April 25, 1798, appears to be the only answer the legislature gave to the protagonists, state and individual, in the case. At that point, Congress responded simply and on the merits; its reference to the Eleventh Amendment was limited to the section of the report in which it recharacterizes Trezevant's petition (or later assertions to the committee), quoted above.

The Committee on Claims noted that it would be "difficult at this late period to determine" whether the articles purchased from Farquhar had gone for the use of the United States and added that no evidence had been produced to that effect. The committee admitted that "probably they were applied in a manner which would have authorized a charge of the amount of them by the state of Georgia to the United States," but pointed out that "whether such charge was made by the State and allowed by the commissioners who settled the accounts between the United States and the individual states" was impossible to determine. The committee then rejected the liability offered it by the claimants as a liability inconsistent not with the institutional capacity of the legislature, but with the settlement of war debts it had already endorsed. "If however, it could be ascertained that the amount of said articles ought to have been allowed to the State of Georgia in said settlement, and that they were not," the committee concluded, still "an allowance cannot be now made, without breaking up all the principles on which that settlement has been made."[140] The committee similarly disposed of Trezevant's claim, noting that he did not contend "that there ever was a contract between him and the United States." "He has," the committee concluded "no foundation for any claim against them."[141] The committee recommended that the House

[139]Report of the Committee on Claims, Apr. 25, 1798.
[140]Ibid.
[141]Ibid.

neither agree to the motion nor grant the petition. On May 1, 1798, the House accepted the committee's recommendation.[142]

By protecting the unique quality of their authority to determine the Farquhar claim, state and federal legislatures rebuffed the first real challenge to a constitutionalism that defined politics as the source animating the economy. But the challenge had occurred. Its roots lay in the approach to funding and public contract advocated by Robert Morris in the 1780s. Its logic was in fact articulated and extended in the very settlement Congress defended when it rejected Trezevant's petition, a settlement that expanded the amount of public debt funded according to rules newly restrictive of legislative flexibility. Its potential for the future appeared in the court suit attempted by Chisholm and Trezevant. Constructing a constitutional system around the new understanding of public obligation, written in economic rights of individual choice and commitment, in remedies available from a court without legislative intervention, and in a popular sovereignty founded in a government of separated powers that protected an apparently independent market, was a matter of the nineteenth century. The denouement of the Farquhar claim suggests the history that remains to be explored.

The Denouement

It took almost another century before Georgia or the United States fully dispatched their liability for the war debt incurred by Robert Farquhar. The Chisholm claim was revived by petition in the state legislature in about 1838; payment, long due on the settlement, was finally obtained in 1847, when the state of Georgia passed "an act for the relief of Peter Trezevant." The act provided that Trezevant be issued bonds worth the amount of the contractual claim without interest, a total of $22,222.22 as converted. The bonds were payable with interest in ten years ($35,555.42); on January 1, 1858, the state redeemed the bonds and paid the estate of Peter Trezevant.[143]

---

[142]Ibid. I have not yet found any surviving records of the Senate debate on Trezevant's petitions or on a state claim such as that made in the House. It is, however, apparent that neither request succeeded.

[143]See U.S. House, *Money Due the State of Georgia,* p. 2; An Act for the Relief of Peter Trezevant, Dec. 25, 1847, *Acts of the State of Georgia,* 1847 (Midgeville, 1848), p. 255;

After Georgia paid the original heir to the claim, it returned to Congress, again by the petition route, arguing that the federal government should reimburse the state after all since the original contract was for Revolutionary War supplies. The state was on the brink of recovery, favorable committee report in hand in 1860, when it seceded instead. After the Civil War, the petitioning began again. It was ultimately rewarded by a private bill providing for Georgia's reimbursement. On March 3, 1883, Congress passed "an act to refund to the State of Georgia certain money expended by said State for the common defense in 1777."[144]

Just when it seemed to be over, the U.S. treasurer declined to pay Georgia, claiming that a Civil War debt owed by the state should be set off against the award appropriated. In an ironic and appropriate confirmation that it was now a new constitutional era, Georgia turned to the newly established U.S. Court of Claims. The case was litigated and finally resolved there, when Georgia won its suit in 1889.[145] The United States paid the state of Georgia on October 6, 1890, one hundred and thirteen years after Robert Farquhar contracted with the state for the delivery of war supplies.[146] In fact, the era of legislatively centered popular sovereignty had long since passed, and the ascendancy of the courts in a new liberal order was well on its way.

Conclusion

Perhaps the most surprising aspect of this essay is that it can still be written. One would think that the importance of legislative remedy in the American tradition, as well as its connection to contract, would be

---

Certificate of Treasurer of Georgia, May 5, 1874, RG 46, Senate 43A-H25, NARA (certifying issuance of bonds amounting to $22,222.22 to Peter Trezevant in 1848, and payment of bonds at maturity on Jan. 1, 1858); Memorial of James A. Green, Agent of the State of Georgia to the U.S. Senate, Mar. 17, 1874, RG 46, Senate 43A-H25, NARA.

[144] 22 Stat. 485.

[145] *Georgia* v. *United States,* 24 Ct Cl. 402 (1889).

[146] Records of the Accounting Officers of the Department of the Treasury, Records of the Misc. Divisions, Records Relating to Accounts and Claims, Sept. 6, 1790–Sept. 29, 1894, vol. 19, entry 345, RG 217, NARA.

a well-developed story.[147] After all, the trail is littered with evidence of the significance of the political role: the archives of claims left in legislative files,[148] the insistence by judges and commentators that the legislatures were the appropriate arenas for redress,[149] the Eleventh Amendment's complementary prohibition forbidding a citizen of one state from suing another state, and the practice of sovereign immunity by the early states generally.[150] Likewise, contract is clearly the salient issue for Americans seeking remedies against the state, judging from the subject matter of the early cases and the pressure to remedy contract rather than other causes of action against the state in the nineteenth century.[151]

By the end of the nineteenth century, however, the fact that legislative remedy could have functioned as part of a coherent constitutional design had been obscured, as had the singularity of contract as the kind of claim initially at issue. The vehicles of legislative remedy, special bills and specific appropriations, had become notorious sources of political corruption,[152] while the claim of the courts to deliver neutral enforcement of law was at a peak.[153] By 1862, President Abraham Lincoln could pronounce in sweeping terms that "the investigation

---

[147]Floyd Shimomura's excellent article seems to be alone in the field. Aspects of the Chisholm story told here are recorded in volume 5 of *DHSC* and in Doyle Mathis, "The Eleventh Amendment: Adoption and Interpretation," *Georgia Law Review* 2 (1968):207–45.

[148]For example, a three-volume index of private claims records all those submitted to Congress. *Digested Summary and Alphabetical List of Private Claims* (1853; reprint ed., Baltimore, 1970).

[149]See, e.g., Alexander Hamilton, *Federalist* No. 81, in Bernard Bailyn, ed., *The Debate on the Constitution,* 2 vols. (New York, 1983), 2:489–90 (identifying contract claims against states to political remedy alone); *Filor* v. *United States,* 76 U.S. 45 (1869); *Gibbons* v. *United States,* 75 U.S. 269 (1868) (both asserting legislative redress for estoppel claims after delegation of contract claims to Court of Claims).

[150]See, e.g., Martindale, "The State and Its Creditors"; Davie, "Suing the State."

[151]Five of the suits filed in the Supreme Court against states in the early republic involved debt or contract claims, *Van Staphorst* v. *Maryland; Oswald* v. *New York; Chisholm* v. *Georgia; Cutting* v. *South Carolina;* and *Brailsford* v. *Georgia.* See *DHSC,* 5:1 n. 1, 7, 57–60, 450–58. When Congress did move out of the business of adjudicating claims for money against them, they do so first in the context of contract. See Shimomura, "History of Claims against the United States," pp. 651–60.

[152]See, e.g., Charles Chauncey Binney, *Restrictions upon Local and Special Legislation in State Constitutions* (Philadelphia, 1894).

[153]See, e.g., Thomas Grey, "Langdell's Orthodoxy," *University of Pittsburgh Law Review* 45 (1983):1–53.

and adjudication of claims, in their nature belong to the judicial department."[154] And by the end of the twentieth century, the legislative court that Congress had created to resolve contract claims was reordained an Article III court, that is, a court within the judicial branch.[155] Both federal and state legislatures had waived their traditional immunity from court suit and delegated a variety of cases to their courts. Legislative organs once designed to produce remedies for individual claims atrophied.

These developments have left courts and legal scholars to puzzle over the residue of the early republic. The courts have been caught between an obligation to preserve the increasingly incongruous commands of an earlier tradition, frozen in the Eleventh Amendment, and the relentless logic of a modern state committed to a functional separation of powers and economic dealings insulated from politics; they have produced a contorted and unwieldy jurisprudence.[156] Legal scholars, steeped like the courts in a modern world of judicially enforced rights, have been at the same time committed with only slightly more flexibility than the courts to an ideal of constancy to early constitutional authority. Their problem has been that the more vibrant the legislatively dominated tradition in the early republic, the more conspicuous would be the change required for a modern reform. They have hunted therefore for evidence that the skepticism of judicial remedies demonstrated by Americans in the early republic had been narrowly instrumental to certain ends or, at least, motivated by unworthy considerations. The underlying premise of those efforts is that the alternative, legislative remedy, was neither a meaningful nor viable element of the earlier tradition.

---

[154]*Congressional Globe,* 37th Cong., 2d sess., (1862), app. 2, as cited in Shimomura, "History of Claims against the United States," p. 655. The Court's action in 1896 to define congressional power over claims as based in the legislature's power to "pay the debts" of the United States, as opposed to its power over appropriations, may be part of this same change. See *United States* v. *Realty Co.,* 163 U.S. 427 (1896); *cf.* Shimomura, "History of Claims against the United States," pp. 668–70.

[155]Compare, e.g., *Williams* v. *United States,* 289 U.S. 553 (1933) with *Glidden* v. *Zdanok,* 370 U.S. 530 (1962).

[156]In a string of cases from the late nineteenth century through the twentieth, the U.S. Supreme Court enforced quite rigorously the prohibitions left on suing governments by earlier generations and, at the same time, expanded methods of evading those prohibitions by various means, including permitting suits against government officials. See *DHSC,* 5:4.

The dilemma of the courts and the scholars is a product of the development of modern economic liberalism and a tribute to its power. That paradigm made legislative power over economic relations with the state, epitomized by cases of public contract, untenable. The relocation of such cases to the judicial realm, by contrast, facilitated the isolation of contractual relations from continuing and unpredictable changes in social and economic circumstance, the reduction of those relations to bipolar exchanges (as opposed to agreements involving and affecting many people), and the insulation of the decision makers from popular means of expression and pressure.[157]

To that end, the controversy in *Chisholm* was a monument well suited. It was crisp, discrete, and bipolar, a case with few of the attributes inviting legislative calibration for circumstance and all the potential vulnerability to legislative abuse. It remained from Wilson's time to the late twentieth century a perfect vehicle for driving down legislative legitimacy and advocating the mandate of the courts to do justice or, put in somewhat later terms, the institutional competency of the courts to enforce legal rights. Contract rights, delegated to and defined by the courts, became the model for other rights, and the business of the judicial branch, operating under the premises identified above, to resolve. As the plausibility of another kind of remedy—in this case, legislative—faded, rights became increasingly and essentially identified with the remedies associated with and available in the judicial arena.

The judicialization of public contract rights greatly strengthened the hands of individuals whose claims could be clearly presented in a court forum: as practices that revalued public debt on rationales of social need faded, nominal obligations took on added sanctity and named parties wielded rights against the state independent of other

---

[157]The best demonstration of the importance of these factors is the debate over discrimination in the payment of the public debt, conducted in the First Federal Congress. See *DHFFC,* 12:181–490 (Feb. 8–Feb. 22, 1790). According to those defending legislative prerogative in that context, Congress had to consider the larger political and social circumstances in which the debt was incurred and had to be paid, if it was to do justice to the creditors who had originally contributed their services or money to the United States. The argument involved multiple parties in the settlement of individual contracts. Finally, it assumed an exposure to popular response, a kind of political reactivity on the part of the public, that was substantial. For an initial investigation, see Christine Desan, "Constituting Capitalism: From Political Economy to the Law of the Market" (paper presented at the American Society for Legal History, Oct. 2000).

claims.[158] Those who had different kinds of claims against the public, claims dependent on equitable evaluations of sacrifice in paying taxes, for example, fared less well. The judicialization of economic relations with the state in turn supported the idea that market relations with the public as well as with private individuals was an affair insulated from politics.

Those developments have helped to obscure both the political process that engendered the shape of the economic realm and the particularity of the institutional commitments that continue to determine the way it operates. The challenge for modern Americans is to understand the relationship between politics and the market itself as a public constitutional matter, intricately connected to both informed and informing matters of right, remedy, and popular sovereignty. Like those abstractions, it is also susceptible to change not acknowledged in the odd discourse of liberal constitutionalism.

---

[158]See Desan, "Constituting Capitalism."

David J. Siemers

The Electoral Dynamics of Ratification

Federalist and Antifederalist Strength and Cohesion, 1787–1803

Don Quixote is known as a fool and a charlatan. Yet his creator, Miguel de Cervantes, also expressed valuable insights through this famous character's voice. Quixote reminds readers that "they who lose today may win tomorrow," an important lesson when applied to politics.[1] Its corollary is also of value: they who win today may lose tomorrow. Eras are defined by the rise and fall of politicians and the political movements they constitute.

There is much more to these observations, however, than the simple acknowledgment that political fortunes wax and wane. Implicit in these maxims is the notion that winning and losing are intimately bound to each other. One group's political victory is necessarily another's loss, of course. But more importantly, adversity can help germinate the seed of victory and victory may initiate breakdown and decay. Political losses frequently force a reexamination of a movement's tactics and message, yielding innovations that may prove more successful. Political victories are advantageous on their face, but are fraught with potential danger. Electoral success shoulders the recipient with accountability. Constituents expect positive, tangible results. If the winner fails to produce beneficial changes, a backlash may ensue. Further,

[1]Miguel de Cervantes, *Don Quixote* (1615; reprint ed., trans. Peter Anthony Motteux and John Ozell, London, 1743), 1.1.7.

even when politicians are successful in bringing change, they may be punished. Electoral success frequently emboldens politicians to attempt more and to act more quickly than is desirable.

In no recent figure have the intertwining dynamics of winning and losing been more readily apparent than Newt Gingrich. Early in his congressional career, the former history professor realized that the Republican minority's accommodationist stance was self-defeating. Gingrich believed that the seemingly permanent Republican minority could become a governing majority. Attempting to make winners out of losers required adopting an abrasively partisan strategy to highlight the differences between Republicans and Democrats.[2] This aggressive strategy paid off, eventually producing the first Republican-led House since the early 1950s. Gingrich himself became the leader of the House majority, and in the first one hundred days of his speakership oversaw the passage of almost all the items in the Contract with America. In 1995 Newt Gingrich knew himself to be the most influential Speaker in nearly a century. His decision to rush major legislation through the House, however, proved counterproductive. The more deliberative, individualistic Senate stymied several contract items, as did the Democratic president.[3] In the wake of the Republicans' stunning victory, Speaker Gingrich understandably pressed forward quickly on all fronts. But it was too much too fast, and, in large part because of his strategic errors, Gingrich faced a revolt within his own party a few years later. In the wake of the 1998 elections, Gingrich could not hold the Republicans together. A sufficient number of his own party were so opposed to his leadership that they vowed not to support his reappointment as Speaker, even if it came to a full vote on

---

[2]Bruce I. Oppenheimer, "Abdicating Congressional Power: The Paradox of Republican Control," in *Congress Reconsidered,* 6th ed., ed. Lawrence C. Dodd and Bruce I. Oppenheimer (Washington, D.C., 1997), pp. 371–76.

[3]There are several worthwhile accounts of the 104th Congress, including Richard F. Fenno's *Learning to Govern* (Washington, D.C., 1997) and Barbara Sinclair's *Unorthodox Lawmaking* (Washington, D.C., 1997), pp. 96–100, 175–216, passim. Gingrich and the other House Republicans' zeal to pursue an electoral mandate is best exemplified by their decision to twice force the shutdown of nonessential government operations. This gambit, designed to force President Clinton to agree to a quicker deficit reduction timetable, badly misfired. Indeed, it provided Clinton the key issue for the '96 campaign, in which he portrayed Republican candidate Robert Dole as an extremist by linking him with Gingrich.

the House floor. Gingrich resigned from the House; he had initially found opportunity in adversity but then discovered adversity amid triumph.

This essay traces the electoral fortunes of the Federalists and Antifederalists vying to represent the American people in Congress. Chronologically distant from Gingrich and our own time, these groups experienced familiar political dynamics. The Federalists' successes and failures were closely tied to the Antifederalists' in an inverse relationship. During the ratification debate and in the first few federal elections, one group's loss was the other's gain. There is also a distinct pattern to how that inverse relationship developed through the 1790s. Initially, the Antifederalists were a sizable group, perhaps a majority by some measures.[4] Federalists nevertheless succeeded in ratifying the new Constitution and so enhanced their stature that it enabled them to dominate the earliest federal elections. In the first, they were so successful that they did not feel a need to hold together their diverse coalition. Federalists had been fairly well united over the political process the national government should employ, but they were much less united on the policies that should result from such a process. Most supported an aggressive legislative agenda in the First Federal Congress. That agenda alienated some Federalists, particularly those from the Middle Atlantic and southern states. Because ratification had vaulted them into an overwhelming majority, though, Federalists

---

[4]Antifederalists may have been a majority at the grassroots level and perhaps even among political elites. Because of the recognition Federalists receive from their role in ratification, one is easily led to the faulty conclusion that far more political elites were Federalist than Antifederalist. It is clearly the case that the two most prominent figures in the United States, George Washington and Benjamin Franklin, were ardent Federalists. They lent their considerable weight to the cause, but it was clear neither would ever serve in the new Congress. Washington was slated to be the first president, and Franklin was too old to be interested in elective office—something which had never appealed to him. Other prominent political figures, both Federalist and Antifederalist, were far below the stature of these two. The next tier of leaders included many Antifederalists: Patrick Henry, Elbridge Gerry, George Clinton, and Samuel Adams were among these household names. If anything, there were probably more Antifederalists immediately below the stature of Washington and Franklin, because most of the leaders of the Federalist movement, such as Hamilton and Madison, were comparatively young newcomers on the national scene. The measure of relative strength I use in my analysis—those who served as delegates in ratification conventions—is designed to avoid easily mistaken impressions in favor of something more comprehensive and accurate. Even this measure is skewed against the Antifederalists, as I explain later in this chapter.

passed those aggressive policies without the breakaway faction. The rift between those two groups proved enduring. Success thus served to split the Federalists' fragile ratification coalition, ultimately to the great detriment of those who initially held the reins of the American government.

The early Federalist victories came at the expense of the Antifederalists. Antifederalists responded to their numerical weakness by allying with the breakaway Federalists, together organizing an opposition party. During the 1790s, the former Antifederalists' fortunes turned, and they recovered much of their initial strength once the nation became comfortable with its new constitutional raiment. The Republican alliance eventually surged past the Federalists into a majority during the so-called Revolution of 1800. By then Federalists had found adversity in victory, and Antifederalists gained opportunity amidst adversity. These phenomena, occurring in logical progression, profoundly shaped the American regime. The Federalists' initial victory allowed the national government to set out on a sound footing, while the Republicans' triumph in the early 1800s served to limit the scope and reach of that government well into the nineteenth century.

Trolling between Disciplines

Prior to discussing the macrolevel political phenomena that attended ratification, it seems appropriate first to comment on why neither historians nor political scientists, for reasons understandable within their disciplines, have presented — nor perhaps fully appreciated — the phenomena discerned here. Each mode of social science has strengths and weaknesses; awareness of them helps remedy systematic flaws. Political historians offer rich explanations of particular contexts. Their narratives self-consciously privilege depth over breadth. Historians frequently provide very detailed and accurate information about a narrowly defined time and place, such as New York's ratification convention or Rhode Island's politics during 1790. However, their devotion to in-depth knowledge makes them reticent to conduct sweeping research or engage in comparisons. Exhaustive attention to a particular context effectively prohibits attention to other contexts. Moreover, if one context is thought to be like another, historians fear it may not be fully understood—or understood for itself intrinsically. Grasping the essence of a place and time, many feel, requires knowing what is unique to that setting. Thus while historians have introduced us to individuals whose political aspirations were benefited or thwarted by ratification, they have not dealt with how widespread that phenomenon was across the nation, collectively advantaging or disadvantaging the two identifiable camps.

Thanks to historians, we do possess scattered evidence suggesting that ratification effected a political earthquake, but these sources are fragmentary and impressionistic. In Connecticut, for instance, Jeremiah Wadsworth related in a late 1788 letter that "the Anties have lost all their influence in our Assembly."[5] Jonathan Trumbull, Jr., conveys the same idea in a contemporaneous letter to George Washington: "the triumph of Foederalism has been great in Connecticut since last Winter. The Opposition which then existed, is now dwindled into meer unimportance."[6] These documents are among the thousands published by historians in four useful multivolume collections. Documentary projects on the federal convention, ratification, the first federal elections, and the First Federal Congress yield a wealth of information about the politics of the time. However, their chronological scope is limited to less than four years, from the time that the Constitutional Convention met in 1787 to the adjournment of the First Congress in 1791. Through the rest of the 1790s the published documentary record is spotty: we know little of how Federalism and Antifederalism were dealt with by leaders or were perceived by the public after 1791. Commentary in these multivolume collections displays the historians' sensitivity to context. But because each event is treated separately, integration suffers. Researchers and casual users may easily lose sight of the logical progression of events during these years; for example, geographic compartmentalization diverts attention from the cumulative outcome of the first federal elections. That collective outcome heavily influenced what the First Congress attempted and accomplished. The

---

[5]Jeremiah Wadsworth to Henry Knox, Nov. 2, 1788, *The Documentary History of the First Federal Elections, 1788–1790,* 4 vols. (Madison, 1976–89), vol. 2 (Gordon DenBoer and Lucy Trumbull Brown, eds.), p. 27, hereafter cited as *DHFFE.*

[6]Jonathan Trumbull, Jr., to George Washington, June 20, 1788, ibid., 2:9.

documentary building blocks in these histories logically point to a comprehensive treatment of the electoral dynamics of ratification—even if that kind of study probably would not be undertaken by historians themselves because of its breadth.

Political scientists attempt what historians avoid by privileging breadth over depth. They tend to compare multiple contexts and broad stretches of time. In so doing they often discern patterns of political conduct and development. One obvious drawback to this approach is that it can threaten historical accuracy. A less obvious difficulty is that political scientists shy away from research where comparisons prove cumbersome. Assessing the electoral effects of ratification involves two major problems of comparison. First, there is no constant national institution in which to judge the phenomenon. One cannot assess ratification's effect by looking at the changing composition of Congress, because it did not exist before ratification.[7] Second, Federalists and Antifederalists are difficult to study through time. In some states the divide over the Constitution did not correspond with state party affiliations. In others, parties were not well defined to begin with. Frequently, positions on the Constitution were ambiguous or have been obscured by the passage of time. Thus it is difficult to assess ratification's impact by studying the composition of state legislatures.

Complicating matters further, the Federalists' ratification coalition broke apart quickly. Since some Federalists allied with Antifederalists, many political scientists have thought the divide over ratification irrelevant after 1791. When political scientists have dealt with the 1790s, most often they have studied the nascent party system, which they find only tangentially related to the ratification divide.[8] Thus political

---

[7]For a variety of reasons it is fruitless to gauge Federalist and Antifederalist strength through time by comparing the Federal Congress to the Confederation Congress. The division between Federalists and Antifederalists became clear only in the last months of 1787, very late in the life of the Confederation Congress. By the time the next year's delegates were chosen, the Congress was clearly a lame-duck institution (its powers had always been severely circumscribed anyway). Attendance was thus sparse and who was selected to serve not particularly consequential. The composition of the two bodies is very different as well: the Confederation Congress was unicameral and each state determined the size of its at-large delegation, ranging between three and seven individuals, independent of the state's size.

[8]John H. Aldrich and Ruth W. Grant assess political science's treatment of the 1790s

scientists have not attached research on party dynamics during the 1790s to the ratification debate. They overlook how a reputation as an Antifederalist or Federalist had an enduring impact in the years beyond ratification by directly leading to the formation of the first party system.

Because the ratification coalition broke apart quickly, political scientists have not applied their "critical election" concept to the first federal election. First articulated by V. O. Key in 1955, a critical election is one in which voting patterns differ markedly from those immediately previous, with subsequent elections confirming that change.[9] A great deal of research has employed this concept, with a general consensus that the elections of 1800, 1828, 1860, 1896, and 1932 fit the bill.[10] In those five elections, major shifts in the partisan composition of Congress are easily shown and highly instructive. In each, cross-time comparisons are easily made — the party affiliations of representatives are readily apparent both before and after the election. What political scientists may be missing for lack of easy demonstration is that the critical shift following ratification is also of the highest magnitude.[11]

---

this way: "focusing on party development has distorted the picture of the politics of the immediate postratification period and has led to a serious misunderstanding of the continuities of the politics of the 1780s and those of the 1790s," in "The Antifederalists, the First Congress, and the First Parties," *Journal of Politics* 55 (1993):296. Aldrich and Grant's corrective for political science squares with the past thirty-plus years of historical research on the era inaugurated by Kenneth R. Bowling's dissertation, which reinforced the congruence of individual stances before and after ratification. Bowling writes that the issues faced by the First Congress "are deeply rooted in the 1780s if not the 1770s. It was not simply that the same men were still working with the same issues. More, it was that these men, almost invariably [took] the same positions they had taken earlier" (Bowling, "Politics in the First Congress, 1789–1791," Ph.D. diss., University of Wisconsin-Madison, 1968, p. 272).

[9] V. O. Key, "A Theory of Critical Elections," *Journal of Politics* 17 (1955):3–15.

[10] Walter Dean Burnham, *Critical Elections and the Mainsprings of American Politics* (New York, 1970), p. 1. Much attention to critical elections was inspired by a devotion to the New Deal and the hope for strong parties that would provide systematic, compelling alternatives to voters. In the late 1960s researchers often commented on the regular periodicity of realigning phenomena, noting that a major realignment occurred every thirty years or so and thus the United States was due for another. While some have argued that 1968 or 1980 fit the bill, it seems that the hopes of these early scholars have gone unfulfilled.

[11] Key's original paper analyzed the 1928 election in New England. He argued that contrary to the conventional wisdom that 1932 brought a sea change, the previous

The critical shift I find accompanying ratification is at least as pronounced as the five mentioned above; it is just more difficult to discern and present.

The ratification realignment is not precisely the same as the agreed-upon realignments above. But comparisons of those five critical elections show that they are each different from the others in some way.[12] Like other critical elections in American history, the ratification realignment "enable[d] the majority party to legislate significant policy changes" and was relatively enduring.[13] As I will demonstrate, even after the breakup of the Federalist coalition, Federalists were still advantaged and Antifederalists disadvantaged well into the 1790s. Demonstrating this shift requires a bit of creativity. Unfortunately, we do not know the affiliations of all who ran for Congress through the 1790s. Nevertheless, we can limit our view to known Federalists and Antifederalists and discern ratification's effect on them. Also needed is a way to approximate the relative strength of Federalists and Antifederalists in the states before and after ratification.

Another useful concept in discerning what transpired as a result of ratification is introduced by Charles O. Jones. In a well-known article about the limits of congressional leadership, Jones draws a distinction between the majority party's "procedural majority" and its "substantive majority." The procedural majority is "necessary to organize [the

---

presidential election had altered voting patterns in New England. He also briefly commented on the election of 1896. In subsequent analyses, various authors comment on the elections of 1860, 1896, and 1932. None have analyzed the elections immediately after ratification. Burnham deals with a broad sweep of time in *Critical Elections and the Mainsprings of American Politics,* with analysis reaching as far back as 1824. David Brady presents three case studies of how critical elections affected policy outcomes in *Critical Elections and Congressional Policymaking* (Palo Alto, 1988): the Civil War realignment, the 1896 critical election, and the New Deal realignment. A recent anthology of classic studies of Congress contains several studies: the alignments beginning with the elections of 1860, 1896, and 1932 are all treated by more than one article in Joel Silbey, ed., *The United States Congress: The Electoral Connection* (Madison, 1991).

12One political scientist, James L. Sundquist, developed a typology of critical elections, showing that many different kinds of realignment could occur. Sundquist mentions five different kinds of critical elections, including elections where a third party is absorbed by the major parties and where one of the two major parties is replaced by a third party. The ratification era provides us with an example of a critical election type not discussed by Sundquist, one accompanying the adoption of a framework of government. See Sundquist, *Dynamics of the Party System* (Washington, D.C., 1983).

13Brady, *Critical Elections and Congressional Policymaking,* p. 2.

party] for business and maintain its organization." After internal consultation, party members typically agree to unanimously support favored leaders and rules of conduct in anticipation of employing them to pass key agenda items. Meanwhile, "substantive majorities are those necessary to pass legislation."[14] In other words, it is important that the majority party hold itself together as an organization as well as on particular legislative proposals. Jones's article focuses on leaders so intent on fully employing their substantive majorities that they faced an internal revolt. As mentioned above, Newt Gingrich faced a comparable situation at the end of the 105th Congress when several Republicans vowed not to support his reappointment as Speaker. A similar dynamic was at work in the First Congress. Federalists were so concerned with passing their substantive agenda that they alienated members who had originally formed their dominant procedural coalition.

Seeking Cover and Exploiting Advantages after Ratification

Those in elective office owe their position to public esteem. Quite naturally, politicians cultivate public acclaim and are interested in how their actions are perceived. In this regard, the politicians of the ratification debate were little different from those of our time. Public figures knew their stance on ratification could affect their subsequent career. Thus, state convention delegates in particular acted in image-conscious ways. A ratification convention vote was easily the most visible any would cast, one that could make or break a political career. With that type of vote, politicians lay themselves on the line. Public acclaim or humiliation depends on subsequent events which they cannot control. Both before and after ratification, constituent reactions were an important factor in crafting political stances. Leaders instinctively felt what historical research has shown to be true for several individuals: ratification convention delegates would be held accountable for their positions. Delegates were forced to deal with uncertainty.

---

[14]Charles O. Jones, "Joseph G. Cannon and Howard W. Smith: An Essay on the Limits of Leadership in the House of Representatives," *Journal of Politics* 30 (1968):617, 618.

Their own ideas about the Constitution were well formed and they had a good idea what their constituents thought, but they were unsure how the ratification process would turn out.[15] The Constitution could be approved or it could be voted down. If implemented, the Constitution could succeed or it could fail. One's position on the Constitution was thus something of a calculated gamble. Most delegates based their votes on a combination of personal philosophy and constituent wishes. Such a vote, however, left delegates vulnerable. On highly visible issues where individuals are forced to take a clear, unequivocal stance, there is no escaping accountability.

Federalists felt ratification would aid the nation, but they also believed it would enhance their own standing. They knew it would do so in an immediate sense because their constituents supported the Constitution. In the long term, the payoff was potentially much greater: they dreamed of being acclaimed as the nation's Founders. Needless to say, if the Constitution was not ratified, Federalists would not enter the American political pantheon. Antifederalists had their own set of mixed motives. They were genuinely concerned about securing the benefits of self-rule won by the Revolution, but they also calculated that vocal opposition to distant, centralized power would resonate with their constituents.[16] If the proposed government was voted down, they might be called on to formulate a more palatable substitute. If ratification occurred, they would have to stake their reputations on a slim

---

[15]This statement is particularly applicable in the eight states that held conventions before June 1788. After South Carolina's approval in late May, the whole nation knew that the next state to ratify the Constitution would fulfill Article V's criteria allowing its implementation. Thus delegates from the last states to ratify knew that the Constitution was the law of the land. While their uncertainty about the Constitution's fate was lowered, it was far from nonexistent, as they could not tell whether it would work out in the long term.

[16]Neo-Progressive scholar Jackson Turner Main starkly demonstrated that Antifederalist strength was inland, in areas more remote from the Federalists' coastal strongholds in *The Antifederalists* (Chapel Hill, 1961). Main attributes that disparity to differing economic conditions: backcountry dwellers did not rely on mercantile markets as much as their coastal counterparts and thus were not interested in the Constitution's ability to break down commercial barriers. While this different political economy is an important factor, isolation likely created an ideological reason to oppose the Constitution as well: it is very likely that fears of a distant, controlling national government were greater in the less cosmopolitan backcountry. Local politicians were aware of this tendency and emphasized this argument accordingly.

reed: they had predicted the Constitution would imperil citizen liberties. If that prediction came true, the Antifederalists would be considered so prescient that only they could right the ship of state.

From the work of two historians, we know that the public lives of several important Antifederalists ended because of ratification. Also of note in these cases is the attempt of other Antifederalists to shield themselves from the fallout of ratification. In the wake of ratification, individual politicians actively protected their own political viability and exploited the weaknesses of their opponents in ways similar to contemporary politicians. After ratification, Federalists and Antifederalists engaged in a public relations contest that mainly benefited the former group.

Robin Brooks tells the story of Antifederalist Melancton Smith, one of Gov. George Clinton's political lieutenants in New York. While the state convention met in Poughkeepsie, New Hampshire and Virginia became the ninth and tenth states to ratify. In order not to lose the seat of federal government (the Confederation Congress had been meeting in New York City since January 1785), Antifederalists from the southern part of the state decided to allow ratification. Unfortunately for them, Antifederalists held a clear majority in the convention and their constituents had elected them to vote against the Constitution. The delicate task of engineering acceptance fell to Smith, who had been acting as the Antifederalists' floor leader. To secure ratification, Smith volunteered to take the "wrong" position and vote for the Constitution, along with his fellow delegates from Dutchess, a southern county. That vote probably cost him a seat in the first United States Senate and ended his promising political career.[17]

It is of crucial importance to note what other New York Antifederalist delegates did in this situation. The great majority voted against the Constitution, despite their tacit acquiescence. They agreed to allow ratification, but they were not letting that be known publicly. As many Antifederalists as possible voted against ratification, fulfilling the expectations of their constituents. Taking such a public stance saved them from embarrassment. To them, taking a clear, defensible stance

[17]Robin Brooks, "Alexander Hamilton, Melancton Smith, and the Ratification of the Constitution in New York," *William and Mary Quarterly,* 3d ser. 24 (1967):339–58.

congruent with their prior commitment was more important than winning the ratification fight.[18]

Even with the Dutchess delegates voting for the document, there were too many Antifederalists to allow for ratification. Accordingly, several delegates abstained to allow a three-vote Federalist majority. Individuals who absented themselves from the final vote could not be blamed directly for ratification. To use a late-twentieth-century phrase, the Antifederalists who voted against ratification or abstained had "political cover." They could face their constituents saying they fought the good fight but ended up short. Melancton Smith and his fellow Dutchess County delegates were not so lucky; they could not hide from their vote. Most Antifederalists, however, were allowed to engage in what was essentially a public ritual designed to prevent damage to their political prospects.

John P. Kaminski relates a similar tale about Rhode Island. The state was firmly Antifederalist throughout the ratification period and, in fact, still had not ratified by the time Congress achieved a quorum in April 1789. By that late date Antifederalists in Rhode Island knew ratification was necessary; however, they were still in a majority and knew constituents would not look kindly on a blatant about-face. "Their problem, then, was to allow the Constitution to be ratified while making it appear that they were not responsible for ratification and simultaneously preventing Federalists from receiving undeserved credit."[19]

Rhode Island's majority party had insistently refused to call a convention for two years and thus feared the repercussions of agreeing to one. Nevertheless, this obstacle was eventually overcome when Antifederalists found a way to divert attention from the two political parties, thus avoiding collective responsibility. Antifederalist Gov. John Collins had cast the decisive vote for a convention. Other Antifeder-

---

[18]For elective officials, it is usually far more important to be on the right side of an issue than to be on the winning side. As a legislator one easily controls one's own vote, but building coalitions is arduous. Congressional scholar David R. Mayhew puts it this way: "the blunt fact is that congressmen have less of a stake in winning victories than they normally appear to have. It is natural for politicians to put more effort into being right than winning" (Mayhew, *Congress: The Electoral Connection* [New Haven, 1974], p. 118).

[19]John P. Kaminski, "Political Sacrifice and Demise—John Collins and Jonathan J. Hazard, 1786–1790," *Rhode Island History* 35 (1976):91.

alists saw an opportunity to cut their losses by blaming their titular leader. They dumped Collins from the gubernatorial ticket in the upcoming election and branded him a turncoat. This move focused attention away from the Federalists and Antifederalists as groups, serving to soften any collective attribution. Governor Collins thus played the role of sacrificial lamb for the Antifederalists, one on whom blame could be heaped to keep it from being distributed generally.[20]

Turning on Collins was sufficiently successful to be repeated on another prominent Antifederalist once the Rhode Island convention finished its work. Under conditions more favorable for Antifederalists, Jonathan J. Hazard might have been chosen the state's first federal senator. Instead, his political career ended when the rest of the party abandoned him, as they did Collins. They accused Hazard of consorting with the enemy, moderating his opposition to the Constitution to garner Federalist support for a Senate post.[21] In this scenario, Hazard's duplicity and personal ambition were to blame for ratification, rather than Antifederalist incompetence or Federalist skill.

As these examples indicate, the Antifederalists were greatly concerned with ratification's effect on their image. This concern became acute as the first federal elections drew near. Antifederalists proclaimed their opposition to the Constitution had ended. They were willing to work within the system the people had chosen but asked constituents to send them to Congress so beneficial amendments could be secured.[22] Meanwhile, Federalists worked to parlay their success, saying that the "friends of the Constitution" should be given a chance to implement the new government. Federalists warned constituents that Antifederalists might sabotage the system they had opposed.[23] While circumstances in each state differed, what happened in New York and Rhode Island occurred in many states: while Antifederalists scrambled for cover, Federalists sought to use ratification to their advantage. In only three states was this dynamic entirely inapplicable: the Delaware,

---

[20]. Ibid., p. 93

[21]Ibid., pp. 95–96.

[22]David J. Siemers, " 'It Is Natural to Care for the Crazy Machine': The Antifederalists' Post-Ratification Acquiescence," *Studies in American Political Development* 12 (1998):383–410.

[23]*DHFFE,* vol. 1 (Merrill Jensen, Robert A. Becker, and Gordon DenBoer, eds.), pp. vii–xii and vols. 1–4, passim.

Georgia, and New Jersey conventions had unanimously favored the Constitution; ratification did not distinguish rival politicians there and thus could not be raised in subsequent electoral contests. In the other states, many Federalists derided their opponents as "Antis," well into the 1790s. Massachusetts's Fisher Ames can be found complaining as late as 1804 that the "anti-federalist party" was misleading the public in calling themselves "Republican."[24] It should come as no surprise that politicians in the ratification debate acted in these image-conscious ways. Scapegoating others and exploiting opponents' vulnerabilities often makes sense in regimes where the support of an imperfectly informed public determines political success. As practicing politicians, leaders in the founding era also employed these tactics.

Less certain than their use are the results these tactics effected. While historical research clearly points to the possibility of a Federalist surge and an Antifederalist decline following ratification, the pervasiveness and duration of that shift, as well as its ultimate impact, has yet to be chronicled. Were Antifederalists generally able to avoid opprobrium? How well did the Federalists build on ratification to enhance their own prospects in state and federal elections? In short, how did ratification affect the subsequent political careers of individuals and aggregate election results nationwide? The evidence to be presented here shows that the first federal elections (1788–89) should be classified as "critical" and led to the Federalist split, inaugurating the United States' first party system.

Documenting the Critical Shift

Determining the size of an electoral shift requires cross-time comparison. Figuring out Antifederalist strength after ratification is easy. Eleven of sixty-five members of the first House and three of twenty-six senators had opposed the Constitution. All remaining representatives and senators were Federalists.[25] Thus, approximately one in six repre-

---

[24]Fisher Ames as "The Republican," originally printed in the *Boston Gazette,* Aug. 13, 1804, Seth Ames, ed., *The Works of Fisher Ames,* 2 vols. (1809, reprint ed., Indianapolis, 1983), 1:321–25.

[25]*The Documentary History of the First Federal Congress, 1789–1791,* 14 vols. to date

sentatives and one in nine senators had been Antifederalists. Figuring out Antifederalist strength before ratification is more difficult. Ratification convention votes provide a useful approximation of the relative strength of the Antifederalists and Federalists, but one that is skewed in favor of the Federalists. All told, 1,650 individuals voted in ratification conventions, 577, or 35 percent, of them voted against ratification. This simple ratio indicates that Antifederalists were a much larger minority than their strength in the First Congress indicates. But this ratio is also somewhat misleading. The numbers above count Federalist majorities for states clearly controlled by Antifederalists during the ratification period: New Hampshire, Virginia, New York, North Carolina, and Rhode Island. Not coincidentally, these were the last five states to ratify. Many Antifederalists in these states ultimately came to conclude they would need to ratify to avoid being left out of the Union. In some states, moderate Antifederalists were won over by the promise of future amendments. The passage of recommended amendments marginally changed voting patterns in several states: Massachusetts, South Carolina, New Hampshire, and Virginia.[26] Finally, aggregating

---

(Baltimore, 1972–), vol. 14 (William C. diGiacomantonio, Kenneth R. Bowling, Charlene Bangs Bickford, and Helen E. Veit, eds.), pp. 489–932, hereafter cited as *DHFFC.* These numbers are a bit misleading, serving to slightly overstate the Antifederalist presence in the new legislature. Representatives from North Carolina and Rhode Island were late to arrive to the First Congress because the states were late to ratify. None participated in the first session of the First Congress, and none were present at the beginning of the second session, convened January 4, 1790. North Carolinians John Baptista Ashe and Timothy Bloodworth arrived on March 24 and April 6, respectively. Rhode Island's Joseph Stanton, Jr., arrived on June 25, in time for crucial votes on the assumption of state debts and the site of the seat of government. William Grayson, an Antifederalist senator from Virginia, was in ill health during almost half of the first session of Congress and unable to participate in the proceedings. Grayson died before he could attend the second session of the Congress and was temporarily replaced by a Federalist. Only in the third session of the First Congress did an Antifederalist, James Monroe, take Grayson's place.

[26]These are the states in which Federalists offered to back a list of recommended amendments for enough moderate Antifederalist votes to obtain ratification. The conventions of three other states, New York, North Carolina, and Rhode Island, also recommended amendments, but because of their unique circumstances one cannot simply attribute Antifederalist support for the Constitution there to the amendments: as mentioned above, New York Antifederalists were a clear majority in the Poughkeepsie convention. In the wake of ratification they endorsed the document to keep the seat of federal government in New York City. Passing recommended amendments was important to them substantively and to provide political cover, but it was not the sine qua non of ratification. Nor was it so in North Carolina or Rhode Island, where late conventions

convention results is problematic because the size of each convention was different and not tied to a state's population, which determined the composition of the new House.[27] Taking these factors into account, Antifederalist strength among political elites rivaled that of the Federalists in 1787.

Obtaining more accurate tallies of Antifederalist strength in the several states is possible. New York's two political parties were sufficiently distinct and polarized over the issue of ratification to give us an accurate ratio. Of sixty-five individuals selected to attend the convention, forty-six were Antifederalists.[28] In March of 1788, Rhode Island's towns voted 48–16 against holding a convention, a fair approximation of Antifederalist strength there. North Carolina held two separate conventions to consider the Constitution. While the second one ratified, the composition of the first gives a more accurate picture of the state's disposition. Though the first convention did not vote directly on ratification, it did vote on whether to adjourn or continue meeting. Adjournment was favored by Antifederalists and opposed by Federalists. The final count was 193–75 in favor of adjournment. The number of delegates won over in other states is a bit more difficult to judge. Nevertheless, that task has been accomplished probably as accurately as it can be by Jackson Turner Main. In his book, *The Antifederalists,* Main estimated the composition of ratification conventions had recommendatory amendments not passed. I use his estimates for New Hampshire, Massachusetts, Virginia, and South Carolina.

Table 1 estimates the number of Antifederalists who would have been elected to the First Congress from each state given the more accurate figures outlined above. Had a critical shift not occurred, a good estimate is that around twenty-seven Antifederalists would have been elected to the House (sixty-five seats total) and eleven selected to serve in the twenty-six seat Senate. In other words, the Antifederalists would have been much more than a small minority, controlling approximately 40 percent of the seats in both the House and Senate.

---

endorsed the already functional Constitution. Meeting with the federal Congress already in session, Antifederalists in each state knew there was little choice but to ratify.

[27]Unlike the other two estimation problems, this last one does not significantly skew the ratio of Antifederalists to Federalists.

[28]Main, *The Antifederalists,* p. 288.

Table 1. Projection of Antifederalist Strength in the First Congress without a Critical Electoral Shift

State	*Convention Vote (F–AF)*	*Estimate of Actual Strength (F–AF)*	*Projected House Delegation (F–AF)*	*Projected Senate Delegation (F–AF)*
New Hampshire	57–47	30–77*	1–2	0–2
Massachusetts	187–168	170–190*	4–4	1–1
Connecticut	128–40	128–40	4–1	2–0
Rhode Island	34–32	16–48	0–1	0–2
New York	30–27	19–46	2–4 or 1–5	0–2
New Jersey	39–0	39–0	4–0	2–0
Pennsylvania	46–23	46–23	6–2 or 5–3	2–0 or 1–1
Delaware	30–0	30–0	1–0	2–0
Maryland	63–11	63–11	5–1	2–0
Virginia	89–79	84–84*	5–5	1–1
North Carolina	195–77	75–193	1–4	0–2
South Carolina	149–73	126–98*	3–2	2–0 or 1–1
Georgia	26–0	26–0	3–0	2–0
Total	1073–577	852–810	38–27	15–11

Note: During state ratification conventions and the First Congress, Maine, Kentucky, and Tennessee were districts of Massachusetts, Virginia, and North Carolina, respectively. Projected delegation numbers were arrived at by choosing the ratio of representatives and senators (Federalist to Antifederalist) that most closely corresponded with their actual strength, presented in the second column.

* Jackson Turner Main's estimates of Antifederalist strength from appendix D of *The Antifederalists,* p. 288.

Group strength in a legislative body helps determine the way it does business. Obviously, a majority is able to act differently from a minority, but large minorities also act much differently than small minorities. For a large minority, killing the majority's policy proposals simply takes convincing a few in the majority that the proposed policies are faulty. Without a critical shift, Antifederalists would have been strong enough to directly oppose Federalist policies in Congress. On the other hand, a minority as small as the Antifederalists were in the early Congresses could not hope to win simply by pointing out flaws in

Table 2. Estimated vs. Actual Antifederal Strength in the First Congress

State	*NH*	*MA*	*CT*	*RI*	*NY*	*NJ*	*PA*	*DE*	*MD*	*VA*	*NC*	*SC*	*GA*
Total House Seats	3	8	5	1	6	4	8	1	6	10	5	5	3
Projected AF Reps	2	4	1	1	4–5	0	2–3	0	1	5	4	2	0
Actual AF Reps	0	2	0	0	2	0	0	0	0	3	1	3	0
Projected AF Sen.	2	1	0	2	2	0	0–1	0	0	1	2	0–1	0
Actual AF Sen.	0	0	0	1	0	0	0	0	0	2	0	0	0

Federalist policies. The small Antifederalist minority thus attempted to take on Federalists in a way where the size of one's coalition is not as important: the realm of constitutionality. In the American conception of fundamental law, not passing constitutional muster trumps majority advocacy. Constitutional challenges are often countermajoritarian—the refuge of minorities who have little hope of commanding a majority. The Antifederalists in the earliest Congress liberally employed such constitutional challenges.[29]

Discerning where the ratification shift was most pronounced requires comparing projected and actual Antifederalist strength in the First Congress. As indicated in table 2, the three states with unanimously Federalist conventions elected all Federalists as expected. Of the ten states with a viable Antifederalist opposition, nine had fewer Antifederalists in their House delegations than expected. Disparities of two seats or more occur in New Hampshire, Massachusetts, New York, Pennsylvania, Virginia, and North Carolina. The sole exception—actually electing more Antifederalists to the House than projected—is South Carolina. Only one state exceeded expectations in selecting opposition figures to the Senate. Virginia's state legislature was controlled by Antifederalists, and it selected two of their own to the upper chamber. Rhode Island, New York, North Carolina, and New Hampshire proved the biggest disappointments to Antifederalist hopes in the Senate. The overwhelming Federalist majority in the Senate indicates that Federalists were in firm control of most state legislatures after ratification. In all, the only states that did not dash Antifederalist

[29]Stanley Elkins and Eric McKitrick, *The Age of Federalism* (Oxford, 1993), p. 234, and David P. Currie, *The Constitution in Congress* (Chicago, 1997), pp. 55–115, passim.

hopes were already unanimously Federalist. Perhaps Virginia and South Carolina were less disappointing than other states with a viable Antifederalist population, but only relatively so. Among the voting public and in state legislatures a major electoral shift took place in the wake of ratification. The move away from Antifederalists to Federalists occurred nationwide; this was, in fact, the first nationwide electoral phenomenon.

To gauge how enduring the electoral shift was, I compared Federalist ratification convention delegates and Antifederalist delegates in three ways: determining how many individuals received votes in early House elections, how many were credible candidates in those elections, and how many won seats in the House.[30] In figure 1, Federalists and Antifederalists who received votes in House elections are compared. An individual need not have attained any particular number of votes to be included. Clearly, many more Federalists garnered votes than Antifederalists in early House elections. The disparity between the two groups is quite large through the first four congresses, as more than twice as many Federalists received votes than Antifederalists in each of those elections. At the same time, there is a clear drop in the number of Federalists receiving votes through the era. Meanwhile, the

---

[30]In order to fulfill the requirements for a critical election, the shift exposed has to be relatively enduring. Electoral phenomena similar to those exposed in the first federal elections must be shown to hold in subsequent elections. I base my observations here strictly on those we know to be of either group: delegates who voted in ratification conventions. For the purposes of this analysis, I count mild Antifederalists won over to the Constitution by amendments as Federalists. Because they voted as Federalists, they may have reaped the benefits of the electoral sweep—or at least were not damaged by their Antifederalism, something they could clearly deny being. There were delegates who served in both North Carolina conventions who voted for adjournment initially but for the Constitution later. I count their first vote, indicative of an Antifederalist stance, as definitive. In compiling the information for these graphs I used Michael J. Dubin's new compilation of electoral statistics, *United States Congressional Elections, 1788–1997* (Jefferson, N.C., 1998), and Kenneth Martis, *The Historical Atlas of Political Parties in the United States* (New York, 1989). I cross-referenced the individuals in those works with lists of ratification convention voters compiled by the documentary history of the ratification of the Constitution at Madison, Wisconsin. In a few states, particularly in Virginia and South Carolina, Dubin's evidence is spotty. In the first two graphs, therefore, there might be some who received votes and had credible candidacies that we cannot be aware of. However, this problem would not cause these graphs to be systematically biased for or against either group. Since senators were selected by state legislatures until the early part of the twentieth century, I do not include them in the analysis.

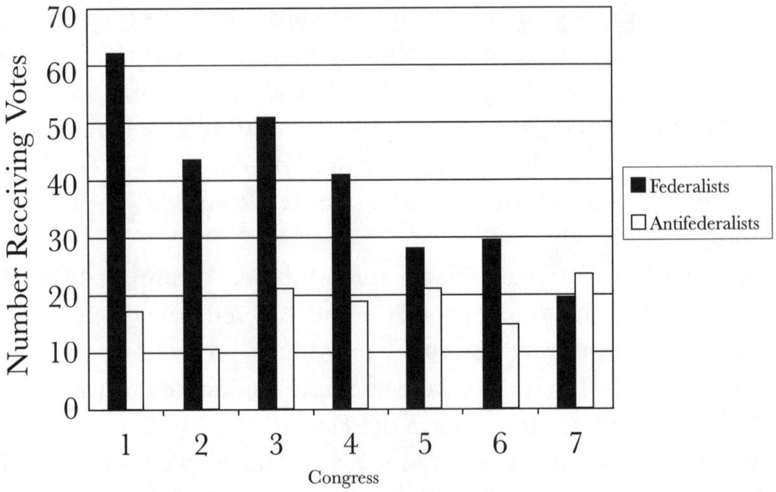

FIG. 1. State Ratification Convention Delegates Receiving Votes in Early House Elections

number of Antifederalists receiving votes in House elections rises somewhat. In the Fourth through the Sixth Congress, the relative number of each group receiving votes is roughly congruent with their overall strength. For the first time, in the seventh federal elections more Antifederalists receive votes than Federalists. Judging by this measure, House elections immediately following the first repeat the pattern of Federalist advantage. That advantage, and thus the critical shift, however, seems not to have lasted much beyond the fourth congressional election. A second way of judging the durability of the Federalist advantage is to restrict our purview to credible candidacies (fig. 2). Naturally any line distinguishing a credible candidacy from one that is not credible is somewhat arbitrary. I included any candidate who received at least 20 percent of the popular vote. Once again, many more Federalists were credible candidates than Antifederalists through the first four congressional elections. Similar to figure 1, more than twice as many Federalists were credible candidates than Antifederalists in each of the first four federal elections. The Federalist advantage is preserved through the sixth federal election, but in races for the Seventh Congress more Antifederalists were credible candidates than Federalists. Judging by their relative ability to muster votes in House races, the shift to the Federalists lasted through the Fourth Congress.

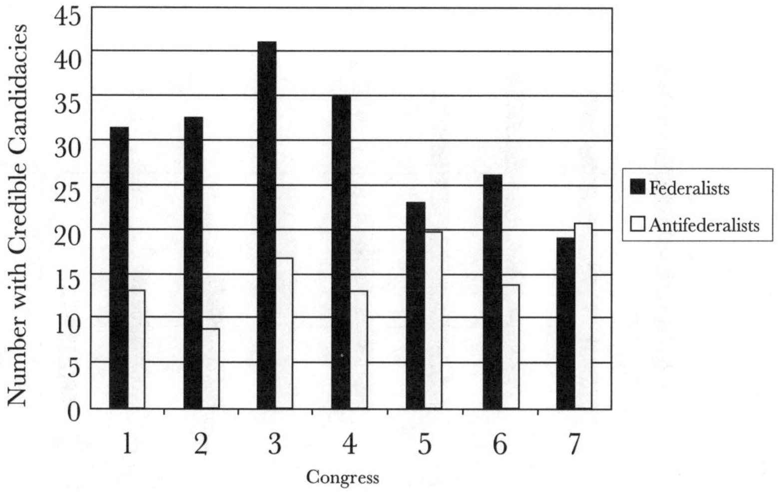

FIG. 2. State Ratification Convention Delegates with Credible Candidacies in Early House Elections

The ultimate test of electoral viability is winning election. As a final measure of the durability of the Federalist surge, I compiled data on who won House seats (fig. 3). As in the other graphs, Federalists clearly had an advantage over Antifederalists in the first four congressional elections. In each, at least twice as many ratification delegates who voted for the Constitution won congressional seats as those who voted against. That changed significantly in the contest for seats in the Fifth Congress. In those elections, held in 1798 and 1799, more Antifederalist convention delegates were elected than their Federalist colleagues. This change is not replicated in elections to the Sixth Congress, though relative strength remains close. In each of the succeeding three elections, more Antifederalists were elected to the House than Federalists. By the eighth and ninth congressional elections, the disparity is pronounced.

Judging by these three measures of Federalist and Antifederalist strength, it would seem that the Federalists were advantaged by their ratification stance through the fourth federal election, a phenomenon independent of party affiliation, a readily understood voting cue by the fourth federal election. Afterward Antifederalists surged back to equal or exceed their strength at the time of the ratification conventions. Judging from the electoral data presented here, active opposition to

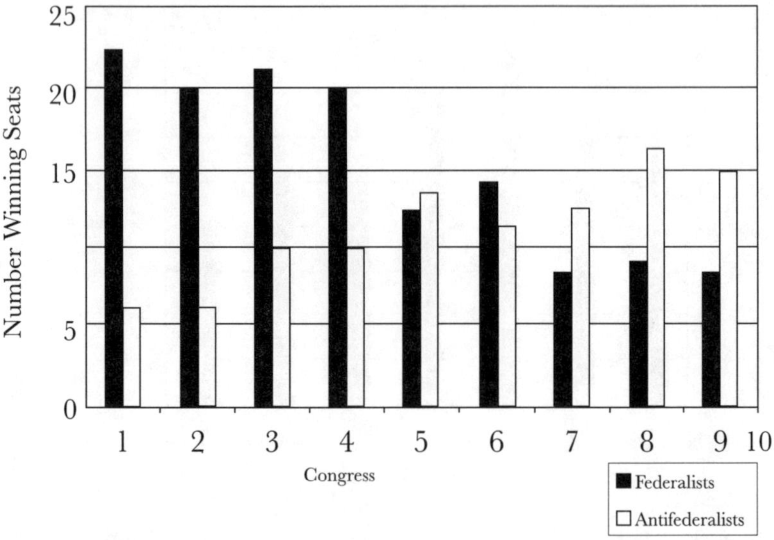

FIG. 3. State Ratification Convention Delegates Winning Seats in Early House Elections

the Constitution during the ratification debate hurt one's electoral prospects for upwards of a decade. However, it also shows that the surge was fairly transient. Political scientists have often noted that the coalition advantaged by a critical election typically stays a clear majority for about thirty years. This critical shift was of much shorter duration. The Federalists may have been hindered by the tint of illegitimacy associated with parties during this period. But the transient nature of the Federalist advantage also indicates that they were a more fragile coalition than is generally acknowledged and that they did a relatively poor job institutionalizing their vision of the future, failing to consolidate their critical shift.

Fallout of the Critical Ratification Shift

The Federalists' failure to institutionalize their post-ratification advantage was the result of strategic choices made very early in the new regime. The First Congress was so dominated by Federalists that many in their number felt emboldened not only to ignore Antifederalist calls for structural changes in the government but also to pursue items not uniformly endorsed by their own coalition that would establish a strong national government.[31] The Federalist legislative agenda revolved primarily around domestic economics. The Constitution clearly gave Congress the power to regulate commerce, but the constitutionality of other Federalist proposals was more questionable. Moderate Federalists, primarily from the South, were set on edge in the second session of the First Congress by the proposed federal assumption of state debts. Though this measure commanded a slim majority after a last-minute compromise, the result indicated to some that certain Federalists could not be trusted to fulfill their ratification debate pledge: that they would only pursue powers explicitly granted them in Article I, section 8, of the document.[32]

In the third session of the First Congress the fears of some Federalists, including James Madison, seemed confirmed by passage of a bill chartering a national bank. Secretary of the Treasury Alexander Hamilton had proposed the bank to spur commerce. In the course of the lengthy debate over this proposal, Madison and others laid out a case against the national bank. The Philadelphia convention had discussed whether to include an incorporation provision in the Constitution and the measure had failed. Since the power to incorporate a bank was not mentioned in Article I, section 8, Congress lacked the power to charter.[33] If the Federalists had possessed only a slim majority in Congress, Madison's qualms would have been determinative. His Federalist faction could have prevented the charter from becoming law and Hamilton's proposal would have been deferred. But because of their great majority, Hamilton and his supporters knew they could establish the bank over the objections of Madison and his colleagues. That is

[31]Most Federalists in the First Congress, even those instructed to do otherwise, were willing to forego amendments. Only James Madison's consistent prodding led to their endorsement, see Kenneth R. Bowling, " 'A Tub to the Whale': The Founding Fathers and the Adoption of the Federal Bill of Rights," *Journal of the Early Republic* 8 (1988):223–51, and Robert A. Goldwin, *From Parchment to Power: How Madison Used the Bill of Rights to Save the Constitution* (Washington, D.C., 1997), chap. 5, passim.

[32]This was James Wilson's argument in a widely reprinted speech delivered in Philadelphia on October 6, 1787. Wilson's speech was the most well-known Federalist defense of the Constitution during the ratification debate.

[33]*DHFFC,* 14:368–75, 378–81, 409–12, 424–29, 436–41.

precisely what the Hamiltonian Federalists did, destabilizing their procedural majority through their substantive victory. With the approval of a charter for the national bank, the Madisonian Federalists' earlier suspicions were confirmed: not even constitutional bounds would stop the Federalist majority in its pursuit of a strong national government.[34] Such a majority threatened the compromise Madison believed characterized the new federal system: dual sovereignty.[35] In the months between the meeting of the First and Second Congresses, Madison, along with Secretary of State Thomas Jefferson, persuaded his former Princeton classmate Philip Freneau to found and edit an opposition newspaper.[36] It was a signal there was to be no turning back. The ratification coalition was at an end.

In the First Congress, the Hamiltonian Federalists chose to press as far as they could on substantive issues, in spite of strenuous objections from members of the procedural majority responsible for helping them ratify and implement the Constitution. The size of their majority in the First Congress allowed them the luxury of employing this strategy. In so doing, the Federalists set the tone for an energetic national government. In the long term, however, this strategy drove those who might have been kept in the Federalist fold into an alliance with the former Antifederalists. By temporarily conceding on the national bank, the Hamiltonian Federalists could have reassured Federalist moderates that the national government was not bent on aggrandizing power. Had these Federalists displayed some restraint, they may have had a much longer run as the majority party and have been able to accomplish much more. The very magnitude of the electoral shift accompanying ratification obscures its critical nature: the shift itself allowed a new cleavage to take hold, one which split those formerly allied over the Constitution.

---

[34]Approximately half of the breakaway Federalists, or Madisonians, I identified hailed from Virginia and North Carolina. Other states with multiple Madisonian representatives in the first seven congresses include Georgia, South Carolina, Pennsylvania, Massachusetts, and New Hampshire. I found just one Madisonian in New York, Delaware, and Maryland. My analysis covers only those federal representatives who voted in ratification conventions, so it is not exhaustive. Even so, such a truncated sample suggests a relative regional prevalence while reinforcing that Madisonianism was, to a certain extent, a nationwide phenomenon.

[35]Lance Banning, *The Sacred Fire of Liberty* (Ithaca, N.Y., 1995), passim.

[36]Elkins and McKitrick, *The Age of Federalism*, p. 240, 264, 282–92.

Hamilton and his supporters surely realized the seriousness of Madison's qualms. Their decision to press forward without one who so ably aided them in securing ratification stems from two problematic assumptions. First, the Hamiltonians gambled that the Federalists' surge was so solid that leaving a few moderates behind was relatively unproblematic. With the majority of their own group intact (Madison's faction was dwarfed by Hamilton's), they concluded they would continue to be electorally advantaged. Calling Madison's bluff, they presumed that a union with the Antifederalists would taint him. But the personal reputations of the two architects of the new coalition, Madison and Jefferson, were too strong to be sullied by linking them to the Antifederalists. Instead of tainting them, Madison and Jefferson's defection lent credence to continued Antifederalist fears of a runaway national government. Second, Hamilton and his colleagues determined that setting an energetic tone for the new government early was far more important than biding one's time and attempting to do so gradually, as moderates became more comfortable with the new regime. Their unspoken assumption in doing so was that either one established expansive national power very early or one lost the opportunity to ever do so. Given the expansiveness and elasticity displayed by the national government through two centuries, that assumption seems faulty.[37] Hamilton and his colleagues gambled that setting the substantive tone of a regime early was far more important than consolidating one's procedural majority. That strategy, made possible by an overwhelming victory in the first federal election, ultimately prevented the "Age of Federalism" from being long-lived.

The range of issues on which the Madisonian Federalists and the Antifederalists agreed was broad, including every major issue decided by Congress from 1790 to 1800. In the Second Congress, Madison and Jefferson's group voted with the Antifederalists to expand the size of the House. In the Third Congress, they voted together to pass an embargo against Great Britain. In the Fourth Congress, they voted against the Jay Treaty in the Senate and pronounced it "objectionable" in the House. During the Fifth Congress, Republicans opposed President Adams's

---

[37]Or perhaps the Hamilton group was correct and their early actions led directly to our elastic regime. If that is the case, then the Hamiltonians seemingly sacrificed their own long-term political ambitions for what they thought would most benefit the nation, a European-style centralized regime.

entreaties to increase military preparedness against France and bitterly opposed the Alien and Sedition Acts. Those two items remained front and center during the Sixth Congress, the Republicans repeatedly but unsuccessfully calling for the repeal of both acts.

Throughout the 1790s, the cohesiveness of this Republican coalition was impressive. When the former Antifederalists opposed Hamilton's faction, more breakaway Federalists, or Madisonians, voted with the Antifederalists 90 percent of the time (table 3).[38] After the First Congress, a majority of the Madisonians voted with the Hamiltonian Federalist majority just more than 5 percent of the time. During the period from 1791 to 1800 only one in six of the Madisonians' individual votes was cast with the Federalist party. Further, the deeper into the 1790s one gets, the more cohesive the Antifederalists and the Madisonians became. In the Fifth Congress, sitting between 1797 and 1799, the majority of Madisonians sided with the former Antifederalists 97 percent of the time and cast ten votes with the Antifederalists for every one they cast with the Federalists. Not only did the majority of Madison and Jefferson's supporters side with the Antifederalists, but almost all of them did on nearly every single issue. Meanwhile, almost all of the critics of the Constitution remained united. Of forty-nine Antifederalist convention voters later elected to Congress, only two were Federalists.[39]

In the long term, the unity of the former Antifederalists and their stable alliance with the breakaway Federalists spelled trouble for the Hamiltonian Federalists. For two centuries commentators have thought of the Alien and Sedition Acts as an incredible Federalist blunder. There was surely a good deal of partisan folly in those acts. And yet there may also have been something more calculated. The Federalist party surely realized that its hold on power was increasingly tenuous. As indicated by the graphs above, Antifederalists reemerged in force during the fifth federal election. Such a drastic change in voting patterns must have been noted by Federalists and interpreted as

---

[38]This analysis is based on roll-call data compiled from those known to be Federalists or Antifederalists because of their ratification convention votes. Party affiliations are based on Martis's compilation in *The Historical Atlas of Political Parties.*

[39]Antifederalists John Williams of New York, who served in the Fourth and Fifth Congresses, and William F. Strudwick, a North Carolinian who served in the Fourth Congress, became Federalists.

Table 3. Alignment of Breakaway Federalists (Madisonians) on Controversial Issues, 1789–1801 (by percentage)

Congress	*Madisonians with Federalists*	*Madisonians with Antifederalists*	*Madisonians Neutral*
1	30	60	10
2	9	88	3
3	4	91	6
4	7	91	2
5	3	97	0
6	4	84	12

Source: Roll-call data from the Inter-University Consortium for Political and Social Research. This table first appeared in "The Birth of the Constitutional State," Ph.D. diss., University of Wisconsin, 1997. *Controversial issues* are votes where a majority of the Antifederalists were opposed to a majority of the Hamiltonian Federalists.

an ominous sign. The reapportionment accompanying the second census was only a few years away, and it would give more clout to the Republicans because of a burgeoning inland population that was almost uniformly Republican. Federalists gambled, taking drastic steps to cripple the opposition party before it became a majority. This gamble was bound to fail. The Sedition Act effectively outlawed the de facto party system that had been accepted by voters for nearly ten years, and the Alien Act distanced key constituencies the Federalists needed to stay a majority. Rather than the horrific blunder they are often portrayed to be, these two acts were the desperate effort of a majority party that rightly feared its days were numbered.

Factors behind the Critical Ratification Shift

As with most complicated political phenomena, there are several reasons behind the Federalists' post-ratification surge. Federalists were advantaged and Antifederalists disadvantaged through the first four congresses through a complex mixture of popular sentiment, practical politics, and the law.

In the wake of ratification, the Federalists' efforts at electioneering were much more compelling than the Antifederalists'. During the first congressional campaigns, Federalists observed that the friends of the Constitution should have a chance to implement it. A Federalist Congress, they reasoned, would do its best to make the new regime work. Electing those who opposed the Constitution would be risky, as they might have an incentive to sabotage the system they had opposed. Federalists continued to label their opponents "Antis," linking them to a losing cause. This tactic of linking a present opponent with past failures is used in politics all the time, of course. Republicans have labeled their opponents "Mondale" or "McGovern Democrats." Democrats returned the favor in the 1996 presidential election by linking the Republican nominee, Bob Dole, with Newt Gingrich, whose national approval ratings were abysmal. Even those slightly aware of politics in 1788 knew that the Antifederalists had lost on ratification. Reminding voters of this fact was good strategy by the Federalists, even if it lowered the level of political discourse. When Federalists continued to deride their opponents with the epithet *Anti* well into the 1790s, they virtually disqualified them from holding public office in some areas.

Meanwhile, Antifederalists in the first federal election campaigns made a much less compelling argument for election. Choose critics of the Constitution, said their broadsides, so that amendments can be framed, making the Constitution secure. But for most voters amendments had become a secondary issue. Successful implementation of the Constitution, the stated goal of Federalist candidates who wanted to prevent amendments, took precedence. Federalists were thus elected to the House and to state legislatures in surprising numbers, the voters being aware that the state legislatures would select senators.[40]

The Antifederalists' problem was compounded by their own awareness of it. Savvy Antifederalist politicians knew that they would have a hard time getting elected. They realized that their stance on the Constitution would be used against them. Rather than risk defeat, many critics of the Constitution refused to stand for office. Political scientists point to candidate recruitment as being key to winning elections. Upsets are very unlikely without politically experienced, high-quality chal-

[40] *DHFFE*, vol. 1, vii–xii and vols. 1–4, passim.

lengers.[41] Few prominent Antifederalists were willing to risk defeat in the earliest congressional elections. Many of the most well known, Patrick Henry and George Clinton, for instance, preferred to stay in state offices. Some who chose to run were embarrassed by the result, including arch-patriot Samuel Adams, who lost a seat to newcomer Federalist Fisher Ames. Adams's loss in the first federal election probably served to discourage fellow Antifederalists from actively pursuing national office in the subsequent election.

Adding to the Antifederalists' recruitment problem was the fact that the entire project of the new Congress was not terribly appealing to them. The Philadelphia Convention had been dominated by Federalists, and the reason is readily apparent: those less interested in expanding national power were understandably less excited about a four-month summer conference designed to increase national power. By disposition the Antifederalists were state-centric politicians. They were much less excited about Congress's mission than were the Federalists. And they also realized that for the foreseeable future they would almost surely be toiling in a minority, with little chance of stopping the Federalists. Thus, individual Antifederalists had good reason not to run in the earliest congressional elections and Federalists dominated the field.

One can see graphic evidence of this in the success Federalist legislators had in districts whose delegates had voted against the Constitution. Figure 4 shows the Federalists' success through time in districts variously categorized by their delegates' ratification votes. The Federalists' success in districts where they had been a clear majority is high throughout this period. In such districts their success rate starts out above 90 percent and never falls below 70 percent. Surprisingly, none of the more mildly Antifederalist districts sent an Antifederalist to the First Congress, evidence of a popular shift toward the Federalists and the fact that few quality Antifederalist candidates ran in those areas.

As the solid line indicates, however, Federalist success at winning Antifederalist-oriented districts declined through the 1790s. Federalists won a solid majority of such districts through the Fourth Congress,

---

[41]Gary C. Jacobson, *The Politics of Congressional Elections,* 4th ed. (New York, 1997), pp. 34–47, 70–80, passim.

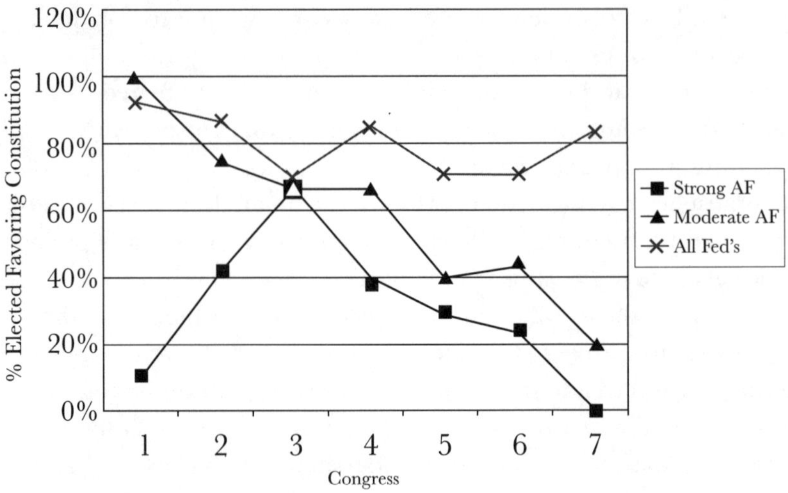

FIG. 4. Representation by District Type: First through Seventh Congresses

but only 40 percent of them in the elections of 1796 and just 14 percent in the election of 1800. The tale in strong Antifederalist districts is a little different, as indicated by the bottom line. While Antifederalists won almost all of the strong Antifederalist districts in the first federal election, Federalists did quite well in the Second through Fourth Congresses. Federalist strength in strong Antifederalist districts peaked in the Third Congress when two-thirds of those districts selected Federalist representatives. After that there was a steady decline in Federalist fortunes. By the Sixth Congress, Antifederalists were just as likely to win seats in Federalist districts as Federalists were in Antifederalist areas. Critics of the Constitution did not do particularly well on their own home turf in early congressional elections. Ultimately, however, they regained electoral dominance there and made inroads into Federalist areas as well. Federalist state legislatures determined the Senate's composition, and enough states were solidly Federalist through the Sixth Congress to keep the Federalist party's majority intact. Those same state legislatures also framed election laws. In several notable cases, these election laws minimized the prospects of the Antifederalists and maximized those of the Federalists. Since each state was given free rein in determining how its representatives were selected, it is only natural that partisan majorities would write laws for their own benefit, as examples from the first election demonstrate. Pennsylvania and Connecticut, with their clear Federalist majorities, opted to elect representatives at large—each voter cast a ballot for an entire delegation. Such electoral laws ensured that the Antifederalists would be outvoted and the state delegations would be uniformly Federalist. States where Antifederalists might have swept an at-large or general ticket race, such as New York, Virginia, and North and South Carolina, were districted. Early election laws skewed to favor Federalists gave them, in turn, the advantage of incumbency in subsequent elections.[42]

Malapportionment was another problem, particularly in states such as South Carolina, which had traditionally had problems with adequate representation of western districts.[43] According to numbers compiled from the first census, the population of South Carolina's westernmost district, the fifth, was 69,301. Two of the coastal districts had less than 30,000 inhabitants. South Carolina's westernmost district had 2.6 times the population of its smallest district. Since Antifederalist strength was concentrated away from the coast, this disparity enhanced Federalist electoral prospects. Though the South Carolina example is extreme, malapportionment was an issue in several states. The population of Antifederalist districts in the 1790s was generally larger than that of Federalist districts. In the First Congress, the average Antifederalist district had 30.7 percent more voting-age white males than the average Federalist district.[44] This great disparity in district size diminished through time. The first census was conducted in 1790 and its data were used to draw more equitable district lines. Several states redistricted during the 1790s to reflect changing population distributions. By the Sixth Congress, the male voting age

---

[42]A notable exception to Federalists taking advantage of their newfound majority is in Massachusetts. Bay State Federalists would likely have won a general ticket race but opted for districts instead, allowing two Antifederalists, Elbridge Gerry and Jonathan Grout, to be elected.

[43]South Carolina traditionally had major apportionment problems, *DHFFE,* 1:147.

[44]I compiled this figure using the district typology developed earlier and data from the first census: Daniel J. Boorstin, ed., "Return of the Whole Number of Persons within the Several Districts of the United States" (1802; reprint ed., New York, 1976). For the purposes of this analysis I counted slaves as three-fifths of a person for purposes of apportionment, precisely as the Constitution dictated.

population in Antifederalist districts was just 12.7 percent higher than that in Federalist districts.[45] Most of that disparity was caused by a single state, New York, the congressional districts of which simply could not keep up with the rapid influx of people settling in the western part of the state.

Election laws are never neutral devices; they help determine who gets elected and who does not. In several individual states and in the aggregate, the earliest election laws disadvantaged the Antifederalists. Most of these laws were framed by Federalist state legislatures, which also sent an overwhelming Federalist majority to the Senate. By virtue of the bellwether elections in the states that populated state legislatures with friends of the Constitution, most Antifederalists chose to sit out the earliest congressional elections. Those Antifederalists who did run knew the weakness of their own arguments, and they rarely were successful outside the most Antifederalist areas. When Federalists dominated the earliest federal elections they were almost assured of retaining majorities for some time, given the strength of incumbency and the long and staggered Senate terms. In the first half of the 1790s, the Antifederalists were bowed but not broken, for none of these hindrances posed as much of a problem later in the decade.

Conclusion

The great majority of those who served in Congress during the 1790s are now utterly obscure; nevertheless, they formed the majorities which decided national policy and determined constitutional precedents. Two of these obscure figures are men from the same part of western North Carolina, both named Joseph McDowell. We know precious little about either. The elder Joseph McDowell was born in 1756 in the northernmost part of Virginia, near what is today the West Virginia border. He was just two years old when his family moved to western North Carolina, close to present-day Asheville. He fought for the patriot cause during the Revolutionary War and participated actively in state politics afterward, being selected to serve in the Confederation Congress in 1787. Around that same time McDowell was

[45]This figure is based on data from the Second Census, Boorstin, "Return of the Whole Number of Persons within the Several Districts of the United States."

chosen as a delegate in North Carolina's first ratification convention. He did not approve of the Constitution.[46] Antifederalists preferred to adjourn the convention rather than vote down the Constitution. McDowell accordingly voted to adjourn North Carolina's first convention. He was again selected to serve in the second North Carolina convention, where he voted against the Constitution outright.

This Antifederalist had a cousin two years younger, also named Joseph McDowell. They lived within ten miles of each other. The younger McDowell had also served in the Revolutionary War. Like his cousin, this man was involved in state politics, being elected to the state house of commons for the first time in 1785. The younger McDowell was also selected as a delegate to North Carolina's ratification conventions. Unlike his Antifederalist cousin, this Joseph McDowell voted in favor of the Constitution.[47]

The Federalist Joseph McDowell ran for Congress in 1792. He was elected and served in the Third Congress. Like many others, he probably found the prestige of serving in the national legislature more than offset by financial and emotional burdens. Legislators were away from their work and loved ones for months at a time. McDowell declined to run for reelection in 1794. Waiting in the wings was his elder cousin, who ran in his place. The Antifederalist James McDowell did not win, but two years later he ran again and won. Once again, North Carolina had a Joseph McDowell in its congressional delegation during the Fifth Congress. Like his cousin, this Joseph McDowell found that a single term in Congress was enough and declined renomination.

These two men shared a great deal. They hailed from the same part of the same state. They were members of the same extended family and almost surely shared role models and political beliefs as a result. Both had a keen interest in politics and an ambition to serve in high political office. The same constituents elected them to Congress. They even shared a name. One crucial difference is the divergent position they took on the Constitution. In these two men, we have something of a natural experiment, a litmus test, revealing the composition of

---

[46]The biographical information presented here comes from the files of the Documentary History of the Ratification of the Constitution project and the *Biographical Directory of the American Congress, 1774–1996* (Washington, D.C., 1996), passim.

[47]The younger McDowell had voted to adjourn during the first convention, but during the second convention he voted to ratify.

congressional politics in the 1790s. The Federalist, the man judged to have been on the "right side" in the wake of ratification, succeeded in the first half of the 1790s. It took the Antifederalist Joseph McDowell until the late 1790s to win a congressional seat. In rough outline, that is precisely what happened to the Federalists and Antifederalists nationwide. Those who had opposed the Constitution suffered electorally until about the Fifth Congress, precisely when the Antifederalist Joseph McDowell was elected. Initially, those who had championed the Constitution were selected to administer the new government, only to see their strength ebb several years into their experiment. A third Joseph McDowell also factors into this story. Joseph Jefferson McDowell served in Congress during the 1840s. He was the son of the Antifederalist Joseph McDowell. His presence in Congress is an indication of the enduring nature of Antifederalist influence on the early republic. His full name bears witness to the great alliance forged by the Antifederalists and Jeffersonian Republicans in the 1790s, which set the tone for American politics into the Jacksonian era.

With a resurgence in the willingness of quality Antifederalist candidates to stand for election, by a gradual shift away from the Federalists on the state level, by the more equitable drawing of district lines, and through their alliance with the Madisonians, the Antifederalists ultimately won back the ground they had lost in the wake of ratification. The story of the Antifederalists in the 1790s is one of resurgence. In the early 1800s, the Antifederalists would move beyond resurgence to participate in governing at the highest levels. Rarely do we pause to think that the two presidents after Jefferson and Madison, James Monroe and John Quincy Adams, had opposed adoption of the Constitution they ultimately came to administer.[48] They who lose today, may win tomorrow.

---

[48]The young Monroe was a moderate Antifederalist who went to the trouble of writing a pamphlet explaining his opposition to the new framework of government but did not circulate it, instead having all but a few copies destroyed. Nevertheless, Monroe did oppose the Constitution as a delegate in Virginia's ratification convention. John Quincy Adams, even younger than Monroe, took the Antifederalist position in a debate at Harvard College against his cousin William Cranch and made Antifederalist statements in his letters and a diary, becoming a supporter of the Constitution only after Massachusetts ratified it.

Terri D. Halperin

The Special Relationship

The Senate and the States, 1789–1801

THE CONSTITUTION SEEMINGLY CREATED a Senate with the trappings of state representation since each state had an equal vote in the body and state legislatures elected senators. Yet, the 1787 Constitutional Convention also adopted several provisions that undermined a close relationship between the Senate and the states—including no recall of senators by state legislatures, long terms, voting by individual and not state, and salaries paid by the federal government. During the ratification debates, the Constitution's opponents complained of the weak link between the Senate and the states. They argued that senators would be tempted to act contrary to their states' interests and states would be powerless to counteract such actions. The weak defenses of the Senate offered by the Constitution's proponents could not completely allay these fears, and the Senate began its existence under a cloud of uncertainty.

To guarantee the success of a republican form of government, the citizenry had to be watchful of its elected officials. As the Senate's electors, state legislatures were charged with the responsibility of ensuring that their representatives acted honorably. The questions were how the states would perform this task and how much influence states would have over their senators. Since senators met in secret for the first six years of the new government, states' efforts to monitor the institution were even more difficult. When states demanded that the Senate open its doors in order to fulfill their republican duty of vigilance, senators rebuffed these entreaties, which often arrived in the form of instructions. These senators believed that both open doors and instructions prohibited free deliberation and restricted the Senate's independence. Other than periodically publishing its legislative journals as required by the Constitution, the Senate offered no other official accounts of its proceedings. A combination of new members and a successful public debate convinced senators that open doors would not be detrimental to the institution. After the Senate opened its doors to the public in 1796, however, it neither made arrangements to record its own proceedings nor for others to do so. The Senate did not make it any easier for states to gather information. With no direct access to Senate proceedings, state legislatures had to rely on the journals and on the senators themselves for information — a role that most senators readily filled.

Throughout the first decade of the new government, senators, state legislators, and governors negotiated the parameters of their relationship. Some states directly challenged the Senate and their senators. Other states were quietly satisfied with their senators' service. Where conflict existed, state legislatures and senators were often associated with different parties or factions within the state. As the first party system of Federalists and Republicans took shape, different ideas about the Senate-state relationship emerged, loosely correlated to partisan divisions. Republican legislators more often sought a superior-inferior relationship with senators, whereas Federalists senators resisted such dictation from the states. Fundamentally, these conflicts and negotiations involved a debate about the nature of the Senate and representation in the young republic.

As it emerged from the Constitutional Convention and ratification debates, the Senate seemed to represent the states. It was the sole federal feature of the new government. On closer examination, however, the relationship between the Senate and the states proved to be much more ambiguous. Delegates to the federal and state constitutional conventions, state legislators, governors, the first senators, and the people had varied expectations about the nature of the special relationship between the Senate and the states.

Even while still in session, delegates to the Philadelphia Convention did not fully understand the institution or the government they were creating. For the first three months, delegates worked their way through James Madison's "Virginia Plan," but no decisions could be finalized until they resolved the issue of who or what would be represented in the lower and upper houses. Originally, Madison proposed proportional representation in both houses, but small state delegates remained resistant to this arrangement. After finally defeating the "New Jersey Plan," which called for a one-chamber legislature representing states, delegates confronted one of their most intractable problems—the basis of representation in the second house. On July 16, 1787, delegates settled the issue with the Great Compromise.[1] Thereafter, they remained committed to equal representation of the states in the Senate. The people would elect the representatives, and state legislators the senators. Presumably, the compromise meant that the Senate would be a council of states, but the convention adopted several proposals that directly weakened this role. Long terms without the possibility of recall, per capita voting, and salaries paid from the national treasury all undermined the idea of senators as their states' ambassadors. The issue of senatorial pay best illustrated delegates' confused vision for the Senate, especially Oliver Ellsworth's changing views on the subject. Before the compromise, this Connecticut delegate advocated payment by the states. In June, Ellsworth argued, "If the Senate was meant to strengthen the Govt. it ought to have the confidence of the States. The States will have an interest in keeping up a representation and will make such provision for support[ing] the members as will ensure their attendance."[2] After the compromise's adoption, Ellsworth opposed this mode because it made senators too dependent upon the states.[3] In June, he wanted to secure the states a voice in the government, but once he achieved this goal, he believed it necessary to increase senators' independence. Thus he embodied the conflicting desires of the convention to have the Senate represent

---

[1]On the Great Compromise, see Jack N. Rakove, *Original Meanings: Politics and Ideas in the Making of the Constitution* (New York, 1996), pp. 62–83, and idem, "The Great Compromise: Ideas, Interests, and the Politics of Constitution Making," *William and Mary Quarterly*, 2d ser. 44 (1987):424–57.

[2]Max Farrand, ed., *The Records of the Federal Convention of 1787*, 4 vols. (New Haven, 1911), 1:427.

[3]Ibid., 2:290.

both the states as political entities and to check the popular passions exhibited by state legislatures and expected to be expressed by the House of Representatives.

After the convention, the same ambivalence existed among even the Constitution's most ardent supporters. John Jay, one of the authors of the *Federalist Papers,* presumed that state legislatures would instruct their senators and senators would correspond regularly with state executives.[4] Jay implied that senators would heed the states' sentiments. Madison dismissed any thorough discussion of the meaning of the Great Compromise, and the Senate as the representatives of the states. He argued that since the compromise was a product of circumstance and not some well-thought-out theory, proponents and opponents should not waste their energy debating it. He certainly would not.[5]

Despite Federalists' effort to stifle this discussion, Antifederalists issued complaint after complaint that the Constitution did not really protect the states or give the states meaningful representation in the new government. At the New York Ratification Convention, Melancton Smith proposed giving the states the power to recall their senators.[6] In support of the amendment, John Lansing reasoned that "if it was the design of the plan to make the Senate a kind of bulwark to the independence of the states, and a check to the encroachments of the general government, certainly the members of this body ought to be peculiarly under the control, and in strict subordination to the state who delegated them."[7]

In Virginia, Patrick Henry warned that under the present system, states could both recall and instruct their delegates, but under the new system, "You *cannot* recal them.—You may instruct them, and offer your opinions;—but if they think them improper, they may discard them."[8] In Maryland, Luther Martin feared that the senators' long

---

[4]Jonathan Elliot, *The Debates in the Several State Conventions,* 2d ed. (1880; reprint ed., Salem, N.H., 1987), 2:283.

[5]Madison, *Federalist* No. 62, in *The Federalist Papers,* ed. Clinton Rossiter (New York, 1961), pp. 376–82.

[6]On ratification in New York, see John P. Kaminski, "Adjusting to Circumstances: New York's Relationship with the Federal Government," in *The Constitution and the States,* ed. Patrick T. Conley and John P. Kaminski (Madison, 1988), pp. 225–49.

[7]Elliot, *Debates,* 2:289.

[8]*Documentary History of the Ratification of the Constitution,* 14 vols. to date (Madison,

terms would encourage them to remove to the seat of government and therefore abandon their home states. Senators then would be more likely to vote the interest of the capital city than their states. Thus Martin echoed Henry's concern that the Senate did not in fact represent the states, but senators represented nothing and no one in particular.

Henry's Federalist colleagues responded by claiming that there was sufficient security against outrageous behavior by senators, but the "dread of being recalled would impair their independence and firmness," and the same was likely to be true if states could instruct them as well.[9] Like James Wilson of Pennsylvania, these Virginia delegates stressed that the Senate could never act alone and thus could never accumulate the power that Henry and others feared it would. Wilson argued, "Thus fettered, I do not know any act which the Senate can of itself perform, and such dependence necessarily precludes every idea of influence and superiority."[10] The Senate could indeed be all things to all people. It could not act alone, and thus no danger could arise from it. Wilson and other Federalists could not explain how the Senate would effectively represent the states. Alexander Hamilton attempted to do so by assigning a particular role to the states. He designated the states as the sentinel over the Senate.

Some states wanted to ensure a closer relationship between the Senate and the states and proposed several amendments to this end. The New York convention approved three such amendments, two of which would have strengthened the state legislators' influence over senators. One amendment prohibited senators from serving more than six years in any twelve years. Thus delegates guarded against the creation of a de facto aristocracy by preventing senators from serving for life. Another gave state legislatures the power to recall senators and elect others to serve out their terms. Senators, therefore, would have been beholden to state legislatures. In addition, New Yorkers proposed stripping governors of the power to fill Senate vacancies during the recess of state legislatures. Again, they wished to enhance

---

1976–), vol. 10 (John P. Kaminski and Gaspare J. Saladino, eds.), p. 1248, hereafter cited as *DHRC.*

9George Nicholas, *DHRC,* 10:1252.

10James Wilson, Speech in the State House Yard, Oct. 6, 1787, *DHRC,* vol. 2 (Merrill Jensen, John P. Kaminski, and Gaspare J. Saladino, eds.), pp. 169–70.

the state legislatures' power over senators. The Virginia and North Carolina conventions proposed amendments that aimed to reduce Senate power and enhance the powers of the House of Representatives, but, although implied, they did not explicitly attempt to dictate a close relationship between the Senate and the states.[11] All of these proposals failed, but they highlighted the Senate's ambiguous representative character.

The Philadelphia Convention created a Senate with an ambivalent relationship to its electors. The ratification debates did not clarify this issue, but instead obscured the terms of the relationship even more. Depending upon the nature of the attack, Federalists defended the Senate as both the representative of the states and as the promoter of national interests.

North Carolina was the first state to explicitly attempt to define its relationship with the Senate. It was the second to the last of the original thirteen states to ratify the Constitution. In fact, it needed two conventions to do so. When North Carolina finally joined the Union, President George Washington rewarded the pro-Constitution men with federal offices—perhaps contributing to the continued rift between the factions while shoring up important support for the new government.[12] North Carolina's Antifederalists issued the first challenge to the notion of complete senatorial independence from state legislators shortly after North Carolina took its place in the new government.

Even before the North Carolina legislature could express its displeasure with its federal senators, the governor announced what he thought his role should be in the exchange of information between the federal and state governments. Like most governors, Alexander Martin expected to initially receive all correspondence, which he would then lay before the legislature. In addition, he saw his role as a gatherer of information for the legislature. Hence, Martin insisted on regular correspondence from both senators and representatives. Rep. Timothy Bloodworth thought such correspondence superfluous because Mar-

[11]"The Ratifications of the New Foederal Constitution," Richmond, 1788 (Evans, *Early American Imprints,* 21529).

[12]Washington also distributed offices in reluctant Rhode Island on the basis of support for the Constitution. Gaillard Hunt, "Office-Seeking during Washington's Administration," *American Historical Review* 1 (1896):270–83.

tin received "necessary information from the Senators, whose duty compels them to correspond with the Executive and the Representatives more particularly with their constituents."[13] Bloodworth, a future senator, thought that senators had a special relationship and obligation to the state's governor and legislature that representatives did not have. He did not wish to take on any additional responsibilities or obligations. Martin appeared to accept Bloodworth's explanation for his failure to write; legislators would not so easily forgive the senators for their transgressions.

During the winter 1790 legislative session, the North Carolina House of Commons passed a series of resolutions demanding Senators Benjamin Hawkins and Samuel Johnston's obedience to its instructions to open the doors of the Senate, correspond regularly with the legislature and executive, reduce the "monstrous" salaries of public officers, and oppose "every excise and direct taxation law."[14] Despite newspaper reports that the state senate sensibly rejected these resolutions, the senate actually passed them with only one amendment to change the description of public salaries from "monstrous" to "enormous." Some North Carolinians thought the legislature had gone too far. The editors of the *State Gazette* blamed the unfortunate resolutions on the poor quality and youth of the legislators.[15] The minority published their own resolutions protesting the legislature's actions. They believed the best mode for expressing grievances was through "spirited remonstrances and firm resolves," not instructions. The minority assigned good reasons for the senators' lack of communications to the legislature. Most significantly, they did not "conceive the necessity of such correspondence [was] expressed or implyed in the nature of the office of Senator." Finally, they expressed their "confidence in the appointments when made" and willingness to rely "upon the zeal and virtue of the

[13]Timothy Bloodworth to Alexander Martin, June 19, 1790, *Governors' Letterbooks*, vol. 10, North Carolina Department of Archives and History, Raleigh. For letters from senators to Martin, see Benjamin Hawkins and Samuel Johnston to Martin, Apr. 11, 1790; Benjamin Hawkins to Alexander Martin, June 13, 1790, Dec. 30 and 31, 1790, Jan. 13, 1791, in *North Carolina Governors' Letterbooks*, vol. 10. In the succeeding volumes, there is a large correspondence between governors and senators.

[14]*State Gazette of North Carolina* (Edenton), Dec. 17, 1790. This issue reported the legislative proceedings of November 24.

[15]"Extract of a letter from Fayetteville," ibid., Dec. 17, 1790.

Senators in supporting the *public good*."[16] Thus these North Carolina Federalists recognized that senators did not just represent their state. In fact, they condemned their colleagues who insisted on privileging local interests and were frankly embarrassed by their actions.[17]

The senators themselves were stung by what they considered unwarranted criticism. Hawkins and Johnston wrote Governor Martin jointly in February 1791 to respond to the charges against them. They vigorously defended the Senate's right to decide its own rules, including whether to open its debates to the public. The Senate, they argued, could judge under what conditions it could best "deliberate on public measures with more attention and unbiased minds to decide with more wisdom and decision to transact the public business with greater or equal dispatch and with more correctness and accuracy."[18] They did not deny the state the right to be informed of federal legislation and thought they had fulfilled this responsibility when the Senate arranged for three copies of its *Journal* to be sent to each state. When Hawkins and Johnston had arrived in Philadelphia for the third session of the First Congress the previous December, they learned the *Journals* had not been sent and quickly rectified the situation.[19] They thought this should have vindicated them from at least some of the charges. Although they did not think they had neglected their duties, they pledged "to inform the Legislature and Executive departments of the state of all measures necessary for them to act on[,] where information is not conveyed through the channel of public offices . . . and punctually to answer all letters written."[20]

In response to the charge of disobedience, the North Carolina senators felt compelled to explain their view that instructions would "so far as they are confined to measures affecting the State individually . . . have all that influence on our conduct which they have the right to expect."[21] Hawkins and Johnston were purposely ambiguous. Cer-

---

[16]"A Member," ibid., Dec. 31, 1790.

[17]Ibid., Jan. 28, 1791.

[18]Benjamin Hawkins and Samuel Johnston to Alexander Martin. Feb. 22, 1791, *North Carolina Governors' Letterbooks,* vol. 10.

[19]Although states began to acknowledge receipt of the *Journal* on September 17, 1790, North Carolina apparently never received its copies.

[20]Benjamin Hawkins and Samuel Johnston to Alexander Martin, Feb. 22, 1791, *North Carolina Governors' Letterbooks,* vol. 10.

[21]Hawkins, whom Norman Risjord describes as "mild-mannered," probably toned

tainly, some state legislators expected a lot more than the two men were ever willing to deliver. Although Hawkins and Johnston welcomed the assembly's opinions, they reserved the right to act contrary to that opinion. The senators professed their respect for the legislature regardless of whether they conformed to its demands or not. They stressed their responsibility to represent national interests above local concerns. At the seat of the federal government, senators, congressmen, and others exchanged information from every state and territory—information to which the North Carolina legislature did not have access. Hawkins and Johnston gently suggested that the state legislature's policy recommendations suffered from "the want of that minute and particular information" that they had at their disposal as senators.[22] Thus, they embraced the hope expressed by many of the Constitution's proponents that the Senate would be a moderating force against the people's passions.

While Hawkins and Johnston were not willing to follow instructions on these issues, they readily offered their services and obedience when it came to "measures affecting the state individually." They stated one area in which they pledged their unlimited aid. They were only too happy to help with obtaining the most advantageous settlement of the state's accounts with the federal government. They fulfilled their promise by closely consulting with the state's agent at the seat of government and with the governor when they needed further guidance about what was expected of them.[23]

---

down the language in the final letter. C. L. Grant identifies Hawkins as a Republican; whereas Risjord puts him in the Federalist camp. Hawkins was certainly not as ardent a Federalist as Johnston, if he was one at all. On Hawkins's political affiliation, see C. L. Grant, "Senator Benjamin Hawkins: Federalist or Republican?" *Journal of the Early Republic* 1 (1981):233–47; Risjord, *Chesapeake Politics, 1781–1800* (New York, 1978), p. 358; Samuel Johnston, "Notes on Instructions," [1790], Hayes Collection, Johnston Series Manuscripts, 1786–1799, microfilm edition, reel 4, Southern Historical Collection, University of North Carolina at Chapel Hill; Benjamin Hawkins and Samuel Johnston to Alexander Martin, Feb. 22, 1791, *North Carolina Governors' Letterbooks,* vol. 10.

[22]Benjamin Hawkins and Samuel Johnston to Alexander Martin, Feb. 22, 1791, *North Carolina Governors' Letterbooks,* vol. 10.

[23]Samuel Johnston and Benjamin Hawkins to Col. Abisha Thomas, Mar. 6, 1792; Abisha Thomas to Samuel Johnston and Benjamin Hawkins, Mar. 12, 1792; and Samuel Johnston and Benjamin Hawkins to Alexander Martin, Mar. 13, 1792, Governors' Papers, series 2, box 4; and Benjamin Hawkins to Alexander Hamilton, Nov. 26, 1791; Benjamin Hawkins to Alexander Martin, Dec. 2, 1791; and Benjamin Hawkins and Samuel Johnston to Alexander Martin, Dec. 10, 1791, Governors' Papers, vol. 19, North Carolina Department of Archives and History, Raleigh.

Johnston, who had drawn a two-year term, had to face the assembly's direct judgment much sooner than Hawkins.[24] Therefore, Johnston felt the need to explain his actions individually. Furthermore, Hawkins, who was milder in both temper and politics than Johnston, had probably toned down the language of their joint letter too much for Johnston. In his letter, Johnston conceded that he disobeyed instructions on at least two occasions—when he voted for an excise on domestically distilled whiskey and against opening the doors of the Senate. On the former, Johnston argued that an excise was necessary and this one would be most fair to North Carolina. He provided a much longer and stronger defense on the other issue. He declared himself firmly attached to liberty and denied the Senate's intent was secrecy and its connotations of conspiracy. Contrary to this view, Johnston "never saw business transacted with so much decency propriety dispatch nor with a more deliberate attention to the right of the people in any assembly of which [he had] had the honour to be a member."[25] He assured legislators that he did not act as he did because he felt his judgment superior to theirs. He even admitted that if he had only the information the assembly possessed, he would have voted for the resolutions, but he had more information and voted according to his convictions.[26] As in their joint letter, Johnston stressed his greater knowledge of events and circumstances in justifying his defiance of the legislature's instructions. In some notes on the subject, Johnston would have fur-

---

[24]The Constitution requires that the terms of one-third of the senators expire every two years. Shortly after the first Senate achieved a quorum, senators drew lots to determine whose term would expire after two, four, and six years. Same-state senators could not have terms that expired on the same day. When Hawkins and Johnston entered the Senate in January 1790, they drew lots. Johnston's term expired on March 3, 1793, Hawkins's on March 3, 1795. Hawkins did not run again in 1795. Grant surmises that Hawkins did not think his chances for reelection were very good because North Carolina was becoming increasingly Republican. Hawkins's more moderate Republicanism did not sit well with the new leadership. Perhaps also influencing his decision was the 1790 censure resolutions. Shortly after retiring from the Senate, Hawkins embarked on a twenty-year career as a federal Indian agent. Grant, "Senator Benjamin Hawkins," pp. 246–47.

[25]Johnston served in the North Carolina colonial assembly, state senate, Continental Congress, state constitutional conventions, and the U.S. Senate. Samuel Johnston to Alexander Martin, Mar. 9, 1791, *North Carolina Governors' Letterbooks,* vol. 10. For a draft of the letter, see Hays Collection.

[26]Samuel Johnston to Alexander Martin, Mar. 9, 1791, *North Carolina Governors' Letterbooks,* vol. 10.

ther restricted the legislature to matters "where an Act of Congress is necessary to give validity to an Act of the Legislature as sometimes is the case."[27] It is telling that at least this Federalist thought states should have only a limited say in national affairs. The rest they should leave to their senators, who knew better. Johnston's plea for forgiveness, however, fell on deaf ears. The Republican-leaning assembly did not reelect the Federalist, but instead elected Republican Martin, who upon his victory hired bagpipers and paraded through the streets of Fayetteville in celebration.[28] Here, the legislature took swift action against an errant senator and replaced him with a man much more amenable to its views. Thus, through the right of election, the legislature attempted to force its own terms on the relationship with senators. Yet, the relationship remained troublesome. Two years later, rumors spread as far as Rhode Island that North Carolina had recalled its senators.[29]

In this first attempt to define the relationship between senators and their states, the North Carolina state legislature demanded a close relationship in which it would hold the upper hand. Their senators—Hawkins and Johnston—resisted the state's dictates. They offered a counterproposal where they would independently determine their views on the vast majority of issues, but the state would be able to offer its sentiments on matters that affected it directly. Through the right of election, the North Carolina legislature guaranteed that its next senators would be more amenable to its views.

Many state legislatures empathized with North Carolina's feeling of neglect by its senators. Since the Senate met behind closed doors for its first six years, the states could only learn about its deliberations from the periodic publication of the terse legislative journal and the senators themselves. Some senators took this task very seriously. William

---

[27]Samuel Johnston, "Notes on Instructions," [1790], Hayes Collection.

[28]The Senate election depended very much on the governor's election and the location of the state capital. The assembly session was tempestuous to say the least. Fistfights broke out on the floor of the House of Commons, after which the assembly adjourned to let tempers cool. Grant argues the legislature chose Martin over Johnston because it thought Martin would be more amenable to their views, which is a correct assessment. J. Dawson to Samuel Johnston, Dec. 15, 1792, Hays Collection; Grant, "Senator Benjamin Hawkins," p. 238; Risjord, *Chesapeake Politics,* p. 411.

[29]Arthur Fenner to Theodore Foster, Feb. 26, 1792, Theodore Foster Papers, Rhode Island Historical Society, Providence.

Maclay of Pennsylvania kept a diary for the purpose of keeping this constituents, particularly the Pennsylvania legislature, informed of his and the Senate's actions.[30]

Most states seemed pleased with the information senators sent home about the Senate, government, and their activities, but still some states wanted reports from other sources. If they had a special connection to the Senate and if they were responsible for holding senators accountable for their actions, some state legislators believed they should know what went on inside the chamber.

Because of states' interest in Senate decisions, the issue of open doors cannot be separated from that of instructions. Fundamentally, both involved the representatives' relationship with their constituents. On the one hand, open sessions and instructions would force a closer association between the two with senators sacrificing a measure of their independence. On the other hand, open sessions and instructions made senators more accountable to both the people and state legislators than if they did not observe either of these conventions. The first calls for open doors came in the form of instructions. New York City officials, the first hosts of the new government, assumed the Senate would meet behind closed doors because they provided no galleries in the Senate chamber. The configuration of the Senate chamber produced the circumstances under which the Senate discussed the propriety of instructions for the first time.

The first debate regarding instructions, however, did not occur in the Senate but in the House of Representatives when it considered a constitutional amendment giving the people the right to instruct their representatives. While the debate focused largely on the effects this amendment would have on the House, congressmen entered into a general discussion of instructions' merits before rejecting the proposal. Thomas Tudor Tucker of South Carolina proposed adding the words "to instruct their Representatives" into what is now the First Amendment. Tucker provided no verbal defense of his motion, but he received aid from his Virginia, Massachusetts, and North Carolina colleagues. These advocates stressed the inseparable connection between

---

[30]Kenneth R. Bowling and Helen E. Veit, eds., *The Diary of William Maclay and Other Notes on Senate Debates,* vol. 9 of *Documentary History of the First Federal Congress,* 14 vols. to date (Baltimore, 1972–), p. xiv, hereafter cited as *DHFFC.*

instruction, representation, and republican government.[31] Most saw instructions as an additional check against abuses of power. Elbridge Gerry of Massachusetts argued that just including the right would be enough and would not produce the dire consequences that his colleagues predicted. He stated, "A knowledge of the right will operate to check a spirit that would render instructions unnecessary."[32]

In the course of the debate, Samuel Livermore of New Hampshire asked for a clarification. He wanted to know to whom the right was being given—townships, districts, or state legislatures. If it was state legislatures, Livermore thought instructions would carry great weight, even though he would not consider them binding. But Livermore did raise a troubling point: in states where representatives were elected at large, as in his state, how would instructions be procured?[33] Theodore Sedgwick of Massachusetts immediately rejected the idea that state legislatures would have the right to instruct members of the House. If they had such a right at all, it would be to instruct senators. These two future senators agreed that the source of instructions was inherently problematic. For instructions to be valid, most congressmen believed the majority of their district had to explicitly endorse the instructions without coercion or encouragement from politicians. At-large districts made this exercise virtually impossible, but even where states were divided into districts, collecting the majority's sentiments would be an extremely difficult task.[34] Both Livermore and Sedgwick recognized the difficulties and as congressmen wished to be excused from having to obey instructions. Sedgwick asserted, "If instructions are to be of any efficacy, they must speak the sense of the majority of the people, at least of a state." And in a state as large as Massachusetts, this would not be feasible.[35]

---

[31]See speeches of John Page of Virginia and Elbridge Gerry of Massachusetts in *DHFFC*, vol. 11 (Charlene Bangs Bickford, Kenneth R. Bowling, and Helen E. Veit, eds.), pp. 1266–67, 1272–74.

[32]Gerry argued that giving people the right to instruct their representatives did not presuppose that representatives would have to obey. Ibid., 11:1273.

[33]Ibid., 11:1274–75.

[34]Edmund Morgan, *Inventing the People: The Rise of Popular Sovereignty in England and America* (New York, 1988), pp. 210–33; J. R. Pole, *Political Representation in England and the Origins of the American Republic* (New York, 1966), pp. 72–73, 541–42 (Appendix 1: "A Fallacy in the Theory of Instruction").

[35]Fisher Ames of Massachusetts agreed with Sedgwick. New Yorker John Laurence asserted he represented the whole Union as well, *DHFFC*, 11:1275–76, 1279.

Opponents argued that instructions, if binding, destroyed the idea of an independent and deliberative body. After reviewing the dangers of instructions, James Jackson of Georgia stated most succinctly: "It will give rise to such a variety of absurdities and inconsistencies, as no prudent Legislature would wish to involve themselves in."[36] Others warned that instructions would only be used for party purposes and not for the general good.[37] Perhaps the deciding factor for many congressmen was James Madison's insistence that the issue was too fraught with ambiguity and controversy to be included in the Constitution. The Constitution would be weakened by Tucker's proposal and Madison did not want to jeopardize either his proposed amendments or the experiment in republican government.[38] When the final vote was taken, only ten members rose in its favor.

The House of Representatives explicitly rejected granting the people the right to instruct them. It refused to relinquish independence of action or debate. But there were strong dissenting voices in the House, and while many representatives did not themselves want to be instructed, they made no such determination for senators. At least one member pointed out that the different bases of representation for the House and Senate produced distinctive relationships between electors and elected. When the Senate considered opening its doors in April 1790, it would also confront this issue of instructions.

During the First Federal Congress, North Carolina and Virginia instructed their senators to open the Senate's doors, but only the Virginia senators dutifully brought the matter to the Senate floor. All senators who spoke against instructions opposed opening the Senate doors. North Carolina's Hawkins and Johnston most likely made the same arguments on the floor as they did to their state legislature. Certainly, similar sentiments were expressed during debate. Connecticut's Oliver Ellsworth thought that instructions were no more than a wish and should be treated as such. Ralph Izard of South Carolina and Robert Morris of Pennsylvania did not think state legislatures had a special claim to their vote. Izard equated legislators with presiden-

[36]Also see speech by Pennsylvanian George Clymer, ibid., 11:1275, 1267.
[37]See speech by Thomas Hartley of Pennsylvania, ibid., 11:1264–66.
[38]Ibid., 11:1270, 1279–80.

tial electors, who it would be absurd to think had the right to instruct the president. Morris exclaimed, "We were Senators for the United States and had nothing to do with One State more than another." He thought his charge was to represent national interests. In addition, some senators may have feared for their and the institution's safety while the federal government depended on a host city. Johnston did not think the Senate would reverse its decision to meet in secret until Congress removed "to the Federal City, where they will be more effectively secured from insult and intrusion on their debates and deliberations, than in a City where they have no Jurisdiction or power to carry into effect their Regulations for preserving order and decorum."[39] These senators were concerned that if the Senate opened itself to both the public and instructions they would compromise, and perhaps endanger, the Senate's deliberative responsibilities.

Not only would instructions preempt debate, but many senators feared public sessions would produce endless, perhaps meaningless, speeches meant to impress the galleries and not to sway colleagues. William Maclay thought that the Senate should indulge the states in their request. If senators played to the galleries and public prints, if "they waged war in Words and Oral Combats, if they pitted themselves like Cocks or play'd the Gladiator for the Amusement of the Idle & curious," Maclay argued the fault lay with the people who chose such men to be their senators.[40] He did not think it would necessarily reflect poorly upon the institution. Opponents of instructions and open doors presumed these reforms would lead senators to privilege public opinion and popularity over the national interest and thus subvert the institution. Hence senators wanted to distance themselves from their electors. They refused to recognize a privileged position for the states by defeating the resolution for public sessions twice during the First Congress. On the first attempt, only Maclay and the Virginia senators, Richard Henry Lee and John Walker, voted for the resolution.[41]

---

[39]Samuel Johnston to Alexander Martin, May 15, 1792, Governors' Papers, vol. 19, North Carolina Department of Archives and History.

[40]Maclay does not record any arguments explicitly favoring instructions, Feb. 24, 1791, Bowling and Veit, *Maclay's Diary*, pp. 388–89.

[41]In February 1791, nine senators voted for a resolution introduced by Virginian James Monroe, ibid., p. 389 n.

After the First Congress, states continued to pass instructions and resolutions entreating the Senate to open its doors. While the majority of states in 1790 and 1791 that passed such resolutions were southern, states outside of the region supported this effort. Virginia, North Carolina, South Carolina, Maryland, and New York instructed their senators to use their utmost endeavors to open the Senate's doors. In January 1791, the Pennsylvania House of Representatives passed a resolution calling for open doors, but the state senate defeated the resolution.[42] Samuel Henshaw reported that in the Massachusetts legislature "there will be a vast majority in favour of the Measure [opening the Senate's doors]. For I have heard no body oppose it."[43] Despite Henshaw's prediction, the legislature never formally expressed its sentiments to Congress. Although Henshaw personally opposed open sessions for the Senate, clearly he thought the majority in the Massachusetts legislature supported such accessibility. Like the 1790 North Carolina legislature, these states felt that to be faithful to the Constitution they had to keep watch on the Senate. They did not think they were capable of carrying out such vigilance when the Senate's doors were closed.

The Senate defeated motion after motion for opening its doors throughout the first half of the 1790s but by increasingly smaller margins. In April 1790, the first resolution garnered only three votes. Less than a year later, nine senators voted for public sessions. A growing and dedicated number of senators were determined to open the Senate's legislative sessions to the public. North Carolina's Alexander Martin, one of these senators, explained:

> To please our fellow citizens to prevent jealousies and murmers rising in the public mind from secret legislation a number, at present the minority[,] wish to render the veil that has heretofore concealed the Senate, and bring them into public view [so] that the bugbear their

[42]Elizabeth G. McPherson, "The Southern States and the Reporting of Senate Debates, 1789–1802," *Journal of Southern History* 12 (1946):223–46; Gerald L. Grotta, "Philip Freneau's Crusade for Open Sessions of the U.S. Senate," *Journalism Quarterly* 48 (1971):667–71; Bowling and Veit, *Maclay's Diary,* p. 389 n.

[43]Samuel Henshaw to Theodore Sedgwick, Feb. 6, 1791, Sedgwick Family Papers, Massachusetts Historical Society, Boston.

secrecy has created may no longer threaten terrors to a nation vigilant over their liberties.

Martin believed that secret sessions threatened the people's liberties and thus the Republic. He pledged to continue his efforts to open the Senate to public scrutiny. Although he thought that the vote would have been nearly equal if taken in December 1793, he hoped that he would soon be able to announce more positive results.[44] When the Senate finally agreed to open its doors in February 1794, the vote was 19–8, but not before the vote on the unamended motion to open the doors passed by one vote. Thus the final vote reflected both a difference in personnel and a realization that further resistance would be futile. Of the four senators who opposed the motion in 1791 and were still members in 1794, only Ellsworth switched sides—probably because he did not want to be associated with the losing side. No one defected from the pro-open session contingent.[45] Senators no longer thought such publicity would adversely affect their legislative proceedings, and, in fact, they recognized the benefits openness could bring.

In 1794, the Senate's first open session was successful enough to ameliorate most lingering fears about public access to the institution. The Senate opened its debates for the first time during consideration of a challenge to Albert Gallatin's election. When the Pennsylvania legislature elected the Geneva-born Gallatin to the Senate in 1793, his Federalist opponents questioned whether Gallatin met the Consti-

---

[44]Alexander Martin to Gov. Richard Dobbs Spaight, Dec. 30, 1793, *North Carolina Governors' Letterbooks.*

[45]The Senate first voted on a resolution to open the doors, but the date on which the doors were to be opened was left blank. According to Martin, this motion lost by a majority of one. However, one senator, whom Martin did not name, claimed to have misunderstood the motion. He voted against the resolution because he believed that the Senate doors would be opened immediately before galleries could be built. Once he realized his error, he moved for a reconsideration. Both the motion for reconsideration and the resolution passed. The Senate then amended the resolution by declaring the next meeting of Congress to be the date on which the resolution would become effective. Martin reported this vote as 18 to 9; the *Journal* reported it as 19 to 8. Senators voted to open their doors on February 20, 1794. Izard was the only southerner to oppose the motion, and he voted against the similar motion in 1791. *Senate Legislative Journal,* 1st Cong., 3d sess., Feb. 25, 1791; *Senate Legislative Journal,* 3d Cong., 1st sess., Feb. 20, 1794; Alexander Martin to Gov. Richard Dobbs Spaight, Feb. 21, 1794, *North Carolina Governors' Letterbooks.*

tution's citizenship requirements. Gallatin himself invited the challenge by publicly admitting to potential problems. The Federalist majority in the Senate referred the petition to committee on two separate occasions. Both committees supported Gallatin's opponents. Significantly, the Senate decided to open this debate to the public in order to preempt accusations of misconduct and conspiracy that Federalists thought a secret session on Gallatin would precipitate, especially in Philadelphia.[46] At the same time, the Senate tentatively endorsed the opening of its doors for all its legislative sessions and directed a gallery to be built. The mere fact that the Gallatin debate did not lead to more than the expected criticism or seemingly to the corruption of deliberative principles helped to give the Senate the confidence to open its doors to all its legislative procedures. With the galleries completed at the beginning of the Fourth Congress, the Senate quickly agreed to adhere to its previous resolution.

Even once the doors opened, states did not have direct access to Senate proceedings. Senators did not hire any stenographers to record their speeches, but instead (like the House) relied on newspaper reporters to chronicle proceedings. Samuel Henshaw warned Sedgwick that if the Senate hired a stenographer, "the greatest mischief will be, that days & weeks & months of precious time will be sacrificed merely to figure in a Newspaper!"[47] Although public sessions did not seem to have produced protracted speeches, some, like Henshaw, transferred their fears of public sessions onto the employment of stenographers. In addition, the Senate frequently met in executive session, which remained closed to the public. When John Quincy Adams served in the Senate in the early 1800s, he complained that the Senate often went into executive session when the only purpose was to give the appearance of employment rather than to conduct any substantive business.[48] Even before the Senate endorsed public sessions, it would

[46]Anne M. Butler and Wendy Wolff, *United States Senate Election, Expulsion and Censure Cases* (Washington, D.C., 1995), pp. 3–5.

[47]Samuel Henshaw to Theodore Sedgwick, Feb. 16, 1796, Sedgwick Family Papers, Massachusetts Historical Society.

[48]In 1804, Adams complained that Stephen R. Bradley moved that the Senate go into executive session "merely for the sake of having on the *printed* Journals an *appearance* of doing business, though there was really none to do." Adams was the only senator to vote against the motion. John Quincy Adams, *Memoirs of John Quincy Adams,*

adjourn "on pretence of doing business in committees."[49] Thus the Senate pretended to be employed while avoiding the embarrassment of repeated early adjournments. Not surprisingly, reporters did not flock to the Senate, but continued to find House debates much more lively and interesting. When one enterprising newspaper editor, William Duane, proposed that the states contract with him to provide stenographers for the Senate who would in turn provide reports directly to them, he received no responses.[50]

States continued to rely on regular correspondence from their senators for information about the Senate and the government in general. Like North Carolina's Hawkins and Johnston, senators reported back to the state legislatures through their governors. Governors would then turn the letters over to the legislatures. In these letters, senators publicized their service to the state while paying homage to their special relationship to the legislatures. Senators' letters ranged from routine accounts of bills passed and lost to more detailed explanations of their votes and actions. They often sent the president's messages, congressional journals, and newspapers to public officials and their friends at home.[51]

Senators did not necessarily confine themselves to a recounting of events. Frequently, they offered unsolicited advice about how best to deal with the national government and other states. In 1796, during the controversy over funding the Jay Treaty, Connecticut Sen. Jonathan

---

ed. Charles Francis Adams, 12 vols. (Philadelphia, 1874), 1:315. For similar comments see diary entries of Nov. 7, 1803, and Nov. 3, 1807, ibid. 1:272, 472. See also, James Hillhouse to Rebecca Hillhouse, Nov. 19, 1807, Hillhouse Papers, Department of Manuscripts and Archives, Yale University, New Haven, Conn.

[49]Upon adjournment, Maclay headed to the House of Representatives to watch its debates, Apr. 28, 1790, Bowling and Veit, *Maclay's Diary*, p. 255.

[50]Duane made this proposal in his *Aurora* in 1800, claiming he did not have the resources to report proceedings in both the Senate and House. He specifically called on Republican state legislatures to hire him to monitor the Federalist Senate. He even calculated his costs and how much each state would have to contribute. In 1814, Ebenezer Cummins decided to devote a whole newspaper to the Senate. Within months he ran out of material and began publishing House debates. The paper folded at the end of the session. *The Senator* (Washington, D.C.), Jan. 1 to Apr. 23, 1814; *Aurora* (Philadelphia), Mar. 13, 1800.

[51]From 1797 to 1808, when Jonathan Trumbull served as Connecticut's governor, he carried on extensive correspondence with the state's senators, Correspondence with Congressmen, vols. 1 and 2, 1780–1818, Connecticut Historical Society, Hartford.

Trumbull advised the governor not to appoint anyone from the House of Representatives to fill Ellsworth's Senate seat because they needed every vote in that chamber. When funding was safely secured, Trumbull advised the governor to make the appointment.[52] Senators offered advice about how to best achieve the state's objectives. Connecticut instructed its senators to secure a favorable settlement of the state's account with the U.S. government. Reporting their success in obtaining passage of such a law, Sen. James Hillhouse suggested the legislature pass a law itself to take full advantage of the federal law.[53]

These letters served the same purpose as congressmen's circular letters, which were an established means of informing the public of the business Congress conducted while in session. These letters were usually published in various local newspapers or as broadsides.[54] In contrast, only occasionally did senators arrange for the independent publication of their letters.[55] They saw their responsibility as keeping their electors and immediate constituents informed of their activities rather than the people at large.

Although the Senate did not open any of its executive proceedings to the public until well into the twentieth century, the Jay Treaty represented an important episode with regard to the Senate's relationship with both the states and the people. The Jay Treaty precipitated not only individual state challenges to senators, but also an effort orchestrated by Virginia to radically reduce the Senate's powers. With the Senate's approval, President Washington sent Chief Justice John Jay to England to negotiate a commercial treaty in 1794. While few if any senators were fully satisfied with the resulting product, the Senate conditionally ratified the treaty in a closed-door, special session in June 1795.[56] Following publication of the treaty, public debate about its

---

[52]Jonathan Trumbull to Jeremiah Wadsworth and William Williams, Mar. 5, 7, 26, and May 4, 1796, ibid.

[53]James Hillhouse to Jonathan Trumbull, Apr. 11, 1798, ibid.

[54]Noble Cunningham, ed., *Circular Letters of Congressmen,* 3 vols. (Chapel Hill, 1978), 1:xv–xlv.

[55]Ralph Izard asked his friend to arrange for the publication of his letter declining to be a candidate for reelection in 1794. Ralph Izard to John Owen, July 15, 1795, and John Owen to Ralph Izard, Aug. 5, 1794, Ralph Izard Family Papers, microfilm reel 1, Library of Congress, Washington, D.C.

[56]The Jay Treaty temporarily settled some issues related to commercial relations between England and the United States. The Senate struck out Article 12, which

merits continued for months. Treaty opponents urged representatives to insist on a House role in treaty making through the appropriations process. While House members attempted to execute this plan, some states—particularly Kentucky and Virginia—heightened their protests. Kentucky took aim at one of its senators; Virginia assailed the entire Senate.

Sen. Humphrey Marshall felt the wrath of the Kentucky legislature and people when he voted to ratify the Jay Treaty. During its session immediately succeeding the Senate's ratification, the Kentucky legislature received numerous petitions asking it to instruct Marshall to vote against further ratification. Petitioners made no mention of Kentucky's other senator, John Brown, because he had voted against the treaty and they trusted him to do so in the future. The freemen of Mercer County, however, thought Marshall had "betrayed the trust reposed in him." Not only did they insist on instructions, but they declared the six-year Senate term "dangerous to the liberties of America, [that it] destroys their [senators'] responsibility, and may enable them to carry into execution schemes pregnant with the greatest evils." Hence, they wanted their representatives instructed to propose a constitutional amendment giving state legislatures the power to recall senators by a two-thirds vote.[57] The legislature responded by instructing both senators to vote against the treaty in all subsequent considerations, although initial proposals did not mention Brown. As a Federalist facing the ire of a Republican legislature, Marshall decided to appeal directly to the people.[58] In a series of articles published in the

---

related to trade with the West Indies. Many people thought that since the Senate altered the treaty, it would have to reconsider the treaty in light of any action taken by King George III. Thus anti-treaty men thought the Senate would have an opportunity to reject the treaty. England accepted the treaty as changed, and President Washington decided it was unnecessary to resubmit it to the Senate. On the Jay Treaty, see Stanley Elkins and Eric McKitrick, *The Age of Federalism* (New York, 1993), pp. 388ff; Samuel Flagg Bemis, *Jay's Treaty* (1923; reprint ed., New Haven, 1962); and Jerald A. Combs, *The Jay Treaty* (Berkeley, 1970).

[57] *Kentucky Gazette* (Lexington), Oct. 3, 1795. See also, Meeting of Masons of Winchester Lodge, Resolutions from Barbour County, Resolutions from Scott County, and Meeting of the Inhabitants of Clarke County (Winchester) in *Kentucky Gazette,* Oct. 24, Nov. 5 and 16, 1795; and *Stewart's Kentucky Herald* (Lexington), Sept. 22, 1795.

[58] Marshall has been described as "an aristocratic lawyer who possessed a sarcastic tongue, [and] a great disdain for the rabble." Given these sentiments it is surprising that Marshall appealed to the people directly. On the other hand, in this instance,

Kentucky Gazette, Marshall explained the treaty and his vote.[59] Marshall closed his defense by asserting that he did not avoid his responsibility to the people, but acted as any public servant should, not according to what would please the people, but what was the best course for the nation. Adhering to this criterion, Marshall declared, "I discharged my duty faithfully—that is, *according to my own judgment.*"[60] Significantly, Marshall did not pay homage to a special relationship with the state legislature, but instead, when faced with an uncooperative legislature, resorted to the public prints and directly to the people. The Federalist Marshall viewed the Senate as above local and parochial interests; whereas the Republican legislature thought that senators should be amenable to the legislature's views—that senators were obliged to follow their legislatures' dictates.

The people proved just as unsympathetic as the legislature. At one point, a mob dragged Marshall from his house in Frankfort with the intention of dunking him in the river.[61] While Marshall talked himself out of this particular humiliation, he was driven out of Georgetown, Kentucky, under the threat of being tarred and feathered. Since Marshall's term did not expire until March 1801, the legislature could only wait until then to replace him. His political enemies, however, had recourse and several other reasons to move against him. Not only had Marshall voted against the legislature's sentiments with regard to the treaty, but he also was involved in several other disputes.[62] His enemies revived perjury charges, which had been lingering against him for years. State Judges George Muter and Benjamin Sebastian brought the case to the legislature's attention through a petition. While simulta-

---

Marshall probably felt more contempt for the rabble in the legislature than in the streets. Butler and Wolff, *Senate Election, Expulsion, and Censure Cases,* pp. 8–9. For a biography of Marshall see, A. C. Quisenberry, *The Life and Times of Hon. Humphrey Marshall* (Winchester, Ky., 1892).

[59]Marshall's series consisted of eleven installments, of which two through eleven appeared in the *Kentucky Gazette* from October 5, 1795, to January 2, 1796. The first installment appeared in *Stewart's Kentucky Herald,* but Stewart refused to publish more because he deemed Marshall's articles too long for a weekly paper. Unfortunately, the issue in which the first article appeared is not extant. "A Freeman" answered Marshall installment by installment, which the *Gazette* also published over this same period.

[60]*Kentucky Gazette,* Jan. 2, 1796.

[61]Quisenberry, *Life and Times of Humphrey Marshall,* pp. 58–62.

[62]Richard E. Ellis, *The Jeffersonian Crisis: Courts and Politics in the Young Republic* (New York, 1971), pp. 133–36.

neously considering the Jay Treaty instructions, the legislature passed a resolution forwarding its concerns about Marshall's conduct to the Senate with the suggestion that Marshall was not worthy of a seat in that body.[63] Though nothing ultimately came of these charges, Marshall could not rescue his national political career, which depended upon the good will of a Republican legislature. Because of senators' long terms and the absence of recall, the Kentucky legislature could only wait until Marshall's term expired to replace him with a man more amenable to their views. Marshall, who retired from the Senate in 1801, spent the rest of his political career in the state legislature.

Unlike Kentucky, Virginia approved of both of its senators' conduct. Like Kentucky, Virginia disapproved of both the Jay Treaty and the Senate. In the wake of the treaty's ratification, the Virginia General Assembly proposed four constitutional amendments—three of which aimed to reduce senatorial power. It wanted to give the House of Representatives a share of the treaty-making power by requiring the House's approval of all treaties, reducing senators' terms to three years, and giving the power to try impeachments to another tribunal.[64] Clearly, Virginia did not trust the Senate. It wanted to make the Senate both more dependent on the states and the will of the people by giving congressmen a say in treaties and by cutting senators' terms by half. Virginia instructed its senators, Henry Tazewell and Stephens T. Mason, to obtain approval of these amendments. Only one other state, Kentucky, gave any support to Virginia, and then it only endorsed the shortening of senators' terms. By supporting only this amendment, Kentucky privileged the state's relationship to the Senate over the Senate's relationship to the people. Virginia's intent seemed to be a wholesale reduction in power rather than simply a closer relationship between senators

[63]*Journal of the Kentucky House of Representatives* in *Record of States of the United States*, Microfilm, Library of Congress; and *Kentucky Gazette*. For Senate records see Record Group 46: Sen 4A-B3 (Motions), 4A-D1 (Committee Reports), and 4A-F6 (Communications to the President of the Senate), National Archives and Records Administration, Washington, D.C.

[64]This last amendment was a holdover from the recommendations made by the Virginia Ratification Convention in 1788. Neither the general assembly nor the convention specified who it thought should have tried impeachments if not the Senate. The Fourth Amendment would have prohibited federal judges from accepting any other office. Thomas J. Farnham, "The Virginia Amendments of 1795," *Virginia Magazine of History and Biography* 75 (1967):75–88.

and the states. The New Hampshire, Rhode Island, New York, Pennsylvania, and Delaware legislatures rejected Virginia's overture. Massachusetts went one step further by declaring that Virginia had violated the Constitution by the manner in which it made its proposal.[65] Massachusetts objected because Virginia proposed the amendments directly to the states instead of to Congress or by a call for another constitutional convention. Faced with certain rejection, Virginia's senators suggested that the general assembly not aggressively push for the amendments. They assured the legislature that they would do what they could to procure the desired ends but necessarily by different means.[66]

The Senate survived both Virginia's challenge to its powers and its attempt to redefine the Senate's relationship with the states and the House. No other proposed amendments to alter the Senate succeeded.[67] Senators and states would have to negotiate the terms of their relationship outside of formal institutional arrangements, just as Kentucky had tried to do with Marshall.

In conclusion, the Senate's relationship with the states remained contested and imbued with expectations held by senators, state legislators, governors, and the people. As it emerged from the Philadelphia Convention and ratification debates, the Senate seemed to represent the states; yet, the delegates did not fully endorse this role by denying states the right to recall senators, giving senators long terms, making senators vote individually and not by state, and giving the federal government the responsibility for paying senators. Thus delegates expressed ambivalence toward the Senate's representative character. It would be left to the first senators and the states to negotiate the terms of their relationship. While instances of conflict can more often than

---

[65]James Madison to James Monroe, Dec. 20, 1795, and Feb. 16, 1796, in *The Papers of James Madison,* 17 vols. (Chicago and Charlottesville, 1962–91), vol. 16 (J. C. A. Stagg, Thomas A. Mason, and Jeanne K. Sisson, eds.), pp. 170, 232.

[66]Henry Tazewell and Stephens T. Mason to Robert Brooke, Nov. 1, 1796, Record Group 79, Office of the Speaker [Executive Communications], Library of Virginia, Richmond.

[67]There were two more attempts to reduce Senate powers through the amendment process. In 1808, Virginia instructed its senators to obtain an amendment to the Constitution granting states the power to recall senators. The Georgia legislature proposed reducing senators' terms to four years in 1816.

not be attributed to nascent partisanship or factionalism, these cases demonstrated the persistence of Antifederalist concerns about the nature of the Senate. The Senate as the sole federal feature of the new government would bear the burden of both having to prove itself loyal to the states and to the national interests as well.

Clearly, states had certain expectations about how their senators would act. All states insisted on regular correspondence with their senators, and senators willingly complied—almost always to the satisfaction of the state legislature. In 1790, North Carolina found fault with their senators who attempted to explain their view of the relationship; they wanted more independence than the legislature wanted to grant them. In this case, the legislature prevailed when it replaced one with a man more friendly to their views and encouraged the other to retire when his term expired two years later, but it could not guarantee that all future senators would adhere to its dictates. Kentucky did not have such success with its senator, who had only just been elected when he defied the legislature's will. Virginia attempted to impose more sweeping changes upon the relationship between the Senate and the states; not simply satisfied with the terms of its relationship to its own senators, Virginia sought to establish the terms for all states and senators. Not surprisingly, the Senate did not accede to Virginia's wishes. Perhaps more surprisingly, no state fully supported Virginia.

States not only tried to define their relationship with senators through instructions but also sought greater and direct access to the Senate. Hence, they instructed and requested that the Senate open its legislative debates to the public. Once the Senate opened its doors in 1795, this immediate access did not become manifest. In fact, the Senate, compared to the House of Representatives, continued to work in relative obscurity until the second decade of the nineteenth century. States still had to rely upon senators for information about Senate proceedings. Thus, state legislators and senators would continue their exchanges of information, sentiments, and sometimes instructions, and would continue to negotiate the terms of their relationship on an individual basis. The relationship would change with every state legislative and senatorial election.

Richard A. Baker

The United States Senate in Philadelphia

An Institutional History of the 1790s

> It is wise to remember that Parliament, in its final structure, was not the result of careful planning or deliberate organization but rather the result of time, chance, and constant compromise.
>
> — GOLDWIN SMITH, *A History of England*

Definition

TODAY, WE PRETTY MUCH TAKE for granted the way the Senate operates as an institution. It has one hundred popularly elected members, seventeen standing committees, a majority leader, a minority leader, and seven thousand staff members. It is a profoundly subtle institution that outsiders, including House members and journalists, generally never come close to understanding. The Senate meets almost year-round in open session and accomplishes 95 percent of its business through the parliamentary expedient of unanimous consent agreements. At any time, a single member can object to these delicately negotiated agreements. Such objection can prove fatal to the matter in question. Consequently, each senator has enormous life-or-death power to shape legislative proceedings. When all else fails, members may slow or halt the Senate's processes by threatening to engage in extended debate—a process known as a filibuster.

The two centuries separating the 1790s from 1990s have brought profound changes to the Senate as an institution. Two hundred years ago, the above-cited numbers, percentages, structures, and procedures would certainly have bewildered members of the United States Senate then meeting at Congress Hall in Philadelphia. Yet, in any discussion of change, we must also remember, as the Constitution's Framers intended, that the Senate is a profoundly conservative, change-resistant, stability-enforcing institution. The Framers placed it as a barrier to momentary fads in policy or process. In James Madison's words, it was designed "to protect the people against the transient impressions into which they themselves might be led."[1] There is much about the Senate of our time that senators of the 1790s would certainly recognize—its passion for deliberation, its untidiness, its equalizing of influence among the states irrespective of their populations, its aloofness from the House of Representatives, and its suspicion of the presidency.

Our visit to the institutional Senate of the 1790s will include an account of its physical setting, administration, membership, leadership, and procedures. We will then examine four milestones that demonstrate the institution's growth during this decade. These four milestones tell us a great deal about the Senate's capacity for responsive change over a short period of time. They also remind us how far the Senate has come in two centuries and how resilient is our framework of government—the United States Constitution.

Setting

In the autumn of 1790, wagons ascended Philadelphia's Chestnut Street from Penn's Landing on the Delaware River. They carried the records and associated paraphernalia of the Congress just arrived from New York City, the former national capital. Their destination was an imposing Georgian brick building at the corner of Sixth Street. Recently named "Congress Hall," this two-story structure had been completed only the year before to serve as the Philadelphia County

---

[1]Max Farrand, ed., *The Records of the Federal Convention of 1787*, 4 vols. (New Haven, 1937), 1:421.

Court House. It was designed in a style to complement the State House—Independence Hall—directly to its east.

When Congress decided in 1790 to relocate the national government to Philadelphia until 1800, workmen hastily refitted and refurnished the courthouse's first and second floors. This provoked a New Yorker to observe bitterly that the Philadelphia city fathers had "hooked up [their] little court house . . . in humble imitation of our city-hall."[2]

New York had reason for its envy. Philadelphia, then Pennsylvania's capital and the nation's largest city with a population of 42,000, was rapidly developing as a prosperous commercial center, with well-lighted, well-paved, and regularly laid-out streets. As one member of Congress observed, Philadelphians "believe themselves to be the first people in America as well in manners as in arts, and like englishmen, they are at no pains to disguise this opinion."[3]

Porters bearing the Senate's meager belongings entered Congress Hall and passed through the large, plainly furnished former courtroom reserved for the House of Representatives. They ascended a staircase to smaller, more ornate quarters. A hallway opened into the Senate chamber, which occupied the second story's southern half. When outfitted for the Senate's opening session, the chamber contained two semicircular rows of mahogany writing desks, divided by a center aisle, to accommodate the body's twenty-six members. Second-row desks were at the same level as those in the first row, unlike the arrangement on the floor below, where the sixty-five House desks were placed in tiered rows. Just as in the New York chamber, each member was provided an arm chair covered in red morocco leather. Both the desks and chairs were built by Philadelphia cabinetmaker Thomas Affleck. A specially woven, neoclassically patterned Axminster carpet featuring the Great Seal of the United States elegantly covered the plain board floor.[4]

---

[2]Robert J. Colborn and staff of Independence National Historical Park, "Furnishing Plan for the Second Floor of Congress Hall," typescript, October 1963, p. 72. I have relied on this report for much of the physical description of the Senate's Congress Hall quarters. A copy is on file in the U.S. Senate Historical Office.

[3]Independence National Historical Park, *Congress Hall* (Philadelphia, 1976), [p. 1].

[4]Susan H. Anderson, *The Most Splendid Carpet* (Philadelphia, 1978).

We do not know if there was any pattern to members' seating assignments. While the Senate was meeting in New York City, Pennsylvania Sen. William Maclay had proposed that members sit according to their states' geographical arrangement, with New Englanders to the right of the presiding officer and Southerners to his left.[5] Although the Senate rejected this plan as a formal rule, there is casual evidence that members tended to cluster by regions. Maclay noted in his diary that he could whisper to senators from the adjoining states of New Jersey, Delaware, and Maryland.

Three bay windows, centered on the chamber's southern wall, framed the presiding officer's desk, which stood on a raised platform. Separated—literally and symbolically—from the members' desks by a railing that ran parallel to the windows, the presiding officer sat in a modest chair behind a small mahogany table covered on three sides with green silk. In the center window, carpenters had attached a wooden frame that supported a modest crimson damask canopy. The chamber's ten other windows, hung with green wooden Venetian blinds and crimson damask curtains, provided added daytime illumination, while candles placed on members' desks lit the chamber for rare late afternoon and evening sessions. The secretary of the Senate's plain mahogany writing desk stood to the presiding officer's right, on the members' side of the railing.

The chamber's most striking and incongruous features were two giant portraits of France's King Louis XVI, by Antoine François Callet, and Marie Antoinette, most likely the work of Elisabeth Marie Vigée-Lebrun. The French government had donated these paintings to the Confederation Congress in 1784. Copied from the originals, they measured approximately twelve feet by six feet. Hung facing the presiding officer on the north wall and flanking the chamber's curtained entrance, they were outfitted with silk damask curtains that could be drawn when members wished not to be reminded of these hated symbols of prerevolutionary France. Given the general anti-French attitudes of the Senate's Federalist majorities during most of the 1790s,

---

[5]Kenneth R. Bowling and Helen E. Veit, eds., *The Diary of William Maclay and Other Notes on Senate Debates* (Baltimore, 1988), vol. 9 of *Documentary History of the First Federal Congress,* 14. vols. to date (Baltimore, 1972–), p. 403, hereafter cited as *DHFFC.*

these artworks' continuing presence in such a choice location attested to the persisting sense of gratitude for the crucial aid the monarchs had provided during the not-so-distant Revolutionary War.[6]

Two smaller rooms, each measuring twenty-eight feet by eighteen feet, filled the remainder of the second floor, north of the chamber. The room on the eastern side served as the Senate's secretary's office, a combined administrative center, record storage facility, and reference library. To the west, separated by a wide hallway, was a general purpose room used for committee meetings. This committee room contained simple pine tables, twelve Windsor chairs, and several bookcases. Each room had a single fireplace.

Congress Hall provided less than half the floor space that had been available at Federal Hall in New York.[7] Within three years of settling in, the Senate and House agreed that the structure needed to be enlarged to relieve initially crowded conditions made worse with the arrival in 1791 and 1792 of members from the newly admitted states of Vermont and Kentucky. The resulting expansion, completed in 1793, was accomplished by extending the building twenty-six feet into the State House yard to the south. The Senate chamber remained on the second floor's south side. With only thirty members, the upper house's needs for chamber space were not as urgent as that of the body on the floor below, whose numbers, thanks to the 1790 census, had risen by 50 percent, from 69 to 105. Accordingly, the Senate added only six feet to its existing chamber and, from the remaining new space, fashioned two additional committee rooms, each eighteen feet square. The original committee room became a much-needed library and document storeroom—a most visible indicator of the new institution's early expansion.

Members

As the Constitution then provided, the new congressional session was set for the first Monday in December. On Monday, December 6, 1790,

[6]Colborn, "Furnishing Plan," pp. 18–27. It is believed these portraits moved with the Senate to Washington, D.C., in 1800. Visitors to the chamber commented on them from time to time. These comments ceased in the years following the 1814 Capitol fire.

[7]Bowling and Veit, *Maclay Diary*, p. 337 n. 9.

fifteen of the twenty-six eligible senators climbed to Congress Hall's second floor to begin the First Congress's third session. This gave the Senate just a one-member margin above the required quorum for conducting business.

Seldom were all twenty-six members—the number would soon increase to thirty-two with the admission of Vermont, Kentucky, and Tennessee—simultaneously present. Although most members attended faithfully in the early months of a session, which then coincided with the winter's dormant agricultural season, they tended to slip away as the spring and early summer growing seasons approached. During the 1790s, in the final weeks of each Congress's first session, as many as one-quarter of the Senate's members failed to participate in votes. Prevalent illness, difficulty of travel, the press of business at home, and the attraction of other public office placed a premium on maintaining a quorum.

The members who inaugurated the Senate's Philadelphia chamber were an experienced lot. Among the twenty-six, more than three-quarters had served in the Continental and Confederation Congresses and in state legislatures. Ten had served in the Constitutional Convention and another seven of that body's fifty-five members would arrive later in the decade. In other words, nearly one-third of the Framers of the Constitution became senators. At a time when few enjoyed the privilege of obtaining a higher education, nearly half were college graduates; two-thirds had some legal training.[8]

Despite Philadelphia's social and cultural attractions, senators encountered significant hardships. The high cost of living—rent increases of 100 percent were reported following announcement of Congress's decision to move there[9]—the greater attractiveness of state legislative service, and the hardship of a six-year severance from one's livelihood conspired to keep many members from serving out their full terms. One-third of the eighty-six senators who filled the thirty-two seats during the Philadelphia years resigned before their terms expired. It was not uncommon for as many as four senators to successively

---

[8]U.S. Congress, Senate, *The United States Senate: A Dissertation on the First Fourteen Years of the Upper Legislative Body, 1787–1801,* by Roy Swanstrom, S. Doc. 99–19, 99th Cong., 1st sess., pp. 36–38.

[9]John Fenno to Samuel A. Otis, Sept. 5, 1790, Records of the Secretary of the Senate, Record Group 46, National Archives and Records Administration (NARA).

fill a seat during a six-year term. Only three senators served all ten years that the Senate met in Philadelphia.[10]

Administration

By the time the Senate had settled in Philadelphia, it had established its basic operational procedures. During its previous fourteen months of actual meeting time in New York City, the body had adopted a code of rules, established procedures based on the presiding officer's interpretation of those rules, hired its officers and a small clerical force, and tested its various constitutional prerogatives.

The Senate of 1790 had access to a good deal of information and precedent to guide its institutional operations. Senators of the First Congress were generally familiar with the operations of the British Parliament and their respective state legislative bodies. As one scholar of early legislative practices has concluded, "Whatever names they adopted, House of Burgesses, House of Representatives, or Commons House of Assembly, from New Hampshire to Georgia these colonial assemblies were all very much alike in external features and general structure. . . . They had similar officers: speaker, clerk, sergeant-at-arms, and doorkeepers; with few exceptions their procedure in passing bills was similar."[11] Rather than being a brand new legislative invention, the Senate blended the Constitution's Framers' and its members' late-eighteenth-century understanding of how representative bodies were supposed to function.

Leadership

Given the high turnover in membership, responsibility for developing and maintaining institutional continuity rested heavily on the Senate's presiding officer—the vice president of the United States—and the Senate's two elected officers—the secretary and the doorkeeper.

[10]James Gunn of Georgia, John Langdon of New Hampshire, and Theodore Foster of Rhode Island.

[11]Ralph Volney Harlow, *The History of Legislative Methods in the Period before 1825* (New Haven, 1917), p. 2.

The presiding officers performed the basic leadership functions—today the province of elected floor leaders—which consisted of keeping members informed on issues, agenda, and timing of votes; maintaining decorum; establishing an order of business; and disposing of legislation in a timely manner. The elected officers managed the flow of legislation, communicated with the House of Representatives and the president, and handled routine administrative and security chores.

Presiding Officers

In the Senate's ornate chamber, a wooden railing separated the vice president from the officers and members. As Senate president, the vice president had few powers beyond the constitutionally prescribed role of breaking tie votes and the right to determine which member would address the Senate if two or more senators sought recognition at the same time. His word was final in maintaining order. Beyond this, the Senate chose to limit the authority of the vice president, over whose selection and political views it had no control.

JOHN ADAMS. In pairing John Adams of Massachusetts with George Washington of Virginia in the first presidential election under the Constitution, the nation's political leaders intended that he would provide politically desirable regional balance. By the time the government settled in Philadelphia, a year and a half after their April 1789 inaugurations, the two men had established a cordial but distant relationship. Adams's province was entirely the chamber of the United States Senate.[12]

During his two terms of office, ending in March 1797, Adams supported the Washington administration through informal consultation with senators and by breaking twenty-nine tie votes in eight years, a record still in place after more than two centuries. Several of these votes proved highly significant. One protected the president's sole authority to remove his appointees; another influenced location of the national capital; and a third prevented war with Great Britain. With few precedents to guide him, Adams initially tried out an activist role,

[12]Swanstrom, *United States Senate, 1787–1801*, pp. 253–57.

lecturing senators on matters of policy and procedure. Recognizing that this might undercut member support for his own presidential bid in years to come, Adams soon adopted a more subdued approach. When he signed official documents as "John Adams, Vice President of the United States," senators gently reminded him of his duty to certify enacted legislation as "president of the Senate." For the remainder of his tenure, Adams tried to have it both ways, signing "John Adams, Vice President of the United States and President of the Senate."

THOMAS JEFFERSON. Hardly a legislative day passed during the Senate's earliest years without some member trying to establish a new rule, precedent, or order. When Thomas Jefferson took his oath as the Senate's president on March 4, 1797, he determined to bring some regularity to this increasingly confused scene.[13] While Adams could rely on the memory of his direct personal participation from the Senate's first day of operations, Jefferson lacked such firsthand experience. The Virginian had spent that eight-year period first as secretary of state and then as a private citizen in a world far removed from that of the Senate chamber. Placing great value on orderliness in his personal life and business affairs, Jefferson sought to avoid the criticism leveled against Adams for the inconsistency of his Senate rulings.

Twenty years earlier, Jefferson had drafted the rules for the Continental Congress that so deeply influenced the shape of the Senate's initial rules. As he approached the duties of the Senate's presiding officer, Jefferson grew concerned. He worried that the existing rules failed to offer him and his successors sufficient detailed guidance for making procedural decisions, noting that "this places under the discretion of the President [of the Senate] a very extensive field of decision, and one which, irregularly exercised, would have a powerful effect on the proceedings and determinations of the [Senate]." It was essential for the presiding officer to be able to consult "some known system of rules, that he may never leave himself free to indulge caprice or passion, nor open to the imputation of them." What system,

[13]Wilbur Samuel Howell, ed., *Jefferson's Parliamentary Writings: "Parliamentary Pocket-Book" and a Manual of Parliamentary Practice* (Princeton, 1988), pp. 9–28.

Jefferson asked, would serve as a suitable guide? The answer resided within the experience of the British House of Commons. "Its rules are probably as wisely constructed for governing the debates of a deliberative body, and obtaining its true sense, as any which can become known to us."[14]

Jefferson's unhurried duties as Senate president left him plenty of time to turn his creative energies to a project of monumental importance and enduring influence—his *Manual of Parliamentary Practice.* To prepare the *Manual,* Jefferson examined several dozen treatises on English history and parliamentary practice, including the first three volumes of John Hatsell's *Precedents of Proceedings in the House of Commons.* He arranged his work into fifty-three categories, from "Absence" to "Treaties," with twenty-three sections devoted to the management of bills. "I have here endeavored to collect and digest so much of these [Senate and House of Commons rules] as is called for in ordinary practice, collating the Parliamentary with the Senatorial rules, both where they agree and where they vary."[15]

He believed the *Manual*'s contents would help the Senate operate with more fairness and consistency than was evident in the House of Representatives or the previous Continental Congress. Jefferson's objective was "to deposit with the Senate the Standard by which I judge and am willing to be judged." He noted that the product may not be perfect, "but I have begun a sketch, which those who come after me will successively correct and fill up, till a code of rules shall be formed for the use of the Senate, the effects of which may be accuracy in business, economy of time, order, uniformity, and impartiality."[16] Jefferson completed the *Manual* as Congress prepared to move from Philadelphia to Washington. The first edition appeared in 1801.

None of Jefferson's successors as Senate president has come close to making such a profound contribution to the institution's self-definition and legislative operations. In 1993, the Senate published a special edition to commemorate both the 250th anniversary of Jefferson's

[14]U.S. Congress, Senate, *A Manual of Parliamentary Practice for the Use of the Senate of the United States,* by Thomas Jefferson, S. Doc. 103–8, 103d Cong., 2d sess., preface.

[15]Ibid.

[16]Ibid.

birth and his unique contribution to a richer understanding of the Senate's rules.[17] In October 1998, Sen. John Glenn carried a copy of the *Manual* with him on the space shuttle *Discovery* as a symbolic representation of his ties to the United States Senate.

President pro tempore

In the vice president's absence, the Constitution allowed the Senate to select one of its own members as temporary presiding officer—president pro tempore. Throughout its decade in Philadelphia, the Senate, on fifteen occasions, elected twelve individuals president pro tempore. In selecting these officers, the Senate paid no particular attention to seniority or party loyalties, contrary to the modern practice of automatically filling that post with the majority party's senior member. Personality rather than politics determined the selection. The brevity of the president pro tempore's term and the randomness of his selection worked against any one individual being able to use the office as a pulpit for leadership.[18]

The reason the Senate even bothered to fill this office in the 1790s is found in the Constitution's requirement for a line of succession in the event neither the president nor vice president is able to discharge the presidency's duties. At a time of high mortality rates and short life spans (consider Philadelphia's 1793 yellow fever epidemic), the possibility that both the president and vice president might die or become incapacitated during a nine-month congressional adjournment was far from remote. The 1792 Presidential Succession Act determined which officers would follow in the line of succession. Overriding House desires to place cabinet officers directly behind the vice president, the Senate inserted two congressional leaders—the Senate president pro tempore and the House Speaker, in that order. Senators did this to minimize chances that Secretary of State Thomas Jefferson or Treasury Secretary Alexander Hamilton, both increasingly unpopular with the Federalist majority, would reach the high office through succession. With this requirement in mind, the Senate took special pains after

[17]Ibid.

[18]Swanstrom, *United States Senate, 1787–1801*, pp. 257–60.

1792 to ensure the election of a president pro tempore for adjournment periods. During these periods, practically speaking, the Senate consisted of two on-call officials: its president pro tempore and its secretary.

Senate Officers

SAMUEL A. OTIS, SECRETARY. In selecting Samuel A. Otis as its secretary, the Senate acknowledged the value of prior legislative institutional experience. Soon after convening for the first time in the spring of 1789, the Senate had chosen the forty-eight-year-old Otis because of his ties to the Senate's president, Vice President John Adams, and for qualifications gained while deputy quartermaster of the Continental army, speaker of the Massachusetts House of Representatives, and member of the Confederation Congress. Despite Otis's obliging and deferential manner, however, not every senator thought highly of the new secretary.[19]

Otis had not been the obvious candidate for the job. Early in 1789, as plans went forward for establishing the new Congress, a spirited contest had developed. Underscoring the recognized value of continuity, the presumed heir to the office was dapper sixty-year-old Charles Thomson, secretary of the soon-to-expire Continental and Confederation Congresses during their entire fifteen-year existence. But Thomson sought a loftier position, thereby fatally weakening his candidacy.[20]

As he began to outline his duties, Otis had reason to be grateful to Thomson. The early Senate's desire to follow traditional organizational models, rather than devise completely new structures, is particularly evident in the inherited nature of those duties. More than a decade earlier, in 1777, the Continental Congress had spelled out Thomson's

---

[19]For biographical information on Otis, see Bowling and Veit, *Maclay Diary,* p. 5 n. 5. For letters relating to the contest for the Senate secretaryship, see *DHFFC,* vol. 15 (forthcoming). *The Papers of George Washington, Presidential Series,* 7 vols. to date (Charlottesville, 1987–), vol. 6 (Mark A. Mastromarino, ed.), pp. 155–57. William Maclay was a severe critic, see Bowling and Veit, *Maclay Diary,* passim.

[20]Boyd Stanley Schlenther, *Charles Thomson: A Patriot's Pursuit* (Newark, Del., 1990), pp. 185–89.

secretarial responsibilities.[21] Those early assignments, drawn from members' experiences in state legislatures, included keeping the journal, managing committee papers, preparing accurate versions of enacted legislation, contracting for printing services, protecting secret documents, communicating with others on the Senate's behalf, and serving as the body's financial officer. Although the Confederation Congress expanded Thomson's role beyond this early model in the 1780s, Otis closely followed the 1777 pattern.

By December 1790, as he settled into his comfortable second-floor Congress Hall quarters, Otis supervised the work of a principal clerk, who kept track of legislation, and an engrossing clerk, who recopied marked-up drafts of Senate-passed legislation into a clean version for presentation to the House of Representatives, or the president. Otis served as financial clerk, paying the Senate's bills and disbursing senators' compensation of six dollars for each day they attended Senate proceedings. His other functions included acting as the Senate's liaison with state legislatures, with whom he routinely exchanged copies of laws; communicating with the president, to whose secretary he similarly sent Senate journals and "authenticated" transcripts of Senate executive records; and furnishing a Philadelphia newspaper copies of the Senate's journal each week for publication.[22] As the Senate authorized each member to subscribe to any three newspapers from around the country, Otis paid for, changed, and renewed these orders—undoubtedly a continuing source of aggravation.[23] He arranged for purchase of paper and stationery, quill pens and ink, pencils, wax sealing wafers, red tape to tie packages, blotting sand, India rubber to make erasures, and pen knives to sharpen quills. Otis was a one-man

---

[21]*Journals of the Continental Congress,* Mar. 22, 1777. Congress revised and expanded these duties in 1782 and 1785, as described in Kenneth R. Bowling, "Good-by 'Charle': The Lee-Adams Interest and the Political Demise of Charles Thomson, Secretary of Congress, 1774–1789," *Pennsylvania Magazine of History and Biography* 100 (1976):314–35. The same source discusses the Otis-Thompson relationship. For the quotation, see Otis to John Adams, May 11, 1789, Adams Family Trust, Massachusetts Historical Society.

[22]Records of the Office of the Secretary, 2d Cong., RG 46, NARA, Jan. 27, 1792, and Mar. 12, 1792; *Senate Journal,* Mar. 30, 1792.

[23]*Senate Journal,* Dec. 9, 1795.

Senate research service. In one typical instance, he requested Treasury Secretary Alexander Hamilton to provide an annual report listing names and salaries of all the government's civilian officials, excluding judges. Nine months later, Hamilton presented a detailed accounting, from President Washington down to the humblest lighthouse keeper.[24]

Although senators and Senate clerks were paid by the day, the secretary, as a year-round official, received an annual salary. At $1,500, Otis's compensation exceeded that of even the most diligently attending senators. Three years after moving to Philadelphia, however, Otis petitioned the Senate for a raise. He noted that comparable government officials had received one raise in four years and had been promised another. He and the clerk of the House had not been so favored. The Senate secretary and House clerk hoped it would "not be deemed improper to state that the enhanced prices of all the necessities of life render their present stipend a bare subsistence insomuch that within that line of decency, which becomes their station, and the necessary support of their families, in this expensive city, they find themselves unable to defray the small additional charge of keeping a horse, for the purpose of necessary exercise, in the preservation of their health."[25] The Senate ignored this woeful appeal.

During a Senate session, which customarily began at eleven each morning—including Saturdays—the secretary's small office attracted more members and visitors than it could comfortably accommodate. In winter, members gathered before its fireplace, outfitted with a Franklin stove, to warm themselves and take the political temperature for their legislative objectives. Clerks labored at three green baize-covered pine tables, paper scattered everywhere.

JAMES MATHERS, DOORKEEPER. Among those routinely encamped in the secretary's office was doorkeeper James Mathers. Unlike Charles Thomson, Mathers successfully made the transition to the Senate from the Confederation Congress, where he had served in its latter days as

---

[24]Reports and Communications Submitted to the Senate, 2d Cong., RG 46, NARA, May 7, 1792–Feb. 27, 1793.

[25]"Petition of Samuel A. Otis and John Beckley for an augmentation of their compensation, March 2d, 1793," 2d Cong. (Sen 2A-G3, folder 246), RG 46, NARA.

doorkeeper. Born in Ireland, Mathers immigrated to America before the Revolution and settled in New York City. He joined the Continental army at the outbreak of hostilities and served throughout the war. He compiled a record of bravery and was once seriously wounded. On the day after it organized in April 1789, the Senate elected the forty-five-year-old Mathers as its doorkeeper. That he was the first staff member to be selected underscored the importance of the doorkeeper's role in a body that intended to conduct all its proceedings behind closed doors.

Close in age, Mathers and Otis differed greatly in background and education. A first-generation American, Mathers lacked Otis's educational opportunities and financial backing. Otis had earned his bachelor's and master's degrees from Harvard College more than a quarter-century earlier. Prior to the Revolution, as Mathers was establishing himself in a new land, Otis flourished as a Boston merchant and state legislator. In the Senate, Otis and Mathers followed a division of labor similar to that of the Continental Congress's secretary and doorkeeper. As Otis and his assistants were keeping the financial accounts and legislative records, Mathers and an aide tended the chamber door—keeping strangers and House members out and senators in. They also looked after the Senate's two horses and kept an adequate supply of firewood. The doorkeeper received a three-dollar daily compensation while the Senate was in session and, with Senate approval after the fact, a lump sum for his services during adjournment periods.

Mathers's security functions evolved during the Senate's residence in Philadelphia. When the Senate decided to open its legislative sessions to the public and completed a gallery for that purpose in 1795, the doorkeeper was expected to maintain order among the visitors. Three years later, in 1798, when the Senate needed an official to arrest an uncooperative target of an impeachment trial, it conferred on Mathers's formal police powers and the expanded title of sergeant at arms and doorkeeper.[26]

---

[26] *Annals of Congress,* Feb. 5, 1798. For biographical information on Mathers, see *DHFFC,* vol. 8 (Kenneth R. Bowling, William C. diGiacomantonio, and Charlene Bangs Bickford, eds.), p. 517.

Rules

In April 1789, the Senate had adopted a code of twenty rules to supplement the operating procedures implanted in the Constitution. Early in the Second Congress, on November 1, 1791, it appointed a three-member committee to review those rules and recommend changes and additions. Although there is no evidence that this committee fulfilled its assignment, that action suggests an appreciation for continuous monitoring.

During the 1790s, the Senate added only five rules. These additions represented a fine-tuning of the 1789 rules based on the lessons of day-to-day experience. The first, adopted in February 1792, indicated problems of accuracy in preparing Senate-passed bills before they were sent to the House for action. The rule assigned responsibility for a measure's correctness to the committee that originated or last reviewed it—a small but significant step in the expansion of committee authority.[27] Within two weeks, the Senate agreed to a second rule designed to keep documentation of its legislative action free from errors. This rule required concise and accurate recording of floor proceedings in the Senate Journal.[28] A third rule, agreed to in February 1794, provided a mechanism for calling closed sessions after the Senate agreed to abandon its practice of conducting all proceedings in secret. The fourth new rule, established in April 1798, similarly sought to guarantee orderly floor proceedings. With the opening of a public gallery in December 1795, petitioners sought floor access to read their petitions or to listen while a senator or clerk read them. Running out of patience, the Senate finally banned this increasingly time-consuming and annoying practice. The final rule of the 1790s also highlighted an increasingly chronic problem: end-of-session absenteeism. Under the rule of June 26, 1798, adopted as the Senate was preparing to debate the Sedition Act, the body authorized those senators who were present, assuming that they were fewer than the quorum required to transact business, to direct the sergeant at arms to arrest

---

[27] *Senate Journal,* Feb. 27, 1792.
[28] Ibid., Mar. 12, 1792.

and return absent members. Unless a summoned member had an acceptable excuse, this rule required him to pay all expenses connected with his arrest.[29]

Legislative Process

Several generations of colonial and state legislators would surely have recognized the Senate's legislative process that gave rise to the above-noted rules between 1789 and 1800. Following state experience, the Framers of the Constitution generally expected the House of Representatives to serve as the principal legislative workshop. Like colonial and state governors' councils, the Senate would review the popularly elected body's handiwork, polishing and reworking in consideration of what were presumably the nation's broader and longer term interests. In practice, however, the Senate took the initiative in certain areas, including the judiciary, organization of state and territorial governments, foreign affairs, and banking.[30]

How a 1790s Bill Became Law

Here is a step-by-step accounting of the process by which a 1790s' Senate bill became law.

1. INTRODUCTION. Individual senators seldom introduced bills. Instead, they requested Senate appointment of temporary committees to investigate the issues involved and draft suitable legislation. This arrangement limited the number of bills introduced to those likely to be actually passed. In the Fourth Congress's first session, the Senate passed thirteen of the eighteen bills formally presented.[31] Although committees served as the principal source of bill introductions during the 1790s, the Senate from time to time allowed individual members that privilege, provided they gave one day's advance notice and obtained specific permission. Occasionally, the Senate agreed to same-

---

[29]Ibid., June 25, 1798.

[30]Lane W. Lancaster, "The Initiative of the United States Senate in Legislation, 1789–1809," *Political and Social Science Quarterly* 9 (1928):67–75.

[31]Swanstrom, *United States Senate, 1787–1801*, p. 224.

day introduction, but it also refused some requests.[32] The incidence of single-member introductions increased slightly through the decade.[33]

2. SELECT COMMITTEES. The full Senate voted on all committee assignments. On major issues, the Senate often made its committee appointments following general floor debate open to all members. This discussion guided committee members in measuring the Senate's collective opinion before sitting down to draft specific language. The word *select* defined two features of these panels: they were made up of a small, select group of senators and their objectives were limited to the specific proposal. After the select committee reported to the full Senate, its duties were at an end.

Following in the traditions of the British House of Commons and the Confederation Congress, the Senate relied on these specially formed committees whenever it wished to examine broad issues, specific proposals, individual nominations, or legislation sent upstairs from the House of Representatives. While some state legislatures had already developed permanent—or standing—committees to expedite handling of petitions and government expenditures, the Senate during the 1790s preferred the flexibility of these temporary committees to provide the substantive expertise needed to fashion specific legislative language.[34]

Select committee sizes ranged from three to nine. In a session or two, several committees with major responsibilities included one member from each state, but this practice ended in the early 1790s.[35] Panels created to consider politically sensitive matters usually had more members—from five to nine—than those with essentially technical and routine missions. At least five members sat on the panels that handled the individual sections of the president's annual message.[36]

The Senate determined each committee's membership by individual ballot among those who advocated the proposition. According to

---

[32]For an example of the Senate's refusal to allow a member to introduce a bill, see *Annals of Congress,* Apr. 2, 1800.

[33]Swanstrom, *United States Senate, 1787–1801,* p. 223.

[34]Harlow, *Legislative Methods before 1825,* pp. 64–70.

[35]George Lee Robinson, "The Development of the Senate Committee System," Ph.D. diss., New York University, 1954, pp. 22–23.

[36]Swanstrom, *United States Senate, 1787–1801,* pp. 226–27.

custom, although not specified under Senate rules, the highest vote-getter, or the measure's leading proponent, served as chairman. Those receiving the next highest number of votes filled the committee's remaining slots.[37] Under this system, senators opposed to the proposition were effectively excluded from committee participation, but they had plenty of opportunity to express their views later in the process. Although the Senate discharged its committees from further responsibilities after they completed their specific assignments, many of their members served on successor committees created to explore identical or related matters. Intelligent, hard-working, and highly motivated members tended to draw a proportionally larger share of committee assignments than their less engaged colleagues. Despite the temporary nature of the Senate's early committees, the budding committee system recognized and accommodated specialization.[38]

3. THREE READINGS. When a select committee completed its work—usually in the designated committee rooms, but if those were occupied, then on the Senate floor or in a convenient nearby location—it reported the measure to the full Senate as a new bill. The Senate clerk then read the bill, in full or by title, for the first time. At this point, if the bill or committee report was either complex or of wide interest, the Senate sent the handwritten copies to John Fenno's nearby shop to be printed in quantities usually ranging from fifty to one hundred so that members could distribute the draft for comment by colleagues, executive branch officials, or their respective state legislatures.[39]

Unless a member successfully moved to table the bill, an action that ended the measure's chances of further consideration and would have been highly unlikely for legislation considered important enough to be drafted by a select committee, the Senate ordered that the measure "pass to a second reading." This reflected the legislative practice, dating at least from England's late-sixteenth-century Parliament, of re-

---

[37]See vote of February 21, 1791, on the land office bill in *DHFFC,* vol. 5 (Charlene Bangs Bickford and Helen E. Veit, eds.), pp. 1231–32.

[38]An excellent source of information on legislative flow for the First Congress is contained in volumes 4–6 of *DHFFC.*

[39]Swanstrom, *United States Senate, 1787–1801,* pp. 230–32.

quiring three readings, each separated by at least one day.[40] The delay, a common procedure in state assemblies, was designed to frustrate passage of hasty and ill-formed legislation and to afford all members reasonable opportunity to participate in its consideration. The Senate then "committed" the measure by entrusting it to a committee, some or all of whose members may have been involved in the measure's original drafting. When the Senate resumed consideration following committee review, it customarily did so as a "Committee of the Whole House."

4. COMMITTEE OF THE WHOLE. Within a month of adopting its first twenty rules in April 1789, the Senate responded to a significant omission by adding a rule providing "that all bills on a second reading shall be considered by the Senate in the same manner as if the Senate were in a Committee of the Whole, . . . unless otherwise ordered."[41]

Initially employed in the English House of Commons two centuries before the Senate first convened, the committee of the whole evolved from members' necessary practice of taking a brief recess for a casual discussion of the issues under consideration without the constraints of formal rules or quorum requirements. Although not technically a committee, this structure allowed the entire Senate to follow the more relaxed procedures that traditionally governed committee operations. Published proceedings do not clearly establish that the Senate followed the model common to other legislatures. Vice President John Adams's reluctance to turn over his duties as presiding officer may have produced a modified version giving emphasis to the governing rule's provision that "all bills on a second reading shall be considered in the same manner *as if* the Senate were in Committee of the Whole."[42]

---

[40]Jennifer Loach, *Parliament under the Tudors* (New York, 1991), pp. 46–52. The process of three readings may have had its origin in the reign of Edward I, 1272–1307.

[41]*Senate Journal,* May 21, 1789.

[42]The Senate's journals for the 1790s contain few references to the Committee of the Whole. Swanstrom speculates that the Senate's small size and John Adams's reluctance to allow a member to replace him as presiding officer presented few identifying "contrasts between procedures of the Senate in Committee of the Whole and in ordinary session" (*United States Senate, 1787–1801,* p. 232).

5. FINAL PASSAGE. After voting on the amendments, the Senate proceeded to the third and final reading of the amended bill. If the passed bill had originated in the Senate, a clerk prepared a handwritten *engrossed* copy on parchment, for Secretary Otis's signature attesting to its accuracy. The Senate presented the engrossed copy to the House of Representatives for its consideration. If the House agreed to language different from that of the Senate, each body appointed up to three members to a conference committee to work out the differences in the second-floor committee room across from the secretary's office. If they reached agreement, a clerk prepared a clean copy for approval first by the House Speaker and then the vice president. If, however, the House initially agreed to the exact version passed by the Senate—a highly unlikely outcome for significant legislation—the House clerk prepared a final *enrolled* copy for signature by its Speaker. The act (once a measure passes one body, it is termed an *act*) was returned to the Senate for the vice president's signature. The Senate secretary then took the act to the joint Committee on Enrolled Bills for final examination. The joint committee, including two members from each house, subsequently transmitted it to the president for his approval or rejection.[43]

6. LEGISLATIVE AGENDA. In modern times, the Senate's party floor leaders attempt to set and achieve a defined legislative agenda. Two centuries ago, long before these leadership posts became firmly established, the Senate employed at least two devices to shape its output. At the start of each new session, the Senate appointed a committee to examine legislation not acted on in the previous session. That committee reported a short list with the understanding that any item on the list could be taken up at a member's request. At the other end of the legislative cycle, as the session neared its anticipated completion date, the Senate occasionally formed a joint committee with the House "to consider and report what business is necessary to be done by Congress in the present session, and what part of the business now depending

[43]A similar process applied to acts received from the House. The Senate either referred the entire act, or questionable portions thereof, to a select committee; or debated the measure first and adopted amendments before sending it to committee for formal revision; or passed it as received.

[pending] may be, without great inconvenience, postponed until the next session; that the proceedings may be so regulated as to close this session by the first Monday in April."[44] (Despite these efforts in March 1794, the session continued for more that two months beyond the targeted adjournment date.)

The Developing Senate: Four Shaping Controversies

Four controversies of the 1790s illuminate the Senate's institutional development during this formative decade. Like the 1999 impeachment trial of President William Clinton, each of these dramatic events placed the Senate under intense public scrutiny and caused senators to consider carefully the ways in which the institution does its constitutional business. The first, in 1794, grew out of a partisan fight to deny a Senate seat to a troublesome minority party member. The second involved one of the decade's most explosive policy issues: the 1795 ratification debate over John Jay's treaty with Great Britain. The third, related to the second, surrounded the Senate's 1795 rejection of President Washington's nominee to be chief justice of the United States. The fourth, in 1798 and 1799, marked the Senate's first exercise of its impeachment powers.

"Each House Shall be the Judge of the Elections, Returns, and Qualifications of Its Own Members": Albert Gallatin and Open Sessions

In the 1790s, Philadelphia served as the capital not only of the United States but also of Pennsylvania. That state's legislature held its sessions at the State House, next door to Congress Hall. When that assembly in 1793 elected the Swiss-born Albert Gallatin, a brilliant, aggressive, and outspoken Republican, to a seat in the Federalist-controlled U.S. Senate, members expected fireworks. Gallatin added fuel to this explosive situation by publicly wondering whether he met the nine-year American citizenship requirement for senators. While various Senate committees investigated the matter, Gallatin launched an attack on the financial policies of Federalist Treasury Secretary Alexander Hamilton.

---

[44] *Senate Journal,* Dec. 17–18, 1795; Mar. 7, 1794.

Gallatin proved to be a formidable adversary. As his attacks increased, so, too, did the desire of the Federalist majority in the Senate to be rid of him. On February 28, 1794, for the first time in its brief history, the Senate exercised its power to determine a member's constitutional fitness to serve by voting along party lines to unseat Gallatin on citizenship grounds.

As the Gallatin debate would take place just yards away from the chamber of the body that had elected him, senators temporarily set aside their closed-door policy to avoid the predictable charges of operating as a "star chamber." This revived the festering debate over the appropriateness of closed sessions. Under that policy, not even House members were permitted to observe Senate debates. As state legislatures increasingly expressed their frustration at not being able to monitor the senators they had elected,[45] the Senate revised its rules, by a more than two-to-one margin, to permanently open legislative sessions as soon as a suitable gallery could be installed.[46]

At the start of the Fourth Congress, on December 9, 1795, the doors opened, but the press and public seemed to prefer viewing vastly more colorful action in the House chamber, one floor below. Press coverage for this period proved to be "inaccurate, distorted, and incomplete." As one scholar has explained, "The newspaper editors found that there was little public interest in the Senate debates and that these lacked the partisan flavor they desired in the columns of their highly partisan papers." Today, sadly, we have only the *Annals of Congress,* pieced together from fragmentary sources decades later, to give us a sense of what happened on the Senate floor during these important developmental years.[47]

---

[45]Virginia and North Carolina acted first. Then, on December 13, 1791, the Maryland House of Delegates instructed Senators John Henry and Charles Carroll as follows: "We, your immediate constituents, satisfied that this free communication of our sentiments will produce the desired effect, assure, that we deem a compliance with wishes expressed from the various parts of the union, that their doors be opened whilst sitting in their legislative capacity, as essential to the preservation of the entire confidence which the whole union ought to repose in that honorable body" (*Votes and Proceedings of the House of Delegates of the State of Maryland,* November Session, 1791, 89–90). For additional information on state action, see the chapter by Terri Halperin in this volume.

[46]*Senate Journal,* Feb. 20, 1794.

[47]Elizabeth Gregory McPherson, "The History of Reporting the Debates and Proceedings of Congress," Ph.D. diss., University of North Carolina, 1940, chaps. 1–2; Swanstrom, *United States Senate, 1787–1801,* pp. 249–51.

Within slightly more than two years of Gallatin's exclusion, the Senate again exercised its powers over members' credentials by refusing, for patently political reasons, to seat Tennessee's two senators on the day the president signed legislation admitting that state to the Union. The Senate's Federalist majority, aware that Tennessee was certain to produce two Republican senators, nonetheless argued that no legislature existed to elect those senators until its statehood was formalized. Within two months, the state's legislature again elected the two senators and the Senate seated them without further dispute.[48]

"[The President] Shall Have Power, by and with the Advice and Consent of the Senate, to Make Treaties, Provided Two-thirds of the Senators Present Concur": Jay's Treaty

Debate over John Jay's 1794 peace treaty with Great Britain placed the spotlight of national attention on the Senate's treaty powers and its evolving party divisions. No other issue in the closing years of the eighteenth century so inflamed partisan animosities and revived fears expressed during the Constitution's ratification debates that the Senate could misuse these powers to subvert the interests of various states, regions, and economic alliances. Recognizing the precedent-setting nature of these delicate negotiations, Atty. Gen. Edmund Randolph advised President Washington to consult with the Senate about Jay's instructions before the envoy's departure. Washington ignored the advice, but a committee of senators informally met with Jay to discuss their concerns. On Jay's return, rumors of the treaty's provisions, perceived as favorable to the hated British, circulated widely before Washington called the Senate into special session on June 8, 1795. Following two weeks of bitter closed-door executive-session debate, the Senate followed party lines in conditionally approving the treaty by a vote of 20 to 10, precisely the required two-thirds majority. Although the Constitution says nothing about conditional agreement to treaties, the majority counted on the president's goodwill to achieve removal of an offensive provision rather than risking a repeat of the contentious process months later.

Several days later, Virginia Republican Sen. Stevens Mason, a treaty

---

[48]U.S. Congress, Senate, *Senate Election, Expulsion and Censure Cases, 1793–1990*, S. Doc. 103–33, 103d Cong., 1st sess., pp. 10–12.

opponent, sold his copy of the still-secret document to the French minister, who handed it to a Philadelphia newspaper. An intense public outcry resulted. Senators who had voted in favor became targets of angry mobs, while the "virtuous and patriotic ten" who had opposed it became national heroes for their refusal to sign this "death warrant of America's liberties." While House members debated President Washington's possible impeachment for signing it, the Senate sank to its lowest point in public esteem. This premature disclosure confirmed administration fears that the Senate was institutionally incapable of keeping secrets and, several years later, caused President Adams to remark that secret instructions were likely to reach a foreign government "sooner than we could send them [to] our minister [there]."[49]

In establishing its prerogatives, the Senate faced a strong challenge to its treaty powers from the House of Representatives and one of its newly elected members, Albert Gallatin. While two-thirds of the Federalist Senate had supported the treaty on the condition that the objectionable feature be renegotiated, the House Republican majority was decidedly against it. Gallatin led those who argued that no treaty could force the House to appropriate funds against its collective will. This constitutional requirement, they contended, gave the House a say in how the treaty would be put into effect. After debating withholding funds, the House demanded treaty documents, which President Washington refused to provide. Members ultimately agreed to the appropriation by a 51–48 margin. Had the House refused, the Senate's treaty prerogatives, and the Constitution itself, would have been in serious trouble.[50]

"[The President] Shall Nominate, and by and with the Advice and Consent of the Senate, Shall Appoint . . . Judges of the Supreme Court": Rejection of John Rutledge

In the early 1790s, the Senate confirmed executive and judicial nominations without open controversy. When it rejected a customs collector in August 1789, President Washington urged closer consultation to avoid further such embarrassing situations. Perhaps the threat of rejec-

[49]Quoted in Henry Adams, *History of the United States of America,* 9 vols. (New York, 1889–91), 8:542 n.

[50]Stanley Elkins and Eric McKitrick, *The Age of Federalism* (New York, 1993), pp. 388–96; David Currie, *The Constitution in Congress* (Chicago, 1997), p. 211.

tion caused the president to reconsider a choice or two before sending the Senate a formal nomination, but he gave the legislators little opportunity to say no. This changed abruptly in late 1795.

When John Jay resigned as chief justice in June 1795, the president selected South Carolina's John Rutledge, who had earlier served briefly as an associate justice. His nomination raised questions about the order of succession to the chief justiceship. Some argued that the appointment should have been made from the ranks of the sitting associate justices, with preference given to the senior justice. Others contended that the best available man should be found for the job. As the Senate was in recess until winter, Rutledge received a temporary commission.

Several weeks after his appointment, Rutledge delivered a speech highly critical of the Jay Treaty, which the administration and the Senate's Federalist majority had supported. Many in the administration cited this ill-timed speech as evidence of Rutledge's advancing mental incapacity. Ignoring the swirling controversy, Rutledge arrived in Philadelphia in August 1795 and took his seat. When the Senate convened several months later, it promptly rejected his nomination. Rutledge thus became the first Supreme Court justice to be rejected and the only one among the fifteen justices who would gain their offices through recess appointments not to be subsequently confirmed. In rejecting Rutledge, the Senate made it clear that an examination of a nominee's qualifications would extend beyond his personal qualifications to his political views. Those who differed substantively from the majority of senators could expect rough going.[51]

"The Senate Shall Have the Sole Power to Try All Impeachments": Trial of William Blount

On two notable occasions in the 1790s, the Senate defined its power to remove members. As we have seen, it ruled in 1794 that Gallatin had not satisfied the Constitution's senatorial residency requirement. Three years later, in July 1797, it expelled Tennessee Sen. William Blount for conspiring with Great Britain against the interests of Spain. This action came the day after the House of Representatives informed

---

[51]Maeva Marcus and James R. Perry, eds., *The Documentary History of the Supreme Court of the United States, 1789–1800,* 5 vols. to date (New York, 1985–), 1:15–18, 94–100.

the Senate it had impeached Blount and would be presenting formal articles as soon as they could be drawn up.

These developments forced the Senate to define the form and scope of its impeachment powers, although not necessarily to answer decisively questions such as: Did the Senate even have to accept the House articles? Or having accepted them, was it obligated to conduct a trial? Was a senator a "civil officer" subject to removal through conviction in an impeachment trial? Were former senators, or other government officials, beyond the reach of the impeachment process? The Senate chose not to answer "no" to any of these questions at the time the House action first raised them. Consequently, it moved ahead with trial preparations by establishing rules of trial procedure. As in other procedural matters, the Senate adopted practices customary to the various states and in the British House of Commons. The need for an officer with the power to serve summons and arrest uncooperative parties produced an expansion in the duties of Senate Doorkeeper James Mathers, who, as previously noted, on February 5, 1798, became the Senate sergeant at arms and doorkeeper.

On that same day, the Senate adopted its first impeachment rule, commanding all persons attending the trial to keep silent "on pain of imprisonment." Several days later, the Senate adopted an impeachment trial oath, as required by the Constitution. When the Blount trial began in later December 1798, the Senate adopted further rules, including one requiring voting behind closed doors. The rules of 1798 remained very much a part of the rules that governed the Clinton trial of 1999. In January 1799, the Senate dismissed the Blount case on jurisdictional grounds. Without explicitly saying so, this action seemed to say that members of Congress and former officials are not impeachable.[52]

Assessment

The Senate took up residence at Philadelphia's Congress Hall with its basic rules and procedures in place. During its decade there, those

---

[52]Peter Charles Hoffer and N. E. H. Hull, *Impeachment in America, 1635–1802* (New Haven, 1984), pp. 146–63; Buckner F. Melton, Jr., *The First Impeachment: The Constitution's Framers and the Case of Senator William Blount* (Macon, Ga., 1998).

rules and procedures evolved at a measured pace. As they were based on long-established parliamentary practice, they had already stood the test of time and required little significant change.

Change also came gradually to the operations of the Senate's leadership structure—the presiding officer and elected officials. Thomas Jefferson's contribution came not in expanding his office's power—that was not likely given his awkward constitutional position between two branches of government—but rather in validating vitally important Senate procedures.

The Senate's two officers developed their duties day by day, without radical innovation. When the Senate in 1798 added the title of sergeant at arms to that of its doorkeeper, it was simply following established practice in the House of Representatives and British Parliament.

Substantial institutional change came, however, in the realm of the Senate's unique constitutional responsibilities for nominations, treaties, and impeachment trials. Rejecting a nominated chief justice, facing down the House as it made a bid to insert itself into the profoundly sensitive matter of treaty making, and implicitly deciding who was an impeachable officer played an essential part in laying the groundwork for the period after the 1820s when the Senate would become the federal government's most powerful component for the remainder of the nineteenth century. Add to these moves the decision to open legislative sessions and you have an adjustment that made the Senate of 1800 significantly more potent than the body that ascended those Congress Hall stairs on the sixth of December 1790.

And consider the Senate chamber itself. This ornate sanctuary, closed even to House members for the first half of the Philadelphia sojourn, served as an incubator for the idea of a national Senate. No one in 1790 knew how it would work out. For ten years, up to thirty-two senators, drawn from an ever-shifting concatenation of eighty-six statesmen, in their every word and deed, worked to define the infant institution's culture. By 1800 the Senate's future was that much easier to predict.

For countless decades after the Senate moved to Washington, its succeeding generations would look to the Philadelphia years as they explained what then seemed to be the certain evolution toward the institution that we know today and its distinctive constitutional role. As early as 1805, Vice President Aaron Burr, who had served as a senator for most of the 1790s, described the institution as "a sanctuary; a citadel of law, of order, and of liberty." "It is here," he said, "here in this exalted refuge; here, if anywhere [that] resistence [will] be made to the storms of political phrensy and the silent arts of corruption." Nearly two centuries later, Senate President Pro Tempore Robert C. Byrd committed Burr's remarks to memory and recited them on appropriate occasions. That Byrd could speak in the same vein as Burr demonstrates the institution's continuity between the two centuries. Observing the Senate's 1989 bicentennial, Byrd proclaimed, "After two hundred years, [the Senate] is still the anchor of the Republic, the morning and evening star in the American constitutional constellation."[53]

[53]U.S. Congress, Senate, *The Senate, 1789–1989,* by Robert C. Byrd, S. Doc. 100–20, 100th Cong., 1st sess., vol. 2 (1991), p. 539.

Raymond W. Smock

The Institutional Development of the House of Representatives, 1789–1801

MORE THAN THIRTY YEARS AGO the distinguished political scientist Nelson W. Polsby declared the process of institutionalization to be one of the "grand themes in all of modern social science." Polsby studied the institutional development of the House of Representatives and provided a framework for thinking about the process. Without organization and institutionalization, Polsby wrote, a political system would be "unstable and weak," and unable to respond effectively to its constituents.[1]

Polsby defined an institutionalized organization as having three major characteristics: "1) it is relatively well bounded, that is to say, differentiated from its environment. Its members are easily identifiable, it is relatively difficult to become a member, and its leaders are recruited principally from within the organization. 2) The organization is relatively complex, that is, its functions are internally separated on some regular and explicit basis, its parts are not wholly interchangeable, and for at least some important purposes, its parts are interdependent." Polsby's definition of institutionalization also stated that the organization should have divisions of labor and specified roles for some individuals. Finally, his third major characteristic of institutionalization was

[1]Nelson W. Polsby, "The Institutionalization of the U.S. House of Representatives," *American Political Science Review* 62 (1968):144–45.

that "precedents and rules are followed; merit systems replace favoritism and nepotism; and impersonal codes supplant personal preferences as prescriptions for behavior."[2] Or, to put it in plainer English, members learned to follow the rules.

Polsby's is a good definition for beginning a discussion of institutionalization. It tells us the things we should be looking for, but it does not necessarily tell us that we will find all of them at any given point in the history of the House or that all of these characteristics will be apparent without the passage of some time.

Polsby found that the House institutionalized itself early on and then continued to become more complex over time. Other scholars have since expanded on his work and found that much, but certainly not all, of the important work of institutionalization occurred in the first dozen years of the House, from the First Congress in 1789 to the Seventh Congress that convened in 1801. The rules of the House, the patterns of leadership, and the development of the standing committee system that emerged in these early congresses established precedents and procedures that would, with some variation, last for centuries. Other aspects of institutionalization, such as the seniority system and the procedure for introducing bills, would appear later in the history of the House.[3]

Fisher Ames, one of the most brilliant, articulate, and prominent members of House from 1789 to 1797, could worry himself to death over the inability of the House to get down to business or to focus on important issues, yet in 1800, in a eulogy to George Washington, he described the beginnings of government this way: "No sooner did the new government begin its auspicious course, than order seemed to arise out of confusion."[4] Was Ames overstating the case in part to praise the greatness of Washington? Probably not; he certainly believed this observation would ring true to his contemporaries. What

---

[2]Ibid., p. 145.

[3]See Garrison Nelson, "Partisan Patterns of House Leadership Change, 1789–1977," *American Political Science Review* 71 (1977):918–39; Michael Abram and Joseph Cooper, "The Rise of Seniority in the House of Representatives," *Polity* 1 (1968):52–85; Joseph Cooper and Cheryl D. Young, "Bill Introduction in the Nineteenth Century: A Study in Institutional Change," *Legislative Studies Quarterly* 14 (1989):67–105.

[4]W. B. Allen, ed., *Works of Fisher Ames as Published by Seth Ames*, 2 vols. (Indianapolis, 1983), 1:526.

Ames said about the government in general could be applied to the House where he served in the 1790s. Order did seem to arise out of confusion. The second time around, the Framers of our government got it right. After the failure of the Articles of Confederation, our first government, there appeared to be a powerful desire on the part of the men who had the task of making the new Constitution work to see that the institutions of government were successfully launched.

From the earliest beginnings in 1789, the House had to figure out ways to be responsive to the people, to work with the other institutions of government, especially the executive branch (and also the Senate), to follow the Constitution's description of the powers granted to Congress, to devise rules and procedures for making laws, to elect their own leaders, and find ways for political opposition and differences of opinion to exist and even flourish as a vital part of the institution. It was a tall order when you think about it. It could have gone sour but it didn't.

If Fisher Ames, or James Madison, or any of the other House members from those early congresses could be transported to Washington, D.C., today, what would they think about the House of Representatives? Except for the television cameras, the funny clothes, and a few new words and phrases that they might not understand, like *Internet* or *stealth bombers,* they would probably feel right at home. They would look down upon the floor of the House from the gallery and see a friendly Speaker about the same size and shape as the first Speaker 210 years ago. They would recognize the parliamentary procedure. They would know about the Committee of the Whole, which is still in use. They would probably be surprised at the size of the House—some thinking too large; others, too small. There were 65 members in the first House, compared to 435 today; but they knew the House would grow in size. At the end of its first decade, as the government prepared to leave Philadelphia and move to Washington, D.C., the size of the House had already increased to 106 members.

Most of all, those members from the early congresses, observing the House today, could say with some satisfaction: "By God, they are still following the Constitution and the Rules of the House." Behind this simple statement lies a tale, and the subject of the pages that follow. In some ways the House is like a time machine. Its rules and practices have roots that go back more than two centuries. The way the House organized itself more than two centuries ago still affects the way it operates. The issues may be different, but in reality they are not that much different. Then, as now, the House struggled with issues of war and peace, with taxation, with budgets, with monetary policy, and the like. When we study the institutionalization of Congress two centuries ago, it is not an antiquarian exercise into the quaint and distant past. It is also current events. What Fisher Ames or James Madison would be able to detect if they returned to the House today would be the shape of a familiar institution—an institution that has survived and functioned much as it was intended to function from the very beginning.

The key to understanding the institutional development of the House of Representatives can be found in the Constitution, which provides the blueprint of powers of the legislative branch, and it can be found in the story of how the members of the House in those early congresses took the Constitution to heart and made it work.

So how did they do it? Perhaps it is easiest understood in the form of a recipe. It is a simple recipe to state, but, like all recipes, different cooks will have different results with the same ingredients. If you plan to study the institutional development of the House, you take the Constitution, add House rules, slowly add committees, political parties, traditions, the biographies and personalities of members of the House, and parliamentary procedure—then mix these ingredients vigorously with United States history and a dash of world history and finally fold in the desires of the American people. It doesn't sound too difficult, does it?

Earlier books in this series have discussed in depth the monumental work of the First Federal Congress; this one extends the look beyond the First Congress to examine how subsequent congresses during the Federalist period either broke with the institutional development achieved in the First Congress or found ways to carry on its precedents. A few words about the First Congress are in order here if for no other reason than to set the stage for what followed. Beginning a discussion of Congress in the 1790s without mentioning the First Congress would be like starting the Bible with the book of Exodus. You would always be wondering how it all got started.

The First Congress left a legacy of important legislation and precedent that established the new government on a solid foundation. The First Congress was an important link with the Framers of the Constitution, and it could be said that the first House and Senate completed the work of the federal convention and put flesh on the bare bones of the Constitution.[5] Nineteen members of the First Congress, nine in the House and ten in the Senate, were delegates to the convention. All the debate, all the theorizing about the nature of government, had to be settled as the members of the First Congress invented a working House of Representatives and a working Senate.

The Constitution said the "House shall chuse its Speaker and other officers," and on the first day it had a quorum, the House elected its Speaker and a clerk and began the process of establishing a framework for conducting legislative business. Soon it had elected or appointed other officers, a doorkeeper and one assistant doorkeeper, a sergeant at arms, a chaplain, and two assistant clerks. The first House also authorized the creation of a symbol of House authority, called the mace. There were just a few rules; you could print them out in just a couple of pages. They dealt with the duties of the Speaker, the proper decorum of debate, how bills would be introduced and passed, and how the House would conduct most of its business through a parliamentary device known as the Committee of the Whole House on the State of the Union, which provided a less formal way of amending and debating bills. The current House rule book, including footnotes to two centuries of precedents, changes, and additions, and including Thomas Jefferson's *Manual of Parliamentary Practice,* runs to 1,250 pages,[6] all of it built on those original rules from the first House. In 1999 the House approved a major codification of its rules and reduced them considerably in number. The House, unlike the Senate, revisits all of its rules every two years at the beginning of each Congress. It is regularly reinventing itself.

---

[5]The best short study of the First Federal Congress is Charlene Bangs Bickford and Kenneth R. Bowling, *Birth of the Nation: The First Federal Congress, 1789–1791* (New York, 1989), which draws on the multivolume work of Bickford and Bowling and their fellow editors, Helen Veit and William C. diGiacomantonio, on the *Documentary History of the First Federal Congress, 1789–1791,* 14. vols. to date (Baltimore, 1972–).

[6]William Holmes Brown, *Constitution, Jefferson's Manual, and Rules of the House of Representatives of the United States,* H. Doc. 102–405 (Washington, D.C., 1993).

The members of the first House, and the public who was watching them, knew something very important was under way. One of those present to observe the earliest session of the House open to the public was a twenty-six-year-old lawyer from New York, James Kent, who accompanied Alexander Hamilton into the House gallery. He described the galleries as packed with "all ranks and degrees of men," eager to see the government in action. "I considered it to be a proud & glorious day," Kent wrote, "the consummation of our wishes; & that I was looking upon an organ of popular will, just beginning to breathe the Breath of Life, & which might in some future age, much more truly than the Roman Senate, be regarded as 'the refuge of nations.' "[7]

As the only popularly elected branch of government, the House immediately became a clearing house for citizens and groups who could hardly wait for the new government to get under way before they sent petitions on a variety of topics. These petitions, addressed to the House, the Senate, and sometimes the executive branch, show clearly and often dramatically what was on the minds of the citizens of the new nation.

The petitions reveal what the people expected of government. They also demonstrated a remarkable acceptance of the new government as a national institution. The fact that the House was able to organize successfully and pass important legislation quickly made it a dynamic force that fostered nationalism in a country where it was still more common to refer to the state you were from when asked your about your citizenship. That was rapidly changing. Citizens of the 1790s were not just Virginians or New Yorkers, they were becoming Americans.

Petitions arrived during the 1790s urging Congress to support American manufacturing and the American maritime industry. Citizens wrote urging the abolition of slavery. Native Americans pleaded not to be driven from their ancestral land. Women even wrote complaining they could not get a divorce in the District of Columbia. All eyes were on the new Congress.[8]

---

[7]James Kent to Elizabeth Hamilton, Dec. 2, 1832, Hamilton-McLane Papers, Library of Congress, cited in Bickford and Bowling, *Birth of the Nation,* p. 18.

[8]Approximately ten thousand petitions, dating from the First Congress in 1789 through the 1820s, are housed in Record Group 233 at the National Archives and Records Administration in Washington, D.C. A compilation of some of the earliest

The petitions to the early congresses, most of which are sitting unused at the National Archives, are an important untapped source for understanding the institutional development of the House, as well as the social and economic history of the early republic. The petitions sent by ordinary citizens helped shape the committee structure of the House during the first two decades of the new government. Another way of saying it would be that the "voice of the people," through their petitions, had much to do with how the House organized itself to do the people's business. When we think of institutionalization we have to go outside of the House and look also at the constituents of the House members—the people themselves and their expectations.

The development of the standing committee system in the House (and later in the Senate) is the great institutional change in the early decades of the new government that sets it apart from the history of the First Congress. The first House was a small body, and the 143 bills it originated were handled without a standing committee system. The House considered each bill by a select committee created for that particular bill. More than three hundred committees were formed during the First Congress alone. In subsequent congresses, as the House grew in size and the workload of the members expanded, the House developed a standing (or permanent) committee system, and members began to specialize in certain areas of legislation. Doing legislative business in committees was a natural development and outgrowth of practices in colonial legislatures and in the pre-1789 Congress. But neither the House nor the Senate rushed to create a standing committee system. The idea of standing committees developed slowly. In the first House there was only one standing committee, the Committee on Elections, a basic housekeeping committee that verified the credentials of members. It was not a legislative committee.

The first major select legislative committee that evolved into a standing committee was the Committee on Ways and Means.[9] In the first

---

petitions can be found in U.S. Congress, House Committee on Energy and Commerce, *Petitions, Memorials, and Other Documents Submitted for the Consideration of Congress, March 4, 1789, to December 14, 1795*, 99th Cong., 2d sess., Committee Print 99-AA, 1986. See also, Raymond W. Smock, "The House of Representatives: First Branch of the New Government," *Prologue* 21 (1989):287–97.

[9]Donald R. Kennon and Rebecca M. Rogers, *The Committee on Ways and Means: A Bicentennial History, 1789–1989* (Washington, D.C., 1989).

House in 1789, the Committee on Ways and Means was a temporary committee that lasted just two months. The House had not yet settled on the committee's role in determining national financial policy or even setting the federal budget, small as it was. In those early years much of the financial policy and budget planning for the United States came from the new Treasury Department and its creative, talented, and always ambitious secretary, Alexander Hamilton. It is hard to say who should get the title of the first "policy wonk," but certainly Hamilton would be in the running. From 1789 to 1794, Hamilton worked closely with the House on financial matters, leading it most of the time. The separation of powers that we have come to see as a major feature of our government was less clearly defined in those early years. The House relied on Hamilton to provide most of the ideas and most of the numbers.

Alexander Hamilton, through a series of brilliant papers still studied in American history courses today, determined, for all practical purposes, the ways and means of the commercial and financial development of the country as he dealt with the complex issue of public credit. It was Hamilton who made recommendations about the state and federal debt, federal excises, a national bank, a sinking fund, manufacturing, and even revisions in the amounts and methods of collecting the tariffs established by Congress before his appointment.

The United States, however, was rapidly becoming a nation whose finances could not be run out of one brain and one set of books, as brilliant as Hamilton was. By 1794, in the Third Congress, tensions between Hamilton's Treasury Department and the House had become so strained that political parties started to emerge in the House, dividing on broad matters of financial policy as well as on the issue of Hamilton himself. As a response to this situation the House revived the Committee on Ways and Means in 1794, then reestablished it again in 1795. It has operated continuously from that point on, becoming a standing committee in 1802. This important committee, a keystone in the development of the committee system of the House, was not created overnight but through an evolutionary process that took more than a decade. In creating this committee and wresting some control from the Treasury Department the House exerted its role in the budget process and staked out its own power and authority in relationship to the executive branch.

In doing so, the House was beginning to institutionalize at yet another level. It was becoming more republican, with both a small *r* and a capital *R* (Jeffersonian Republicans). In establishing a ways and means committee, the House, as the people's branch, exerted its authority to conduct the people's business and did not rely too heavily on the executive branch, the favorite of the Federalists. The House and the nation were moving toward a new party that would emerge with the election of Thomas Jefferson in 1801.[10]

Other standing committees had similar origins, arising out of perceived need, political pressure, the desire not to be subsumed by the executive branch, and the desire to fulfill the mission of the House as described in Article I of the Constitution. The second standing committee of the House from the 1790s was the Committee on Commerce and Manufacturing, established on December 1, 1795, during the Fourth Congress. Its original jurisdiction was "all such petitions and matters of things touching the commerce and manufactures of the United States."

Members quickly grasped the trade-offs that would result from such committees and some opposed their creation. Committees created specialists. More important, they gave certain members more clout than others in shaping national policy and determining priorities. Other members argued that difficult legislative issues required specialization and the mastery of details. The House needed members who would become experts in certain policy areas. Specialization, so the argument went, would result in better legislation.

The committee system grew to fill specific needs as the country grew. It is no coincidence, for example, that two years after the purchase of the Louisiana Territory, which doubled the size of the United States, the House created a Committee on Public Lands. Major events in American history have continued to play an important catalytic role in the creation of committees in the House.

House leadership is another major way to explore the institutionalization of the House. In the First Congress the House elected as its first Speaker, Frederick Augustus Conrad Muhlenberg of Pennsylvania,

---

[10]Mary P. Ryan, "Party Formation in the United States Congress, 1789–1796," *William and Mary Quarterly* 3d ser. 28 (1971):523–42. See also H. James Henderson with a reply by Mary P. Ryan, "Quantitative Approaches to Party Formation in the United States Congress: A Comment," *William and Mary Quarterly* 3d ser. 30 (1973):307–24.

but there was virtually no guidance in the Constitution about what a Speaker would do. This important office had to be invented and institutionalized by House rules. The personality and style of each elected Speaker also has contributed to the nature of the office. There was, however, a considerable body of precedent about at least some of the things a Speaker would do. It was an office familiar to the Framers and the members of the early Houses. It originated in the thirteenth-century British Parliament and was carried to the new world in the colonial assemblies. The First Congress elected Muhlenberg in large part because he had previous experience as Speaker of the Pennsylvania Assembly and was the presiding officer of the state convention that ratified the Constitution.[11]

Once in office, Muhlenberg, who also served as Speaker in the Third Congress, set his stamp on the office largely by playing down the formality of the position. It was the practice of the early Houses to copy the style of the British House of Commons and to be quite formal about the appearance of the Speaker on the floor of the chamber. All would rise when he entered the room. None would sit down until the Speaker sat down. We still see vestiges of this behavior in the current Congress, which rises at the opening of the session when the Speaker, accompanied by the mace of the House, enters the room. Muhlenberg was uncomfortable with the pomp surrounding the office and played down the need for excessive formality. He seemed to be embarrassed by it. This was a republic, after all, and Speakers, Muhlenberg thought, should not be treated as royalty. The Speaker was paid more, eight dollars a day as opposed to six dollars for the other members. Again, Muhlenberg played down this distinction by noting how expensive everything was in New York City and Philadelphia and complaining that he spent his extra pay on oyster suppers for the members.

More significant than the formality surrounding the early Speakers was the slow evolution of the office from one of impartial parliamentarian and presiding officer of the House into an office that had both administrative and political clout. This process of institutionalization took time. During the 1790s and into the first decade of the nine-

---

[11]See Ronald M. Peters, Jr., *The American Speakership: The Office in Historical Perspective*, 2d ed. (Baltimore, 1997).

teenth century, Speakers were, for the most part, figureheads and presiding parliamentarians. The real action of setting national policy and exercising legislative leadership rested with the executive branch and with House floor leaders, who took their lead not from the House but from the president.

The early Speakers of the House, all the way to Henry Clay, who assumed the office for the first time in 1811, are all but invisible men in the history of Congress. This is unfortunate; closer study may show that they played a larger role in House institutional development than they have been given credit for.[12]

Why do these early Speakers deserve more attention? Mainly because none of them were mere ciphers in the early political history of the nation. Jonathan Trumbull of Connecticut, the second Speaker, sandwiched in between Muhlenberg's two terms, had succeeded Alexander Hamilton as Gen. George Washington's aide and confidential secretary in 1781 and later served as senator and governor for Connecticut. He was a man with political ambition, but we know virtually nothing of his impact on the House during his one-term speakership. The third man to hold the job, Jonathan Dayton of New Jersey, is even more fascinating. He was the youngest Framer of the Constitution, only twenty-seven years old when the federal convention sat. He was a colorful, ambitious man who, while serving as Speaker, engaged in western land speculation. He was close friends with both Hamilton and Hamilton's arch-rival, Aaron Burr. Dayton used the influence of the Speaker's office to appoint one of the judges of the Northwest Territory and then speculated with the judge in land in the territory. Dayton, Ohio, bears his name.

The fourth man to be Speaker, Theodore Sedgwick of Massachusetts, the last of the Federalist speakers, took office in 1799 on the eve of the first major shift in American political alignment that would sweep Thomas Jefferson and his Republicans into power in 1801. Sedgwick fought a rear guard action against the rising Republican sentiment in the land. He may have been the first Speaker to overtly use his office for political ends. He seemed impatient with being an impartial

---

[12]Raymond W. Smock, "Kings of the Hill: The Speakers of the United States House of Representatives," *OAH Magazine of History* 12 (1998):26–31.

parliamentarian, and his rulings from the chair often favored the Federalists. Sedgwick had the uncomfortable duty of announcing the election of Jefferson, whom he considered a rascal and a traitor. Sedgwick's partisanship was so blatant that when his term of office was completed, the House, which had formally thanked previous Speakers for their service, refused to do so for Sedgwick. The lives of these men need to be explored from the standpoint of what they may have contributed to the institutional development of the House, especially in how the growing tensions between Federalists and Republicans played out in the formative years of the House.

There were no developed political parties as we know them today during the Federalist era, although most members of the House called themselves Federalists, while others (including many former Antifederalists) called themselves Republicans or Democratic Republicans. The political stew was beginning to thicken, however, and two parties, loosely defined as (Hamiltonian) Federalists and (Jeffersonian) Republicans, were discernible by the mid-1790s. The House was a seedbed for their development. Yet, it is fair to say that parties happened accidentally in the House. No one planned them. They had less to do with ideology and more to do with specific issues that unfolded over time. If there was a prevailing ideology in Federalist America, it was that factions or parties had no place in republican government. This early amorphous, reluctant, accidental, political division, however, shaped how the House developed for twenty years, affecting committee assignments, the election of Speakers, relations between the House and Senate and between the House and the executive branch, and led to the important institution of party caucuses.

Thomas Jefferson wrote to a friend in 1798 wondering if perhaps political parties were inevitable and necessary and grew out of conflicts contained in human nature itself. During the Federalist era, however, it is very difficult to put precise political labels on House members. Political scientists and historians have found House political divisions in the 1790s based on sectional differences between Northern, Middle, and Southern states. They have found that voting blocs emerged over foreign policy issues such as pro- or anti-British or pro- or anti-French sentiment. In 1794, when it looked like the United States and

Great Britain would go to war again, John Jay negotiated a treaty that kept us out of war, but the treaty caused a great deal of political controversy that divided the House.

Also in 1794 the House divided sharply over the Whiskey Rebellion in Pennsylvania when farmers in the state's western counties objected to a tax on their corn liquor, and George Washington led 13,000 troops into the state to guarantee the collection of federal taxes, the only time in American history that the commander in chief took the field with his troops. In 1798, about the time that Thomas Jefferson was pondering the notion that political parties might be an inevitable part of human nature, the House experienced its first major brawl when Matthew Lyon of Vermont spit tobacco juice in the face of another House member, Roger Griswold of Connecticut. Lyon, a backwoods roughneck Antifederalist, did not like the fact that the aristocratic Griswold, a Federalist, had called him a coward. Behind this brawl was a marked difference of opinion between the two men over a potential war with France. Griswold supported President Adams's plan not to declare war on France but only to prepare for war. Lyon feared preparations for war would lead to war.

While the House investigated the incident, Griswold got tired of waiting and decided to beat Lyon with a cane. Lyon defended himself with tongs from the House fireplace. Neither man was expelled for his behavior, but the incident could certainly be cited as a sign that strong political differences, if not well-defined parties, were emerging in the House.[13]

External to Congress but affecting party development in the House was the rise of newspapers that took a strong position for or against certain national issues. John Fenno, the editor of the *Gazette of the United States,* a New York and then Philadelphia newspaper, was a strong supporter of Alexander Hamilton. To counter the views of the *Gazette,* Thomas Jefferson and James Madison urged the poet Philip Freneau to start a pro-Republican newspaper—the *National Gazette.* During the time that Congress met in Philadelphia, the city had twelve

---

[13]Alvin M. Josephy, Jr., *On the Hill: A History of the American Congress* (New York, 1979), pp. 109–10.

newspapers. The war of partisan words had begun, and it has never abated in American history.[14]

As the House established itself internally through its rules and procedures, it also had to institutionalize its dealings with the executive branch and with the Senate. During the 1790s, the relationship between the House and the executive branch was much cozier than would be true later. Perhaps *cozy* is too informal a word but it conveys a sense of familiarity and closeness that would change over time. Physical proximity helped account for closeness of the House and the executive. When the government moved to Washington, D.C., in 1800, that physical proximity was severed.

Behind the formal institutional developments between the House and the executive branch were less visible but equally important institutional developments. It was not uncommon for members of Congress to seek favors of the executive branch, such as a job for a friend or relative. With Jefferson's election in 1801, House Republicans were easy prey to Jefferson's favors, and many of them became, in effect, his agents in the House. This affected their relationship with the executive branch, and it affected the independence of the committees of Congress in relationship to the executive branch. The physical proximity between the House and the executive branch may have been severed with the move to Washington, but the coziness that came from political favors remained. Nathaniel Macon, the first Republican Speaker, aggressively saw to it that the House committees were stacked with supporters of Thomas Jefferson.

Looking back on the formative years of Congress one continues to be amazed that things turned out as well as they did with the successful launching of the legislature and the firm establishment of the system of government described in the Constitution. David P. Currie, in his book *The Constitution in Congress: The Federalist Period 1789–1801,* expressed a similar sense of amazement when he looked at the successful launching of the federal government, especially Congress. He wrote:

> After the relative honeymoon of the First Congress, debates became more partisan; one is less confident that many of the participants were

[14]Donald A. Ritchie, *Press Gallery: Congress and the Washington Correspondents* (Cambridge, Mass., 1991), pp. 7–11.

> dispassionately seeking to determine what the Constitution meant. Yet the quality of the argument remained astoundingly high, and on the whole there is considerable cause for satisfaction with the results. Most of the time, despite extreme statements on one side or the other, Congress and the President seemed to have been faithful to the Constitution. Most of the time Congress displayed both a willingness to exercise the authority the Framers had given it and a sensitivity to the demands of federalism and the separation of powers.[15]

Currie concluded that the most important thing to come out of the institutionalization of Congress was the institutionalization of free expression—the members of the Federalist era Congresses gave us, he said, "the indispensability of speech to the political process and the marketplace of ideas."[16]

In institutionalizing free expression in the House, the Federalists may have helped to do themselves in. The House quickly became the institution of government most receptive to the idea of democracy, the thing the Federalists loathed because it represented to them the mob, the masses of people who were easily swayed by demagogues. It was these new democrats who coalesced into a party that put Jefferson in the White House and many of his supporters in the House of Representatives. Fisher Ames, always the consummate Federalist, did not like what he saw by the late 1790s, with Jefferson's Republicans on the march. He said: "We are sliding down into the mire of democracy, which pollutes the morals of the citizens before it swallows up their liberties."[17] The Federalists began to fear the growing political forces of ordinary citizens in the cities.

There were, however, plenty of checks against democracy that the Framers had built into the new government, not the least of which was the Senate, still more than a hundred years away from direct election by the people. The electoral college was also designed to check democratic impulses by filtering the presidential election through smaller, supposedly less democratic electors. The House, the Framers of the Constitution thought, would probably elect most presidents because it

---

15. David P. Currie, *The Constitution in Congress: The Federalist Period, 1789–1801* (Chicago, 1997), p. 296.

16. Ibid., p. 297.

17. Fisher Ames, "The Mire of Democracy," in Allen, *Works of Fisher Ames,* 1:7.

would be difficult to get a majority in the electoral college. But the Framers did not see how quickly political parties would change the way we elected presidents and eventually members of Congress. In 1801, with Jefferson's election, the House did in fact have to vote to ensure his election over Aaron Burr. By then, however, there were enough Jeffersonians in the House to guarantee his election: 70 of the 106 members of the House were Republicans. The Federalists after 1801 would be relegated to minority status. They would survive as a political force in the House for another two decades but never in the majority. The dire consequences the Federalists predicted for the country as a result of the movement toward democratization of government did not materialize. While they did not like it, even the Federalists recognized the power of public opinion. The forces of democracy would continue to affect and shape the ongoing institutionalization of the House. They still do, some two centuries later.

Contributors

Richard A. Baker has been director of the U.S. Senate Historical Office since 1975, when the office was created. His books include *Conservation Politics: The Senate Career of Clinton P. Anderson* (1985); *The Senate of the United States* (1988); and *Vice Presidents of the United States, 1789–1993* (coauthor, 1997). Among his articles related to the early history of Congress are "The Senate of the United States: 'Supreme Executive Council of the Nation,' 1787–1800," *Prologue* (1989); and "The 'Great Departments': The Origin of the Federal Government's Executive Branch," in *Well Begun: Chronicles of the Early National Period* (1989), ed. Stephen L. Schechter and Richard B. Bernstein.

Christine A. Desan is a professor of law at Harvard Law School. She is the author of several articles that explore the way law, politics, and rights took shape in American constitutional history, including "The Constitutional Commitment to Legislative Adjudication in the Early American Tradition," *Harvard Law Review* (1998). Her current research enters the debates over capitalism by examining how the definition of the modern liberal democratic state came to include, as an important component, an apparently autonomous market sphere.

William C. diGiacomantonio is associate editor of the Documentary History of the First Federal Congress, 1789–1791, a project of the National Historical Publications and Records Commission of the National Archives and The George Washington University in Washington, D.C. His publications include articles on Quakers' antislavery lobbying, District of Columbia governance, and federal support for the arts and sciences in the First Federal Congress.

Terri D. Halperin completed her graduate studies at the University of Virginia in 2000. Her dissertation is entitled "Dangerous to Liberty: The United States Senate, 1789–1821." She is currently a visiting assistant professor at the University of Richmond in Richmond, Virginia.

Richard R. John is an associate professor of history at the University of Illinois at Chicago. His many publications include *Spreading the News: The*

American Postal System from Franklin to Morse (1995). He is currently working on a history of communications in industrial America.

John P. Kaminski is director of the Center for the Study of the American Constitution in the Department of History at the University of Wisconsin-Madison. He also is project director of the Documentary History of the Ratification of the Constitution. In addition to the sixteen volumes of the ratification series published to date, he has written, edited, or coedited eleven other books. At the center he directs an extensive program of judicial education, and he holds a visiting faculty position at the National Judicial College in Reno, Nevada. He is currently compiling a 3,000-page documentary edition entitled "The Founding Fathers on the Founding Fathers."

Jeffrey L. Pasley is assistant professor of history at the University of Missouri-Columbia. He has taught at Florida State University and in the history and literature program at Harvard University. His works include *"The Tyranny of Printers": Newspaper Politics in the Early American Republic* (2001) and " 'A Journeyman, Either in Law or Politics': John Beckley and the Social Origins of Political Campaigning," *Journal of the Early Republic* (1996), along with various other articles and reviews on early American political culture. He is currently coediting "Beyond the Founders: New Approaches to the Political History of the Early American Republic," a collection of original essays that will be published by the University of North Carolina Press.

David J. Siemers is an assistant professor of political science at the University of Wisconsin-Oshkosh, where he teaches courses in American politics and American political thought. He is author of *Ratifying the Republic: Antifederalists and Federalists in Constitutional Time* (forthcoming) and several articles on the founding period, including " 'It is Natural to Care for the Crazy Machine': The Antifederalists' Post-ratification Acquiescence," *Studies in American Political Development* (1998). Siemers has served as a visiting professor at Wellesley College and Colorado College and is currently at work on an edited volume of Antifederalist works.

Raymond W. Smock, historian of the U.S. House of Representatives from 1983 to 1995, is the editor of *Landmark Documents of the U.S. Congress* (2000) and *Masters of the House: Leadership in the House of Representatives over Two Centuries* (1999). He also is coeditor of the fourteen-volume documentary edition *The Booker T. Washington Papers* (1972–83).

Marion Nelson Winship is completing a doctoral dissertation at the University of Pennsylvania. Her recent publications include "Kentucky in the New Republic: A Study of Distance and Connection," in *"The Buzzel about Kentuck": Settling the Promised Land* (1999), ed. Craig Thompson Friend; and "Safety and Danger in a Puritan Home: Life in the Hull-Sewall House, 1676–1716," in *The American Home: Material Culture, Domestic Space, and Family Life* (1998), ed. Eleanor McD. Thompson.

Christopher J. Young is a doctoral candidate in history at the University of Illinois at Chicago. His dissertation explores the use of public opinion during the presidency of George Washington. He is the author of "Mary K. Goddard: A Classical Republican in a Revolutionary Age," *Maryland Historical Magazine* (2001).

Index